PETER MARTYR VERMIGLI AND THE EUROPEAN
REFORMATIONS: SEMPER REFORMANDA

STUDIES IN THE HISTORY
OF
CHRISTIAN TRADITIONS

FOUNDED BY HEIKO A. OBERMAN †

EDITED BY

ROBERT J. BAST, Knoxville, Tennessee

IN COOPERATION WITH

HENRY CHADWICK, Cambridge
SCOTT H. HENDRIX, Princeton, New Jersey
BRIAN TIERNEY, Ithaca, New York
ARJO VANDERJAGT, Groningen
JOHN VAN ENGEN, Notre Dame, Indiana

VOLUME CXV

FRANK A. JAMES III

PETER MARTYR VERMIGLI AND THE EUROPEAN
REFORMATIONS: SEMPER REFORMANDA

PETER MARTYR VERMIGLI AND THE EUROPEAN REFORMATIONS: SEMPER REFORMANDA

EDITED BY

FRANK A. JAMES III

BRILL

LEIDEN · BOSTON

2004

This book is printed on acid-free paper.

Library of Congress Cataloging-in-Publication Data

Sixteenth Century Studies Conference (1999 : St. Louis, Mo.)
  Peter Martyr Vermigli and the European reformations : semper reformanda / edited by
Frank A. James III.
    p. cm. — (Studies in the history of Christian traditions, ISSN 1573-5664 ; v. 115)
  Includes bibliographical references (p.) and index.
  ISBN 90-04-13914-1
  1. Vermigli, Pietro Martire, 1499-1562—Congresses. I. James, Frank A. III. Title. III.
Series.

BR350.V37S59 1999
270.6'092—dc22

2004045781

ISSN   1573-5664
ISBN   90 04 13914 1

© *Copyright 2004 by Koninklijke Brill NV, Leiden, The Netherlands*
Koninklijke Brill NV incorporates the imprints Brill Academic Publishers,
Martinus Nijhoff Publishers and VSP.

All rights reserved. No part of this publication may be reproduced, translated, stored in
a retrieval system, or transmitted in any form or by any means, electronic,
mechanical, photocopying, recording or otherwise, without prior written
permission from the publisher.

Authorization to photocopy items for internal or personal
use is granted by Brill provided that
the appropriate fees are paid directly to The Copyright
Clearance Center, 222 Rosewood Drive, Suite 910
Danvers, MA 01923, USA.
Fees are subject to change.

PRINTED IN THE NETHERLANDS

CONTENTS

PART I

REFORMERS IN COMMUNITY

PART II

BIBLICAL AND THEOLOGICAL REFLECTIONS

PART III

CHURCH AND REFORM

PREFACE

Several years ago, the late Heiko A. Oberman, wrote to me:

> Your intention to place Peter Martyr Vermigli in the wider context of the Reformation movements racing through sixteenth-century Europe makes your volume the ideal candidate for inclusion in the series *Studies in the History of Christian Thought*.[1]

Oberman's professional judgment certainly comports with the original purpose of this volume. In 1999, there were several international celebrations of the 500th anniversary of the birth of Vermigli—in Padua, Zurich and St. Louis at the Sixteenth Century Studies Conference. Most of the essays included in this volume arose out of the celebrations in St. Louis. Additional essays were subsequently invited to form this particular collection. What makes this volume so fascinating is that it explores new avenues of research in Vermigli's thought, which in turn illuminate new aspects of the European Reformations. This collection of articles is divided under three rubrics: community among Reformers, biblical and theological reflections and church reform. Each of these depicts a vital aspect of Vermigli's life commitments as well as demonstrate something of his contribution to the European Reformations. But for Vermigli, the Bible was not merely the repository for theological knowledge, but was also the touchstone for a wide variety of issues—societal, political as well as theological. His theological insights (or thoughts generated from his biblical studies) range from his views on dancing, happiness, suicide, friendship, combat, the treatment of war captives, canon law and the role of women. We have tried to capture some of that immense variety in this collection of essays.

I want to extend special thanks to my graduate assistants, Ryan Reeves and Lori Ginn, for their kind assistance in completing this project. Both Lori and Ryan display superb academic instincts and are already scholars in their own right.

---

[1] Personal letter from Professor Oberman, 25 July 2000.

IN MEMORIAM: HEIKO AUGUSTINUS OBERMAN, 1930–2001

Heiko Augustinus Oberman, one of the leading Reformation scholars of the past half-century and a longtime supporter of Vermigli studies, died 22 April 2001 in Tucson Arizona where he taught at the University. He was by all accounts, a scholar's scholar.

Oberman and Peter Martyr Vermigli have a long and distinguished history. Professor Oberman began his formal affiliation with this Italian reformer when he published Father Donnelly's early monograph on Vermigli in 1976,[1] and continued his support by including my first major essay on Vermigli in a volume he and I edited in 1991.[2] It was rather daring and exceedingly gracious for a scholar of his stature to agree not only to publish a volume but to serve as co-editor with a still very young scholar. Despite all the horror stories of working with this demanding and perfectionistic Dutchman, I found him to be a generous colleague who treated me with enormous, if underserved, respect. I recall having lunch with Professor Oberman at All Souls College in Oxford and delighted in his strong opinions. I heard him lecture and was mesmerized, like everyone else, at his vast knowledge, expertise and unwavering assurance that he was correct.

Oberman's support for Vermigli research continued until his death. Over the last years he again provided his enthusiastic endorsement for another collection of essays, of which this volume is the fruit. For his longstanding support for Vermigli studies and his personal generosity to me, it is with gratitude and delight that this volume is dedicated to the memory of Heiko Oberman. *Requiescat in pace.*

---

[1] John P. Donnelly, *Calvinism and Scholasticism in Vermigli's Doctrine of Man and Grace*, Studies in Medieval and Reformation Thought 18 (Leiden: E. J. Brill, 1976).

[2] "A late Medieval Parallel in Reformation Thought: *Gemina Praedestinatio* in Gregory of Rimini and Peter Martyr Vermigli," in *Via Augustini: Augustine in the Later Middle Ages, Renaissance and Reformation.* Studies in Medieval and Reformation Thought 48, edited by Heiko A. Oberman and Frank A. James III (Leiden: E. J. Brill, 1991), 157–188.

ABBREVIATIONS

BIBL   *A Bibliography of Peter Martyr Vermigli*. Sixteenth Century Essays and Studies, XIII. Ed. John Patrick Donnelly with R. M. Kingdon and M. W. Anderson. Kirksville, Mo.: Sixteenth Century Publishers, 1990.

CAS   *Calvinism and Scholasticism in Vermigli's Doctrine of Man and Grace*. John Patrick Donnelly. Leiden, 1976.

CP   *The Common Places of Peter Martyr Vermigli*. "Translated and partly gathered" by Anthony Marten. London, 1583.

DIAL   *Dialogue on the Two Natures of Christ*. Ed. and trans. John Patrick Donnelly, Peter Martyr Library, vol. 2. Kirksville, Mo.: Thomas Jefferson University Press, 1995.

EW   *Early Writings: Creed, Scripture, Church*. Trans. Mariano Di Gangi and Joseph C. McLelland, ed. Joseph C. McLelland, Peter Martyr Library, vol. 1. Kirksville, MO.: Sixteenth Century Journal Publishers, 1994.

HHR   *Peter Martyr Vermigli: Humanism, Republicanism and Reformation*. Emidio Campi, Frank A. James, III and Peter Opitz. Geneva: Librairie Droz, 2002.

JAP   *Theological Loci: Justification and Predestination*. Trans. and ed. Frank James III, Peter Martyr Library, vol. 8. Kirksville, Mo. Truman State University Press, 2003.

LC   *Loci Communes of Peter Martyr Vermigli*. London: R. Masson, 1576; Basle: P. Perna, 1580–82 (3 vols.).

LLS   *Life, Letters, and Sermons: Peter Martyr Vermigli*. Trans. and ed. by John Patrick Donnelly, SJ. Peter Martyr Library, vol. 5. Kirksville, Mo.: Thomas Jefferson University Press, 1999.

PMI   *Peter Martyr in Italy: An Anatomy of Apostasy*. Philip Mcnair. Oxford, 1967.

PMIR   *Peter Martyr Vermigli and Italian Reform*. Ed. Joseph C. McLelland. Waterloo, Ont.: Wilfrid Laurier University Press, 1980.

PMRD   *The Peter Martyr Reader*. Ed., John Patrick Donnelly, S. J., Frank A. James, III and Joseph C. McLelland. Kirksville, MO: Truman State University Press, 1999.

PMRE   *Peter Martyr Vermigli: A Reformer in Exile (1542–1562): A*

        Chronology of Biblical Writings in England and Europe. Marvin
        W. Anderson. Nieuwkoop, 1975.

PPRED *Peter Martyr Vermigli and Predestination: the Augustinian Inheritance
        of an Italian Reformer.* Frank A. James, III. Oxford, 1998.

PW   *Philosophical Works of Peter Martyr*, Peter Martyr Library, vol.
        4. J. C. McLelland. Kirksville, MO: Sixteenth Century
        Essays and Studies, 1996

VWG   *The Visible Words of God: An Exposition of the Sacramental Theology
        of Peter Martyr Vermigli, AD 1500–1562.* Joseph C. McLelland.
        Edinburgh: Oliver and Boyd, 1957.

NUNC PEREGRINUS OBERRAT: PETER MARTYR IN CONTEXT

Frank A. James III

I. *Peter Martyr's Portrait*

Portraits are not always flattering. The woodcut of Peter Martyr Vermigli in Theodore Beza's *Icones*, is almost grotesque.[1] His bloated, somewhat distorted, face with its bulbous nose looks more like a gargoyle than a Protestant Reformer. This is in striking contrast to the portrait by Hans Asper in the National Portrait Gallery in London, which shows a rather distinguished Peter Martyr who gazes serenely beyond the frame. The two foci of the painting are his flushed face with its forked beard and his disproportionately large hands. In his left hand he holds a crimson book to which he points with his right forefinger. Although the book is not specifically identified, there is little doubt that it is his Bible. Martyr does not look at the Bible, but stares intently beyond the painting resulting in a somewhat stilted portrait. It would appear that the intent is to portray Vermigli in the act of teaching. It is as if time has stopped just as he is preparing to quote the famous words from the *Confessions* of his precious Augustine: "*tolle lege, tolle lege.*"

II. *Peter Martyr and the European Reformations*

Asper's portrait belongs to a collection of paintings of prominent Zurich divines.[2] This beautiful painting contains a tetrastich inscribed above Vermilgi's head that reads:

---

[1] Theodore Beza, *Icones, id est Verae Imaginis virorum doctrina simul et pietate illustrium* (Geneva: C. Froschauer, 1580), 2.

[2] Torrance Kirby, "*Vermilius Absconditus*? The Iconography of Peter Martyr Vermilgi," in HHR, 296–298.

HVNC GENVIT FLORENTIA, NVNC PEREGRINVS OBERRAT
QVO STABILIS FIAT CIVIS APVD SVPEROS
ILLIVS EFFIGIES, MENTVM SCRIPTA RECONDVIT
INTEGRITIS PIETAS PINGIER ARTE NEQVIT.

"Florence brought him forth, Now he wanders as a foreigner/That he might forever be a citizen among those in heaven./This is his likeness; [but] a painting cannot reveal his heart/[for] integrity and piety cannot be represented by art." The tetrastich recalls Vermilgi's dramatic flight from his Italian inquisitors and his sojourns among the reformations in Strasbourg, England and Switzerland. The Florentine theologian (*HVNC GENVIT FLORENTIA*) was doomed to professorial itinerancy for his scriptural convictions. It is not surprising that in his portrait he would point literally to the reason for his exiles—the Bible. The second part of the first stanza (*NVNC PEREGRINVS OBERRAT*) in particular underscores his émigré status and his peripatetic Protestant career.

A. *The Phoenix of Florence*

The French reformer, Theodore Beza, once described Vermigli as a "phoenix born from the ashes of Savonarola."[3] Although hyperbole, this sentiment rightly suggests that Vermigli, like Savonarola, saw the Roman church in moral decline.[4] Pietro Martire Vermigli was born in Florence on 8 September 1499. Little is known of his early years except that he had an abiding affection for the Bible. Reflecting back on his youth in his inaugural speech at Zurich in 1556, Vermigli revealed: "from an early age when I was still living in Italy, I decided to pursue this one thing above the other human arts and studies—that I should learn and teach primarily the divine Scriptures."[5] Following this conviction, even though it went against

---

[3] Theodore Beza, *Icones, id est Verae Imaginis virorum doctrina simul et pietate illustrium* (Geneva: C. Froschauer, 1580), 2: "Petrum Martyrem . . . Florentinae natum et a Savonarolae veluti cineribus prodeuntem phoenicem . . ." Cf. Klaus Sturm, *Die Theologie Peter Martyr Vermiglis während seines ersten Aufenthalts in Strassburg 1542–1547* (Neukirchen: Neukirchener Verlag, 1971), 41.

[4] PMI, 68–69, finds no evidence that Vermigli family had any connection to Savonarola.

[5] Peter Martyr Vermigli, *Loci Communes . . . ex variis ipsius authoris scriptis, in unum librum collecti & in quatuor Classes distributi* (London: Thomas Vautrollerius, 1583), 1062. A new English translation of this oration is found in LLS, 9–64.

the wishes of his father, Vermigli joined the Lateran Congregation of Canons Regular of St. Augustine in 1514. Academically precocious, the young Florentine was sent to study at the University of Padua, at that time one of the most famous universities in the world. At Padua he lived a dual intellectual existence. On the one hand, he was inundated with the ideas of Aristotle in the faculty of theology at the University; but on the other hand, he imbibed Renaissance humanism at his monastery, S. Giovanni di Verdara. His years of study at Padua culminated in priestly ordination and a doctorate in theology (1526).[6] But he encountered more than ideas at Padua. He acquired also a proclivity for action, for among his Paduan friends were Pietro Bembo, Reginald Pole and Marcantonio Flaminio—all future leaders of the abortive Italian reform movement. It is interesting that nearly every prominent Italian leader in this failed venture was linked to the University of Padua at roughly this the same time.[7] During the Italian phase of his career Vermigli was well known as a distinguished young theologian and eloquent preacher. Indeed the April 1540 records from his own Augustinian order characterized him as "*Predicatorem eximium*" (an exceptional preacher).[8] He was also an active reformist within the Catholic Church. He was the confidante of powerful prelates under Pope Paul III, served as consultant to the famous *Consilium de emendanda ecclesia*[9] (Council on the reform of the Church) in 1537 and was appointed by Cardinal Gasparo Contarini as a member of delegation to engage in dialogue with the Protestants at the Colloquy of Worms in 1540.[10] At Spoleto, Naples and especially Lucca, he actively pursued a reformist agenda.[11]

---

[6] PMI, 116–117.

[7] Fr. de Santa Teresa Domingo, O.C.D., *Juan de Valdés, 1498 (?)–1541. Su pensamiento religioso y las corrientes espirituales de su tiempo* (Rome: Apud Aedes Universitatis Gregorianae, 1957), 401.

[8] PMI, 192, derived from the records of the order, the *Acta Capitularia* (1540). These records are housed in the Biblioteca Classense in Ravena.

[9] PMI, 130–138. Cf. Elisabeth Gleason, *Gasparo Contarini: Venice, Rome and Reform* (Berkeley: University of California Press, 1993), 129–157.

[10] McNair, *Peter Martyr in Italy*, 197–199.

[11] Salvatore Caponetto, trans. Anne C. and John Tedeschi, *The Protestant Reformation in Sixteenth-Century Italy* (Kirksville, MO: Truman State University Press, 1999), 277–280, 327–331. Cf. PMI, 127–130, 139–179, 206–238. In 1681, Cardinal Giulio Spinola sent a letter to the Lucchese refugees in Geneva inviting them to return

So successful were his reforms in Lucca that the ire of papal con-
servatives was stirred to resolute action. Philip McNair provides com-
pelling evidence that the reconstitution of the Roman Inquisition was
directly connected to Vermigli's reforming efforts in Lucca.[12]

Vermigli's critical theological transformation was initiated during
his Neapolitan abbacy (1537–1540) by the Spanish reformist, Juan
de Valdés. It was in the Valdésian circle in Naples that he encountered the Italian reform movement, first read Protestant literature
and embraced the pivotal doctrine of justification by faith alone.[13]
Evidence of his theological reorientation manifested itself during his
Priorate in Lucca, where he established "the first and last reformed
theological college in pre-Tridentine Italy."[14] With Martyr as his
mentor, Girolamo Zanchi was introduced to the works of Bucer,
Melanchthon, Bullinger, and Calvin.[15] Willem van't Spijker has drawn
attention to a letter in which Zanchi, recalling his training in Lucca,
reported that both he and Martyr regarded Bucer as the most learned
of the new theological voices arising in Germany.[16] Zanchi himself
acknowledges Vermigli's role in exposing him to key themes in the
theology of Calvin.[17]

With the reinstitution of the Roman Inquisition under the iron
hand of Cardinal Carafa (later Pope Paul IV), whose advocacy for
moral reform gave way to repression of suspected heretics within the
Church, Vermigli experienced a personal crisis of conscience.[18] In

---

to the Roman fold. In reply, the Lucchese still remembered Vermigli's role in con-
verting their forebears. See E. Campi and C. Sodini, *Gli oriundi lucchesi di Ginevra e
il Cardinale Spinola* (Chicago: Newberry Library, 1988), 180.

[12] PMI, 249–250.

[13] Charles Schmidt, *Peter Martyr Vermigli: Leben und ausgewalte Schriften* (Elberfeld:
R.L. Friedrichs, 1858), 20, deduces that it was Valdés who provided writings from
Bucer and Zwingli to Vermigli.

[14] PMI, 221.

[15] Joseph N. Tylenda, "Girolamo Zanchi and John Calvin: A Study in Discipleship
as Seen Through Their Correspondence," *Calvin Theological Journal*, 10 (1975): 104.

[16] Willem van't Spijker, "Bucer als Zeuge Zanchis im Straßburger Prädestinationsstreit," in H. A. Oberman, E. Saxer, A. Schindler, and H. Stucki, eds., *Reformiertes
Erbe: Festschrift für Gottfried W. Locher zu seinem 80 Geburtstag* (Zurich: Theologischer
und Buchhandlungen, 1992), 332.

[17] In an undated letter to Calvin, Zanchi invokes Peter Martyr as a witness to
his deep affection for the Genevan reformer. See Zanchi's *Opera Theologica* (Geneva:
Stephanus Gamonetus, 1605–13), vol. 2, *Liber Epistolarum*, 331.

[18] PMI, 239–268. Vermigli was not alone in his apostasy. The Vicar General of
the Capuchins, Bernardino Ochino, also fled the Inquisition with Vermigli's encouragement. For background on Ochino see, Karl Benrath trans. H. Zimmern *Bernardino*

the summer of 1542, he was ordered to appear before a Chapter Extraordinary of the Lateran Congregation of the Canons Regular of St. Augustine in Genoa. Warned by highly placed friends, he found himself on the horns of a dilemma: would he flee his homeland for the sake of freedom to declare the gospel according to the Holy Scriptures, or would he hold his tongue and conform to the authority of a church he no longer respected? Weighing the consequences, he forsook Rome for a life in exile.

B. *The Peripatetic Protestant*

Almost immediately after his apostasy in the summer of 1542, he was propelled into prominence as a biblical scholar and Protestant theologian. But the transformation was not without its trials. Former Italian Catholic theologians were not quickly welcomed into the Protestant community without caution. At Zurich he was carefully scrutinized by Heinrich Bullinger, Konrad Pellikan and Rodolph Gualter and then vetted again by Oswald Myconius and Boniface Amerbach in Basel. Convinced of his Protestant orthodoxy, lifelong friendships were formed but there was no academic post available. Not until October 1542 did Vermigli find a position succeeding the late Wolfgang Capito as professor of Divinity in Strasbourg. There too he forged a close personal alliance with the Alsacian Reformer Martin Bucer. So valuable was he to Bucer, that Johann Sturm stated the veteran Reformer made no decisions without first consulting with his Italian colleague.[19] As a teacher, Vermigli was judged by all "to surpass" Bucer.[20]

After five productive years in Strasbourg, Vermigli's reputation as

---

Ochino of Siena: A Contribution Towards the History of the Reformation (New York: Robert Carter and Bros., 1877), 105 ff.

[19] Letter from J. Sturm to J. Marbach in Zanchi, *Opera Theologica*, vol. 2, *Liber Epistolarum*, 163.

[20] Simler, *Oratio*, 4. The English translation is found in Donnelly, *Life, Letters and Sermons*), 29. Likewise, Zacharias Ursinus in a letter (10 March, 1561) to Abel Birkenhahn, praises Vermigli's writing as clearer than Zwingli or Oecolampadius, see Eerdmann Sturm, "Brief des Heidelberger Theologen Zacharias Ursinus Aus Wittenberg Und Zurich (1560/61)," *Heidleberger Jahrbucher* 14 (1970): 90–91. Even Catholic detractors, such as Cornelius Schulting argue that Vermigli was clearer and more learned than Calvin. See Schulting's *Bibliotheca catholica et orthodoxae, contra summam totius theologiae Calviniae in Institutionibus I. Calvini et Locis Communibus Petri Martyris, breviter comprehensae* (Cologne, 1602), 1: 1.

a Protestant theologian was substantial enough that Archbishop Thomas Cranmer invited him to England to help inculcate a generation of Anglican priests with Protestant theology. To this end he was appointed Regius Professor of Divinity at Oxford University (1547–1553). His nearly six years in England were among the most fruitful of his career. He single-handedly upheld Protestant Eucharistic teaching at the famous Oxford Disputation of 1549, consulted with Bishop Hooper in the Vestarian controversy in 1550, assisted Cranmer in the revision of the 1552 Prayer Book and in the formulation of the Forty-Two Articles of Religion in 1553, and played a pivotal role in writing the *Reformatio Legum Ecclesiasticarum* from 1551–1553.[21] Vermigli's name would no doubt have been better remembered today if his sojourn in England had not been cut short by Mary Tudor's ascension to the throne in 1553.

After his banishment from England, Vermigli was received back in Strasbourg. But the atmosphere in Strasbourg, once so hospitable, had become contentious. Bucer was dead (1551), and the Lutheran faction under the leadership of Johann Marbach was on the ascendancy. Vermigli had anticipated the Lutheran opposition to his sacramental theology, as indicated in letters written to Calvin and Bullinger just a few days after he arrived in Strasbourg.[22] Led by Marbach, the Lutherans objected to Vermigli's reappointment because they judged him to have departed from the Augsburg Confession.[23] To ensure Vermigli's theological conformity, the Lutherans demanded that he sign both the Augsburg Confession and the 1536 Wittenberg

---

[21] John Frazier Jackson, "The *Reformatio Legum Ecclesiasticarum*: Politics, Society and Belief in Mid-Tudor England," (D.Phil. dissertation, Oxford University, 2003). Cf. *Tudor Church Reform: The Henrician Canons of 1535 and the Reformatio Legum Ecclesiasticarum*, ed. Gerald Bray (Church of England Record Society 8, 2000).

[22] Vermigli had arrived in Strasbourg on 30 October 1553. On 3 November, he wrote to Bullinger: "Hence it is that I am now here, but I do not yet know whether I shall again be received in this church and school; for, as I suspect, the sacramentary controversy will occasion some difficulties; however, I am not very anxious about it." *Original Letters Relative to the English Reformation, 1531–1558*, ed. Hastings Robinson for the Parker Society (Cambridge: Cambridge University Press, 1846–1847), 2: 505.

[23] On 15 December 1553, Vermigli wrote to Bullinger: "My own affairs are in this condition. Our friend Sturm, and the principal professors, with the greater portion of the clergy, have made strenuous exertions for my remaining here . . . But two or three of the ministers . . . object . . . on account of my opinions respecting the sacrament and have raised such an opposition that the matter cannot yet be resolved." *Original Letters*, 2: 509.

Concordat between Luther and Bucer. In his formal statement to the governors of the Strasbourg Academy, Vermigli was willing to embrace the Augsburg Confession, "if rightly and profitably understood," but not the Wittenberg Concordat.[24] Despite Lutheran opposition, he was reinstated in his former faculty position and began lecturing on the Book of Judges.[25]

Though Vermigli was restored to his faculty position, the controversy with the Lutherans continued unabated. Besides the matter of the Eucharist, Vermigli's doctrine of predestination also became a bone of contention. There in Strasbourg, he found a capable ally in his fellow countryman Girolamo Zanchi. The bond between these two Italians had long been established, for Zanchi had been converted in Lucca under Vermigli.[26] The relationship forged in the heat of battle was so close that Bullinger coined a new term to describe Zanchi's teaching—*Martyrizet*.[27]

Vermigli's troubles in Strasbourg soon led him to accept the invitation of Bullinger to succeed the recently deceased Konrad Pellikan at Zurich in 1556.[28] Vermigli was again welcomed to Zurich, as he

---

[24] Vermigli's statement, "Clarissimis atque Magnificis Dominis Scholarchis Argentinensi," is found in *Loci Communes*, 1068. Vermigli was willing to sign the Augsburg Confession, "*si recte atque commode intelligantur*," that is, according to the 1540 Augsburg Confession (the *Variata*). Vermigli refused to sign the Wittenberg Concordat (1536) because he was unwilling to acknowledge that the wicked actually ate the body of Christ in the sacrament.

[25] Vermigli was not officially restored to his faculty position until 22 January 1554. See his letter to Bullinger, *Original Letters*, 2: 511.

[26] For general background on Zanchi see PMI, 227–231; Luigi Santini, *La communità evangelica di Bergamo: Vicende storiche* (Rome: Torre Pellice, 1960), 228–239; and Christopher Burchill, "Girolamo Zanchi: A Portrait of a Reformed Theologian and His Work," *Sixteenth Century Journal* 15 (1984): 185–207. For some of the more significant writing on Zanchi's theological orientation see John L. Farthing, "Patristics, Exegesis and the Eucharist in the Theology of Girolamo Zanchi," in *Protestant Scholasticism: Essays in Reassessment*, eds. C. R. Truman and R. S. Clark (Carlisle, Cumbria, Paternoster Press, 1999), 79–95; idem, "*De coniugio spirituali*: Jerome Zanchi on Ephesians 5.22–33," *Sixteenth Century Journal* 24 (1993): 621–52; idem, "Christ and the Eschaton: The Reformed Eschatology of Jerome Zanchi," in *Later Calvinism: International Persepctives* (Kirksville, MO: Sixteenth Century Journal Publishers, 1994), 333–354; John Patrick Donnelly, "Calvinist Thomism," *Viator* 7 (1976): 444–448 and his "Italian Influences on Calvinist Scholasticism," *Sixteenth Century Journal* 7 (1976): 96–100; Joseph N. Tylenda, "Girolamo Zanchi and John Calvin," *Calvin Theological Journal* 10 (1975): 101–141.

[27] Bullinger's letter to Zanchi on 30 August 1556, Zanchi, *Opera Theologica*, vol. 2, *Liber Epistolarum*, 84.

[28] The controversies in Strasbourg escalated until May 1556, when Vermigli accepted the invitation from Zurich. On 13 July 1556, Vermigli, accompanied by

had been fourteen years earlier having just escaped from the clutches of the Roman Inquisition. If Vermigli thought Zurich a refuge from the storm, he was mistaken. Vermigli arrived in July and soon found himself embroiled in yet another controversy.

Vermigli found a cordial environment for his Eucharistic views in Zurich, especially since Calvin and Bullinger had forged the *Consensus Tigurinus* in 1549, but the reception was less than warm for his doctrine of predestination.[29] Bullinger had been quite moderate and cautious in his formulations, preferring a doctrine of single predestination.[30] A few years earlier, Bullinger had provided only lackluster support for Calvin in the Bolsec affair in 1552 and had also refused to sign the *Consensus Genevensis*, which contained the strong Calvinian view of predestination.[31] Although not an advocate of *gemina praedstinatio* like Vermigli, Bullinger was tolerant of his view.[32] Theodore Bibliander, Bullinger's colleague at Zurich, was not.[33]

Vermigli had always maintained a desire to avoid unwarranted controversy[34] and so, upon his arrival in Zurich, he took great pains

---

his English disciple, John Jewel, departed for Zurich. See Christina H. Garret, *The Marian Exiles: A Study in the Origins of Elizabethan Puritanism* (Cambridge, Cambridge University Press, 1938), 367.

[29] CAS, 182, rightly points out, "the *Consensus Tigurinus* brought agreement on the Eucharist but it did not unite the two churches on the equally crucial question of predestination." Cf. Schmidt, *Leben*, 215.

[30] J. Wayne Baker, *Heinrich Bullinger and the Covenant: The Other Reformed Tradition*, (Athens, Ohio: Ohio State University Press, 1980), 27–47. For a complete historiography on Bullinger and predestination, see Peter Walser, *Die Prädestination bei Heinrich Bullinger im Zusammmenhang mit seiner Gotteslehre* (Zurich: Theologischer Verlag Zurich, 1957), 9–22.

[31] The *Consensus Genevensis*, otherwise known as *De aeterna Praedestinatione*, was approved by the Genevan Syndics but was never accepted by the other Swiss churches. Philip Schaff, *History of the Christian Church* (New York: Scribner's Sons, 1910; reprint Grand Rapids: Eerdmans, 1976), vol. 8, *Modern Christianity: The Swiss Reformation*, 210–211.

[32] For an account of Bullinger's tolerance for other predestinarian views, both more and less rigorous than his own, see Baker, *Bullinger and the Covenant*, 39–44.

[33] Theodore Bibliander, professor of Old Testament at Zurich, had long been an opponent of Calvin, but had restrained himself from public attack. Bibliander held to a view of predestination much like that of Erasmus. See Schmidt, *Leben*, 215.

[34] Despite their differences, neither Bullinger nor Vermigli wanted to make predestination a subject of controversy. One gets a sense of their mutual reluctance to quarrel over predestination in two letters exchanged in late 1553. To Bullinger, Vermigli writes: "May God of His goodness grant us all to feel, respecting predestination, that what ought to be the greatest consolation to believers, may not

to praise Bibliander and tactfully published his commentary on Romans in Basel rather than Zurich.[35] However, even if Bullinger could count on Vermigli's good nature, he still had to contend with Bibliander's brooding hostility.[36] The desire for peace went unrequited. Vermigli began lecturing on I Samuel on 24 August 1556, and, by June 1557, Bibliander had begun openly to attack Vermigli's doctrine of predestination.[37] A full-blown *"Prädestinationsstreit"* ensued.[38] The controversy became so intense that Bibliander challenged Vermigli to a duel with a double-edged axe.[39] Eventually, Bibliander was dismissed from his duties as professor in February 1560. According to Vermigli scholar John Patrick Donnelly, Vermigli's victory in the Bibliander affair "marks an important stage in Zurich's adhesion to a full Reformed teaching on grace and predestination."[40]

The Zurich years (1556–1562), although not entirely tranquil, were productive. His lectures on Romans (1558) and Judges (1561) were published, along with his massive *Defensio Doctrinae veteris & Apostolicae de sacosancto Eucharistiae Sacramento . . . advesus Stephani Gardineri*[41] opposing the Eucharistic theology of Stephen Gardiner, bishop of Winchester (1559). With Theodore Beza, he attended the Colloquy of

---

become the painful subject of pernicious contention!" Cf. *Original Letters* 2: 506. Bullinger writes to Vermigli in December 1553: "I know you [and] I am not concerned that you will cause dissension over this doctrine. I know that your reputation would set aside such controversy regardless of whomever might raise the issue." This citation is found in Alexander Schweizer, *Die Protestantischen Centraldogmen in Ihrer Entwicklung Innerhalb Der Reformierten Kirche* (Zurich, 1853), 1: 275.

[35] CAS, 183.

[36] Schmidt, *Leben*, 218, writes: "Bibliander wurde nicht pensioniert wegen seiner Lehre, sondern weil er geisteskrank war."

[37] Bullinger's diary specifically provides the date when Vermigli began lecturing on 1 Samuel as 24 August 1556. Emil Egli, ed. *Heinrich Bullingers Diarium (Annales vita) der Jahre 1504–1574* (Basel, 1904), 48, quoted in Marvin Anderson, *Peter Martyr Vermigli: A Reformer in Exile (1542–1562)* (Nieuwkoop: B. De Graaf, 1975), in 380. On 1 July 1557, Vermigli wrote to Calvin: "I have begun to treat predestination, and shall continue with it the whole week. Not only does the inducement of the passage move me to declare it, but also because my College, as you know, is widely separate from me in regard to this, and has spoken against the doctrine in lectures this past week." Cf. Joseph C. McLelland, "Reformed Doctrine of Predestination according to Peter Martyr," *Scottish Journal of Theology* 8 (1955): 266.

[38] Joachim Staedtke, "Der Züricher Prädestinationsstreit von 1560," *Zwingliana* 9 (1953): 536–546.

[39] Schmidt, *Leben*, 218.

[40] CAS, 183.

[41] Peter Martyr Vermigli, *Defensio Doctrinae veteris & Apostolicae de sacrosancto Eucharistiae Sacramento . . . adversus Stephani Gardineri* (Zurich: C. Froschauer, 1559).

Poissy (1561) where he conversed with the queen mother, Catherine de'Medici, in her native Italian tongue and tried to win her to the Protestant side. Edmund Grindal, bishop of London, spoke of Vermigli's important role at Poissy to Sir William Cecil saying: "I am of the judgment that no man alive is more fit than Peter Martyr for such a conference . . . for he is better versed in old doctors, councils and ecclesiastical histories than any Romish doctor of Christendom."[42]

Vermigli was successful in the eyes of at least one Catholic bishop present at the Colloquy of Poissy. Antonio Caracciolo, bishop of Troyes (France), was so impressed with Vermigli that he converted to Protestantism and attempted to bring his whole diocese into the Reformed faith. He was the first bishop in the history of the French Reformed Church.[43] Vermigli lived out his final days in Zurich where he died on 12 November 1562 attended by his closest friends, including Bernardino Ochino, Heinrich Bullinger and Josiah Simler.

Only the lofty words of Plato for his mentor Socrates would suffice to express Josiah Simler's esteem for his theological tutor. To him, Vermigli was *"viri omnium quos ego noverim optimi et sapientissimi atque iustissimi"* (the best and wisest and most righteous of all the men I have known).[44] To his child in the faith, Girolamo Zanchi, he was *"praeceptor carissimus"* (beloved teacher).[45] John Hooper called him "a brave and godly solider in the army of the Lord."[46] Even the older Reformers proffered their own accolades. Heinrich Bullinger, Vermigli's colleague in Zurich, said: "This man was incomparable . . . The loss felt in his death is not ours alone, but more surely an irreparable

---

[42] *The Remains of Edmund Grindal, D.D.*, ed. William Nicholson for the Parker Society (Cambridge: Cambridge University Press, 1843), 244–245. I have modernized slightly the English to make it clearer. Cf. Marvin W. Anderson, "Peter Martyr on Romans," *Scottish Journal of Theology* 26 (1973): 401.

[43] Vermigli letter to Beza, 6 November, 1561, in *Correspondance de Theodore de Beze*, ed. F. Aubert, H. Meylan et al. (Geneva: Libriarie Droz, 1960–), 3: 209. See also VWG, 64 and Schmidt, *Leben*, 272–273.

[44] Josiah Simler, *Oratio de vita et obitu viri optimi praestantissimi Theologi D. Peteri Martyris Vermilii, Sacrarum literarum in schola Tigurina Professoris* (Zurich: C. Froschauer, 1563), xvi. My translation differs slightly from Donnelly in LLS, 61. Reference is to Plato, *Phaedo*, 118A.

[45] Zanchi, letter to John Calvin, 18 April 1563, Zanchi's *Opera Theologica* (Geneva: Stephanus Gamonetus, 1605–13), vol. 2, *Liber Epistolarum*, 292: ". . . quamdiu vixit meus vere observandus pater et praeceptor carissimus, Peter Martyr. . . ."

[46] *Original Letters*, 1: 97.

one for the church universal."[47] Calvin called him "the miracle of Italy."[48] Many more such laudatory remarks can be read in the *testimonia* of the various editions of the *Loci communes*.

III. *Peter Martyr in Retrospect*

Vermigli found life as an immigrant theologian difficult, but even he had to admit that exile had its benefits, since it put him into direct contact with other reformers and their reformations. Repeated exiles meant that he was constantly entering into the reforming efforts of others, each with their own particular political, social and ecclesiastical concerns. Recurring expulsions also meant that Vermigli was in some degree or another always reforming (*semper reformanda*)—that is, always having to rethink and to nuance his theology in new contexts. This is not to suggest that he compromised on his core theological values, but that different circumstances demanded different theological applications. As I have noted elsewhere with regard to his doctrine of justification, his understanding of this doctrine developed in significant ways throughout his Protestant career under varying theological, political and geographical contexts.[49] Vermigli also exercised considerable theological influence on other Protestant reformers. His Eucharistic exchanges with Calvin for instance, led Calvin to reconfigure his understanding and to declare: "The whole [doctrine of the Eucharist] was crowned by Peter Martyr, who left nothing more to be done."[50]

---

[47] *Corpus Reformatorum (CR)*, (Berlin/Leipzig/Zurich, 1835–), 48: 3879. Cf. PMRE, 266.

[48] VWG, 1. McLelland also mentions a letter to Cranmer, in which Calvin describes Vermigli as "*optimus et integerrimus vir*" (*Visible Words*, 279).

[49] Frank A. James III, "*Dei Iustificatione*: The Evolution of Peter Martyr Vermigli's Doctrine of Justification" (Ph.D. Dissertation, Westminster Theological Seminary, 2000).

[50] Treatise of Calvin to Tileman Heschusius entitled: "True Partaking of the Flesh and Blood of Christ in the Holy Supper," in *Selected Works of John Calvin: Tracts and Letters*, edited by Henry Beveridge and Jules Bonnet (Edinburgh: Calvin Translation Society, 1849; reprinted: Grand Rapids: Baker Book House, 1983), 2: 535. See also the work of W. Dunkin Rankin, "Carnal Union with Christ in the Theology of T. F. Torrance," Ph.D. Dissertation, University of Edinburgh, 1997), 175–193.

It has become customary to divide the study of the Reformation into four principal movements—Lutheran, Reformed, Radical and Catholic. Within each of these are, of course, further gradations and variations of reform. This diversity in beliefs, core values and practices warrants what has been described as the "plurality of Reformations."[51] It is this plurality of Reformations that underscores the uniqueness of Vermigli. He was a major "shaper" of both the Italian reform movement of Cardinal Contarini and Juan de Valdés within the Roman church as well as Reformed Protestantism along with Calvin, Bullinger, Bucer and Cranmer.[52] While he was not an insider of the Lutheran movement, he was a valued correspondent with Philip Melanchthon[53] and a significant interlocutor with the Gnesio-Lutherans after Luther. He served alongside and resisted pressures of Johann Marbach and the Lutherans at Strasbourg.[54] Vermigli also found himself involved with one of the more intriguing and eccentric figures associated with the Radical reformers—Bernardino Ochino.[55] Vermigli provided a brotherly check on his countryman's more bizarre inclinations (such as polygamy) in Zurich. However, a fellow native of Siena, the radical Laelius Socinus, seems also to have exercised influence on Ochino.[56] After Vermigli's death, Ochino was expelled from Zurich (1563) and descended into obscurity. Upon his departure from Zurich, Ochino was reputed to have declared: "I wish to be neither a Bullingerite, nor a Calvinist, nor a Papist, but simply a Christian."[57] Ochino began to criticize severely the mainstream reformers and to applaud the Anabaptists as the "true" church.[58]

In view of Vermigli's repeated exiles and many associations, few

---

[51] Carter Lindberg, *The European Reformations* (Oxford: Blackwell, 1996), 9.

[52] Richard A. Muller, *Christ and the Decree: Christology and Predestination in Reformed Theology from Calvin to Perkins* (Grand Rapids, Baker Book House, 1988), 67: identifies Vermigli as one of the primary shapers of the "first codification of Reformed theology."

[53] Marvin W. Anderson, "*Register Epistolarum Vermilii*" in *A Bilbiography of the Works of Peter Martyr Vermilgi*, eds. John Patrick Donnelly and Robert M. Kingdon (Kirksville, MO: Sixteenth Century Journal Publishers, 1990), 155–197. Anderson identified correspondence between Vermigli and Melanchthon from 1554–1559.

[54] Cf. James M. Kittelson, "Marbach vs. Zanchi: The Resolution of Controversy in Late Reformation Strasbourg," *Sixteenth Century Journal* 8 (1977): 31–44.

[55] George H. Williams, *The Radical Reformation* (Philadelphia: Westminster Press, 1962), 570, 630 ff.

[56] Williams, *Radical Reformation*, 630.

[57] Schaff, *The Swiss Reformation*, 651.

[58] Williams, *Radical Reformation*, 633.

reformers of his stature had such a notable voice in the European Reformations. He not only allows the modern scholar to peer into the remarkable diversity of the Catholic Church (1517–1542), but equally into the diversity among Lutheran and Reformed and then more specifically, among the various versions of Reformed branches in such places as Strasbourg, Oxford and Zurich. This peripatetic reformer, I would argue, is an untapped medium for a better understanding of the Reformations of Europe.[59]

Shortly after his death, the friends and colleagues of Vermigli commissioned a silver medal bearing his effigy.[60] Having received the medallion, the bishop of Salisbury, John Jewel, wrote poignantly of his beloved Martyr to Josiah Simler. "In the figure indeed, although there is in many respects an admirable resemblance (to the original), yet there was something, I know not what, in which I was unable to perceive the skill of the artist. And what wonder is it, that there should be some defect in producing the likeness of one, the like of whom, whenever I look around me, I can scarce believe ever to have existed?"[61] As reflected in the Asper painting, Peter Martyr did exist and his impact deeply affected the shape of the European Reformations.

---

[59] Joseph C. McLelland, "On Six Degrees Of Reform" in *Peter Martyr News Letter*, eds, Frank A. James III and J. C. McLelland, issue 10 (October 1999), pp. 3–4.

[60] A copy of this medal exists in the Zentralbibliothek of Zurich and was on display at the International Symposium on Peter Martyr Vermigli: Humanism, Republicanism and Reformation, 5–7 July, 1999, sponsored by the Institut für Schweizerische Reformationsgeschichte and the University of Zurich (25 May–10 July, 1999).

[61] Jewel to Simler, 23 March 1563. *The Zurich Letters, Comprising the Correspondence of Several English Bishops and others, with some of he Helvetian Reformers, during the early part of the Reign of Elizabeth*, ed. Hastings Robinson for the Parker Society (Cambridge: Cambridge University Press, 1842–1845), 2: 126.

PART I

REFORMERS IN COMMUNITY

PRAECEPTOR CARISSIMUS:[1]
IMAGES OF PETER MARTYR IN GIROLAMO
ZANCHI'S CORRESPONDENCE

John L. Farthing

Peter Martyr and Girolamo Zanchi

In 1541, Peter Martyr Vermigli succeeded Tommaso da Piacenz as prior of S. Frediano at Lucca. It was also in 1541 that Girolamo Zanchi da Bergamo arrived there. Vermigli's doctrinal reforms, seen especially in his expository sermons on the Psalms and the Pauline epistles, became the principal catalyst for Zanchi's conversion to the Reformed faith. Under Martyr's tutelage, Zanchi was introduced to the works of Bucer, Melanchthon, Bullinger, and Calvin.[2] Willem van't Spijker has drawn attention to a text in which Zanchi, recalling the excitement of his early encounters with Protestant literature, reports that both he and Martyr regarded Bucer as the most learned of the new theological voices arising in Germany.[3] Perhaps even more crucial to an evaluation of Peter Martyr's place in the evolution of the Reformed tradition is his role in making available to Zanchi key themes in the theology of Calvin.[4]

---

[1] *Praeceptor carissimus* is Zanchi's characterization of Peter Martyr in a letter to John Calvin (18 April 1563), *Epist. theol.*, II, in *Operum Theologicorum*, 8 vols. (Geneva: Stephanus Gamonetus, 1613), 292.

[2] Joseph N. Tylenda, "Girolamo Zanchi and John Calvin: A Study in Discipleship as Seen Through Their Correspondence," *Calvin Theological Journal* 10 (1975): 104.

[3] Willem van't Spijker, "Bucer als Zeuge Zanchis im Straßburger Prädestinationsstreit," in Heiko A. Oberman, et al., *Reformiertes Erbe: Festschrift für Gottfried W. Locher zu seinem 80 Geburtstag*, 332, no. 23. The reference is to Zanchi's *Operum Theologicorum* vol. VII, 13.

[4] In an undated letter to Calvin, Zanchi invokes Peter Martyr as a witness to his deep affection for the Genevan reformer. *Epist. theol.*, II, 331: "Credo te, vir ornatissime et mihi colendissime, non nescire quanti ego te ob tuam admirabilem et pietatem et eruditionem faciam. ... [C]erte mihi testis est inprimis Deus optimus, καρδιογνώστης, deinde post Martyrem et Martinengum, omnes illi qui me tam publice in Schola quam privatim inter amicorum colloquia, quotiens data fuit occasio verba de te honorifice faciente audiverunt." "... Fui quidem saepius tuo nomine cum ab aliis permultis, tum a D. Petro Martyro et a Martinengo per literas, salutatus."

Among the leading voices of the early Reformed tradition, Zanchi
and Martyr are linked by the fact that they were both trained in
Thomism before becoming Protestants; they both brought Thomistic
resources to bear on the articulation of a Reformed perspective.
Hinting at the special relationship between the two, especially dur-
ing their time together at Strasbourg, Joseph N. Tylenda claims that
Zanchi was, after Peter Martyr himself, "the most capable of the
Reformed teachers at Strasbourg."[5]

During the years when they were teaching together in Strasbourg,
Zanchi and Martyr lived and worked in an atmosphere of intimate
collegiality (*coniunctissime*).[6] A close working relationship was deepened
through their common struggle against the hyper-Lutheranism of
Johannes Marbach vis-à-vis the Eucharist, predestination, and the
perseverance of the saints. In the early years of the controversy—
until his departure from Strasbourg for Zurich in 1556—Martyr provided crucial support to Zanchi in his conflict with Marbach, and
he continued to make the case for Zanchi's position in letters from
Zurich, including two addressed to Johannes Sturm in Strasbourg.[7]
At the height of the controversy, Peter Martyr welcomed Zanchi
into his home for an eight-day sojourn during Zanchi's travels through
Switzerland to rally the support of Reformed pastors and theologians.[8] Zanchi's report to Beza about his visit in Vermigli's home
provides an intriguing glimpse of Peter Martyr shortly before his
death. Calling the old man "toothless, indeed, but not speechless"
(*edentulo quidem sed non elingui*), Zanchi expresses an almost incredu-
lous delight at the lucidity of his thought and speech.[9]

The personal and intellectual linkages between Vermigli and Zanchi
have been noted in various studies, although no exhaustive analysis
of the relevant texts has yet been made. There has been considerable variation in scholarly assessments of the Zanchi/Vermigli relationship. John Patrick Donnelly, for instance, while acknowledging

---

[5] Tylenda, "Girolamo Zanchi and John Calvin," 101.

[6] CAS, 206; "Italian Influences on the Development of Calvinist Scholasticism,"
Sixteenth Century Journal, 7 (April, 1976): 88.

[7] CAS, 183.

[8] Ibid.

[9] Zanchi to Beza (5 February 1562), *Epist. theol.*, II, 364: "Per septimanum fui
cum nostro Martyro, edentulo quidem, sed non elingui, et incredibilem cepi ex eius
sermone (multa enim de vestra Gallia narraavit) voluptatem."

the humanistic aspect of Peter Martyr's work,[10] remains convinced that Martyr is at heart a scholastic and a key figure in the emergence of Reformed scholasticism. Donnelly acknowledges that Peter Martyr's role in Zanchi's conversion was his most significant contribution to the development of Protestant scholasticism,[11] but he has characterized the shift from Vermigli's perspective to Zanchi's in ways that support the indictment of Zanchi as a betrayer of the original genius of Reformed thought. In a 1976 article, Donnelly interpreted Peter Martyr as a transitional figure between the biblical and humanistic orientation of the Reformers and the unabashed scholasticism—marked by metaphysical rather than biblical modes of argument and presentation—that is instantiated in Zanchi's theology.[12] Vermigli was, in Donnelly's memorable phrase, "the pioneer of Calvinist Thomism."[13] Frank A. James, III has called attention to Vermigli's vehement critique of scholastic theologians, which is far sharper than anything to be found in Zanchi's comments on the usuability of the medieval tradition.[14] Richard A. Muller, on the other hand, has drawn attention to significant commonalities between

---

[10] Cf. Marvin Anderson, "Peter Martyr Vermigli: Protestant Humanist," in PMIR, 65–84. McLelland affirms (with Anderson) that "Martyr was a biblical commentator rather than a Systematiker." McLelland, "Peter Martyr Vermigli: Scholastic or Humanist," in PMIR, 142.

[11] CAS, 189. See also 207: ". . . Jerome Zanchi was the most thorough-going and influential in pioneering Calvinist scholasticism, Theodore Beza was the best known and the most prolific, but Peter Martyr was the first and the inspiration of all who came after."

[12] Donnelly, "Italian Influences," 86: "Martyr represents a transitional stage; his theology has the same basically humanist-biblical orientation as Calvin's, yet there is a strong undercurrent of scholastic elements. Zanchi represents for the first time a fully developed scholasticism." Cf. Donnelly, "Immortality and Method in Ursinus's Theological Ambiance," in Dirk Visser, ed., *Controversy and Conciliation: The Reformation and the Palatinate, 1559–1583* (Allison Park, Pa.: Pickwick Publications, 1986), 182–195, where Donnelly notes that Zanchi, in contrast to Peter Martyr, articulates his doctrine of immortality not in biblical categories or in relation to the resurrection of the body, but rather in abstract metaphysical considerations.

[13] Donnelly, "Calvinist Thomism," *Viator* 7 (1976): 452.

[14] Cf. Frank A. James, III, "Peter Martyr Vermigli: at the Crossroads of Late Medieval Scholasticism, Christian Humanism and Resurgent Augustinianism," in *Protestant Scholasticism: Essays in Reassessment*, Carl R. Trueman and R. S. Clark, eds., 66; Vermigli's *Exhortatio ad iuventem* dismisses Peter Lombard, along with Aquinas, Ockham, and Scotus as untrustworthy guides who "'filled everything with darkness.'" One could hardly imagine a sharper contrast to Zanchi's enthusiasm for Lombard and St. Thomas, in particular, and a variety of other *auctoritates* from the tradition of medieval scholasticism.

Zanchi's perspective and that of Peter Martyr: these include an infra-lapsarianism that suggests a basic continuity with Calvin's theology, an essentially Thomistic way of conceptualizing the efficacy of the death of Christ, an Augustinian view of divine omnipotence (joined, however, with vigorous defense of the freedom of secondary causes), and a fondness for the Pauline/Irenaean theme of recapitulation.[15] Muller warns that the contrast between Vermigli's humanism and Zanchi's scholasticism can easily be overestimated.[16]

Until 1986, with the initial publication of Muller's *Christ and the Decree*, most scholarly studies portrayed the Vermigli/Zanchi relationship as little more than a chapter in the history of the degradation of early Reformed theology. From Brian Armstrong's early thesis about "an unholy triumvirate"—Vermigli, Zanchi, and Beza—who allegedly executed a shift in Reformed scholasticism away from the symmetry and balance of Calvin's biblical, christocentric perspective,[17] to Donnelly's claim in 1976 that Zanchi moved away from Vermigli's critical appropriation of medieval sources toward a more deductive, scholastic methodology,[18] the older view characterized the Vermigli/Zanchi relationship in terms of betrayal or decline. Recent work on Protestant scholasticism has called that interpretation into serious question. Whether it is to be lamented or celebrated, however, the linkage between Vermigli and Zanchi is clearly crucial for our understanding of the dynamics of the transition from Reformation to Reformed Orthodoxy.

Especially in light of the personal rapport between the two, it is remarkable that in Zanchi's wide-ranging topical treatises, explicit Vermigli-citations are fairly scarce. Questions of influence and rela-

---

[15] Richard A. Muller, *Christ and the Decree: Christology and Predestination in Reformed Ttheology from Calvin to Perkins* (Grand Rapids, Mich.: Baker Books, 1988), 112. On Vermigli's infralapsarianism, cf. 65; idem, 118: "Zanchi, much like Vermigli and in contrast to the Scotist position of Calvin, predicates the infinite value of Christ's work on the hypostatic union and the *communicatio idiomatum*"; idem, 117; idem, 118.

[16] Muller, "Calvin and the Calvinists: Assessing Continuities and Discontinuities between the Reformation and Orthodoxy," *Calvin Theological Journal*, 30 (1995): 369.

[17] Brian Armstrong, *Calvinism and the Amyraut Heresy* (Madison, Wis.: University of Wisconsin Press, 1969), 38.

[18] CAS, 28: "Calvin's references [to the medieval scholastics] are almost uniformly hostile and derisive; Martyr cites the opinion of the scholastics nearly as often to agree with it as to oppose it. Martyr's friend Zanchi carried this a step further; his references to particular scholastic authors, particularly St. Thomas, are almost uniformly friendly."

tionship cannot be resolved by a numerical tally sheet of citations, of course. Still it is remarkable that Zanchi refers to Lombard, St. Thomas, and St. Bernard, for instance, far more often than to Peter Martyr.

In Zanchi's correspondence, however, the presence of Peter Martyr begins to loom larger, not only in Zanchi's letters to Calvin, Musculus, Bullinger, and Beza, among others, but also in their letters to him. In addition, there are two letters from Peter Martyr to Johannes Sturm, Zanchi's patron in Strasbourg, written at the height of the Marbach controversy.[19] What patterns emerge from this body of epistolary evidence? What light does it shed on the relation between Zanchi and Vermigli? [20]

Images of Vermigli in Zanchi's Correspondence

A. *In laudem Martyris*

Expressions of gratitude and affection for Peter Martyr constitute a veritable leitmotiv in Zanchi's correspondence. Writing to John Calvin on 18 April 1563, Zanchi expresses his devotion to Peter Martyr in terms that could hardly be more emphatic: explaining why he has not previously written to Calvin, Zanchi explains that ". . . as long as Peter Martyr, my truly reverend father and dearest teacher, was alive, I always took his advice with such seriousness that I did not think it right to disturb other great men, who were engaged in more serious matters."[21] Writing to Musculus, Zanchi says that he embraces

---

[19] To the best of my knowledge, there are no extant epistles from Vermigli to Zanchi, or *vice versa*. Cf. Marvin W. Anderson, "Register of Vermigli's Correspondence," in BIBL, 160–197.

[20] The value of Zanchi's published correspondence as a resource for assessing his relation to Peter Martyr might be called into question in light of the editorial process that preceded their publication in the 1613 edition of the *Oper. theol*: perhaps the letters have been contaminated by Zanchi's heirs and redactors. I can only report that I have been able to uncover no textual evidence to suggest that such a suspicion is warranted. In any case, the correspondence is no more subject to the possibility of redactional distortion than are the commentaries and treatises that appear in the 1613 edition, since they all bear the imprint of the same editorial processes.

[21] Zanchi to John Calvin (18 April 1563), *Epist. theol.*, II, 292: ". . . quamdiu vixit meus vere observandus pater et praeceptor carissimus, Petrus Martyr, illius semper, ut debeam, ita usus sum consiliis ut iudicarim alios magnos viros, et in rebus gravioribus occupatos, haud esse a me molestandos."

"my Martyr" (*Martyrem meum*), along with Musculus and Bullinger, not just with admiration but even with "a certain tenderheartedness" (*amore quodam tenero*) that creates a bond of trust unparalleled in his relationships with others.[22] Writing to Zanchi on 30 August 1556, Bullinger bears witness to Zanchi's special affection for Peter Martyr: "From your letter, most reverend Zanchi, I understood your clearly fervent love, by which your affection is aglow—or rather enflamed— toward our Martyr."[23] Writing to Bullinger on 8 January 1557, Zanchi gives voice to a prayer that God will "keep [Peter Martyr] safe and sound, not just for us but for the whole Church."[24] In 1562, following Peter Martyr's death in Zurich, the search for a successor leads Bullinger to consult Zanchi, who applauds his intention to seek someone who might be worthy to fill Martyr's shoes.[25] Zanchi expresses profound doubts, however, about the prospects of finding someone who fits that description:

> But where on the earth shall another Martyr be found? Others may promise and even render a similar industriousness, diligence, earnestness, sincerity of doctrine, friendship, and peacefulness, but who can both promise and render such doctrinal erudition, so varied and complex, such prudence in giving advice, such a charming lifestyle, such patience in bearing insults, and finally such dexterity not only in interpreting the Scriptures but in all other matters as well?[26]

---

[22] Zanchi to Musculus (undated), *Epist. theol.*, II, 315: "Mi pater Musdcule, ego omnes viros doctos et pios observo et colo. Sed mihi credas, te, Bullintgerum, et Martyrem meum singulari et peculiari non dicam tantum observantia, sed amore quodam tenero complector, ut maiori etiam fiducia mihi videar posse vobiscum quam cum aliis uti."

[23] Bullinger to Zanchi (30 August 1556), *Epist. theol.*, II, 398: "Amorem plane ferventem intellexi ex literis tuis, vererande Zanchi, quo ardes, imo flagras erga Martyrem nostrum."

[24] Zanchi to Bullinger (8 January 1557), *Epist. theol.*, II, 277: "Quae scripsisti de nostro D. D. Petro libentissime legi, precorque Deum ut eum diu non tam nobis quam toti ecclesiae Christi conservet incolumen."

[25] Zanchi to Bullinger (undated), *Epist. theol.*, II, 275–276: "Quod autem attinet ad quartum, talem vos expetere qualis fuit Martyr, vehementer probo vestrum desiderium: ego quoque tales exopto collegas."

[26] Ibid., 276: "Sed ubi terrarum alius invenietur Martyr? Laborem, diligentiam, studium, sinceritatem doctrinae, amicitiam, pacem promittere alli quoque possunt et vero praestare, sed tantum tamque variam et multiplicem eruditionem atque doctrinam, tantam prudentiam in dandis consiliis, tantam morum suavitatem in quotidiana consuetudine, tantam patientiam in ferendis iniuriis, tantam denique non solum in Scripturis interpretandis, set in aliis etiam rebus omnibus dexteritatem, quis possit ita promittere ut etiam reipsa praestet?"

B. *Zanchi, Vermigli, and the Struggle Against Gnesio-Lutheranism*

In the late sixteenth century, a loosely knit group of highly partisan
Lutheran polemicists engaged in wide-ranging controversies with their
more moderate fellow-Lutherans as well as with proponents of a
Reformed vision. They came to be known as "Gnesio-Lutherans,"
who contrasted the purity of their own "genuine" or "original"
Lutheranism with what they condemned as the compromises and
attenuations of the Melanchthonians (sometimes called "Philipists").
One of the points of controversy involved the accusation that some
Lutherans had fallen into a "crypto-Calvinism" by retreating from
Luther's doctrine of the bodily presence of Christ in the bread and
wine of the Lord's Supper. As a result, Gnesio-Lutherans tended to
be emphatic and highly partisan in their rejection of Reformed understandings of the eucharist.[27] From 1553, when he returned from
England, until 1556, when he accepted an invitation to become a
professor of Hebrew at the Zurich academy, Peter Martyr was
Zanchi's principal ally in responding to the resurgence of an aggres-
sive Lutheranism in Strasbourg. Zanchi's position became increasingly precarious when the leader of Strasbourg Lutheranism, the
polemical Johannes Marbach (1521–1581),[28] launched a frontal assault
on various points in Zanchi's Reformed theology, especially his doctrines of predestination and the eucharist. Zanchi's lectures on predestination, which initially provoked Marbach's critique, were prepared
in close consultation with Peter Martyr,[29] and throughout the years
of his second stay at Strasbourg, Martyr was Zanchi's principal ally
in the struggle. The ferocity of Marbach's onslaught may reflect a
Lutheran antipathy toward the Italians (perhaps in imitation of Luther,
who is reported to have dismissed Cajetan by saying, "He is an
Italian and that is what he remains").[30] It is clear that personal ani-
mosity played a significant role in the controversy. James Kittelson
has noted that Zanchi and Marbach "had numerous personal complaints against each other."[31] On the other hand, it may be simplistic

---

[27] Cf. James Arne Nestingen, "Gnesio-Lutherans," *Oxford Encyclopedia of the Reformation*,
II, 177–180.
[28] Cf. James M. Kittelson, "Johannes Marbach," *Oxford Encyclopedia of the Reformation*,
III, 1–2.
[29] Zanchi to Bullinger (undated), *Epist. theol.*, II, 275–276.
[30] *WABr* 1: 209.
[31] James M. Kittelson, "Marbach vs. Zanchi: The Resolution of Controversy in

to minimize the seriousness of the pastoral and theological issues at
stake in this confrontation. Marbach seems genuinely concerned that
Zanchi's doctrine of predestination puts in jeopardy the central position of the Church's day-to-day ministry of word and sacraments.
Kittelson may well be right when he argues that "for Marbach, these
practical and pastoral concerns always took precedence over speculative theology."[32] Whatever the original motivations, however, what
is clear is that Marbach's harassment made Zanchi's life exceedingly
unpleasant. Especially after Martyr accepted a position in Zurich,
Zanchi, deprived of a crucial collaborator, found the conditions under
which he lived and worked at Strasbourg increasingly intolerable.[33]

From Zurich, Peter Martyr continued to give Zanchi critical support. On the twenty-ninth of December, 1561, for instance, he joined
several other Zurich pastors and professors in endorsing fourteen
theses by Zanchi, thereby affirming the positions on eschatology, predestination, and perseverance that had led the Marbach faction to
question his orthodoxy.[34] Peter Martyr joined the other Zurich divines
in speaking of Zanchi with words of deep respect and solidarity, calling him "a man highly esteemed for his outstanding piety and teaching,"[35] and identifying with Zanchi's distress over the assaults on his
orthodoxy.[36] The Zurich manifesto examines each thesis in turn,
affirming most of them and offering only the mildest fine-tuning for
a few.[37] The tone of the response of Zurich's teachers and pastors
is illustrated by their comments on Zanchi's fourth thesis, in which
he asserts that the exact number of the elect—as of the reprobate—
is fixed and unchangeable, since in God's mind there is no uncertainty about his own eternal decree. Peter Martyr and the other
leading voices in the Zurich church unite in pronouncing Zanchi's

---

Late Reformation Strasbourg," *Sixteenth Century Journal* 8, no. 3 (1977): 32. Kittelson
notes that Zanchi conspired with Johannes Sturm to prevent republication of Tileman
Heshusius' sacramental treatise (a critique of Reformed eucharistic theology) at
Strasbourg.
[32] Ibid., 36.
[33] Zanchi to Bullinger (undated), *Epist. theol.*, II, 274–275: "Mihi quidem nihil
molestius, nihil gravius, nihil et vitae meae perniciosius, quam hic inter tot et tales
hostes, qui pugnam tamen et certamen detrectant continuis animi molestiis confici..."
[34] *Epist. theol.*, I, 257–258.
[35] "vir egregria pietate ac doctrina clarissimus" Ibid., 258.
[36] "non sine dolore cum suo tum nostro." Ibid.
[37] Ibid., 259–260.

thesis "beyond controversy" (*citra controversiam*). To reject Zanchi's position, they argue, is to imply that in matters of election and reprobation, God acts randomly (*casu*) or by chance (*temere*). According to the Zurich churchmen, the position of those who have attacked Zanchi in Strasbourg "must be rejected as something that is quite absurd."[38] If a sparrow cannot fall apart from the Father's will, how could it be supposed that God—who knows the exact number of hairs on our heads—could be ignorant of the number of the elect and the reprobate? But if God knows those numbers with an exact certainty, then they are fixed and definite. They are determined, in fact, by acts of the divine will. Since the divine will is eternal and immutable, so is the number of the elect and of the reprobate.[39] The final verdict of Peter Martyr and his colleagues places them squarely on Zanchi's side in his struggle against the Gnesio-Lutherans of Strasbourg:

> After closely and carefully considering the main points of his teaching, we find nothing in it that should be condemned as ungodly or inconsistent with Holy Scripture. On those points of dogma concerning which a controversy has arisen between [Zanchi] and his adversaries, we approve, commend and embrace his position (provided only that his theses are understood in a godly and suitable way), and we conclude that what he deserves is not some penalty but high praise.[40]

In light of Zanchi's deep attachments to his family (reflected by the prominent place of marital metaphors in his spirituality),[41] one cannot help sensing in the language of the Zurich manifesto of December,

---

[38] "Id autem ut absurdissimum reiiciendum est." Ibid.

[39] Ibid., 259: "Nam si duo passeres absque voluntate Patris non cadunt, nec citra eiusdem voluntatem ulli vel servabuntur vel deserentur, cumque voluntas Dei non sit nova sed aeterna, nec ipse mutetur, utqui sit prorsus immutabilis, consectarium est numerum utriusque ordinis iam apud eum esse constitutum. Hinc deinde accedit etiam capillos nostri capitis esse numeratos; quare e multo magis Deo constare necesse est numero servandorum."

[40] Ibid., 258–259: "Capitibus autem eius doctrinae attente ac dextre perpensis et excussis, nihil ibi deprehendimus aut impium aut pugnans cum divinis literis. Quo circa illa dogmata de quibus inter ipsum et adversarios eius orta est controversia, modo pia commodaque interpretatione accipiantur, approbamus, commendamus, et amplectamur, atque illum non poena ulla, sed laude non vulgari, dignum existimamus."

[41] Note that Zanchi conceived of his last published work, the *De religione christiana fides*, as a theological bequest for his children, to whom it is dedicated. Cf. John L. Farthing, "*De coniugio spirituali*: Jerome Zanchi on Ephesians 5.22–33," *Sixteenth Century Journal* 24, no. 3 (1993): 621–652.

1561, a sensitivity not only to the question of Zanchi's integrity and salvation but also to the implications of the controversy for his career and thus for the welfare of his wife and children: "For if he should be deemed guilty of such an offense, not only would the salvation of his soul come into question, which would itself be an occasion for dread and terror, but he would suffer the loss of his reputation, with severe negative consequences for his wife and children."[42] This concern for Zanchi's family reflects a sensitivity that is quite Zanchian, if we may coin such a term. Those, such as Peter Martyr, who knew Zanchi's priorities and sensitivities, and who understood the marital/familial shape of his piety, saw fit to frame their response not only in terms of dogmatic necessities but also in terms of what was at stake for Zanchi as *pater familias* and for the entire Zanchi household.

On 1 January 1562 (three days after the publication of the Zurich churchmen's response to Zanchi's theses), and then again on 24 May 1562, Peter Martyr posted letters to Johannes Sturm, reiterating his solidarity with Zanchi in the conflicts at Strasbourg. The first of these epistles reads as if it had been designed to serve as a cover letter for the report of the Zurich ministers and professors.[43] Martyr begins by noting that Zanchi has subjected his theological positions to the judgment of the Zurich churchmen, explicitly asking for an honest critique that is not adulterated by considerations of personal affection (*omni humano affectu seposito*). The invitation is one that Peter Martyr finds he cannot in good conscience decline.[44] Although he knows full well that nothing he can say will persuade Marbach and his allies, Martyr finds that he simply cannot remain silent.[45]

---

[42] *Epist. theol.*, I, 258: "Nam si tanti sceleris damneretur, non tantum eius animi salus in discrimen veniret, quod horribiliter expavendum est, sed etiam de omni eius existimatione actum esset, idque cum suo uxoris liberorumaque maximo detrimento."

[43] Peter Martyr to Johannes Sturm (1 January 1562), *Epist. theol.*, I, 265: "Proinde quamvis non dubitat praeclaros illos viros, scriptis utriusque partis diligenter perlectis, cognitaque vestri Capituli gravissima sententia, et duarum Academiarum praeclaro iudicio, iam tandem intellegere neque ipsum pro haeretico habendum, attamen pro Christiana charitate requisivit a nobis ut sua dogmata seu theses gravi severaque censura examinaremus, et si quid minus orthodoxum in eis deprehendissemus, omni humano affectu seposito, illum ut fratrem admoneremus, sin vero ea quae docuit vera et sana censeremus, testimonium et quidem conscriptum veritati dare non gravaremur."

[44] Ibid., 266: "Huius autem non minus docti quam pii viri petitioni, per conscientiam et eam fidem qua veritati sumus obstricti, non potuimus non assentari."

[45] Ibid.: "Et quamvis nos haud quaquam latet quod adversarii nostra testimonia sint pro nihilo habituri, quod ab illis in caussa sacramentaria dissentiamus . . ."

He claims that it is an obligation to the truth itself that impels him to reinvolve himself in the Strasbourg disputes.[46] Responsive to the language of Zanchi's request, Martyr insists that he will not let his judgment be tainted by his affection for Zanchi,[47] although he does not hesitate to acknowledge a personal bond between himself and his fellow-Italian expatriate, whom he calls his "best friend" (*summus amicus*). He goes on to express his wholehearted support for Zanchi's position in the conflict with Marbach *et al.* He speaks of Zanchi as one who "in such troublesome times, at considerable expense and through no fault of his own, has been forced to wander from place to place" for the sake of his witness to the truth of the Reformed faith.[48] He expresses his sympathy for all that Zanchi has suffered as a result of the conflict, along with his appreciation for the support that Sturm and the Strasbourg chapters have given Zanchi throughout the long controversy.[49] He reports that while Zanchi is confident of ultimate vindication, he is becoming frustrated over prolonged delays in resolving the case, and over the limited expertise— and the social or political vulnerabilities—of those who are to pass judgment on the issues at stake in the dispute.[50] Finally, Martyr reminds Sturm that Zanchi's teachings are hardly an innovation, since they stand in continuity with the theological perspective of both Luther and Bucer.[51]

---

[46] Ibid.: ". . . non tamen absterreri potuimus quin veritati laboranti opitularemur."

[47] Ibid.: "Necque nos ita in odio esse arbitramur ut putemur in gratiam unius hominis, quantumvis chari atque amici, doctrinam impiam et haereticam voluisse probare."

[48] Ibid., 265: "Fuit hisce diebus, vir clarissime, apud nos communis utriusque nostrum summus amicus, D. Zanchius, a quo cum audierim eius caussae tam longam dilationem, non potui non vehementer dolere, ac sum illius ex animo ac impense miseratus, qui hoc tempore tam incommodo, nec sine magnis sumtibus, praesertim innocens cogitur oberrare."

[49] Ibid.: "Nobis quidem fideliter exposuit tuam tum Capituli suae caussae iustam et fortem defensionem. Qua de re tibi atque tuis venerandis collegis maximas ago gratias."

[50] Ibid.: "Retulit item quinque optimis viris consularibus negotium suum et cognoscendum et definiendum esse commissum, ut auditis nonnullis doctorum virorum sententiis, quid viderentur de tota re pronuntient. Sed interea nihil esse acturum et se vereri ne cunctatio propterea interponatur, quod iudices delecti cum interioris theologiae non sint admodum periti, metuant ne religionis capitibus definiendis nonnullorum hominum reprehensionem incurrant."

[51] Ibid., 266: "Imo vero sumus admirati quare ministri vestrae hanc doctrinam ausi fuerint damnare, cum illam, praesertim quoad praedestinationem, Ecclesiae

In May of 1562, Peter Martyr once again writes to Johannes Sturm. Whereas his earlier letter was filled with explicit references to Zanchi's role in the struggle over predestination and perseverance, now he focuses intently on the eucharistic dimensions of the controversy. Without mentioning Zanchi by name, Peter Martyr places before Sturm a most emphatic vindication of the eucharistic theology that Zanchi has affirmed against the Lutheranism of Marbach and Brentz, who affirm that the Lord's body, while being fully human, is nonetheless capable of being in many places at the same time, going so far as to claim that the body of Christ is equal in ubiquity to his divine nature.[52] Martyr lays out the Reformed case against the claims of the Strasbourg Lutherans who, while rejecting transubstantiation (*metousían*), still posit such an intimate connection between the eucharistic elements and the actual body and blood of Christ that the Savior's bodily presence is conceived as something existing "not only in heaven but also in the bread and wine of the sacred supper."[53] That a body should be in many places at the same time would clearly involve a violation of the laws of physics, which the ubiquitarians explain by appealing to divine omnipotence. Martyr finds that appeal inappropriate and unpersuasive. God's omnipotence, after all, is not absolute. There are some things, Martyr notes, that even God cannot do; for instance, God cannot deny himself or reverse past events, or violate the law of noncontradiction.[54] The appeal to omnipotence, after all, is often the last refuge of heretics seeking to evade the clear import of biblical teachings.[55]

---

nexus, perseverantiam sanctorum, et promissiones aeternae vitae, professi fuerint cum Lutherus tum etiam Bucerus, Evangelii Filii Dei concionatores celeberrimi."

[52] Peter Martyr to Iohannes Sturm (24 May 1562), *Epist. theol.*, I, 234: "Non verentur Domini corpus, quamvis humanum est, affirmare simul eodemque tempore in multis locis esse, imo progrediuntur eo ut illud aeque ad naturam divinam pronuntient esse ubique . . ."

[53] Ibid.: ". . . supponant statuantque carnem et sanguinem Christi non tantum in caelis esse, verum etiam in pane ac vino sacrae Caenae adesse praesentia."

[54] He cites II Tim. 2:13 for this first point of God not denying Himself. Ibid., 235: "Commonefacimus attamen pios divinam omnipotentiam, quam una cum omnibus fidelibus credimus, non esse citra omnem exceptionem credendam. Nam et Paulus excipit, Deum non posse negare seipsum." Idem: ". . . a Deo fieri non posse ut quae facta sunt infecta reddantur." Idem: "In scholis etiam theologis definitum est: ea Deum non posse facere quae, ut loquitur, contradictionem implicant . . ."

[55] Ibid.: "Attenendum praeterea non paucos haereticos isto suffugio esse usos, cum illorum prava et insana dogmata refellerentur a sanctis patribus non solum ut absurda verum etiam ut impossibilia. Respondebant enim, ut se tuerentur: omnia Deo esse possibilia."

Affirming, with Zanchi, that Christ is not absent from the supper, even though his eucharistic presence is not corporeal,[56] Martyr insists that Christ's availability to believers in the Supper must be distinguished from the corporeal or substantial presence that Lutherans affirm.[57] Realities disjoined in space (*i.e.*, believers on earth, the body and blood of Christ in heaven) are indeed brought together in the Supper, not in a bodily but in a spiritual way.[58] The effect of partaking in faith is that the flesh and blood of Christ are present in believers as the fruit of their union with him.

> Hence the body and blood of Christ are present to us by his Spirit, grace, and merits, and by the other wonderful effects that flow by a divine influence from them to us, just as we say that the sun is present to us through the light, the rays, and the good influences that we receive from that source.[59]

Hence Martyr joins Zanchi in affirming the real presence of Christ's body and blood in the eucharist, while insisting, with Zanchi, on the spiritual way in which they become available to believers, who eat and drink with the mouth of faith, not the lips and teeth of the body:[60] "Therefore," he claims, "those who believe, by faith embracing the reality that the flesh and blood of the Lord were given unto death for our salvation, spiritually eat and spiritually drink."[61] Like Zanchi, Martyr underlines the material reality of what is received in this spiritual way, while at the same time denying that the presence

---

[56] Cf. John L. Farthing, "Patristics, Exegesis, and the Eucharist in the Theology of Girolamo Zanchi," in Carl R. Trueman and R. S. Clark, eds., *Protestant Scholasticism: Essays in Reassessment* (Carlisle, UK: Paternoster, 1999), esp. 89–90.

[57] Peter Martyr to Johannes Sturm, (24 May 1562) *Epist. theol.*, I, 236: "Si de ea praesentia loquamur quam corporalem, realem, atque substantialem vocant, corpus et sanguinem Christi abesse fateor."

[58] Ibid.: "Eadem dico adesse fidelibus in Caena praesentia fidei, cuius vis et facultas est ut ea efficiat reddatque praesentia spiritualiter quae locorum spacio longe admodum sunt abiuncta."

[59] Ibid.: "Deinde caro et sanguis Christi nobis praesentia sunt spiritu, gratia, et meritis, et aliis admirabilibus fructibus qui divinitus per ea in nos derivantur, quemadmodum Sol dicitur nobis adesse praesens per lucem, radios, et bonos influxus quos inde percipimus."

[60] Vermigli cites the dictum of Cyprian and Augustine: "Quid paras dentem et ventrem? Crede, et manducasti." (Ibid.).

[61] Ibid., 235: "Qui ergo credunt et fide amplectuntur Domini carnem et sanguinem fuisse nostrae salutis caussa in mortem tradita ea spiritualiter commedunt et spiritualiter bibunt."

is corporeal or that the body and blood of Christ are received in a corporeal way.[62]

Although he does not explicitly invoke Zanchi's name, Martyr's argument is clearly intended as a vindication of the Reformed eucharistic theology that is under massive assault by Zanchi's adversaries in Strasbourg. The notion of the humanity of Christ, he contends, implies a reality that can be present in only one place at one time.[63] Here Martyr's rejection of ubiquity is rooted in biblical rather than abstract philosophical considerations. The women at the empty tomb receive the angelic announcement, "He is not here!" Christ himself told the Apostles that he was going away. According to Peter's sermon in Jerusalem, the heavens must receive the risen Jesus until the last day.[64] Martyr poses the question that a Reformed eucharistic perspective renders inevitable: "If according to his human nature he will be in heaven until the last day, why are we looking for his body on the earth?"[65] But Zanchi's opponents in Strasbourg, according to Vermigli, completely disregard the weight of biblical evidence. At the heart of Martyr's critique is his accusation that the ubiquitarians have abandoned biblical theology for natural philosophy.[66] Thus his ultimate rebuke of the Lutheran polemicists is an admonition that they should "stop making up from their own minds new dogmas and new articles of faith and imposing them on us as things that have to be believed, which arose, however, in the house of the ubiquitarians, but not in the field of the divine Scriptures."[67] Here Peter Martyr articulates the humanist-biblical orientation that unites him to Calvin and allegedly marks a point of divergence from Zanchi.

---

[62] Ibid., 235: "Proinde fatemur ad esum et potationem physicam et propriam exigi esculentae ac poculentae rei praesentiam; alioqui res absentes nec edi neque bibi posse, vicissem autem negamus e spirituali esu et potu elici aut concludi eaque ἀλληγωρικῶς edi et bibi corporaliter ac proprie adesse praesentia."

[63] Ibid., 234: "Ego vero Christi naturam humanam semper certo qauodam loco fuisse comprehensam dico, quem ita occuparit ut eodem tempore alibi non fuerit."

[64] Mark 16.6, Matt. 28.6, Luke 24.6; John 14.28, Acts 3.21.

[65] Ibid.: "Si futurus in caelis est, quoad naturam humanam, usque ad extremum diem, quid eius carnem et sanguinem in terris quaerimus?"

[66] Ibid.: "Non me latet eos in hac tota ratione id nobis exprobare, quod non theologos verum naturales philosophos agamus."

[67] Ibid.: ". . . illos porro sedulo moneo ut ex capite suo nova dogmata novosque articulos fidei cudere desinant, et nobis ea obtrudere credenda, quae domi eorum nata sint, non autem in agro divinarum scripturarum creverint."

Yet when he appeals to the primacy of biblical over philosophical theology, he speaks in the first-person plural, firmly associating himself with Zanchi's defense of a Reformed christology in Strasbourg: "We follow the testimony of the holy scriptures," he says, adding that "insofar as we follow the testimonies of the holy scriptures . . ., to that extent we confess that we do not follow philosophy at all but rather the Word of God."[68] Clearly this use of the first person plural pronoun is intended as a way of expressing Martyr's solidarity with Zanchi. Perhaps such language should give pause to those who are tempted to draw too sharp a distinction between Martyr's methodology and Zanchi's.

C. *De eligendo successore Martyris: Zanchi as Vermigli's Heir*

Zanchi's contemporaries recognized a continuity between his role in the Reformed church and that of his compatriot, Peter Martyr. On 25 February 1553, when Jacob Sturm invited Zanchi to accept a teaching position at Strasbourg, he was emphatic about the continuity that he saw between the perspectives of the two Italian Reformers.[69] Zanchi's letter accepting the invitation is replete with indications of affection for his mentor and compatriot, thus confirming the public perception of continuity between his own career and that of Peter Martyr.[70] Part of the basis for his willingness to go to Strasbourg, he says, is his awareness that this will be pleasing to Martyr.[71] In a 1556 epistle to Bullinger, Zanchi insists that the target

---

[68] Ibid., 235: ". . . quo sanctarum scripturarum testimonia sequimur, ut illa recensuimus, eo minime nos philosophiam sed verbum Dei sequi testamur."

[69] Jacob Sturm to Zanchi (25 February 1553), *Epist. theol.*, II, 269: "Scripsit ad nos Caeluius Secundus te animum a nostra Repub., Hieronyme Zanchi, non alienum gerere, neque recusare nobiscum vivere ea qua fuit Petrus Martyr conditione. . . . Deinde idem tibi quod Petro Martyri, et quod felix faustumque sit Ecclesiae et Scholae nostrae munus, eademque disciplinae functionem damus atque committimus. Promittimus etiam eadem stipendia et laborum consimiles fructus. Et quantum in nobis est, curabimus ut non minus apud nos libenter futurus sis quam Petrus Martyr fuerit."

[70] Zanchi to Jacob Sturm (undated), *Epist. theol.*, II, 269: "Officii vero, quando tam officiose ac perliberaliter mihi, quae vestra est de nobis Italis honestissima opinio (hoc ut caeteris taceam accepto ferimus honestissime Petri Martyris vobiscum consuetudini) eadem et fuctionem et conditionem, quam habuit apud vos idem vir doctissimus, vestrique observantissimus, Peter Martyr, offertis . . .

[71] Ibid., 270: Me enim si vobis morem gererem, Petro etiam Martyri, vestri amantissimo, rem gratam facturum."

of Marbach's assault was not so much Zanchi himself as it was Peter
Martyr (along with Calvin and Beza).[72]

Martyr's departure for Zurich in 1556 left Zanchi to face the Gnesio-
Lutherans alone. Naturally, he was distraught over the loss of his
friend, ally, and fellow-countryman.[73] He comments to Theodore
Beza, in a letter dated 6 July 1556, "Even if I do not mention it,
you can imagine how distressing and upsetting it is for the good
people [of Strasbourg] to have to deal with Martyr's departure. For
you are not unaware of how beloved Martyr was by all good men."[74]
He confides to Calvin that Martyr played a crucial role in the training of the Reformed clergy.[75] He goes on to indicate that his only
consolation in Peter Martyr's departure from Strasbourg is his sense
that divine providence has summoned his old friend to Zurich in
order to combat the Pelagian tendencies of those who are stressing
freedom of the will in such a way as to imperil the truth of predestination.[76] When eventually Zanchi abandoned Strasbourg, he
claimed that he was leaving for the same reasons that led his mentor to precede him to Zurich.[77] Conditions in Strasbourg, he says,
prevented him from fulfilling the terms of his appointment, which
specified that he was to continue the doctrinal tradition of Peter
Martyr.[78] When Bullinger wrote to console Zanchi on his loss of

---

[72] Zanchi to Bullinger (dated only 1562), *Epist. theol.*, II, 272: "In conventu pas-
torum maxima contentione damnavit doctrinam de praedestinatione, et Martyrem,
Calvinum, ac Bezam appelavit sine ullo pudore, non dicam."

[73] Cf. Donnelly, *Calvinism and Scholasticism*, 190.

[74] Zanchi to Beza (6 July 1556), *Epist. theol.*, II, 363: "Quam graviter et moleste
ferant omnes viri boni Martyris discessum tu potes scire, etiam me tacente. Non
enim nescis quam omnibus bonis esset gratus Martyr."

[75] Zanchi to Calvin (1 July 1563), *Epist. theol.*, II, 331: "Ad hanc enim nostram
Scholam . . . confluunt ex omnibus Germaniae partibus studiosi, qui postea in ministros verbi eliguntur. Permultum autem refert huiuscemodu studiosos initio bene in
veris dogmatibus et in sincera scripturarum intelligentia institui. Cum igitur hoc
optime praestaret Martyr noster, et eius auctoritatem plurimum valeret ad veram
doctrinam studiosis persuadendam, vehementer doleo hominis discessum."

[76] Ibid.: "Illud enim me in hoc D. Petru discessu consolatur, quod sciam divina
providentia eum vocatum fuisse Tigurum fortasse in hunc finem, ut praeter alia
Ecclesiae commoda, multos etiam qui in ea sunt Ecclesia pestilentissimam illam (in
sinum tuum hoc repono) de libero arbitrio contra praedestinationem, ideoque contra gloriam Dei doctrinam, dedoceat."

[77] Zanchi to Henricus Knollus (undated), *Epist. theol.*, II, 271: "De discessu meo
Argentina, credo te ab aliis iam pridem intellexisse. Ea fuit, ut uno verbo dicam,
propter quam bonus quoque piae memoriae Petrus Martyr longe ante me disces-
serat . . ."

[78] Ibid.: ". . . cum igitur vidissem mihi non amplius licere libere docere neque

Martyr's assistance in his struggles against the Lutherans in Strasbourg, he felt it necessary to remind him that Zurich's gain was not Zanchi's loss: ". . . since friends have all things in common, Martyr is still yours, because we all belong to you, and we hope that you belong to us as well."[79] The continuity between Martyr and Zanchi is underlined by Bullinger's pun: Peter Martyr, he says, is closely connected to Zanchi, who "is being martyred in Strasbourg."[80]

After Peter Martyr's death in 1562, when a consensus emerged that his successor should be found among those who had been his students, the search turned naturally to Zanchi as one of Martyr's most illustrious disciples.[81] Writing to Zanchi on 15 December 1562, Conrad Gesner made it clear that the position is Zanchi's for the taking.[82] One day later, in a letter dated 16 December, Bullinger notes that Peter Martyr's style of scholarship, churchmanship, and piety constitutes the standard against which candidates to succeed him will be measured:

> We are looking for a man who will be in all respects like our Martyr—
> a diligent man, peaceful, kind, not negligent, contentious, or quarrel-
> some, who will not bring conflict but will nourish peace among the
> brethren. We are seeking, moreover, a man who is both sincere and
> straightforward, not preoccupied with interminable opinions and ques-
> tions or matters of curiosity that have nothing to do with salvation.[83]

---

eam tueri doctrinam quam ante me viri doctissimi, Bucerus, Capito, Martyr, Calvinus, e fonte S. literarum haustam, in ea Schola auditoribus multos annos propinaverant?"

[79] Bullinger to Zanchi (30 August 1556), *Epist. theol.*, II, 398: "Ac quoniam ami-corum omnia sunt communia, Martyr etiamnum vester est, quia nos omnes vestri sumus et speramus vos omnes nostros esse."

[80] Ibid.: "Manet et inhaeret pectori tuo cor tuum. Avulsum non est. Tigurum translatum non est, quia Zanchius insidit cordibus nostris, licet Argentinae Martyrizet."

[81] Bullinger to Zanchi (16 December 1562), *Epist. theol.*, II, 273: "Nunc igitur agi-tur de successore illi surrogando cumque multorum animi in te inclinent, ut qui illius diligens sis discipulus . . ."

[82] Conrad Gensner to Zanchi (15 December 1562), *Epist. theol.*, II, 286: "Convenimus heri, Clarissime D. Doctor, et de substituendo in locum defuncti nuper D. Martyris professore egimus, praesente utroque consule et senatoribus duobus, tandem una-nimiter visum est excellentiam tuam unam omnium optime, doctissime, et gravis-sime, hoc munere fungi posse, et propter tuam erga Ecclesiam nostram benevolentiam de tua voluntate non dubitavimus. Quam facile vero dimittereris dubium nobis fuit. Speramus tamen id quoque non difficulter futurum et primo quoque tempore de voluntate tua certiores fieri cupimus, qua intellecta, res ad senatum deferetur nos-trum, quem non diffidimus sententiam nostram confirmaturum . . ."

[83] Bullinger to Zanchi (16 December 1562), *Epist. theol.*, II, 273: "Requirimus

After summarizing the qualifications for Martyr's successor, Bullinger makes it abundantly clear that, in his view, Zanchi rises to that level. All the ministers and teachers at Zurich, he notes, must swear to say nothing contrary to the canonical Scriptures and to introduce no doctrinal innovations.[84] Then he makes the case that Zanchi, no less than Peter Martyr, fulfills these conditions.[85] Zurich, he says, is looking for someone who will continue Peter Martyr's broad, comprehensive approach to exegesis, without devoting undue time and energy to obscure subplots of the larger biblical message, at the expense of what is essential.[86] He observes that Martyr's stipend has been allotted to his widow "until the Feast of John the Baptist," but expresses his hope that financial arrangements will not prevent Zanchi from coming to Zurich at once to assume the position left vacant by Martyr's death.[87]

Two days later, on 18 December 1562, a similar appeal was addressed to Zanchi by Wolfgang Hallerus, a Reformed minister and president of the Zurich academy. Hallerus laments the death of Peter Martyr as a grievous loss not only to the faithful in Zurich but also to the Church universal: "He was not only a light and a mainstay (*lumen atque columen*) for our church but also a most splendid illumination for the whole Church of Christ in all the world."[88] Now Hallerus and his colleagues are seeking another Elisha to stand in

---

vero talem modis omnibus virum qualis fuit Martyr noster, hominem laboriosum, pacificum, benignum, non neglegentem, contentiosum, et rivosum, qui pacem inter fratres alat, non discordiam ferat. Hominem praeterea requirimus simplicem et expositum, non involutum variis opinionibus et quaestionibus interminabilibus, non intentum rebus curiosis et nihil facientibus ad salutem."

[84] Ibid.: "Iurant autem ministri et professores omnes se nihil dicturos aut asserturos contra scripturam canonicam, se denique perserveraturos in nostra illa doctrina, neque unquam quicquam in hac nostra ecclesia innovaturos aut nova dogmata nondum collata cum synodo scripturisque explicata et confirmata ac recepta proposituros."

[85] Ibid.: "Quae quidem omnia tibi, ut et Martyri, non iniqua sed maxime necessaria videri arbitror."

[86] Ibid.: 273: "Ac progressus est Martyr noster in exponendis literis sacris expedite, non inhaesit uni alicui capiti, nedum loco scripturae alicui, dies aliquot et menses, quod alioqui a doctis viris saepe solet fieri."

[87] Ibid.: 273: "Stipendium tamen huius anni, usque ad natalem Iohan. Bapt. benigne Martyris viduae donatum est. Inde vero et labores et stipendium una progredientur, quanquam mallem te citius, si deligeris, advenire."

[88] Wolfgang Hallerus to Zanchi (18 December 1562), *Epist. theol.*, II, 284: "Fuerat non modo nostrae ecclesiae lumen atque columen, sed totius Christi in toto orbe lampas Ecclesiae splendissima."

Elijah's place; what they are looking for is "a new Martyr,"[89] and in that search they turn to Zanchi:

> And while our scholars are wrestling with this concern, in the end it is you alone, my dear Zanchi, whom they all prefer. For in you we have observed the blessed Martyr's spirit, learning, integrity, humanity and character, which make it possible for us to consider you a worthy replacement for him.[90]

Seeking to overcome Zanchi's reluctance to accept the summons to Zurich, Hollerus appeals to his love for Peter Martyr, who did so much to shape the religious and intellectual life of that city: "Even if our academy is smaller than the one in Strasbourg, still it is by no means less excellent, especially because of Martyr . . ."[91]

In spite of urgent appeals from the Zurich divines, Zanchi finds that he cannot bring himself to forsake his post in Strasbourg. Although he admits to Bullinger and to Hallerus that Zurich looks good to him from his current position in the midst of the Strasbourg controversies, he finds that he cannot bring himself to leave the perils and stresses of Strasbourg for the more congenial atmosphere of Zurich.[92] He despises the conditions under which he lives and works in Strasbourg, but he cannot in good conscience abandon his post.[93]

---

[89] Ibid.: "Sed eccum! Quae nos fors ex eius oblitu assignat? Ut non modo propter illum amissum dolore, sed insuper propter illum ereptum de novo Martyre inveniendo et substituendo modo nos torquere cogamur."

[90] Ibid: "Atque dum ea cura scholarchae nostri torquentur, unus tu, mi Zanchi, es, in quem omnium vota inclinare et desinere videntur. In te enim D. Martyris spiritum, eruditionem, integritatem, magnanitatem atque mores et merito de te substituendo cogitemus hactenus observavimus."

[91] Ibid.: "Nostra quae sit Ecclesia ipse nosti, et quae nostrae Scholae ratio itidem. Ea si minor videatur Argentinensi, nihil tamen ignobilior, propter Martyrem praecipue, qui in ea docuit atque in ea vitam suam claudi cupivit, censenda erit."

[92] Zanchi to Bullinger (undated), *Epist. theol.*, II, 275: "Illa certe est non postrema quod, praeter consensum in vera doctrina, quanta sit et vestra et vestri magistratus benevolentia, cum generatim ad nationem nostram, tum speciatim erga demortuum patrem Martyrem . . . satis diu et multum sensimus ac sentimus."; Zanchi to Wolflgang Hallerus (undated), *Epist. theol.*, vol. 2, 285: "Cur enim non malim inter amicos vivere quam inter non paucos hostes quotidie mori, et isthic quotidianis piisque consolationibus affici quam hic perpetuis animi cruciatibus confici? . . ." 286: "Quin cupiam igitur vobiscum et in Ecclesia isthic Italia vivere non est cur dubites."

[93] Zanchi to Bullinger (undated), *Epist. theol.*, II, 274–275: "Mihi quidem nil molestius, nihil gravius, nihil et vitae meae perniciosius, quam hic inter tot et tales hostes, qui pugnam tamen et certamen detrectant continuis animi molestis, confici: sed spectatis iis, quae prudenter a Sturmio quoque perpensa sunt, qua conscientia possim ante exitium caussae hanc stationem deserere non video."

However much it might have pleased him to replace the controversies of Strasbourg with the concord of the Zurich brethren, Zanchi
concludes that it would be an unforgivable failure of nerve to leave
Strasbourg before seeing the controversy to an appropriate conclusion: he cannot in good conscience abandon the struggle for the
truth in Strasbourg, since that would yield an undeserved victory to
the enemies of the Reformed faith.[94] Zanchi's reverence for his mentor is also suggested by his admission to Hallerus that he has some
anxieties about filling Martyr's shoes.[95]

Less than a year later, in the fall of 1563, the Italian Reformed
church at Lyons, under the leadership of Peter Viret, invited Zanchi
to assume the pastorate there.[96] Zanchi received the invitation, however, only after agreeing to serve as pastor to the Reformed congregation in Chiavenna.[97] Therefore Zanchi had to reject the invitation.
More than two years earlier, Zanchi had been in conversation with
the church in Lyons about the possibility of coming to serve as its
pastor. At that point, he says, he had indicated that he could not
abandon the struggle in Strasbourg to assume this position.[98] Had it

---

[94] Zanchi to Woflfgang Hallerus (undated), *Epist. theol.*, II, 286: "Sed duo tantum
hic consideranda sunt. Unum, An antequam haec nostra diffidia sint composita vel
aliquem habeant finem, liceat mihi hanc meam stationem deserere, fratribus et collegis meis solis in pugna relictis? Non video quomodo per conscientiam possim caus-
sam tam iustam, tam bonam, non privitam, sed nobis et omnibus Christi ecclesiis
communem, deserere aut neglegere. . . . Alterum est an si post exitum huius caussae per dominos mihi licuerit veritatem hic defendere, docere, ac retinere, licitum
mihi sit, veritatis oppugnatoribus meo discessu cedere."; Cf. Zanchi's comments to
Bullinger, *Epist. theol.*, II, 274, 277–288.

[95] Zanchi to Wolfgang Hallerus (undated), *Epist. theol.*, II, 285: "Illud tantum dolet
quod maiorem, ut video, plerique vestrum de me concepistis quam ut ei ego possim unquam satisfacere. Iam dudum quidem enitor ut persequar Martyris eruditionem, pietatem, spiritum, eruditionem. Sed quando unquam assequar? . . . Foret
etiam mihi opus duplo maiore spiritu et doctrina mei Eliae, hoc est, Martyris, prae-
ceptoris mei, cum in dies augeantur hostes contra quos dimicandum et intereant
fortissimi imperatores."

[96] Petrus Viretus to Zanchi (21 September 1563), *Epist. theol.*, II, 375: "Quum
itaque una omnium consensione ad hoc munus ab ipsis electus voceris, nos te
quibuscunque possumus precibus rogamus ut vocationem sequaris et ad nos accedas.
Nam ea est et tua eruditio et pietas, nobis omnibus satis testata, ut non dubitemus
tuam praesentiam in hac urbe non solum tuae genti sed etiam toti huic Ecclesiae,
et caeteris omnibus totius regni huius, magno et adiumento et ornamento fore."

[97] Zanchi to Petrus Viretus (1 November 1563), *Epist. theol.*, II, 376: "Nisi fidem
meam, paulo ante istam electionem, Ecclesiae Clavennensi . . . obstrinxissem, ego
quam libentissime tum vestrae tum Italorum meorum petitionem satisfecissem . . ."

[98] Ibid., 377: "Sunt anni duo et amplius ex quo cum electus fuissem in min-
istrum, respondi me nullo modo Argentinensem stationem deserere . . ."

not been for this determination to see the Strasbourg controversies through to a successful conclusion, Zanchi says, he would have been delighted to accept the call to Lyons (*quam libentissime*). Apparently defending himself against the suggestion that he had agreed to accept the pastorate in Lyons and then failed to live up to that commitment, he calls the Zurich brethren to witness, invoking also the silent witness of *optimus noster Martyr*, in support of his explanation of reasons for refusing to accept the position at Lyons.[99] Even in death, Martyr remains for Zanchi—true to his name—a rock-solid witness to the truth.

A Concluding Suggestion

When Zanchi's formal theological treatises (excluding his biblical commentaries) are compared to Peter Martyr's, it is easy to detect a significant shift in the trajectory of Reformed thought. As Donnelly has noted, Aristotle is a more crucial resource for Zanchi's project than for Vermigli's.[100] Zanchi's training at Bergamo and Padua "was even more heavily Thomist than Martyr's and left an even deeper impression."[101] The impact of Zanchi's greater indebtedness to Aristotle and Aquinas is not hard to discern. Like Calvin's *Institutes*, Martyr's writings include no separate treatise on the nature of God per se, comparable to what St. Thomas does at the beginning of the *prima pars* of the *Summa theologiae*. Zanchi, on the other hand, has not completely abandoned the medieval longing to know God *per se* as well as *erga nos*: especially (though not exclusively) in his *De natura Dei*, Zanchi revels in speculations about the attributes of divinity in itself.[102] In addition, it is beyond dispute that deductive, syllogistic reasoning is far more evident in Zanchi's theology than in Peter Martyr's.[103] Reformed anthropology undergoes a remarkable transformation in

---

[99] Ibid., 377: "Noverant haec fratres Tigurini (vivebat nam adhuc optimus noster Martyr), et tamen defuncto Martyre, illius conditionem mihi obtulerunt, quod certe non fecissent si iudicassent me fratribus qui erant Lugduni, propter illud meum responsum, fide adhuc fuisse obstructum."

[100] Donnelly, "Italian Influences," 93.

[101] CAS, 189–190.

[102] Ibid., 201.

[103] Ibid., 200.

Zanchi's theological writings. Martyr's teaching about life after death (like Calvin's) is based on biblical arguments, to which philosophical considerations are secondary and almost peripheral. Martyr frankly admits that immortality cannot be established by rational proofs, but must be accepted on the basis of biblical revelation. With Zanchi, however, the immortality of the soul is affirmed on metaphysical grounds.[104] At several points, then, one can hardly immerse oneself in the writings of Martyr and Zanchi without hearing a distinct shifting of the gears—if not of the tectonic plates—in early Reformed theology.

Nothing that has arisen in our review of the epistolary evidence requires us to turn a blind eye to these points of contrast. But the evidence provided by Zanchi's published correspondence does suggest that the links between Martyr and Zanchi are complex (if not, in some ways, paradoxical), and that previous analyses of that relationship may have opened up only one side of a multi-faceted reality.

If the books that they published provided the only window through which to catch a glimpse of their relationship, we might well conclude that there is a sharp discontinuity between Peter Martyr Vermigli and Girolamo Zanchi. But the pattern emerging unmistakably from a careful review of Zanchi's published correspondence qualifies that conclusion: the contrast between Martyr and Zanchi, which seems so obvious upon a close reading of their systematic treatises, was not at all apparent to Martyr himself, nor to Zanchi, nor to their contemporaries. Martyr mounts a vigorous defense of Zanchi against his adversaries in Strasbourg. Zanchi, in turn, is clearly devoted to Martyr, his *praeceptor carissimus*. Reformed circles in Zurich and Lyons saw fundamental continuities between Zanchi and Martyr, viewing their relationship as parallel to that between Elijah and Elisha. Somehow the methodological and thematic discontinuities that Donnelly, among others, has noted, seemed less obvious, or less important, to Martyr, Zanchi, and their contemporaries.

At the quincentennial of Peter Martyr's birth,[105] perhaps we can discern the dynamics of change in early Reformed theology more

---

[104] Donnelly, "Italian Influences," 95.

[105] The original draft of this essay was presented to a session of the Sixteenth Century Studies Conference in St. Louis, Missouri (29 October 1999), in celebration of the quincentennial of Peter Martyr's birth.

clearly than could those who reshaped that tradition in the late six-teenth century. Where they saw continuity, we see discontinuity. We may be right, of course; perhaps they were so close to these devel-opments that they could not see a larger pattern that was there all along but too subtle to be noticed except from the distance of nearly five centuries. But the disconnect between our perception and theirs might alert us, at least, to the complexity of the evidence—and the fragility of the assured conclusions of our own scholarship.

STRANGERS IN A STRANGE LAND:
THE ENGLISH CORRESPONDENCE OF MARTIN BUCER
AND PETER MARTYR VERMIGLI

N. Scott Amos

The friendship of Martin Bucer (1491–1551) and Peter Martyr Vermigli (1499–1562) spanned a period of some ten years, from Martyr's
arrival in Strasbourg in 1542 to Bucer's death in Cambridge in
1551—a critically important period in Martyr's career, and the final
decade of Bucer's life. Though it began as a relationship of patron
and beneficiary—it was Bucer who secured for Martyr his first major
post upon the latter's entry into exile—it soon became one of equals,
and the regard they had for one another was a constant throughout the years in Strasbourg. It should thus come as no surprise that
upon Bucer's own exile from Strasbourg and arrival in England it
was, perhaps, Martyr (who had preceded him to England by nearly
two years) more than any other who proved to be a source of encouragement and advice during what was at times a difficult exile.[1]

Bucer's friendships with the leaders of reform in England (and
particularly in Cambridge) have been remarked upon, but what is
often not taken note of is that among his *correspondents* during his
time in exile, it was Martyr more than any other with whom he
exchanged letters. By the same token, Martyr's friendship with Heinrich
Bullinger is rightly emphasized, but for the first years of his sojourn
in England, it was Bucer to whom he had recourse most often in
correspondence and this recourse was only ended by Bucer's death.
The fact that they were both strangers (though not to each other)

---

[1] It is worth noting that whereas in the case of Bucer's English friends we have
a limited amount of direct evidence which testifies to their dealings with him, in
the case of Martyr we have relatively extensive material. I have written elsewhere
on aspects of Bucer's English sojourn and his relationship with his hosts: N. Scott
Amos, "'It is Fallow Ground Here': Martin Bucer as Critic of the English Reformation," *Westminster Theological Journal* 61, no. 1 (1999): 41–52; and an as yet unpublished piece, "The Alsatian among the Athenians: Martin Bucer, Mid-Tudor Cambridge
and the Edwardian Reformation" (presented to the April 2001 Meeting of the
Society for Reformation Studies, Westminster College, Cambridge).

in a strange land—foreigners in what was for them an unfamiliar country, and one which wore its Reformation with a difference[2]— certainly had much to do with the value to each of their continued relationship. However, we miss the point if we see it only in these terms. The important thing was the relationship itself, which ante-dated their English sojourn, and which has been described by Marvin Anderson as one of alter egos.[3] The letters from their English years are particularly valuable because they provide the most substantial evidence for this relationship (at any time during its ten year span), and they enable us to gain a sense of its character and its inner dynamic.

What these letters reveal is a friendship of deep affection between the two, an affection that only increased during their time in England. Further, we find a strong mutual dependence between them, not only for encouragement during the difficult times both faced in their respective universities, but also for advice relating to their work in the furtherance of reform. The letters reveal occasional tensions as well, as one would expect between two formidable theologians in such a tumultuous age of shifting allegiances and doctrinal debate. Yet this also serves to underscore that the relationship was one of parity between equals, and in view of Bucer's senior status as the leading German Reformer after Martin Luther and Philip Melanch-thon, this is testimony to Martyr's emergence as a major theologian. If the English phase of Martyr's career was indeed highly significant for his emergence as a leading theologian, both in print and on the public stage,[4] then the prominence of Bucer as a source of advice and dialogue (and the respect Martyr displayed towards him) must be given its due in any examination of these years of Martyr's life.

---

[2] This latter phrase is borrowed from G. R. Elton's essay on the Reformation in England, found in G. R. Elton, ed., *The New Cambridge Modern History*, vol. II of *The Reformation, 1520–1559*, 2nd ed. (Cambridge: Cambridge University Press, 1990), 262.

[3] Marvin Anderson, "Peter Martyr, Reformed Theologian (1542–1562): His Letters to Heinrich Bullinger and John Calvin." *Sixteenth Century Journal* 4, no. 1 (April 1973): 41.

[4] See Philip M. J. McNair, "Peter Martyr in England" in PMIR, 87, and the assessments of John Patrick Donnelly, S. J., Joseph McLelland, and Marvin Anderson cited by him.

The Historical Context: the Edwardian Reformation

It is necessary first to say something about the immediate historical context of this friendship, specifically the Edwardian phase of the English Reformation (1547–1553).[5] Martyr and Bucer were the most prominent of a number of Continental theologians who took shelter in England in the years following the Holy Roman Emperor Charles V's victory over the Schmalkaldic League at Mühlberg in 1547.[6] During these years, England emerged as the best hope for the continued progress of the Reformation in Europe, which elsewhere had entered a very difficult phase. With the accession of Edward VI, England became the refuge of choice for Protestant theologians and laity fleeing the advance of Catholic armies.[7]

At the same time, Archbishop Thomas Cranmer sought to move England into the forefront of theological leadership of the wider Reformation.[8] It was his hope to make English reform the standard for European reform, and to that end he sought to gather together the leading Protestant theologians of his day into a synod that would produce a statement of doctrine that could unite evangelicals and lead to a renewed advance for their faith throughout Europe.[9] Cranmer issued letters of invitation to a wide range of theologians, and among the first to answer his call was Peter Martyr.[10] Martyr was at the time in Strasbourg, and came to England in December 1547 with

---

[5] The best work for this phase of the English Reformation is that of Diarmaid MacCulloch, specifically: *Thomas Cranmer: A Life* (New Haven and London: Yale University Press, 1996); and *Tudor Church Militant: Edward VI and the Protestant Reformation* (London: Allen Lane/The Penguin Press, 1999). In each of these works, attention is given to the part Martyr and Bucer played in the Edwardian Reformation.

[6] Among the others were: Bernardino Ochino; Immanuel Tremellius; Francis Dryander; John à Lasco; Pierre Alexander; John Ab Ulmis; Paul Fagius; and Vallerand Poullain. See MacCulloch, *Thomas Cranmer*, 351–513 passim. Several of them came at the express invitation of Cranmer.

[7] See MacCulloch, *Thomas Cranmer*, 380; and MacCulloch, *Tudor Church Militant*, 77–81.

[8] See MacCulloch, *Thomas Cranmer*, 393–5. See also 174–6, where MacCulloch describes the early stages of Cranmer's aspirations in this regard.

[9] MacCulloch, *Thomas Cranmer*, 501–2.

[10] Cranmer wrote to John Calvin, Philip Melanchthon, Heinrich Bullinger, Albrecht Hardenberg, John à Lasco, Wolfgang Musculus and Martin Bucer (among others). See MacCulloch, *Thomas Cranmer*, 394–5 and 501–2, for a discussion of Cranmer's plans with regard to a projected Council to produce a comprehensive statement of doctrine.

the blessing and support of his patron and colleague, Martin Bucer.[11] Martyr was installed as Regius Professor of Divinity at the University of Oxford, and immediately found himself on the front line of the Reformation in England, facing down strong opposition from Catholic members of the university.[12] When Bucer himself left Strasbourg for England in 1549—in answer to the same call of Cranmer—he became in turn Regius Professor of Divinity at the University of Cambridge.[13] Both reformers thus became key figures in the promotion of Protestant theology, not only at their respective universities, but also in the wider Reformation in England during these years.

It is against this backdrop that the letters of Martyr and Bucer should be read. Their correspondence did not take place in a vacuum, but rather in the midst of the Edwardian Reformation. This Reformation was characterized not only by conflict with Catholicism, but also by divisions within the ranks of the Protestants over the path of reform to follow.[14] It was a matter of finding the *via media*, although in the case of the Edwardian Reformation it was not a middle way between Rome and Wittenberg, but rather between Wittenberg and Zurich.[15] At the heart of the controversy on the Continent between the two poles of Protestantism was the dispute over the presence of Christ in the Lord's Supper, and it was impossible for Cranmer to prevent completely the importation into England of this dispute while welcoming *émigré* theologians. It was over this issue more than any other that Bucer and Martyr differed (however

---

[11] See the letter of Bucer to Cranmer, 28 November 1547 (Paris, Bibliothèque Ste-Geneviève MS 1458, ff. 173v–175); this letter is discussed by MacCulloch in *Thomas Cranmer*, 381–2.

[12] See Jennifer Loach, "Reformation Controversies" in *The History of the University of Oxford*, vol. III, *The Collegiate University*, ed. James McConica (Oxford: Oxford University Press, 1986), esp. 368–375, for a concise discussion of Martyr at Oxford. See also the article by McNair, "Peter Martyr in England," cited above.

[13] The most recent short study of Bucer in England is Basil Hall, "Martin Bucer in England" in D. F. Wright ed., *Martin Bucer: Reforming Church and Community* (Cambridge: Cambridge University Press, 1994), 144–160. The two most substantial studies are: Constantin Hopf, *Martin Bucer and the English Reformation* (Oxford: Blackwell, 1948); and Herbert Vogt, "Martin Bucer und die Kirche von England" (Ph.D. dissertation, Münster, 1968).

[14] The Vestments Controversy is but one instance of this conflict within the Protestant party during these years. See, for instance, J. H. Primus, *The Vestments Controversy* (Kampen: J. H. Kok, 1960), especially 43–55. See also MacCulloch, *Thomas Cranmer*, 479–81.

[15] See MacCulloch's comment to this effect in *Thomas Cranmer*, 617.

slightly). Bucer and Martyr were roughly at the center point of the spectrum of convictions on this issue, though Bucer leaned towards Wittenberg and Martyr towards Zurich.[16] It is in the tension of this issue, as it is reflected in their letters, that we get the best sense of the true nature of their friendship. Their exchange will form the center of the investigation that follows.

A Statistical Survey

Before moving to a discussion of the content of the letters, some remarks on the statistics of the correspondence are in order, for they are in themselves revelatory both of the strength of the continued friendship of Bucer and Martyr and its importance to each. This is especially true when these letters are considered in the context of what we know of the total correspondence of each for these years. During his time in England, Martyr exchanged letters with a growing number of correspondents, totaling fifteen by the end of February 1551.[17] It is indicative of his increasing importance as a theologian and churchman that leading Continental reformers as well as leaders of reform in England were included in his epistolary circle, though at this point the circle was still somewhat restricted.[18] What is striking is that Bucer was numerically by far and away the most significant of his correspondents during his time in England from December 1547 down to the end of February 1551 (Bucer died on 28 February).[19]

---

[16] In respect of this issue with particular reference to Cranmer, see MacCulloch, Cranmer, 406–7.

[17] In what follows, I have drawn on Marvin Anderson's register of Martyr's correspondence found in BIBL, 161–66. It should be noted that Dr. Anderson's list is not completely accurate, as there are some missing letters, and must be used with some caution. In addition to Anderson's register, I have consulted the register of Bucer's correspondence found in Vogt, "Martin Bucer und die Kirche von England", 175–199. Also important is: Jean Rott, "Le Sort des Papiers et de la Bibliothèque de Bucer en Angleterre." Revue d'Histoire et de Philosophe Religieuses 46 (1966): 346–67. For details of Bucer's and Martyr's correspondence with all others, I refer the reader to these works.

[18] Only four correspondents were on the Continent (if one includes Bucer prior to his arrival in England), for a total of seven letters, and of those with whom he exchanged letters in England four were fellow exiles (again, including Bucer).

[19] Indeed, if you carry the statistical analysis down to the end of Martyr's English sojourn, the correspondence with Bucer still constitutes the largest single percent-

Of the extant correspondence between these dates, Martyr exchanged eighteen letters with Bucer—seventeen to Bucer[20] and one received from Bucer[21]—out of a total correspondence of 41 letters. The Bucer correspondence thus constitutes very nearly 44% of the total, far outstripping that of any other single correspondent. If we include in

---

age of the whole, even compared with that which Martyr had with all the Zurichers combined.

[20] From December 1547 to February 1551, Martyr sent the following letters to Bucer:

1. 26 December 1547, found in Hastings Robinson, ed. *Original Letters Relative to the English Reformation*, vol. II (Cambridge: Parker Society, 1846–7)—hereafter designated *O. L.*—468–73. The Latin text is printed in Hastings Robinson, ed., *Epistolae Tirguinae de rebus potissimum ad Ecclesiae Anglicanae Reformationem Pertientibus conscriptae* (Cambridge: Parker Society, 1848)—herafter *E. T.*—348–49;
2. 22 January 1549 (*O. L.*, II, 474–77; *E. T.*, 312–15);
3. 15 June 1549, printed in G. C. Gorham, *Gleanings of a few scattered ears, during the period of the Reformation in England* . . . (London: Bell and Daldy, 1857), 80–82; translated from Conrad Hubert, ed., *Martini Buceri Scripta Anglicana fere omnia. . . .* (Basel: Petrus Perna, 1577), 545–46;
4. August 1549, (Gorham, *Gleanings*, 97–8; translated from the original in the Parker Library of Corpus Christi College, Cambridge—hereafter CCCC—MS 102, nr 7, fols 103–06);
5. 18 December 1549 (Gorham, *Gleanings*, 123–26; CCCC MS 102, nr. 8, fols. 107–110);
6. 10 January 1550 (*Rogeri Ascham Epistolarum libri quatuor*, ed. Edward Grant [Oxford, 1703], 437–38);
7. 31 March 1550 (Gorham, *Gleanings*, 140–42; CCCC MS 119, nr. 44, fols. 119–20);
8. 10 June 1550 (Gorham, *Gleanings*, 151–56; CCCC MS 119, nr. 40, fols. 107–08);
9. 11 June 1550 (CCCC MS 119, nr. 40, fols. 117–18);
10. 31 August 1550 (Gorham, *Gleanings*, 168–75; CCCC MS 102, nr. 5, fols. 91–4);
11. 6 September 1550 (Gorham, *Gleanings*, 176–79; CCCC MS 119, nr. 38, not paginated);
12. 10 September 1550 (Gorham, *Gleanings*, 180–85; British Library, Add. MSS 19400, nr. 3, fol. 20);
13. 20 September 1550 (CCCC MS 119, nr. 38, not paginated);
14. 25 October 1550 (Hopf, *Martin Bucer*, 162–64; Oxford, Bodleian Library, MS New College 343, fols. 14–15);
15. 11 November 1550 (Gorham, *Gleanings*, 196–99; CCCC MS 119, nr. 37, not paginated);
16. 10 January 1551 (Gorham, *Gleanings*, 227–31; CCCC MS 119, nr. 39, not paginated);
17. 2 February 1551 (Gorham, *Gleanings*, 231–33; British Library, Add. MSS 28571, fols. 47r–48v).

[21] The only letter from Bucer to Martyr for which we have a record is that of 20 June 1549 (Gorham, *Gleanings*, 82–92; the Latin original is no longer extant, but is printed in Hubert, *Scripta Anglicana*, 546–50).

our calculations the letters between the two that are no longer extant
(but the existence of which can be deduced from Martyr's letters),
the total number of letters increases to 30.[22] By contrast, for the
same period there are only three letters from Martyr to Heinrich
Bullinger (letters in response to three Bullinger had sent him, letters
no longer extant), and none to Calvin—both of whom were correspondents who figure prominently in the latter half of Martyr's life.

The sheer frequency of Martyr's letters to Bucer is itself significant
in view of the fact that he was not (by his own admission) an assiduous correspondent. He freely admits to Bullinger in the three letters he wrote from England before March 1551 that he has delayed
in responding to him, and though the reasons given are plausible
one senses that Martyr made no special effort to reply to him with
dispatch.[23] Yet this never seems to have been the case in his correspondence with Bucer. If the number and frequency of letters alone
are to be taken as an indicator of the importance of the relationship, it is clear that Bucer was very important to Martyr during
these years, more so than any other correspondent or group of correspondents, those of Zurich included.

When we turn to Bucer and his English sojourn, it is equally clear
that Martyr was of great importance to him during these years. He
exchanged more letters with Martyr than with any other correspondent—and considering that he was in Cambridge during most
of this time, away from the centers of English politics and as a con-
sequence apart from men such as his patron and friend, Archbishop
Thomas Cranmer, this is of some significance. Of the sixteen letters
between Martyr and Bucer between 1549 and 1551, we have seen
that only one from Bucer is extant (evidently, Martyr was not as

---

[22] If the missing letters are included in our calculations, correspondence with
Bucer constitutes nearly 57% of the corpus of Martyr's correspondence. However,
we must bear in mind that there are likely letters from other correspondents that
have also gone missing, which should qualify any such hypothetical calculations.
See below for a list of Bucer's missing correspondence with Martyr.

[23] See Martyr to Bullinger, 27 January 1550; 1 June 1550; 28 January 1551. All
in *O. L.*, vol. II, 477–480, 481–484, and 486–490 respectively. The Latin text is
in *E. T.*, 315–16, 317–19, 320–2. We find a similar admission in a letter to Conrad
Hubert of 8 March 1551 (*O. L.*, vol. II, 490–492; *E. T.*, 323), and another to the
ministers at Strasbourg of the same date, found in Gorham, *Gleanings*, 237–238.
The Latin text of the letter translated by Gorham is printed in an appendix—
Epistolae Theologicae—to *Loci Communes D. Petri Martyris Vermilii* (Londini: Excudebat
Thomas Vautrollerius Typographus, 1583), 1088–89.

careful in collecting his correspondence as was Bucer). However, we can reconstruct from remarks in Martyr's letters an approximate number of those written by Bucer (eleven further in addition to the one we have today),[24] as well as one further by Martyr to Bucer.[25] By contrast, Bucer had exchanged only three letters with Thomas Cranmer during these years, and only five with John Calvin.

At the same time, and without taking anything away from the significance of Martyr as a correspondent for Bucer, we must note that although Martyr was the person with whom Bucer corresponded the most, the percentages with regard to Bucer's total correspondence are considerably different. Of the extant letters for the period of Bucer's exile from 26 April 1549 to 28 February 1551, correspondence exchanged with Martyr constitutes sixteen of 136 letters that have been identified in Bucer's correspondence, or approximately 11.7% of the total.[26] Rather than suggest that Martyr was relatively less

---

[24] The missing letters from Bucer to Martyr are:
1. 7 August 1549, referred to in Martyr's letter from the end of August 1549 (Gorham, *Gleanings*, 97; CCCC MS 102, nr. 7, fols. 103–06 at 103);
2. after 13 November 1549 and before 18 December 1549, to which Martyr's letter of 18 December 1549 is a response (Gorham, *Gleanings*, 123–26; CCCC MS 102, nr. 8, fols. 107–110 at 107);
3. prior to 31 March 1550, to which Martyr's letter of the same date is a response (Gorham, *Gleanings*, 140–142; CCCC MS 119, nr. 44, fols. 119–20 at 119);
4. 11 May 1550, as noted on Martyr's letter of 31 March 1550 in Bucer's hand (Gorham, *Gleanings*, 142; CCCC MS 119, nr. 44, fols. 119–20 at 120);
5. 2 June 1550, referred to in Martyr's letter of 10 June 1550 (Gorham, *Gleanings*, 151; CCCC MS 119, nr. 40, fols. 107–08, at 107);
6. 16 August 1550, referred to in Martyr's letter of 31 August 1550 (Gorham, *Gleanings*, 168; CCCC MS 102, nr. 5, fols. 91–94 at 91);
7. 30 August 1550, referred to in Martyr's letter of 31 August 1550 (Gorham, *Gleanings*, 168; CCCC MS 102, nr. 5, fols. 91–94 at 91);
8. early September 1550, referred to in Martyr's letter of 10 September 1550 (Gorham, *Gleanings*, 180; original in the British Library, Add Mss 19400, nr. 3, fol. 20);
9. a letter received on 5 November 1550, referred to in Martyr's letter of 11 November 1550 (Gorham, *Gleanings*, 196; CCCC MS 119, nr. 37, not paginated);
10. a letter accompanying Bucer's *Censura* sent in January 1551, referred to in Martyr's letter of 10 January 1550 (Gorham, *Gleanings*, 227; CCCC MS 119, nr. 39, not paginated);
11. and finally, a letter of 22 January 1551, referred to in Martyr's letter of early February 1551 (Gorham, *Gleanings*, 231–33; original in the British Library, Add Mss 28571, fols. 47 recto—48 verso).

[25] The missing letter of Martyr to Bucer was sent some time in November 1549, and is referred to in his letter to Bucer of 18 December 1549 (Gorham, *Gleanings*, 126; CCCC MS 102, nr. 8, fols. 107–109 at 109).

[26] If we include the missing letters of Bucer and Martyr, the figures rise to 28 of 148, or 18.9% of the total.

important to Bucer than vice versa, though, these figures underscore Bucer's continued commanding position as a leading theologian and churchman, both for the Continent and for England.[27]

Two principal points emerge from these statistical comparisons. One, Bucer and Martyr were of tremendous importance for one another during their years in England, as is evidenced by the volume of their correspondence alone relative to that exchanged with others. Two, though it is true that Zurich (and in particular Bullinger) was to become an important source of correspondence for Martyr in future years, it was not so as long as Bucer was alive.[28]

The Epistolary Relationship of Bucer and Martyr

While these numbers do tell a significant story, the content of the letters is of course the more important and revealing of the actual character of the relationship between the two Reformers. The principal aspect of this relationship to which I wish to draw attention is the personal, which provides a necessary context within which to understand the theological exchanges that constitute the bulk of the correspondence—including that dealing with the Eucharist. The two had a profound attachment to one another, and an equally profound personal regard. Martyr gives clear evidence of his deep affection for Bucer, delighting even in his friend's prolixity in writing (a delight to which few have ever admitted).[29] Letters from Bucer appear to have been eagerly awaited by Martyr, and from them he derived much comfort as well as advice. Further, he was often prompt in his response to them (the significance of which I have already sug-

---

[27] The total number of his correspondents for this period was 75 (as opposed to 15 for Martyr), of whom 45 were on the Continent and 30 in England. Of the latter, 20 were English and the remainder fellow exiles or other foreign visitors. The numbers for Bucer are the more impressive relative to those for Martyr, for whereas in the latter's case I included letters from December 1547 to February 1551 (39 months), in the case of Bucer I have only taken account of the period from April 1549 to February 1551 (23 months).

[28] One might also note that while it is clear that Martyr was increasingly important for the wider world of the Reformation, this comparison of correspondence indicates that he had not yet attained the stature of Bucer—nor that which he himself would later achieve.

[29] Martyr to Bucer, 10 September 1550; in Gorham, *Gleanings*, 180; original in British Library, Add Mss 19400, nr. 3, fol. 20.

gested). Given Bucer's often poor health, it is not surprising that this affection should be expressed in solicitude on Martyr's part for his friend, whose numerous maladies prompted deep anxiety in Martyr, anxiety which he expressed on more than one occasion—for he greatly valued both the correspondence and friendship he had with Bucer, and Bucer's role in the affairs of England and of the Church at large.[30]

In the same connection, those occasions on which Bucer evidently gave vent to his deep misgivings about his situation were of nearly equal concern to Martyr.[31] The familiar tone of his letters is further testimonial to the depth of friendship, a familiarity that is less pronounced in his correspondence with, for instance, Heinrich Bullinger from the same time. For his part, Bucer was (if anything) even more familiar and more effusive in his expression of affection for Martyr, writing at one point in the course of a discussion regarding the Eucharistic debates:

> It is my wish, as your very loving friend, very much loved by you, most truly lovingly to transmit to you these suggestions for your consideration, till the Lord shall bring us together again. How is it possible that I should not love most lovingly one who loves me ardently, one so powerful in Christ, one so patient? Such affection—what offences from you cannot it forgive; when you come forward so boldly in every place to assert the glory of Christ?[32]

One rarely encounters such language in other of Bucer's letters from this time, even in those to Calvin with whom he had an equally close relationship.

---

[30] See Martyr to Bucer, 18 December 1549; 31 March 1550; both in Gorham, *Gleanings*, 123–126, 140–142 (originals, CCCC MS 102, nr. 8, fols. 107–09; MS 119, nr. 44, fol. 119 respectively). In the latter letter Martyr refers to an earlier letter in which he expressed sympathy for Bucer's illness and relief (as he thought) at his friend's recovery. Further, he exhorts Bucer to exert himself less in his duties at Cambridge for the sake of his personal well-being.

[31] Martyr to Bucer, 18 December 1549; in Gorham, *Gleanings*, 124–25 (CCCC MS 102, nr. 8, fols. 107–09).

[32] Bucer to Martyr, 20 June 1549; in Gorham, *Gleanings*, 91. Latin text printed in Hubert, *Scripta Anglicana*, 550: "Haec (dum Dominus nos rursus coniunxerit) volui tibi mittere cogitanda, meo amicissimo amicissimus, et vere amicissime. Ecqui te non summe mei amantem, tantumque in Christo potentem, tamque ferentem, non amarem amantissime? Qui amor quas non possit a te remittere offensiones: sic cum te in adserenda ubique gloria Christi praestas?" There is (with some variations in wording) a modern edition of this letter and that of Martyr which preceded it in volume I of J. V. Pollet, *Martin Bucer: Etudes sur la correspondance*, 2 vols. (Paris: Presses Universitaires, 1958–62), 263–272.

Yet underneath the familiarity and the expressions of affection there is evidence of the deep respect each held for the other, and here we turn to the theological dimension of their relationship, and the parity between the two which they themselves tacitly acknowledged. The measure of this respect is seen in part in the number of occasions upon which each sought the advice of the other, demonstrating a mutual reliance in a common cause. For instance, Martyr's desire for Bucer's opinion regarding the disputations at Oxford and his own efforts therein indicates to us the esteem in which he held his friend—both as a source of advice, and as a seasoned debater to be emulated:

> Give me your best advice; for, my strength being small, the matter perplexing, and the adversaries both obstinate and very audacious, in the compass of four days I was unable to effect more than you see. [...] It is not uncommon for veteran soldiers, and for those who, like yourself, have retired with honour from the service, to take delight in looking on while raw recruits are fighting....[33]

On another occasion, again in connection with an impending disputation, he was desirous of Bucer's views on merits, though he was grieved that his request came at a time when Bucer was seriously ill and the effort to answer the request proved to be a strain.[34] Nevertheless, the matter—and Bucer's advice—was in Martyr's view important enough to justify his imposition:

> In truth, I did not put those questions to you hastily: for some of our adversaries think that we are in the greatest possible error, while we inculcate such doctrine; and they are confident that, should a public disputation on these matters take place, I should so hesitate as to be totally unable to answer their arguments.[35]

---

[33] Martyr to Bucer, 15 June 1549; in Gorham, *Gleanings*, 81. Latin text in *Scripta Anglicana*, 545: "Tu boni consules. Nam, ut meae vires sunt imbecillae, res involuta, et adversarii cum obstinati, tum audacissimi, pro quatuor dierum spacio non plus, quam vides, praestare valui. [...] Solet veteranis militibus, et iam, uti tu es, rure donatis, iucundum esse, videre tyrones interdum pugnare...."

[34] Martyr to Bucer, 31 March 1550; in Gorham, *Gleanings*, 141 (CCCC MS 119, nr. 44, fol. 119).

[35] Martyr to Bucer, 31 March 1550; in Gorham, *Gleanings*, 141 (CCCC MS 119, nr. 44, fol. 119). The original reads: "Quandoquidem ea temere non interrogavi: sunt sane aliquot ex nostris adversariis, qui putant nos cum haec docemus toto errare caelo; atque confidunt si ad disceptandum publice de his aliquando veniat, me ita hesitaturum ut ipsorum argumentis respondere minime valeam."

These instances give evidence of Martyr's regard for and reliance upon the advice of Bucer.[36] Further, Martyr's expression of relief that they were of one mind regarding the Vestments controversy,[37] and his pleasure at reading Bucer's critique of the 1549 Book of Common Prayer and finding further evidence of their common thinking[38] provide additional testimony to the value Martyr attached to and his deep respect for the thinking of his friend.

The same measure of respect and regard was true of Bucer for Martyr. In the one letter we have from Bucer's hand for this period, he writes:

> But God, who is Love, in the course of my life has brought me into connexion with no man [but yourself] whose innermost thoughts, both on the whole subject of religion, and on the manner of bringing a State into conformity with it, appear to me more fully to agree with my own judgment of whatever measure it may be: let there, then, be cemented between us no common friendship; on my part, by means of the contemplation of those rare virtues with which Christ has adorned you; on your part, by the consideration of my not altogether worthless endeavours.[39]

He adds later that Martyr, in addition to being "among the dearest of my acquaintance", had in his view "a very great name among the Churches of Christ in every land."[40] And where Martyr submitted

---

[36] There is also an indication that Martyr may have sought Bucer's views on infant baptism (though to what end is unknown), which were contained in a letter written some time in the summer of 1550 but no longer extant. Martyr to Bucer, 31 August 1550; in Gorham, *Gleanings*, 175 (CCCC MS 102, nr. 5, fols. 91–4 at 94).

[37] Martyr to Bucer, 11 November 1550; in Gorham, *Gleanings*, 196 (CCCC MS 119 nr. 37, no folio numbers). Martyr had earlier written to Bucer on the same issue on 25 October 1550: Bodleian Library, Oxford, New College MS 343, fols. 14–15; text printed in Hopf, *Martin Bucer*, 162–69.

[38] Martyr to Bucer, 10 January 1551; in Gorham, *Gleanings*, 227–29 (CCCC MS 119 nr. 39).

[39] Bucer to Martyr, 20 June 1549; in Gorham, *Gleanings*, 83. Latin text in *Scripta Anglicana*, 546: "Atqui nullum mihi Deus, qui est charitas, virum in hac vita obtulit, cuius intima sensa, cum de religione tota, tum etiam de Republ. huic conformanda, mihi eadem visa sint, cum qualicunque meo iudiciolo, plenius congruere, sitque proinde inter nos amicitia haud vulgaris constata: in me, contemplatione virtutum tuarum, quibus pereximiis te Christus ornavit: in te, consideratione studii nonnullius mei."

[40] Bucer to Martyr, 20 June 1549; in Gorham, *Gleanings*, 88. Latin text in *Scripta Anglicana*, 548–9: ". . . qui permagnum hodie ubique gentium apud Christi ecclesias nomen habes, et es mihi, ut nemo magis, charissimus. . . ."

his thinking on the Eucharist to review by Bucer, and sought Bucer's advice on a number of other occasions, so too Bucer appears to have sought Martyr's advice. This is evident from several of Martyr's letters in response to a number of requests from Bucer, though again Bucer's letters are no longer extant.[41] In each instance, the request arose in the context of Bucer's dispute with the Catholics at Cambridge in the summer of 1550, and in each instance Bucer appears to have sought to draw on Martyr's knowledge of the fathers regarding a number of issues, most particularly the matter of justification.[42] Given that Bucer's own Patristic learning was regarded as impressive in his day, these repeated requests are a significant measure of his own regard for Martyr's Patristic learning. It is the *mutual* reliance of the two that is noteworthy. One might well expect that Martyr would have continued to be deferential to his friend and desirous of his advice (out of courtesy to a senior Reformer and former patron, if nothing else), even though he now held a position in his own right— that of Regius Professor of Divinity at Oxford, the equal of Bucer's at Cambridge—and was himself consulted by the English on theological matters. What is perhaps somewhat surprising is the extent to which the same was true of Bucer in regard to Martyr.[43]

Yet, for all the unanimity they professed to find in their thinking, and for all their genuine mutual regard, they were realistic enough to recognize that each held to positions which the other might find displeasing, and their respect for one another was such that neither was unwilling to draw attention to this fact. There were tensions in the relationship. Here we see the sense of parity more clearly, cer-

---

[41] Martyr refers to two letters of Bucer in a response sent on 31 August 1550; the first was dated 16 August, the second 30 August. This latter must have been sent in some haste by Bucer, since it arrived in the space of a day. He sent an additional letter on 6 September 1550 as a further response to Bucer's requests. Bucer then followed up with another request, to which Martyr responded on 10 September 1550. For all, see Gorham, *Gleanings*, 168–175, and 176–179, and 180–183 respectively (CCCC MS 102, nr. 5, fols. 91–4; MS 119, nr. 38; British Library, Add MSS 19400, nr. 3).

[42] Bucer wrote on at least one other occasion seeking Martyr's reading of the church fathers on a question regarding the nature of faith. Martyr's response was dated 11 November 1550; in Gorham, *Gleanings*, 197 (CCCC MS 119, nr. 37).

[43] Though we do have the testimony of Johann Sturm, in a letter to Johannes Marbach, in which he stated that Bucer would seek the advice of Martyr before doing anything that concerned either the Church or Academy of Strasbourg. Cited in John Patrick Donnelly, *Calvinism and Scholasticism in Vermigli's Doctrine of Man and Grace* (Leiden: E. J. Brill, 1976), 174.

tainly on the part of Martyr. The tensions are most obvious in the matter of the Eucharist, that great bone of contention between evangelicals and Catholics (not to mention among the evangelicals themselves). In fact, it is on this issue alone for which we have evidence from the hand of both of an exchange of views on any point of theology, and the temptation is to set them in opposing camps with Martyr tending towards (if not, indeed, fully part of) the mind of Zurich.

But we should consider the exchange within the wider context of their personal relationship, as well as pay careful attention to what they said in this instance. Joseph McLelland has analyzed the theological issues discussed in their correspondence, and finds that the two at heart are in agreement.[44] It is true that their differences can indeed be over-stressed. Bucer and Martyr themselves believed they held to fundamentally the same position (a point that should not be overlooked), and each hastens to emphasize that the difference between them is more apparent than real. It is, however, an indication of Martyr's independence of mind that for all the deference he displays to Bucer, even offering to submit to his judgment on the results of the Oxford Disputation, he does not indicate any uncertainty regarding the rectitude of the position he advanced—though he suspects that Bucer might take exception to it:

> I am inclined to think that you will not be sorry to read these my [papers]; unless, perhaps, I shall appear to differ somewhat from you on that Question; in which, however, on weighing the whole thoroughly, you will easily understand that—when I maintain that the Body of Christ becomes present to us by faith, and, by communicating, we are incorporated with Him, and are transformed into that [Body]—I do not wander far from what you yourself teach.[45]

It is interesting to observe that he also (mistakenly, as it happens) believed that in rejecting the ubiquity of Christ's body he would dis-

---

[44] VWG, 273–78.

[45] Martyr to Bucer, 15 June 1549; in Gorham, *Gleanings*, 81. Latin text in *Scripta Anglicana*, 545: "ita forte puto, ut nostra haec legisse te non poeniteat: nisi forte visus fuero nonnihil in ea quaestione a te dissentire, in qua tamen, si omnia bene perpenderis, facile intelliges, cum ego dem, Fide corpus Christi fieri nobis praesens: nosque illi communicando incorporari, et in illud transmutari, me non multum ab eo, quod ipse doces, aberrare."

please Bucer.[46] He stressed to Bucer that in describing the presence of Christ in the Lord's Supper, he will allow only for that which the language of scripture itself will permit (a position with which Bucer could hardly quarrel), and concluded: "I am persuaded, you will either bear with a candid mind what I have brought forward in disputation, or you will not be silent as to any things which in your judgment I ought to correct."[47]

And indeed Bucer was not hesitant to respond as Martyr anticipated. In response to Martyr's comment regarding the ubiquity of Christ's body, Bucer professed himself astonished at Martyr's suggestion, and indeed sounded quite annoyed towards the end of his letter: "If you have told any one that I maintain that Christ is at the same time in many places, I mean locally—I, who in these Mysteries exclude all idea of place—I entreat you to have the kindness to explain to such an one my sentiment more correctly." That the letter ends shortly thereafter, and abruptly, with a simple "Farewell" is an indication that Bucer was more than a little irritated.[48]

Yet for all his annoyance, it is not the case that Bucer regards Martyr as having gone over to Zurich on this point. It is more the terms that Martyr chose to use than the substance of what he said which Bucer felt impelled to address, wistfully expressing the desire that Martyr had seen fit to consult him prior to the disputation so that he might have suggested terminology he believed more suitable to what he regarded as their common position.[49] However, one also senses a note of concern on Bucer's part in this regard:

> I know what is the prerogative and the due office of friendship, even in communicating the most intimate thoughts of friends, especially in things of such importance. But since you do not *seem* to ask me to give you my serious view on these matters, and my grief on account

---

[46] Martyr to Bucer, 15 June 1549; in Gorham, *Gleanings*, 81. Latin text in *Scripta Anglicana*, 546.

[47] Martyr to Bucer, 15 June 1549; in Gorham, *Gleanings*, 82. Latin text in *Scripta Anglicana*, 546: "unde mihi persuadeo, vel aequo animo te laturum esse, quae disputando protuli: vel quae iudicaveris me debere corrigere, non taciturum."

[48] Bucer to Martyr, 20 June 1549; in Gorham, *Gleanings*, 92. Latin text in *Scripta Anglicana*, 550: "Et certe si alicui dixisses, me statuere Christum in multis locis, qui omnem loci cogitationem in his mysteriis excludo, simul esse, nimirum localiter, rogo velis ei meam sententiam rectius explicare. [. . .] Vale."

[49] Bucer to Martyr, 20 June 1549; in Gorham, *Gleanings*, 83. Latin text in *Scripta Anglicana*, 546.

of the ruin of our Churches in Germany sufficiently exercises my mind; moreover, since I *hear* that you confess with open mouth the exhibition of Christ in the Sacrament, and of his being daily received more fully by faith—I deem it superfluous to continue the discussion of that matter with you—though you would not have declined it, such is your piety towards Christ and your regard for me.[50]

One might be tempted to regard this as wishful thinking. Without rehearsing the contents of this lengthy letter (which displays to the full the prolixity that so delighted Martyr), and at the risk of over-simplification of the issues involved, it can be said that Bucer was concerned with two things. First, he desired that the understanding of the Lord's presence in the Supper be in terms found in scripture *and* in the early fathers, in order that the proper understanding be accepted by the broadest spectrum of the Church—and in particular, not exclude the Lutherans.[51] Second, Bucer was uncomfortable with what he took to be sounds of an extreme Zurich understanding of the issue in the way Martyr expressed himself in the disputation, and was desirous that neither his friend nor the Church of England be identified with a view that held to the absence of Christ in the Supper.[52]

One also senses a pained weariness on Bucer's part in this matter, a weariness that stemmed from a lifetime of contention on this very issue (in which he likened his own attempts at mediation unto the curse of Sisyphus),[53] and he clearly expressed a desire that this dispute not be continued in England. He is further concerned that Martyr is not fully aware of the devastation to the advance of the Gospel such contention can wreak among fellow believers:

---

[50] Bucer to Martyr, 20 June 1549; in Gorham, *Gleanings*, 84. Emphasis mine. Latin text in *Scripta Anglicana*, 546–7: "Novi quid amicitiae ius et debitum officium sit, in communicandis etiam intimis amicorum cogitationibus, praesertim in rebus tantis. Sed cum tu non videreris expetere seriam mecum de his rebus collationem, et me dolor propter ruinas Ecclesiarum nostrarum in Germania satis exerceret: denique audirem te exhibitionem Christi in Sacramento, et fide indies percipiendi plenius pleno ore confitieri, supersedi pluribus rem istam tecum agere, quod tu pro tua et in Christum religione, et in me charitate, non fuisses detrectaturus."

[51] Bucer to Martyr, 20 June 1549; in Gorham, *Gleanings*, 84–86. Latin text in *Scripta Anglicana*, 547–8.

[52] Bucer to Martyr, 20 June 1549; in Gorham, *Gleanings*, 88. Latin text in *Scripta Anglicana*, 548–9.

[53] Bucer to Martyr, 20 June 1549; in Gorham, *Gleanings*, 84. Latin text in *Scripta Anglicana*, 547.

> I am sure, if you were but fully informed of those evils which have sprung up from the single occasion of this controversy; and what neglect of all Sacraments and of the whole discipline of Christ, aye, and even hatred, has been brought in among us—you would be filled with horror whenever you heard that such a controversy was agitated.[54]

Nevertheless, his respect for his friend is such that he does not insist that Martyr rigidly conform to his own understanding, lest he suffer anathema. As he stated at the very outset of the letter (perhaps to reassure his friend of his continued respect for him):

> I feel confident that you will receive these [suggestions] with a mind as grateful and as free from all offence, as I myself have received and perused your Disputation. For, to require that no brother should retain his peculiar sentiments in any degree whatever—*that* would be, either to tyrannize over the mind, or to expect the perfection of the saints here, which belongs to the future world.[55]

Bucer here displays a breadth of mind and a generosity of spirit sorely lacking in this or any other debate in the sixteenth century. Though he was convinced that Martyr was mistaken in thinking he must state his position in such terms as he chose, and though in pointing to his own past experience Bucer implied Martyr's lack thereof, yet he was willing to treat his friend as an equal, and he (characteristically) regarded such differences as there are to be terminological but not fundamental.

Whatever else it may display, what this exchange does illustrate is that Martyr chose to follow his convictions regarding the way in which the Eucharistic dispute should be discussed, and felt himself to be on an equal footing with his friend. It also shows that Bucer was willing to accept this state of affairs, but did not believe that there had been a parting of the ways. Rather than see this as a new development in their relationship and an indication of Martyr's move-

---

[54] Bucer to Martyr, 20 June 1549; in Gorham, *Gleanings*, 91. Latin text in *Scripta Anglicana*, 550: "Scio, si tu ea mala potuisses intelligere, quae apud nos, ex sola huius contentionis occasione sunt exorta, et quantus sacramentorum omnium, totiusque Christi disciplinae neglectus, imo odium etiam apud multos invectum, totus horreres, quoties istam audires agitari contentionem."

[55] Bucer to Martyr, 20 June 1549; in Gorham, *Gleanings*, 83. Latin text in *Scripta Anglicana*, 546: ". . . ea te confido tam grato accepturum animo, ac ita citra omnem offensionem, atque ego tuam Diptutationem accepi ac perlegi. Illud enim esset, vel dominari velle animis, vel etiam sanctorum perfectionem hic requirere, quae futuri seculi est, petere, ut nemo fratrum proprii aliquid retineat."

ment away from Bucer and towards Zurich, perhaps what we witness is an instance of sparring between the two over an issue they discussed early in Martyr's days in Strasbourg, as Simler recounted in his funeral oration for Martyr:

> And Bucer, whom Martyr esteemed and admired, often urged him to use some obscure and ambiguous terminology on the question of the Lord's Supper, as he himself used them, because that good man had persuaded himself that this way the grave controversy about this question could be avoided and the Church restored to the peace she long desired. Martyr finally obeyed him and used the same way of speaking as he did, but he soon recognized the danger of this approach and changed his view. [. . .] So he left Bucer to his own way of speaking, while he himself sought the same clarity in this teaching as in all other matters.[56]

Whether the difference over terminology reflects a more deep-seated difference on the issue at hand is another matter, one that requires much more extensive discussion. I have chosen not to enter the thicket of questions surrounding Martyr's Eucharistic views in relation to those of Bucer or to those of Zurich. But as I have indicated, I think the differences between Martyr and Bucer can be exaggerated.

Moreover, I do think it suggestive that during this time it was to Bucer that Martyr wrote, and his first letter to Zurich subsequent to the affair was well after the event and was in response to a letter of Bullinger (Martyr's letter was not, need I add, soliciting advice).[57]

---

[56] Josiah Simler, "Oration on the Life and Death of the Good Man and Outstanding Theologian, Doctor Peter Martyr Vermigli, Professor of Sacred Letters at the Zurich Academy" in LLS, 30–31. The Latin original, taken from J. Simler, *Oratio de vita et obitu clarissimi viri et praestantissimi Theologi D. Petri Martyris Vermilii . . . à Iosia Silmlero Tigurino* (Tiguri apud Christophorum Froschoverum Iuniorem, Anno M.D.LXIII), 12: "Quin etiam cum Bucerus, quem coluit et admiratus est, saepe illum hortaretur ut in causa coenae Domenicae obscuris quibusdam et ambiguis dicendi formulis uteretur, quibus ipse ideo utebatur, quod vir bonus sibi persuasisset, posse, hac ratione tolli gravem est de hac causa controversiam, et ita ecclesiae, pacem diu desideratam restitui: paruit tandem illi et eisdem cum eo loquendi formis usus est: sed mox periculo huius rei animadverso, sententiam mutavit. [. . .] Quare Bucero suas locutiones concedens, ipse eandem quam in aliis rebus in hoc quoque dogmate perspicuitatem secutus est. . . ."

[57] I should note Marvin Anderson's suggestion that Martyr had sent a report on the disputation to Bullinger, from which was sent a response which Martyr in turn replied on 27 January 1550 (*O. L.*, II, 477–80). See Anderson, "Peter Martyr,

I also think it significant that the matter was not a bone of contention on that other occasion when Martyr took issue with Bucer, in the course of his examination of the latter's *Censura* on the Book of Common Prayer—and this despite the fact that his criticism dealt with Bucer's handling of a Eucharistic issue, in particular the reservation of the sacrament for the sick. The opportunity certainly presented itself.[58] Yet there is nothing in this letter regarding what Bucer had to say elsewhere in the *Censura* about the presence of the Lord in the Supper, which was much the same as what he had maintained the last time they corresponded on the issue. Perhaps Martyr chose—as it were—to let sleeping dogs lie, but given his forthrightness on the earlier occasion one would have expected *some* comment had he seen anything to which he objected. The evidence suggests that he respected his friend too much to do otherwise.

Conclusion

The friendship of Martin Bucer and Peter Martyr, though generally acknowledged, is not always given its due. Yet its importance for the two cannot be overstated. It was a friendship between equals, despite the fact that Bucer was nine years Martyr's senior in age and had been a leading Reformer for twenty years prior to Martyr's conversion to the Protestant cause. At no time does the friendship appear to have been dearer to both than during their respective sojourns in England. Because they were strangers in the land, the friendship was all the more dear. Their correspondence from these years bears witness both to the strength of their continued friend-

---

Reformed Theologian," 44. Martyr does indicate his full agreement with Bullinger, but as McLelland has noted it is in the context of the Zurich consensus to which Calvin had signed up. This should qualify any conclusions drawn regarding the relationship between Martyr's teaching and that of Zurich. See McLelland, *Visible Words*, 277.

[58] In writing to Bucer, Martyr marveled that his friend had nothing to say regarding the practice of taking the elements of Communion to the sick and administering them without the words of the service, since (as he notes Bucer himself has stated), "the words of the Supper belong more to men than to bread or wine...." Martyr to Bucer, 10 January 1551; in Gorham, *Gleanings*, 228 (CCCC MS 119, nr. 39: "...verba coenae magis ad homines, quam aut ad panem aut ad vinum pertinere.")

ship, and to their mutual reliance—both intellectual and emotional. It was perhaps more important to them on a personal rather than a theological level, but no less important for that reason.

It is, moreover, the personal element that comes through these letters most strongly. We have already read Bucer's rather florid expression of the depth of his love for his friend, but perhaps the most poignant statement of Martyr's feelings for his friend (and of just how important Bucer was for him) comes from a letter he wrote to Conrad Hubert shortly after Bucer's death:

> He has now departed in peace to our God and to Christ Jesus, to the universal regret of all good men, and to my incredible sorrow. I am so broken and dismayed by his death, as to seem mutilated of more than half of myself, and that the better half; so that I am almost worn out by anxieties and tears, and seem scarcely to retain my senses by reason of the bitterness of my grief. [. . .] O wretched me! as long as Bucer was in England, or while we lived together in Germany, I never felt myself to be in exile. But now I plainly seem to myself to be alone and desolate. Hitherto I have had a faithful companion in that road in which we were both of us so unitedly walking. I am now torn asunder from a man of the same mind with myself, and who was truly after my own heart, by the most bitter death which has taken him off.[59]

Martyr's first biographer was quite clear on the depth of their friendship and mutual respect, but also on how important Bucer was to Martyr throughout his life in every respect. It is thus fitting that I conclude this essay with Simler's assessment of this friendship as given in his funeral oration for Martyr, which is a continuation of the passage I quoted earlier on their difference regarding the Eucharist:

> Nonetheless the same firm and constant friendship remained between them, for neither did Bucer criticize Martyr's view, nor was Martyr

---

[59] Martyr to Hubert, 8 March 1551; in *O. L.*, II, 490–91. Latin text printed in *E. T.*, 323: "Verum nunc ille ad Deum nostrum et Christum Iesum in pace migravit, communi omnium bonorum lucto, et meo incredibili moerore. Adeo sum ob illius mortem fractus et consternatus, ut plusquam dimidia parte mei, et ea quidem potiori, mihi videor mutilatus: quamobrem aerumnis et lacrymis pene conficior, et prae doloris acerbitate me amplius apud me ipsum esse non arbitror. [. . .] O me miserum! dum Bucerus in Anglia fuit, aut in Germania simul viximus, nunquam mihi sum visus exulare. Nunc plane mihi videor solus esse desertus. Habui hactenus fidum comitem in hac via, qua pariter atque coniunctissime ambulabamus: modo ab homine unanimi, et qui vere secundum cor meum erat, morte amarissima quae intercessit sum divulsus."

ignorant of Bucer's meaning, however ambiguous were the expressions
he used. Even if the way they taught about this matter was different,
they were still in complete agreement about all religious doctrines, and
they enjoyed a lasting friendship, and their lives were intimately linked.
Had I wanted to explain this and to relate all the acts of respect by
which they manifested their mutual love, words would fail me more
quickly than subject matter.[60]

---

[60] Simler, "Oration", 31; Latin from *Oratio*, 12: ". . . mansitque nihilominus inter
eos firma constansque amicitia: nam neque Martyris sententiam Bucerus impro-
babat, neque Buceri sensum, quantumvis ambiguis locutionibus uteretur, Martyr
ignorabat. Itaque etsi diversa eorum in hac causa esset docendi ratio, fuit tamen
summus eorum consensus in omni doctrina religionis, et perpetua amicitia vitaeque
coniunctio: quam si explicare vellem, et omnia eorum officia quibus mutuum amorem
declararunt commemorare, verba me citius quam res ipsae deficerent."

PETER MARTYR AND THE CHURCH OF ENGLAND AFTER 1558

Gary Jenkins

Peter Martyr's asymmetric legacy in England following the ascension of Elizabeth emerged both from his eventful life at Oxford, and also from the students who followed him to the continent after Edward VI's death. The unbalanced property arises from the internecine grappling for Martyr's mantel, as both those who on the one hand embraced the Elizabethan Settlement—and with them those who notwithstanding its inadequacies sought to work within its confines, and those on the other who believed that the Settlement was an essentially flawed arrangement itself in need of drastic reform, made various outright appeals to Martyr and Martyr's thought not only while he lived, but even long after his death in 1562. This varied status nonetheless bears testimony to the esteem in which England's Protestants held Martyr, and gives short shrift to those who may think him a marginal character in the formation of the Protestant, English, religious mind.[1] But Martyr's views on the probity or infamy of clerical garb and episcopal office, the debates for which his authority was first recruited, hardly exhaust Martyr's impact on England. This essay seeks to begin an assessment of Martyr's place in the formation of English, Protestant religion following Mary Tudor's death in November 1558.

"This is the Lord's doing, and it is marvelous in our eyes",[2] Elizabeth proclaimed at the news of Mary's death on 17 November 1558. Peter Martyr echoed Elizabeth in a letter to her on 22 December 1558, no doubt delivered by the hand of returning exiles, as John Jewel left Zurich to return to England some time shortly after

---

[1] M. A. Overell, "Peter Martyr in England 1547–1553: An Alternative View. *Sixteenth Century Journal*, XV.1 (1984): 87–104.

[2] Psalm 117.25. Cecil had brought the word to Elizabeth, who had been kept under close scrutiny during Mary's reign, and probably would have been executed were it not for the protection of her thoroughly Catholic brother-in-law, Philip II of Spain.

Epiphany 1559. "It is therefore fitting" Martyr wrote Elizabeth "that
at this time all godly people should have in their mouths the festive
song of the Psalms: 'This is the Lord's doing; it is marvelous in our
eyes; the stone which the builders rejected has become the head of
the corner.'"[3] Elizabeth's ascension heralded a new day in the life
of the English church, and a notable evidence of God's Providence;
it also signaled the beginning of what Martyr hoped would be a
thorough reform, whereby worship would be "according to what is
prescribed in the divine letters."[4] What this reform entailed in Martyr's
mind can be gleaned from both the letter to Elizabeth, and also his
correspondence with his former students Thomas Sampson and John
Jewel. This included the abolition of all rites and ceremonies that
had no biblical warrant, that smacked of Rome, and that did not
lead to edification. Martyr had disdain for Roman vestments, being
reminded by Jewel that what was being debated among the English
in 1559—"the scenic apparatus of worship"—he and Martyr had
once laughed at, and that such vestments "(that scenic dress. . . .
these trifles) are indeed as you very properly observe, the relics of
the Amorites."[5] Yet Martyr was not beyond employing economy in
such a situation.[6] To Thomas Sampson, who had been the choice
for the bishopric of Norwich, he initially advised that to minister
when such abominations (e.g., the crucifix, altars, popish vestments,
inter alia) were retained would only lead to a dilution of any preaching against them.[7] Yet, with the removal of crucifixes and altars,
Martyr's tone changed, writing Sampson that

> like as altars and images have been removed, so this resemblance of
> the mass may also be taken away, provided you and others who may

---

[3] LLS, 171.

[4] LLS, 173. Later in the letter Martyr invokes the story of Uzzah who died when
he touched the ark of the covenant, i.e., acting against and beyond the precepts of
God.

[5] Jewel, Letter to Martyr, 5 November 1559, *Works*, IV, 1223; and undated,
Works, IV, 1210.

[6] Indeed Martyr's moderation, evident already from a letter to the bishop of
Gloucester, John Hooper, during the first Vestarian controversy in 1550 (this letter shall be repeatedly referenced below), may have done as much to craft Martyr's
legacy in English Protestantism as perhaps anything else he wrote or did.

[7] Martyr to Sampson, 15 July 1559, in *Zurich Letters*, Vol. II (Cambridge: Cambridge
University Press, 1845), 25–27.

obtain bishoprics, will direct all your endeavors to that object, (which would make less progress, should another succeed in your place, who not only might be indifferent about putting away those relics, but would rather defend, cherish, and maintain them;) therefore was I the slower in advising you rather to refuse a bishopric, than to consent to the use of those garments.[8]

And further, that "[u]nless however you are driven to this strait [of ministering with the crucifix on the altar], do not refuse the ministry that is offered you."[9] Regardless, Sampson avoided all appointment, preferring to "[l]et others be bishops; as to myself, I will either undertake the office of a preacher, or none at all." Further, he would have followed Martyr's advice, "but the thing was never carried so far as to compel me to that step."[10] It must be noted that in all of this correspondence Martyr had no necessary problem with the office of bishop. In 1547 he had written to Martin Bucer, upon the prospect of their going to England, his pleasure to see "bishops upon the earth. . . which be truly holy. . . . This is the office of a pastor. This is that bishoplike dignity described by Paul in the Epistles to Timothy and Titus. It delighteth me much to read this kind of description in the Epistles, but it pleaseth me a great deal more to see with the eyes the patterns themselves."[11] This enthusiasm for the perceived Protestant zeal of England's bishops had repercussions for the later reception of Martyr, though he had made no express statement about church polity.

As early as 1559, Jewel had despaired of thorough reform, noting the zeal of some for a "leaden mediocrity" and that whereas "Christ was once exiled by his enemies, he is now kept out by his friends." Nonetheless Jewel followed Martyr's advice, and took up his life as bishop of Salisbury, though always with an eye to Zurich and Martyr. Yet however much Jewel wished again to be in Zurich, and even though he hoped to "behold you face to face", and that "[t]he time I hope, will at length arrive, when we may be able to salute each other in person. Should I ever see that day, and live to

---

[8] Martyr to Sampson, 4 November 1559, in *Zurich Letters* II, 32–33.
[9] Martyr to Sampson, 20 March 1560, in *Zurich Letters* II, 48.
[10] Martyr to Sampson, January 1560, and 13 May 1560, *Zurich Letters* I, 63, 76.
[11] From Martyrs letters, and appended to the Marten translation of the LC, 62–63.

welcome you, I shall think I have lived long enough," it never happened. Though such an idea had been discussed among Elizabeth's counselors, Jewel had grave misgivings about Martyr returning to England:

> Many of our leading men, and those not unknown to you, are fixing their thoughts upon yourself, and are anxious that you should be invited at the earliest opportunity, in spite of all the German leaguers. But I, who most of all mankind anxiously and above all things desire to see you, cannot but recommend you, if you should be invited (which however I scarcely think will be the case in the existing state of affairs), to do nothing in a hurry. . . . I had rather hear of you absent and in safety, than see you present among us and in danger.[12]

Martyr was invited back to England in 1561, but he declined. Jewel's frequent reports on the state of religion and education at Oxford may have had something to do with it, but Martyr was already ensconced at Zurich, a place he had been for five years, and, having been informed by Jewel's and Sampson's missives, one he knew to be far more theologically congenial than England.

Jewel wrote at least twenty letters to Martyr between 1559 and Martyr's death in 1562, many of them filled with the warmest of sentiments for his mentor. In his 1561 *Dialogue on the Two Natures in Christ*, Martyr reciprocated the kindness by dedicating the book to his former pupil. (The *Dialogue* shall be touched on again below.) Other English Protestants wrote Martyr, though Jewel's letters alone outnumber all the rest combined. But Martyr's influence on the English church hardly ended with Jewel and Sampson, for his name and writings became part of the respective arsenals in the religious debates of Elizabeth's reign.

The first of these, the second Vestarian controversy of 1566, initially engaged the Archbishop of Canterbury Matthew Parker against two of Martyr's pupils from Zurich, Sampson, by then dean of Christ Church, Oxford, and the President of Magdalen College Oxford, Laurence Humphrey. Already in 1563 Humphrey had written Heinrich Bullinger in Zurich asking whether *adiaphoron* could still be so after having been so long contaminated by superstition and used to beguile the ignorant; and whether the "command of the sovereign. . .

---

[12] Jewel, letter to Martyr 16 November 1559, *Works* IV, 1225.

for the sake of order" is sufficient to remove any material offense?[13] By 1566, the issues had expanded into both a direct questioning of the right of the prince to prescribe the wearing of vestments, and as well the denial that the surplice was even a thing indifferent.[14] To Sampson and Humphrey, the superstitious abuse of the vestment by Rome had rendered it completely detrimental, and as such a matter beyond civil jurisdiction. Sampson's and Humphrey's initial 1566 letters predate archbishop Parker's actions of 26 March 1566, when he suspended thirty-seven London clergy from their livings for nonconformity.[15] And it was this, Parker's gauntlet, that incited Robert Crowley's response in *A briefe discourse*.[16] After some animadversions on scripture, Crowley turns to the continental Reformers, first citing Bucer, and then Martyr,

> whose judgement hath in this matter bene oftentimes asked, dothe more than once in his writinges call them *Reliquias Amorraeorum*, leavings or remnaunts of the Amorites. And although he do in some case thinke that they maye be borne with for a season; yet in our case, he would not have them suffered to remaine in the church of Christ.[17]

Crowley's work, which also enlisted the names of Ridley and Jewel, was soon answered by the extended *A brief examination for the tyme*, probably written by Archbishop Parker. The author seeks to reclaim Bucer, Ridley, Jewel and Martyr to the side of conformity, and rather disingenuously notes of Martyr that "there is no wryter of these dayse more evidently agaynst you."[18] The author appends five letters to

---

[13] These two appear in Humphrey's 1563 letter, *Zurich Letters*, Vol. I, 134. Humphrey does distinguish the tyranny of the pope from that "just and legitimate authority of the queen."

[14] Humphrey to Bullinger, 9 February, and Sampson to Bullinger, 16 February 1566. *Zurich Letters*, Vol. I, 151–155; and Humphrey again to Bullinger, July 1566, 157–166.

[15] Parker to Cecil, 26 March 1566, *Parker's Correspondence* (Cambridge: Cambridge University Press, 1853), 270. Cf. J. H. Primus, *The Vestments Controversy*. (Kampen: J. H. Kok, 1960), 102–104.

[16] *A briefe discourse against the outward apparell and Ministring Garmentes of the Popishe Church*. 1566. STC 6078.

[17] Crowley, *briefe discourse*. unpaginated. Besides Martyr and Bucer, Crowley also cites Jewel and Ridley, though in Ridley's case it was his refusal to wear "Massing garmentes" at Oxford before his death. In Jewel's case it is a citation from his *Reply to Harding* that the fraction, not being to edification, ought to be abolished. The quotation is taken from the second part of *briefe discourse*, entitled *The unfolding of the Popes Attyre*.

[18] Quoted in Primus, *Controversy*, 120.

the end of the book, one of which is Martyr's 4 November 1550
letter to Hooper enjoining him to conform for the sake of the Gospel.
The letter would have an extended history in Elizabethan and
Jacobean England.

In the midst of the controversy, May of 1566, Bullinger responded
to Humphrey and Sampson with a long letter addressing eighteen
points the two had raised.[19] Bullinger also had Martyr's 1550 letter
to Hooper before him when he wrote, for he quotes it at length:

> Nonetheless there were some rites there so set up that, while they can-
> not technically be called sacraments, they contributed to decorum,
> order and a certain suitability which I think could be brought back
> and retained as congruent with the light of nature and bringing some
> advantage to us. Who does not see that the Apostles commanded the
> gentiles to abstain from blood and strangled meat for the peace and
> more congenial feasting of believers? Unquestionably these prohibitions
> were Aaronic if you wanted to embrace in general all the things which
> were in the Law. None of our people are ignorant that tithes also
> have been established today in an infinite number of places to sup-
> port the church's ministers. You will not easily prove from the books
> of the New Testament that psalms and hymns were sung in sacred
> meetings; it is clearly established that this was done in the Old Testa-
> ment. . . . Lest I omit it, we have feast days in memory of the Lord's
> resurrection and other things. . . . Are all of these to be abolished
> because they are vestiges of the Old Law? I think that you now see
> from all these things that not everything from the Aaronic priesthood
> should be abolished in a way that nothing can be retained and used.[20]

Further, Bullinger cites the same Patristic authorities Martyr had,
demonstrating the early Church's use of distinctive clerical garb. In
an act of cordiality, Bullinger also sent the letter to the bishop of
Winchester, Robert Horne, who then forwarded it to bishops Parkhust,
Plikington, Grindal, Sandys, and Jewel. Subsequently the letter was
published in order to force Humphrey and Sampson into obedience.
Upon hearing of its publication, Bullinger was not amused.[21]

The nonconformists responded to *A brief examination* with their own
catalogue of Continental divines in *The Fortresse of Fathers*, again recruit-

---

[19] *Zurich Letters*, I, 345–355.

[20] The quotation is taken from Donnelly, LLS, letter 48. The ellipses are Bullinger's.

[21] Bullinger and Gualter to Grindal and Horn, 6 September 1566. *Zurich Letters*,
I, 357–360. Cf. Primus, *Controversy*, 125 ff.

ing Martyr, along with St. Ambrose, Erasmus, Bullinger, Gualter, *inter alios*; all being cited as confederate with the nonconformists.[22] The Puritans quoted from Martyr's commentaries on Judges, Kings, Romans, and Corinthians, to show that magistrates could not enjoin that which is evil, and by implication, since vestments were the pagan superstitions of Rome, they should be abrogated.[23] In response to the *Fortresse*, Martyr's letter to Hooper again appeared in the short tract *Whether it be Mortalle Sinne to Transgresse Civill Lawes*.[24] The pamphlet employed the writings of five different continental divines including Melanchthon, Bullinger, Gualter, and Bucer. It clearly was aimed not so much at the question of the licitness of surplices, though this was addressed, but at obedience to authority.[25]

The uses made of Martyr's thought and theology were no less undulating in the Admonition controversy of 1571 and following. Like the second Vestarian controversy, the Admonition controversy followed an attempt, this time by Convocation to enforce subscription to the Articles, the Book of Common Prayer, and the use of the surplice. The Puritan response, a biting piece of invective entitled *Admonition to the Parliament*, Presbyterian in its intent, and antiepiscopal in its ends, had little to nothing to do with Martyr's thought; this came afterwards in the writings of John Whitgift, and in Thomas Cartwright's *A Replie agaynst Master Doctor Vugigifts Ansuer to the Admonition*. The *Admonition*, published by several prominent Puritan clergy—John Field, Anthony Gilby, and Thomas Wilcox—during the 1572 Parliament, in its first part addressed several concerns, most notably the ignorance of the clergy, the wearing of surplices, ancillary and unscriptural rites (e.g. baptismal fonts, godparents, the sign of the cross), the civil dominion of the bishops, and the orders or offices of the clergy. The remainder of the *Admonition* is taken up with what are

---

[22] Leonard Trinterud, *Elizabethan Puritanism* (New York: Oxford University Press, 1971), 95–100.

[23] The definition of the term Puritan is problematic, one whose nuances have even become increasingly shaded. By Puritan I mean not only those who were overtly nonconformists, but also those who subversively and clandestinely worked against particular accidents of the Settlement: those who saw such matters as surplice, Prayer Book, and prelacy as unnecessary evils, and thus felt a bounden duty to fight against them.

[24] *Whether it be Mortalle Sinne to Transgresse Civil Lawes, which be the Commaundementes of Civill Magistrates* (London: Richard Jugge, 1566).

[25] D. J. Mcginn, *The Admonition Controversy* (New Brunswick: Rutgers, 1949), 17–21.

termed *Popishe Abuses*.[26] Whitgift, then dean of Lincoln Cathedral and Professor of Divinity at Cambridge wrote *An ansvver to a certen libell intituled, An admonition to the Parliament*,[27] which was met with Cartwright's *Replie* in 1573.[28] In 1574 Whitgift answered with his lengthy *The Defense of the Aunswere to the Admonition, against the Replie of T. C.*[29]

Cartwright and Whitgift both sought to claim Martyr for their own, and often their polemics seem little more than haggling over what Martyr really intended by his words.[30] But Whitgift, owing to Martyr's letter to Hooper which he cites at several places, and quotes at length once,[31] scores several polemical points, at least as to whom Martyr would have sided with in the present dispute. Most notably Whitgift bludgeons Cartwright with the Hooper letter in respect to vestments, employing Martyr's analogy that as ministers are angels of God, and since angels were clad in white, so ministers should be?[32] Cartwright's response was little more than vestarial Donatism. Whitgift also draws upon Martyr, though with less rhetorical effect, in demonstrating that the nature of ecclesiastical offices is not a fixed thing. Whereas Whitgift's appeal to Martyr's intent in the Hooper letter was effective in that Martyr had been addressing the very thing then under dispute, the case for ecclesiastical government differed. Here Whitgift drew on some of Martyr's commentaries, particularly *Romans*, "that there are many governments in the church;"[33] yet ultimately appealled to Martyr's lack of any apprehensions of the government of the Church when he was in England.[34] Whitgift also employed Martyr with respect to *adiaphora* from his commentary on

---

[26] W. H. Frere and C. E. Douglas, eds., *Puritan Manifestoes: A study of the Puritan Revolt* (London: S.P.C.K., 1954), 1–40. Cf. Patrick Collinson, *The Elizabethan Puritan Movement*, Patrick Collinson, 1967, 117–121.

[27] Whitgift, *An Ansvuere* (London: Henrie Bynneman, for Humfrey Toy, 1573).

[28] Thomas Cartwright, *A replye to an answere made of M. Doctor Whitegifte againste the admonition to the Parliament* (n.p. 1573). Cartwright's *The second replie* was published in 1575, and his *The rest of the second replie* followed in 1577.

[29] In John Whitgift, *Works*, Vols. I–III The Parker Society (Cambridge: Cambridge University Press.

[30] Cf. Whitgift, *Works*, vol. I, 484–485. Following the commonplace of the day, Whitgift reproduces Cartwright's work in his.

[31] Whitgift, *Works*, vol. II, 35–36.

[32] Whitgift, *Works*, vol. II, 63.

[33] Whitgift, *Works*, vol. III, 162. The quotation from Martyr is from ch. xii of *Romans*.

[34] Whitgift, *Works*, vol. III, 545.

I Corinthians on three types of tradition, focusing on the third: "there be other some traditions which we may call neuters; because they be neither contrary to the word of God, nor yet necessarily joined to the same; in which we must obey the church."[35]

Cartwright's meager profit from his use of Martyr, especially in light of Whitgift's far more extensive and effective exercise of him, nonetheless gives evidence that the Puritan saw him not only as an authority, but also as an ally. Cartwright cites him less frequently than Whitgift, but still makes frequent appeals not only to him, but also to Calvin and Bucer. By the time Cartwright publishes his *The rest of the second replie* in 1577 he has all but abandoned the use of Martyr. He makes extensive use of Calvin especially, but also of Bucer; but he appeals to Martyr only three times, and but once does his citation of him go beyond the use of his name:

> Likewise of M, Martyr, who affirming that 'certeyn of the peolpe, vuere ioyned vuith the Pastor in the government of the church:' assigneth the cause, 'for that the Pastor could not doe al himself,' thereby giving to understand, that the Eldership was as general, as the pastor. For he doeth not say, where the Pastor could not doe al, there he had assistance of an Eldership: but 'because the Pastor could not doe al etc.'[36]

Cartwright's slighting of Martyr in the controversy, and Whitgift's more extensive deployment of him, may have foretold Martyr's future among the more precise Calvinists in the British Isles. In Scotland, Martyr's identification with the Church of England put him on the outside of Presbyterian thought, and those who did appeal to him generally were from the Church of Scotland. Further, Martyr's appropriation of Aristotle was also shunned in Scotland where the philosopher of choice was Pierre Ramus.[37]

Cartwright not only employed Martyr in his own polemics but recommended his writings to his students as well. In his letter to Arthur Hildersham "For Direction in the Study of Divinity" he

---

[35] Whitgift, *Works*, vol. I, 252. Quoting Martyr on I Corinthians i.

[36] Cartwright, *Rest of the second replie* (Zurich, or Basle: 1577), 46.

[37] Bruce Gordon, "Peter Martyr Vermigli in Scotland: A sixteenth-century reformer in a seventeenth-century quarrel" in HHR, 280–83.

endorses Martyr's general writings, but then gives a somewhat back-handed endorsement of his commentaries: "Likewise for singular and much reading Mr Martyr; saving that his Commentaries are rather Commonplaces then [sic] Commentaries."[38] This recommendation is all the more guarded than it seems given that Cartwright "would esteem also that the Commentaries might be read before the other Workes, for that by them the Holy Scripture . . . is made more familiar unto us."[39]

Cartwright was not alone in commending Martyr. Richard Rogers, whose Puritan life and mind are laid out in his diary, in his *Practice of Christianity* lists Martyr's *Commonplaces* along with Calvin's *Institutes*, and the writings of Beza and Perkins as containing "the sume of many learned Authors, in a plaine and profitable manner."[40] Martyr appeared in the student notebooks of John Stone of Christ Church, Oxford; and in Alexander Cooke of University College, Oxford, both Puritans. Stone created commonplace books in which he cited Martyr along with Jewel, Oecolampadius, and Rainolds; Cooke quotes Martyr alongside Cicero, Seneca, Erasmus, More, and Petrarch about the nature of the life of learning. We know that he was read by both the arts and the divinity students.[41] From 1558–1602 English students leaned heavily on continental divines: "For instance, the library catalogues of theological students who died in Oxford between 1558–1618 are replete with works by Calvin, Melanchthon, Peter Martyr, Zanchius, Beza, Bullinger, and other continental reformers."[42]

---

[38] Albert Peel andLeland H. Carlson, eds., *Cartwrightiana* (London: Published for the Sir Halley Stewart Trust [by] Allen and Unwin, 1951) *Elizabethan Nonconformist Texts*, Vol. I, 113–114. The inscribed date on the Trinity College Dublin MSS is 1583, the publication year of Martyr's *Commonplaces*, though this gives only at best puzzling insight into Cartwright's comment.

[39] Peel, *Cartwrightiana*, 113.

[40] Quoted in Morgan, *Godly learning: Puritan attitudes towards reason, learning, and education, 1560–1640* (Cambridge: Cambridge University Press, 1986), 156. For Rogers' diary see Knappen, ed., *Two Elizabethan Puritan Diaries* [Richard Rogers and Samuel Ward] Chicago: The American Society of Church History, 1933. Studies in Church History, vol. II.

[41] In Margo Todd, *Christian Humanism and Puritan Social Order* (Cambridge: Cambridge University Press, 1987), 59–60, and fn. 15. Prof. Todd asserts that student references to the continentals was too frequent to try and cite.

[42] Mark Curtis, *Oxford and Cambridge in Transition: 1558–1642. An essay in Changing Relations between the English Universities and English Society. Oxon* (Oxford: Oxford University Press, 1959), 162–163.

Martyr's thought found an influential conduit of dissemination in the Puritan fellow and later president of Corpus Christi College, Oxford, John Rainolds (1549–1607). The assessments of Rainolds' Puritanism vary, but he did dissent from Richard Bancroft's views, first aired in 1588, that bishops were a different and higher office than priests. Further, he represented the Puritan interests before James I at the 1604 Hampton Court conference. In 1577, he wrote a letter of advice, like Cartwright, on the study of divinity.[43] Rainolds gives an index of the more important books of the Old and New Testaments, explicitly indicating St. John's Gospel and the book of Romans as the sum of the New, the Prophets and the Psalms as the sum of the Old. "Howbeit in the rest, you shall doe well also if in harder places you use the judgement of some godly writer, as Calvin and Peter Martyr, who have written best on the most part of the old Testament."[44]

Rainolds confederate in Puritanism at the Hampton Court Conference, Thomas Sparke, erstwhile archdeacon of Stow in the diocese of Lincoln, also made recourse to Martyr, and again like others before him, to the letter to Hooper. Sparke had been a disappointment for the precisian cause at Hampton Court, for though he had dressed the part of a non-conformist, coming, according to Wood, clothed as would a Turkey-merchant,[45] he never spoke a word, at least not in public. He did have a private conference with James I, and this, said Sparke, in his 1607 *A brotherly perswasion to Unity and Uniformity*, was what won him over to conformity. Sparke's *Perswasion* invoked Martyr's authority on four occasions, twice in asides to the now catholic Hooper epistle (p. 12, and a more elaborate use of Martyr on p. 25 concerning the number and meaning of ceremonies), and once to the argument employed by Whitgift that Martyr had no problems with the Prayer book, for, says Sparke citing Whitgift, Martyr never spoke against prelacy while in England (Sparke frequently quoted Whitgift's arguments against Cartwright). The fourth place Sparke draws on Martyr he develops an extended argument about propriety of using the sign of the cross at the baptismal font,

---

[43] John Reinolds, *A Letter of D. Reinolds to his friend concerning his advice for the studie of Divinitie*. London, Iohn Beale, for Ionas Man, 1613, not paginated.
[44] Rainolds, *advice*, unpaginated.
[45] Antony á Woods. *Athenae Oxonienses*, Vol. I, c. 190.

and cites Martyr on the second commandment that the sign of the cross was a benefit to the Christian.[46]

Martyr influenced the English church not just through the teaching and writings of his students and admirers, but also through the continued publication and dissemination of his books. Initially it was the Puritanically sympathetic Londoner, Jon Day who published not only Martyr's works, but also Calvin's, Viret's, Bullinger's, and Zwingli's. It was Day who published the first English translation of the Romans commentary in 1568.[47] Martyr's works went through numerous printings, with the Romans commentary going through six editions: 1558, 1559, 1560, 1568 (both Latin and English), 1612, and 1613. *Romans* was dedicated to Sir Anthony Cooke, Edward VI's governor, and the father-in-law of both Lord Keeper Nicholas Bacon and William Cecil. This dedication was reprinted in every one of the editions of the *Loci communes*. The *Loci communes* went through fourteen editions between 1576 and 1656, the first English edition being in 1583. By 1604 various of Martyr's Old Testament commentaries had gone through twenty-four editions.[48] In all, Martyr's various works and his *Loci communes* went through "110 separate printings."[49] Collinson notes that "English theologians were as likely to lean on Bullinger of Zurich, Musculus of Berne, or Peter Martyr as on Calvin or Beze. . . . But if we were to identify one author and one book which represented the center of theological gravity of the Elizabethan church it would not be Calvin's *Institutes* but the *Common Places* of Peter Martyr . . ."[50]

Some of the Oxford and Cambridge libraries possessed Martyr's works early in Elizabeth's reign, while others acquired them later on. All Souls in Oxford was given £5 by Andrew Kingsmill upon his death for the purchase of the works of Martyr and Calvin, which was done in 1575 buying five of Martyr's commentaries and his *Defensio* against Stephen Gardiner. Corpus Christi College also benefitted

---

[46] Thomas Sparke, *A Brotherly Perswasion to Unitie and Uniformitie in Iudgement and Practise touching the Received and present Ecclesiastical gouerment, and the authorised rites and ceremonies of the Church of England* (London: Nicholas Okes, 1607), 25 (STC 23019.5).

[47] Anderson, *Foundations*, 176.

[48] Anderson, *Foundations*, 310.

[49] CAS, 171.

[50] Patrick Collinson, "England and International Calvinism: 1558–1640," in Menna Prestwich, ed., *International Calvinism: 1541–1715* (Oxford: Oxford University Press, 1985), 214.

from a patron's legacy when Thomas Greenway left it a collection of books "the bias of which inclined towards Zurich rather than Geneva." This included Martyr's commentaries.[51] Magdalen College President Laurence Humphrey purchased John Jewel's library following the bishop's death in September of 1571, which had numerous works linked to Zurich, and apparently all of Martyrs, though since the books were used by students, as they wore out they often were replaced by newer editions, and thus perhaps the reason why none of Calvin's works appear in the bishop's library (though Jewel made no use of Calvin in his own writings).[52] Thanks to archbishop Grindal, who left his library to Queen's College, Oxford, it also possessed a number of Martyr's works. In 1623, Martyr's complete works were given to St. John's College, Oxford.[53] Marvin Anderson noted that c. 1600 the Oxford collegiate libraries had 102 different copies of Martyr's works, and that the Cambridge colleges had 100. St. John's College Cambridge came by most of Martyr's works in Elizabeth's reign, though some that are only known with certainty to be present by 1628 (e.g. the *Defensio adversus [librum] Gardineri*) could have been procured earlier. Nonetheless, in 1579 Edward Grant gave to the college library Martyr's commentaries on Romans, I Corinthians, Samuel, Kings, and Judges. In 1599 Hugo Martin gave St. John's the Genesis commentary and the *Loci Communes*.[54] Emmanuel College Cambridge, founded in 1584, in its first library inventory had two of Martyr's works, Thomas Southaicke between 1605 and 1621 donated to the library Martyr's commentaries in Genesis, Kings, Judges, and I Corinthians. William Sancroft, formerly master of the College, c. 1694, donated the commentaries on Samuel, Romans, the Eucharistic discourses, and the *Loci communes*.[55] The Parker Library

---

[51] Dent, *Reformers in . . . Oxford*, 94.

[52] Neil Ker "The Library of John Jewel" *The Bodleian Library Record*, IX no. 5 (1977), 256–265. Many of the volumes of Jewel's library were discarded as newer editions than those of his appeared. It was only some years subsequent (Ker does not say when) that Jewel's library, both as a collection of rare books and as a former possession of the bishop, was seen as valuable in and of itself. There are some eighty books of the bishop still in the library.

[53] In Margo Todd, *Christian Humanism and Puritan Social Order* (Cambridge: Cambridge University Press, 1987), 59–60, and fn. 15.

[54] This information was provided by Jonathan Harrison of St John's College Library, Cambridge.

[55] This information was provided by the kindness of Dr. H. C. Carron, Librarian of Emmanuel College, Cambridge.

of Corpus Christi College has seven sixteenth-century editions of
Martyr's works, and though there is no certainty when they arrived,
it is assumed they came from Archbishop Parker's own library.[56]
Gonville and Caius College Library acquired nine of Martyr's works
(Commentaries, Prayers, *Loci communes, Defensio, inter alia*) in 1619,
each given by William Branthwaite, Master of the College.[57] King's
college possessed at least three of Martyr's works prior to 1600, one
of which was certainly the Romans commentary given to the library
in 1569.[58] Corpus Christi College was bereft of Martyr until the
1580's when it obtained his commentaries; Merton obtained his fifteen
volume *Opera* in 1584.[59] In the early seventeenth century, the chapter of Peterborough cathedral placed on permanent loan to Cambridge
24 volumes of Martyr's works. In inventories of the libraries of individual students, Martyr was found among many, though relatively
few students actually owned books. Beyond the inventories, Martyr's
works are also found in the extant wills of Oxford students.[60]

Not everyone at the universities or in England for that matter,
was so pleasantly disposed to Martyr: at the end of the sixteenth
century controversy again brought Martyr's name to the fore, but
now it was not between those who, like Whitgift and Cartwright
wished to claim Martyr for their own, but instead, along with Calvin,
Zanchius, and Beza, as a target of the Cambridge chaplain William
Barrett's 1595 anti-predestinarian diatribe delivered at the university, in response largely to William Perkins' *Golden Chain*.[61] Barrett
was so forward as to label Martyr a Calvinist, then a term of oppro-
brium used by Roman Catholics.[62] Barrett's actions eventually prompted
Whitgift, by then archbishop of Canterbury, to issue the Calvinistic

---

[56] This information, and supposition, was provided by Gill Cannell, Parker Sub
Librarian, Corpus Christi College.
[57] This information was provided by Huw Jones, assistant librarian of Gonville
and Caius College.
[58] This information was provided by Mrs. Wai Kirkpatrick, assistant librarian at
King's College. I am indebted to each of the librarians who responded to my
inquiries.
[59] Dent, *Reformers in ... Oxford*, 97.
[60] Dent, *Reformers in ... Oxford*, 96.
[61] Nicholas Tyacke, *Anti-Calvinists: The Rise of English Arminianism, c. 1590–1640*.
(Oxford: Oxford University Press, 1987), 29–30.
[62] Anthony Milton, Anthony Milton, *Catholic and Reformed: The Roman and Protestant
Churches in English Protestant Thought, 1600–1640* (Cambridge: Cambridge University
Press, 1995), 434.

Lambeth articles. Similarly, the Covenanter Robert Baille saw Martyr's name coupled with Calvin's, Beza's, and Bucer's in declamations by the Scottish Arminians in the seventeenth century.[63] Henry Burton, an ardent predestinarian, but no Puritan, nonetheless summons the specter of Martyr against the Arminians in his 1629 *Truth's Triumph over Trent*: "Why should the world, O Lord, complaine and cry where is the spirit of those ancient bishops and martyrs, and learned champions of thy truth, as of Cranmer, Ridley, Latimer, Hooper, Bucer, Peter Martyr, Jewel, and other faithfull witnesses . . .?"[64]

The employment of Martyr by later Puritans was varied, and to an extent diminishing, especially as English Calvinism developed its own idiom. Nonetheless numerous Puritans granted Martyr status both tacitly and overtly in divers ways. Edward Fisher, in his *Marrow of Modern Divinity* (1646) lists Martyr as one of those to whom he owed a theological debt, and from whom he had culled the content of his work. Specifically he uses Martyr's commentary on Romans in arguing for a federal theology with respect to the Christian's status as regards the covenant of Works.[65] John Rogers in his 1603 *Seven Treatises* linked Martyr with Calvin and Beza as the author's of choice as opposed to the blasphemies of Machiavelli. Rogers also, in a series of 103 sermons on the book of Judges essentially simplifies Martyr's commentary for the laity.[66] Fr. John Patrick Donnelly has called attention to John Milton's likely use of Martyr's Genesis commentary in preparation of *Paradise Lost*.[67] Milton in his work on divorce, *Tetrachordon*, three times cites Martyr: once on the licitness of a Christian divorcing a pagan out of fear of religious defilement (this same place out of Martyr's commentary on I Corinthians is also cited by Milton in his *Colasterion*); again when commenting on Martyr's views on divorce, he notes Martyr's bewilderment at why, since Theodosius and the ancient Roman law had the tacit approval even of St. Ambrose, modern magistrates would not likewise permit divorce,

---

[63] Milton, *Catholic and Reformed*, 443.

[64] Quoted in Tyacke, *Anti-Calvinists*, 187.

[65] Edward Fisher, *The marrow of modern divinity: touching both the covenant of works, and the covenant of grace, with their use and end, both in the time of the Old Testament, and in the time of the New etc.* (London: Printed by R. Leybourn, for Giles Calvert . . ., 2nd ed. 1646). Ch II, III. 2.

[66] In Marvin Anderson, *Evangelical Foundations: Religion in England, 1378–1683* (American University Studies, New York: Peter Land, 1987), 310, 275–276.

[67] CAS, 180.

and cites him as seeing both fornication and heresy as grounds for divorce; and finally in noting Martyr's place in the commission of Edward VI for the reformation of the *Reformatio Legum Ecclesiasticarum* that radically altered England's divorce laws, and gave wide latitude for divorce.[68] Milton also in his *The Tenure of Magistrates and Kings*, notes Martyr's approval, drawn from his commentary on Judges, of how England's parliament dealt with Richard II.[69] The Scottish Covenanter George Gillespie, in *A Treatise of Miscellany Questions*, chapter 10 on heresies, quotes Martyr out of the *Loci Communes* delimiting his own views on what heresy is. In *Against the English Popish Ceremonies*, Gillespie cites Martyr nine times, all from his commentaries on Kings and I Corinthians.[70] He is included in William Beale's *An Almanacke* for 1631 as a confessor, along with Luther, Melanchthon, and Pico della Mirandola; Ridley, Latimer, and Cranmer being bishop martyrs.[71] Though esteemed by the Puritans, Martyr in the seventeenth century diminishes as a cited source. In the six volumes of *Puritan Sermons: 1659–1689*,[72] Martyr is cited fourteen times in some 4,000 pages of sermons. By contrast, though not surprisingly, Bellarmine is cited 173 times, St. Augustine 260, while Calvin and Beza are fifty-five times each; Petrarch is cited forty-nine times, Cicero thirty-eight, Seneca sixty-five, and Bernard of Clairvaux seventy-one times. The Puritan divine and sometime chaplain to Cromwell, John Owen, in his sixteen volumes of writings cites Martyr but six times. Similar instances could be multiplied.

A survey, however extensive, of Puritan and establishment rhetoric

---

[68] John Milton, *Tetrachordon: expositions upon the foure chief places in Scripture, which treat of mariage, or nullities in mariage. Wherin The doctrine and discipline of divorce, as was lately publish'd, is confirm'd by explanation of Scripture, by testimony of ancient fathers, of civill lawes in the primitive church, of famousest reformed divines, and lastly, by an intended act of the Parlament and Church of England in the last yeare of Edvvard the Sixth.* London, 1645.

[69] John Milton, *The tenure of kings and magistrates: proving that it is lawfull . . . to call to account a tyrant . . . and . . . to depose and put him to death etc.* (London: Printed by Matthew Simmons . . ., 1649, Second ed. 1650). Milton calls Martyr a "divine of foremost rank".

[70] George Gillespie, *A treatise of miscellany questions: wherein many usefull questions and cases of conscience are discussed and resolved* (Edinburgh: Printed by Gedeon Lithgovv, 1649) and *A dispute against the English-popish ceremonies, obtruded vpon the Church of Scotland.* (Leiden: Printed by W. Christiaens, 1637); reprinted by Naphtali Press, Dallas, 1998.

[71] In Milton, *Catholic and Reformed*, 314, fn. 206.

[72] James Nichols ed. *Puritan Sermons: being the morning exercises at Cripplegate, St. Giles in the Field and in Southwark by 75 Ministers of the Gospel* (Wheaton, Ill: R. O. Roberts, 1981).

and theology, and later Puritan thought, does not exhaust Martyr's legacy. The above-cited recommendation of Martyr made by the Oxford Professor John Rainold he made good in action as well. Rainolds had distinguished himself in the divinity debates with the Catholic John Hart in 1578 (Rainolds was then Lecturer in Greek); and though expelled from Corpus Christi in 1579, he soon found himself reinstated. With him was expelled one of his wards, Richard Hooker. Hooker's first introduction to Martyr did not come via Rainolds, but rather from his uncle John Hooker, erstwhile Marian exile who had been at Oxford, and then also at Strasbourg with Martyr. John Hooker had placed his nephew under the aegis of his fellow countryman from Devon, John Jewel, and it was Jewel who sponsored Hooker and appealed to Rainolds and William Cole,[73] Corpus Christi's president, to take the prodigy on.[74] Rainolds gave Hooker his notes from Martyr, and likewise strongly recommended the study of Aristotle, Martyr's preferred philosopher. But Rainolds was not the only Vermiglian influence on Hooker, for part of his time at Oxford he spent with Laurence Humphrey, then the Divinity chair, and also one of Martyr's protégées.[75] Eventually, Hooker would tutor the son of another of Martyr's students, Edwin Sandys, bishop of London. As with others who defended the Elizabethan settlement, Hooker would also find himself contending with the meaning of Martyr's words. In his well-known exchange with his fellow minster at Temple Church, the Puritan Walter Travers, Hooker echoed the theme's sounded in the Vestarian and Admonition controversies, accusing Travers that, in his zeal to establish the presbyterian polity, he had mishandled Martyr.[76]

Hooker's appropriation of Aristotle, and the place Aristotle obtains in Martyr's theological method, elicits another avenue of inquiry,

---

[73] Cole had been a fellow at Corpus Christi College when Martyr was at Oxford and had followed Martyr to both Strasbourg and Zurich. He ended up in Geneva assisting with the translation of the *Geneva Bible*, before going to Antwerp and preaching in the English stragner churches. See C. M. Dent, *Protestant Reformers in Elizabethan Oxford* (Oxford: Oxford University Press, 1983), 42–43. He was conversant in Hebrew, and according to Marvin Anderson, had imbibed Martyr's "rabbinic exegesis". Anderson, *Foundations*, 159.

[74] Philip B. Secor, *Richard Hooker, prophet of Anglicanism* (Tunbridge Wells, Kent: Burns & Oates; Toronto: Anglican Book Centre, 1999), 43–49.

[75] Dent, *Reformers in . . . Oxford*, 184–190.

[76] Secor, *Hooker*, 200.

and that is the place of Martyr in the formation of what is termed Protestant Scholasticism, especially as it relates to England. For some this phenomena amounted to an admission that *sola scriptura* had definite drawbacks, and that what was needed was some heuristic or theological method that ensured doctrinal integrity. This is the opinion of Bryan Spinks and Brian Armstrong. Spinks, mirroring Armstrong's assessment, sees Protestant scholasticism as built on the presuppositions that reason rightly used, i.e., according to the method of Aristotelian syllogisms, can define and defend a theology coherently conceived and logically constructed. The materials for this of course are drawn from Holy scripture, and scripture itself is a logically coherent record. Consequently, this system lends itself to a metaphysics that applies to the most abstract of doctrines, including that of the Deity.[77] As Yule puts it, this method became

> a defence against heresy on the left as well as an attack on the superstitions of Rome, biblical doctrines were constructed into a logical system and then deductions bolstered up by syllogisms were made from these. This required making priorities of theological importance and this inevitably led to a pronounced interest in metaphysical matters particularly with reference to the doctrine of God and of His will.[78]

To Yule, Armstrong, and Spinks, Protestant scholasticism came to England via Beza and Martyr, and another of Martyr's followers, Jerome Zanchius. Zanchius had left Italy ten years after Martyr did, in 1552, and eventually found himself in Heidelberg. His work on the doctrine of God was deeply indebted to Aquinas, and in this he did not stray far from Martyr.[79] To what extent Martyr embraced or adumbrated Protestant Scholasticism has been debated by recent Martyr scholars, with assertions from John Patrick Donnelly that Martyr indeed was very much the scholastic, Marvin Anderson that

---

[77] Bryan D Spinks *Two Faces of Elizabethan Anglican Theology: Sacraments and Salvation in the Thought of William Perkins and Richard Hooker* Drew University Studies in Liturgy No. 9 (Lanham, Maryland and London: The Scarecrow Press, 1999, 27–34. Cf. Brian Armstrong *Calvinsim and the Amyraut Heresy: Protestant Scholasicism and Humanism in Seventeenth-Centruy France* (Madison: University of Wisconsin Press, 1969, 32 ff.

[78] George Yule, *The Puritans in Politics: The Religious Legislation of the Long Parliament, 1640–1647*. Courtenay Library of Reformation Classics. Sutton Courtenay Press, 1981, 29.

[79] Cf. John Patrick Donelly, "Calvinist Thomism", *Viator*, 7 (1976), 441–455.

rather he was a humanist, and Joseph Mclelland that such cut and dry distinctions cannot easily be made.[80]

Regardless of these debates, Spinks and Armstrong *inter alios*, still correctly point out that the real doctrine affected in all of this, as seen with Zanchius, is Theology proper, or the doctrine of God. This scholastic affinity with syllogism and Aristotle was valorized by Beza, who had refused to allow Ramus to teach against Aristotle at Geneva, while he himself lectured on both the *Politics* and the *Ethics*.[81] Such a theology moves away from Calvin's more Christocentric theology of grace and more humanistic (and dare it be said, Platonic) approach to theology, toward one dominated by the doctrines of absolute predestination, and thus a line is drawn from Beza's *Tabula praedestinationis* to Perkins's *The Golden Chain*.[82] That such a shift as Spinks and Armstrong posit occurred among some English Calvinists has been embraced also by Patrick Collinson:

> It is possible to speak of a 'giant leap' across the chasm separating Calvin, the biblical humanist, from seventeenth-century Calvinist scholasticism while regarding Beza as a transitional and bridging figure, and systematizer, but scarcely a Protestant scholastic. The Aristotelian rot, if that is what it was, seems to have begun not with Beza but with the Italians, Peter Martyr and G. Zanchius.[83]

But whether praise or blame can be laid at Martyr's feet simply because Zanchius was his disciple, and that he praised Beza's *tabula* presents several problems. Martyr certainly held to predestination, even double predestination in a modified form. Martyr's holding the will of God as coterminus with His essence, and holding as well to the Augustinian notion of the primacy of essence *simpliciter* in all definition of God, makes predestination inevitable. Consequently, any attempt to separate Martyr's doctrines of predestination from those

---

[80] Cf. CAS. Marvin Anderson, "Peter Martyr: Protestant Humanist" in PMIR, 65–84 and Joseph Mclelland, "Peter Martyr Vermigli: Scholastic or Humanist" in Mclelland, *Italian Reform*, 141–151. Mclelland, though sympathetic to the concerns Anderson raised, nonetheless falls out more on the side of Donnelly, all the while warning against facile hard and fast distinctions between scholasticism and humanism.

[81] Spinks, *Two Faces*, 30.

[82] Spinks, *Two Faces*, 28.

[83] Collinson, "International Calvinism," 217.

embraced by such Puritans as Ames and Perkins, is futile.[84] But was
he the source, even indirectly, of their doctrine? Even a qualified
yes is hard to give, but that a coincidence of doctrine obtained
between Martyr and later Puritans seems the logical judgement, leaving causality to be inferred.[85]

This brings us back to Jewel, his Eucharistic doctrine, and the
manner in which he chose to defend it, which strongly parallels
Martyr's method as explicated in the *Dialogue on the Two Natures*. As
to any definite assertions of what things the ancient Church truly
taught, aside from the oft repeated "they are more for us than for
you," or how the Fathers could be used as an express dogmatic
canon, Jewel produces little. Jewel's sustained arguments with Thomas
Harding (formerly Regius Professor of Hebrew, the Warden of New
College Oxford,[86] and Treasurer and Canon Residentiary of Salisbury
Cathedral),[87] the extant texts of which occupy about three quarters
of Jewel's four volumes of collected works, dominated his polemical
career in defending both his Challenge Sermon, and the *Apologia
Ecclesiae Anglicanae*.[88] Jewel seldom comments on the scriptures he
proffers to bolster his points even in light of Patristic authority; nor
does he give any precise interpretations by way of alternative to the
writers and points his Catholic nemesis Harding employs; instead
Jewel responds by way of confutation: either through questioning

---

[84] Cf. Peter White, *Predestination, Policy, and Polemic: Conflict and Consensus in the
English Church from the Reformation to the Civil War* (Cambridge: Cambridge University
Press, 1992), 50.

[85] Sts Augustine and Aquinas, to both of whom Martyr owed a theological debt
[Cf. PPRED, 93–150], maintain the same *ordo theologiae* as is present in the Westminster
Confession of Faith, Chapter II, "On the Holy Trinity". The first, two substantial
sections say nothing at all about the Trinity, but treat first the being of God, then
the divine attributes, and only then in the last section (less than twenty percent of
the chapter) treats of the divine Triad. It could just as easily be argued that the
Puritan doctrine of God had just as much, in not more, in common with Aquinas
and Augustine (essence, attributes, Persons) as with Calvin.

[86] Philip M. J. McNair, "Peter Martyr in England" in PMIR, 96.

[87] John le Neve, *Facti Ecclesiae Anglicanae, 1541–1857, VI Salisbury Diocese*. Compiled
by John Horn (London: University of London, Institute of Historical Research,
1986), 12, 95.

[88] The debate sparked by Jewel's Challenge Sermon, and spurred on by the
Apologia Ecclesiae Anglicanae, would eventually produce some ninety-six different works.
The complete bibliography can be found in A. C. Southern, *Elizabethan Recusant
Prose, 1559–1590* (London, 1950), 60–66.

what Harding's quotations assert, or by employing syllogism and logic—and that at times shoddily—to weaken the virtue of his arguments, or in robbing Harding's authorities of the weight he asserted they bore.[89] In commenting upon the sixth proposition of Jewel's well-known Challenge Sermon, that Christ's body is, or may be, in a thousand places or more at one time, Harding had argued that

> although the body of Christ be naturall and humaine in dede, yet through the vnion and coniunction, many thinges be possible to the same now, that to all other bodies be impossible; as to walke vpon waters, to vanishe awaye out of sight, to be transfigured and made bright as the sunne, to ascende vp through clowdes: and after it became immortall, death being conquered, to ryse vp againe out of the graue, and to entre through doores fast shutte.[90]

Harding's response is predicated upon *communicatio idiomatum*, that those attributes which belonged to either nature of the Incarnate Christ, divine or human, could be properly attributed, through the unity of the person, to the other nature. This is the same line of argumentation followed by some Lutherans—most notable Johannes Brenz, at whom Martyr's dialogue *On the Two Natures in Christ* was aimed—in maintaining their peculiar Eucharistic doctrine of consubstantiation. In response, Jewel writes,

> Now let us consider Harding's arguments: Christ's body walked upon waters: It entered through the doors being shut: it Ascended through the clouds: *Ergo*, it may be at one time in sundry places. Although this argument may soon be espied, having utterly no manner sequel in reason, yet the folly thereof may the better appear by the like: St. Peter walked upon the water: Elias was taken up into the clouds: St. Bartholomew entered through the doors being shut; *Ergo*, St. Peter, Elias, and St. Bartholomew may be at one time in sundry places.[91]

---

[89] Professor Richard Rex of Cambridge, once noted in a conversation that Jewel was great at telling one what to believe, but rather poor in telling why, and in this the bishop was far more like Calvin than Martyr; a man, said Rex, who knew how to use a syllogism.

[90] Harding, *Answere to Ivell*, 136.

[91] Jewel, *Replie to Harding*, in *Works* I, 483. Jewel's illogic or his misapplication of theology goes beyond the scope of this essay, but it should be noted that Jewel's argument rests upon Peter, Elijah, and Bartholomew having by nature bodily attributes similarly empowered to supernatural ends in the same was as Christ's body was also supernaturally empowered in his Incarnation; a point Jewel would not have confessed.

Jewel here follows, though with a weak syllogism, the line against
the traditionalist doctrine of the real presence that had been taught
by Peter Martyr in his dialogue, which Jewel referred to in his letters with Martyr as *Orothetes* (Greek: , one who sets boundaries), a
book possessed by Jewel since 1562, Martyr himself having sent Jewel
a copy. In the book Martyr had cast Jewel as Palaemon, the mod-
erator in a dispute between one who held to *ubiquitarianism*—the
Lutheran doctrine that Christ's body was ubiquitous, i.e., everywhere—and a disputant inclined toward Martyr's and Zurich's doctrine of the Eucharist.[92] Essentially, Martyr's argument affirms the
temporal presence of Christ's body in heaven, and that to say it
possessed trans-temporal qualities, i.e., that it is ubiquitous, makes it
more than a human body. Jewel's use of syllogisms, however, hardly
rises to the level of competence of Martyr's logic. But what is most
telling is not that Jewel was somehow theologically unfaithful to his
mentor—he was not—but that whatever Aristotelian methods Martyr
employed were largely lost on Jewel.[93]

Jewel did possess a vast knowledge of the Church Fathers: reading Jewel's polemical works is like going through a florilegium of
Patristic citations. Yet Jewel did not appropriate his sources through
florilegia, for his library was extensive, and the parts of it still extant
in Magdalen College testify to his assiduous note-taking, and the system he had whereby his notes and marginalia were transferred to
notebooks.[94] These citations eventually found themselves in Jewel's
works. This pedantry hardly gives Jewel the title of humanist, however capable his rhetorical and oratorical skills were. But while Jewel
was no humanist, or even that subtle a theologian, he nonetheless
does give Martyr a progeny in England of conforming, Reformed

---

[92] See Jewel, Letter to Martyr, 7 February 1562, *Works* IV, 1245–1246. See also
VWG, 65–67. The antagonist is the personification of one Brentius, dubbed Pantachus
(Greek, everywhere).

[93] The accidents of Jewel's syllogisms, particularly St. Peter and the prophet Elijah,
Martyr explicitly placed in the mouth of Pantachus, in the *Dialogus*, but his manner of argumentation is quite different than Jewel's, and centers on Aristotelian distinctions pertaining to substance and accidents; matters (should I say, categories)
Jewel never touches. Cf. DIAL, 140–142.

[94] Most of the notes are confined to several texts, notably some Greek Ecclesiastical
Historians, and also in a Volume containing several of the works of Nicholas of
Cusa. The most marginalia in Jewel's works is in an early edition of his *Defense of
the Apology* and are simply notes he inserted for a later edition. Cf. Ker, "Library"
256–265, but Ker notes none of this information.

orthodoxy (for this is exactly what he was defending), a lineage no doubt bolstered by the pervasive publishing and distribution of Martyr's *opera*. As his most celebrated English pupil, John Jewel embodied Peter Martyr's humanistic and Patristic legacy to England, however attenuated; and Jewel represents as well, as Elizabeth's dutiful bishop, that element of Martyr that embraced conformity as an aspect of preserving the ministry. Martyr also, along with Beza, left to England, in the Protestant Scholastics, an embrace and use of Aristotle unknown among the first generation of Reformers. So Jewel, and in a sense Rainolds through Hooker, left Martyr's legacy of, if not Patristic scholarship, at least a Reformed understanding and interpretation of the Fathers to the Church of England. Hooker also certainly leaned upon Aristotle, for though surely not the reliance of either medieval or Protestant Scholasticism, it was a dependence garnered from Martyr via Rainolds.[95] Consequently, given his support for conformity both in Edward's and Elizabeth's reigns, his theological presence through Jewel and other of the Marian exiles, and his bequest of Aristotle in whatever form to England's Protestants, Martyr stands as one of the most, if indeed not the most influential of the Protestant, continental divines in the formation of an English Protestant identity.

---

[95] This of course adumbrates Hooker's theological prolegomena of Scripture, Tradition, and Reason, though such a heuristic was neither explicitly nor even implicitly in Vermigli.

THE EARLY REFORMED COVENANT PARADIGM: VERMIGLI IN THE CONTEXT OF BULLINGER, LUTHER AND CALVIN[1]

Peter A. Lillback

Introduction

Since the earliest days of the Reformation, the concept of the covenant has served as the primary idea for expressing the redemptive relationship of God with man. After its initial formulation by Ulrich Zwingli, this covenantal paradigm shaped the Reformed understanding of God's perpetual commitment to the physical and spiritual descendants of Abraham, and provided a biblical-theological structure for redemptive-historical continuity. Jürgen Moltmann offers a working definition of covenantal theology: "a theological method which utilizes the biblical theme of the covenant as the key idea for a) the designation of the relationships of God and man, and b) the presentation of the continuity and discontinuity of redemptive history in the Old and New Testaments."[2] At the heart of the development of this covenant idea, as the Reformers themselves understood it, rests the interpretation of Genesis 17. Heinrich Bullinger viewed this passage of God's covenant with Abraham, the patriarch of Israel, as paradigmatic and John Calvin viewed it as vital, but Martin Luther rejected its theological role concerning the Gospel because of its establishment of circumcision with its conditional (law) implications. Therefore, while the Reformers disagreed *how* Genesis 17 was important, all agreed *that* it was important—for biblical foundation, for

---

[1] This study is an outgrowth of my doctoral research, which has been revised and published as *The Binding of God: Calvin's Role in the Development of Covenant Theology* (Grand Rapids: Baker Academic, 2001). I here express my appreciation to Dr. Frank A. James, III for the opportunity to investigate Martyr's covenantal thought, and to David Garner and Clark Stull, both Ph.D. students at Westminster Theological Seminary for their assistance in perfecting this paper for publication.

[2] J. Moltmann, "Foderaltheologie," in *Lexikon für Theologie und Kirche* (1960), 190, my translation.

theological integration, or for outright rejection in terms of doctrinal construction.

The focus of this essay is Peter Martyr Vermigli's exposition of the covenant in Genesis 17 in the milieu of the early reformation's covenantal discussion of this biblical text. Accordingly, this analysis begins with Zwingli, who, in the wake of the Anabaptist debates, offered an inchoate covenant paradigm in his 1525 Commentary on Genesis. Subsequently, in 1534 two years before Calvin's first edition of the *Institutes*, Bullinger developed Zwingli's covenant paradigm in the first monograph on the covenant, *Of the One and Eternal Testament or Covenant of God*.[3] Therein, he termed Genesis 17, "the target of all of the Scriptures."[4] At almost the same time as Bullinger's exposition, Luther was lecturing on Genesis. In his commentary, he called Genesis 17, "dangerous for the Christian."[5] Within a year or two of Bullinger's work, Calvin wrote the Preface to the *Geneva Bible* that developed a covenant theology that paralleled some of the perspectives of Bullinger.[6] More significantly, of course, is Calvin's covenantal teaching on Genesis 17 and in the *Institutes*. In this broad context, Martyr's views of the covenant in Genesis 17 will be developed and assessed.

---

[3] The first English translation was produced by Peter A. Lillback, "The Binding of God: Calvin's Role In The Development Of Covenant Theology", (Ph.D. diss., Westminster Theological Seminary, 1985) 499–527. Another translation has been made also by Charles S. McCoy and J. Wayne Baker, *Fountainhead of Federalism* (Louisville: Westminster/John Knox Press, 1991), 101–138.

[4] See Bullinger's Of The Testament or Covenant in *The Binding of God*, 507.

[5] *Luther's Works*, American Edition, edited by Jaroslav Pelikan and Helmut T. Lehmann, (Philadelphia: Fortress Press; St. Louis: Concordia, 1955 ff.) will be abbreviated as LW followed by volume, page. D. Martin *Luthers Werke*. Kritische Gesamtausgabe, edited by J. C. F. Knaake, et al. (Weimar: Hermann Bohlaus Nachfolger, 1883 ff.), this will be abbreviated as WA followed by volume, page. The reference here is LW, III, 77; WA, XLII, 603.

[6] The French title is "A Tous Amateurs De Jesus Christ et De Son Evangile, Salut." But its Latin title in Beza's 1576 *Epistolareum et Consilium Calvini* is "Praefatio in N.T. Cuius Haec Summa Est: Christum Esse Legis Finem." These can be found in CO, IX, 791–822. The English translation is *Christ the End of the Law, Being the Preface to the Geneva Bible of 1550* by John Calvin, trans. Thomas Weeden (London: Henry George Collins, 1848.) See also La Vraie Piete, *Divers traites de Jean Calvin et Confession de foi de Guillaume Farel*, ed. Irena Bachus and Claire Chimelli (Geneva, 1986), 17–23.

The Covenant Paradigm of Zurich: Zwingli & Bullinger on the Covenant

The beginnings of a Reformed articulation of the covenant of grace emerged in the debate with the Anabaptists over the biblical legitimacy of paedobaptism.[7] Zwingli concludes, "It has been proved clearly enough that the Christian people also stand in the gracious covenant with God in which Abraham stood with him," and next he presents the following chart.[8]

Abraham's Chart	The Christian's Chart
II. God	II. God all-sufficient
II. is Abraham's God.	II. is our God.
III. He should walk uprightly before him.	III. We should walk uprightly before him.
IV. He is also the God of his seed	IV. He is also the God of our seed.
V. God promised the Savior to Abraham	V. God has sent the Savior to us.
VI. Covenant sign: circumcision of young children and adults.	VI. Covenant sign: baptism of young children and adults.
VII. Nevertheless we first teach the children when they are old enough.	VII. We teach the children when they are old enough.

This is the first paradigm of Reformed covenant theology as it was conceived in the early part of the sixteenth century. When Heinrich Bullinger composed his monograph in October 1534 on the theme of the covenant some nine years after Zwingli's volume, he built it on Genesis 17, using essentially this same outline. Zwingli's model of the covenant was perpetuated wherever Bullinger's *De Testamento Seu Foedere Dei Unico Et Aeterno* was studied. In *De Testamento*, he does not discuss the pre-fall relationship of God and Adam. Nor does he consider the issue of covenant and election as Zwingli had done in

---

[7] For a discussion of the Zurich baptismal debates and their impact on Zwingli's development of his covenantal thought, see *The Binding of God*, 81–109.

[8] ZSW, IV, 637–638. "So nun yetzt Klarich gnug bewart ist, doss's Christenvolck eben in dem gnadigen pundt gegen gott stadt, in dem Abraham mitt in gestanden." Next, Zwingli presents his chart containing "the main points of the earlier covenant and our covenant, so that the unity may be clearly seen."

his final work against the Anabaptists.[9] There is no mention of a pre-temporal covenant of redemption. There is, however, a full consideration of the one covenant of grace throughout the successive ages of redemptive history. It is evident that Bullinger's exposition of the covenant is an amplification of Zwingli's chart from Genesis 17. This makes sense when one realizes that Bullinger believed that Zwingli's focus on the covenant was nothing less than the rediscovery of the "chief point of religion."[10]

The Covenant Perspective of Wittenberg:
The Contrast Between Luther & Bullinger

A comparison of Bullinger and Luther reveals an aspect of the tensions that strained relations between the Zurich and Wittenberg reformations. Significantly, Luther was lecturing on Genesis during 1535–36, only a year or so after Bullinger's *De Testamento* was published.[11] Bullinger builds his explication of the covenant upon Genesis 17. Luther, too, has strong feelings about Genesis 17. "This chapter, therefore, is outstanding because of the institution of circumcision, which the Jews single out for unrestrained praise and are proud of beyond measure."[12] The reference to circumcision is important, but it also poses a problem. It is the basis of the false Jewish pride. "Therefore Paul attacks the Jews so vigorously in order to free them from this carnal presumption."[13] Luther continues, "If someone should diligently stress this chapter, he will find countless supporters and pupils, for in it Moses assembles such powerful arguments in favor of circumcision that St. Paul had to resist with all his might."[14]

Paul's struggle with the Jews of his day was precisely because of

---

[9] See *The Binding of God*, 102–109.

[10] See note 18 below.

[11] LW, III, ix.

[12] LW, III, 76; WA XLII, 602–03. "Est igitur insigne hoc Caput propter institutam circumcisionem, quam solam Iudaei immodice efferunt, et mire de ea superbiunt."

[13] LW, III, 76; WA, XLII, 602–03. "Itaque Paulo tam vehemens contra Iudaeos pugna est, ut hanc praesumptionem carnalem eis eximat."

[14] LW, III, 76–77; WA, XLII, 603. "Si quis enim hoc caput graviter urgeat, inveniet suae sententiae suffragatores et discipulos infinitos. Adeo enim robusta et firma argumenta in hoc Capite pro circumcisione a Mose colliguntur, ut necesse fuerit Divo Paulo omni impetu se opponere."

what Genesis 17 teaches. Rather than "diligently stress" this chapter, one should first learn Paul's arguments against circumcision.
". . . there is no danger among strong Christians and those fortified
by the Word if some fanatic should insist on circumcision."[15] "But
among the weak there is great danger. . . ."[16] The chapter of "the
chief article of religion"[17] for Bullinger is *dangerous* for untrained
Christians in Luther's estimation. While Luther insists that one must
first be fortified by Paul before he reads this chapter, Bullinger
believes that all Scripture aims at the covenant of this chapter.[18]
Thus he provides a "Collation of all of Scripture to the Heads of
the Covenant."[19] Luther and Bullinger are obviously working with
different theological presuppositions.

This difference can be clarified if one considers their interpretations of Genesis 17. For Luther, the chapter contains two different
covenants. One was for both Isaac and Ishmael in that both received
circumcision. The other was an unnamed covenant given only to
Isaac promising the Savior.[20] The first was a covenant for the Jews
only,[21] which served as a temporal covenant and symbolized only
material things.[22] For Bullinger, the chapter contains one covenant.

---

[15] LW, III, 77; WA, XLII, 603. "Non igitur periculum est apud firmos Christianos
et munitos verbo, si quis phanaticus urgeat circumcisionem."
[16] LW, III, 77; WA, XLII, 603. "Apud infirmos autem ingens periculum est . . ."
[17] Cf. Joachim Staedtke, *Die Theologie des jungen Bullinger*. Studien zur Dogmengeschichte und systematischen Theologie (Zwingli Verlag: Zurich, 1962), 49, 50,
287–88. Cf. Jack W. Cottrell, "Covenant and Baptism in the Theology of Huldreich
Zwingli", (Ph.D. Dissertation, Princeton Theological Seminary, 1971), 338–39.
[18] "Further, in these most brief heads of the covenant the whole sum of piety
consists, in fact, no other teaching of the saints of all ages through the whole
Scripture exists than what is included in these heads of the covenant, except that
by the succession of times each one is explained more extensively and more clearly."
The Binding of God, Appendix, paragraph VIII 507.
[19] *The Binding of God*, Appendix, paragraph IX 508–510.
[20] LW, III, 111; WA, XLII, 627–28. "But let us return to the exposition of the
text. Abraham hears that both covenants are being confirmed: the material one
involving the land of Canaan and the spiritual one involving the eternal blessing."
See also LW, III, 116; WA, XLII, 630–31.
[21] Luther considers it to be a covenant only for the Jews. He declares, "Thus
here God's own words refute the argument of the Jews, who maintain that circumcision is to continue forever and want it imposed upon the Gentiles too; for
He expressly says: 'You and your descendants shall keep your covenant.' Hence
this covenant does not concern the Gentiles. In addition, He says: 'Throughout
their generations,' that is, as long as the kingdom and the priesthood continue to
exist."
[22] "This expression, "throughout their generations," should be carefully noted.

Circumcision is a true sacrament of the covenant of grace equal with the Supper and baptism. It is the one eternal covenant of God made with men to save them, and it was continued by Christ's coming. Moreover, it is a covenant of grace consistent with the covenant of Christ.[23] The differences can be stated pointedly—Genesis 17 is *law* for Luther[24] and *gospel* for Bullinger. Luther's "theology",[25] caused him to see the covenant of Genesis 17 as a *promissio legis* rather than a *promissio gratiae*.[26] For one who had "dashed the teeth out of the law",[27] Genesis 17 was no place to build his theology.

The Covenantal Consensus of Zurich & Geneva: A Comparison of Bullinger & Calvin

Scholars have recognized that Calvin employs the covenant idea.[28] From their standpoint, however, Calvin's utilization of the covenant

---

He could simply have said: "My covenant shall be everlasting between you and your descendants after you"; but because He adds "throughout their generations," He indicates its continuance for a fixed time. Therefore the meaning is: this covenant, or circumcision itself, will continue as long as your generation continues. It is also certain that Abraham's descendants no longer continue to exist, for after the capture of Jerusalem no kingdom, no people, no family, and no sacrifice remained."

[23] "He fulfilled the symbolism of circumcision by shedding His blood for man's justification, and by purifying the believer's heart so that he could keep the covenant's conditions. Circumcision is the sacrament of the covenant. In ancient covenants, there was the killing of an animal as a sign of the willingness of the covenanters to be destroyed even as the animal was should they violate the covenant. God is seen in this very action in Genesis 15, while God requires it of Abraham in Genesis 17 in the bloody rite of circumcision. Since God is a testator of a last will just as much as the maker of a covenant, this sign taught that God would one day die when He had assumed flesh by the shedding of His own blood. This is the significance of the two sacraments of baptism and the Lord's Supper." Fountainhead, 130–132.

[24] LW, XXVI, 6; WA, XL, I, 43–44. "Mira autem res est et mundo inaudita, docere Christianos, ut discant ignorare legem, utque sic vivant coram Deo, quasi penitus nulla lex sit. Nisi enim ignoraveris legem et ita direxeris cogitationes tuas in gratiam, quasi nulla sit lex et gratia mera, tum non possum salvus fieri."

[25] Luther says, "This is our theology, by which we teach a precise distinction between these two kinds of righteousness, the active and the passive, so that morality and faith, works and grace, secular society and religion may not be confused. Both are necessary, but both must be kept within their limits. Christian righteousness applies to the new man, and the righteousness of the Law applies to the old man, who is born of flesh and blood." LW, XXVI, 7; WA, XL:1, 45.

[26] See LW, XLVII; WA, LIII, 467.

[27] LW, XXVI, 161; WA, XL:1, 276.

[28] Leonard J. Trinterud, "The Origins of Puritanism", *Church History* 20 (1951):

is not that of the majority of the Reformed theologians. Thus the Rhineland theologians such as Bullinger and Oecolampadius developed a bilateral conditional covenant that was not possible for Calvin. To remain consistent with his unyielding views of election, Calvin was compelled to teach an unconditional unilateral covenant. The difference is a milder form of predestination that accommodates itself to a mutual covenant between God and man by the Rhinelanders, while Calvin's double predestinarianism resisted human response in the covenant. Trinterud claims the interpretation of "covenant" in Calvin's writings can "in no manner be compatible with that meaning" of such terms as "treaty," "alliance," "mutual agreement," "reciprocal agreement," etc. as used in Rhineland-Puritan covenant theology.[29] Lyle Bierma has summarized the alleged contrast between Calvin and the Rhineland theologians led by Zwingli and Bullinger in a most striking manner. For the Genevans, the covenant is unilateral; it is God's unconditional promise to man, with the burden for fulfilling the covenant resting on God, since the covenant is fulfilled in Christ's Incarnation, Crucifixion, and Resurrection. But for the Rhinelanders, the covenant is bilateral; it is God's conditional promise to man requiring man's response (in a mutual pact or treaty), with the burden for fulfilling the covenant resting on man, since the covenant is fulfilled in the obedience of the individual.[30]

Because so many have posited a fundamental dichotomy between Zurich and Geneva on the covenant, it is worth noting that there is in fact, a considerable covenantal continuity between Calvin and Bullinger. Calvin's conformity with Bullinger's covenantal perspec-

---

37–57; J. Wayne Baker, *Heinrich Bullinger and the Covenant*, (Ohio University Press, 1980), pp. xxi–xxiii, 193–98; Charles S. McCoy and J. Wayne Baker, *Fountainhead of Federalism: Heinrich Bullinger and the Covenantal Tradition* (Louisville: Westminster/John Knox Press, 1991), 23–26; Joseph C. McLelland, "Covenant Theology—A Re-Evaluation" *Canadian Journal of Theology* 3 (1957): 184–85. A related viewpoint held by some scholars is that Johannes Cocceius' covenantal theology was developed explicitly to blunt Calvinistic predestinarianism. Cf. J. A. Dorner, *History of Protestant Theology*, trans. G. Robson and S. Taylor, (Edinburgh: T. & T. Clark, 1871), II: 39–42; Ludwig Diestel, "Studien zur Foderaltheologie" in *Jahrbuch fur Deutsche Theologie* 10 (1865): 266 ff.; Otto Ritschl, "Entwicklung des Bundesgedankens in der reformierten Theologie des 16. und des 17. Jahrhunderts" in *Dogmengeschichte des Protestantismus* (Gottingen: Vandenhoeck & Ruprecht, 1926), 3: 430–35.

[29] Leonard J. Trinterud, "The Origins of Puritanism," 56 n. 27.

[30] Lyle Dean Bierma, "The Covenant Theology of Caspar Olevian", (Ph.D. diss., Duke University, 1980), 25.

tive can be observed in various ways. For example, Calvin insists, as does Bullinger, upon the unity and eternity of the covenant. He writes, "The covenant made with all the patriarchs is so much like ours in substance . . . that the two are actually one and the same. Yet they differ in the mode of dispensation."[31] Similarly, Calvin's description of the "one and eternal" covenant comports with the Rhinelander. The covenant is "everlasting" or "eternal",[32] "forever inviolable",[33] "firm and inviolable",[34] and "still in force".[35] It is established "once and for all"[36] and "keeps itself alive by its own strength".[37]

This accords with Bullinger's discussion of the continuity of the Old and New Covenants.[38] Further, Calvin sees the covenant with Abraham as the actual establishment of God's covenant. It is obvious that Calvin believes that the covenant was in existence before Abraham as was indicated above. Yet, the covenant's formal establishment was with Abraham in Genesis 17. Here again one observes the harmony between Calvin and Bullinger.

There are several other aspects of the Abrahamic covenant emphasized by Calvin in the *Institutes* that parallel Bullinger. Both reformers affirm that the covenant is the divine means of separating the world into those who are believers in Christ the Redeemer and those

---

[31] Calvin's Institutes of the Christian Religion are marked by the standard three part designation: Book, chapter, section. The page is to the Battles' translation, and the final reference is to Calvini Opera, volume and page. II. X. 2, 429, CO, II. 313. "Patrum omnium foedus adeo substantia et re ipsa nihil a nostro differt, ut unum prorsus atque idem sit." Cf. II. X. 7, 434, CO, II. 317. "The spiritual covenant was also common to the patriarchs. . . . Adam, . . . Noah, Abraham, and other spiritual patriarchs cleaved to God by such illumination of the Word."

[32] II. XI. 3, 345, CO, II, 250; II. VI. 4, 346, CO, II, 251; II. XI. 4, 454, CO, II, 332; II. XI. 4, 454, CO, II, 332; II. XI. 10, 459, CO, II, 336; II. XVII. 4, 532, CO, II, 388–89; III. IV. 32, 661, CO, II, 484; III. XX. 25, 884, CO, II, 651. "Aeternus."

[33] IV. I. 27, 1039, CO, II, 766; IV. II. 11, 1052, CO, II, 775. ". . . aeternumque manebat inviolabile. . . ."

[34] IV. XV. 17, 1317, CO, II, 972; IV. XVI. 5, 1328, CO, II, 979. ". . . firmum inviolabileque semper manebat. . . ."

[35] IV. XVI. 6, 1328–29, CO, II, 978–79. "Valere etiam."

[36] IV. XVI. 14, 1336–37, CO, II, 985–86; IV. XVII. 1, 1361, CO, II, 1003. "Semel."

[37] IV. II. 11, 1051–52, CO, II, 775. Cf. Psalm 105:6–11, VI, 176–79, CO, XXXII, 98–102; Jeremiah 31:3, X, 57–58, CO, XXXVIII, 644–45; and Jer. 32:40, X, 215, CO, XXXIX, 41–42. "Vim suam retinet."

[38] Cf. Bullinger's Of the One and Eternal Testament, in *Fountainhead of Federalism*, 120–25.

who are not. Calvin asserts, "My readers therefore should remember that I am not yet going to discuss that covenant by which God adopted to himself the sons of Abraham, or that part of doctrine which has always separated believers from unbelieving folk, for it was founded in Christ."[39] He adds, "I do not yet touch upon the special covenant by which he distinguished the race of Abraham from the rest of the nations. For, even then in receiving by free adoption as sons those who were enemies, he showed himself to be their Redeemer."[40] Moreover, the Abrahamic covenant is still in force today. Calvin maintains that it "is most evident that the covenant which the Lord once made with Abraham is no less in force today for Christians than it was of old for the Jewish people. . . ."[41]

Calvin also characteristically teaches that the heart of the Abrahamic covenant is Christ. "For even if God included all of Abraham's offspring in His covenant," Calvin writes, "Paul nevertheless wisely reasons that Christ was properly that seed in whom all the nations were to be blessed."[42] Finally, Calvin emphasizes the existence of two great redemptive benefits contained in the Abrahamic covenant, namely, justification and regeneration (sanctification). ". . . Abraham's circumcision was not for his justification, but for the seal of that covenant of faith in which he had already been justified.[43] Furthermore, "the Lord covenants with Abraham that he should walk before him in uprightness and innocence of heart. This applies to mortification, or regeneration . . ."[44] Significantly, at each point, Calvin's teaching

---

[39] I. VI. 1, 71, CO, II. 54. "Meminerint ergo lectores, me nondum de foedere illo dissere, quo sibi Deus adoptavit Abrahae filios, et de illa doctrinae parte qua proprie segregati semper fuerunt fideles a profanis gentibus, quia in Christo fundata fuit."

[40] I. X. 1, 97, CO, II. 72. "Nondum attingo peculiare foedus quo genus Abrahae a reliquis gentibus distinxit. Num gratuita adoptione recipiens in filios qui hostes erant, redemptor iam tunc apparuit."

[41] IV. XVI. 6, 1328–29, CO, II. 979–80. "Siquidem evidentissimum est, quod semel cum Abrahamo Dominus foedus percussit, no minus hodie Christianis constare, quam olim iudaico populo. . . ."

[42] II. VI. 2, 343, CO, II. 248. "Nam etsi Deus totam Abrahae sobolem in foedere suo complexus est, prudentur tamen ratiocinatur Paulus, Christum proprie esse semen illud in quo benedicandae erant omnes gentes."

[43] IV. XIV. 5, 1280, CO, II. 944. ". . . no fuisee circumcisionem Abrahae in iustitiam, sed eius pacti obsignationem, cuius fide fuerat iam ante iustificatus."

[44] IV. XVI. 3, 1326, CO, II. 978. "Post ab Abrahamo Dominus stipulatur ut ambulet coram se in sinceritate et innocentia cordis, quod ad mortificationem pertinet seu regenerationem."

agrees with Bullinger. Although Calvin's discussion of Genesis 17 does not declare with Bullinger that it is the target of all Scripture, he does assert that it contains the summary of the divine covenant: "Now that word summarily contains this declaration, that God enters into covenant with Abraham: it then unfolds the nature of the covenant itself, and finally puts to it the seal, with the accompanying attestations."[45]

Calvin also maintains a significant emphasis upon the conditionality of the covenant. Calvin says: "In making the covenant, God stipulates for obedience, on the part of his servant ... For on this condition, he adopts children as his own, that he may, in return, obtain the place and the honour of a Father. And as he himself cannot lie, so he rightly demands mutual fidelity from his own children."[46] Commenting on Genesis 17:2, Calvin concurs with Bullinger that there are "two parts" of the covenant.

> We have said that the covenant of God with Abram had two parts. The first was a declaration of gratuitous love; to which was annexed the promise of a happy life. But the other was an exhortation to the sincere endeavor to cultivate uprightness, since God had given, in a single word only, a slight taste of his grace; and then immediately had descended to the design of his calling; namely, that Abram should be upright.[47]

Finally, Calvin and Bullinger agree that Genesis 17 does not teach that the sacrament of initiation, whether baptism or circumcision,

---

[45] Calvin's Commentary on Genesis (Calvin Translation Society: Grand Rapids, Baker, 1979), vol. 1, This will be abbreviated hereafter as: Gen. 17:1, I, i, 442, CO, XXIII, 233–35. "Iam verbum summatim hoc continet, quod Deus foedus paciscitur cum Abram: deinde quale sit foedus ipsum declarat, et tandem obsignat, addita tessera."

[46] Gen. 17:1, Vol. I, i, 443; CO, XXIII, 233–35. "In foedere pangendo stipulatur Deus a servo suo obedientiam. Sed non frustra praefatus est Deus se fortem esse Deum, et instructum virtute ad suos iuvandos: quia revocari ab aliis omnibus oportuit Abram ut totum se uni Deo addiceret ... Nam hac lege filios sibi adoptat ut vicissim patris obtineat locum et honorem. Sicut autem ipse non mentitur, ita iure mutuam fidem a suis exigit. Quare sciamus fidelibus Deum ideo patefieri, ut sub eius conspectu vivant: et illum sibi non operum modo, sed cogitationum arbitrum statuant." See also my, "The Continuing Conundrum: Calvin and the Conditionality of the Covenant," *Calvin Theological Journal* 29 no. 1 (1994): 42–74.

[47] Gen. 17:2, Vol. I, i, 444; CO, XXII I, 235. "Diximus bimembre fuisee Dei foedus cum Abram. Prius membrum erat gratuiti amoris testimonium, cui annexa erat beatae vitae promissio. Alterum vero, exhortatio ad sincerum colendae iustitiae studium."

was required for the salvation of an infant dying in infancy.[48] Both place the curse for neglecting the covenant sign on the adult who fails to take the seal of the covenant.[49] Thus, in the main, there is substantial identity between Bullinger and Calvin in their understanding of the covenant.

Between Wittenberg & the Zurich-Geneva Consensus: Martyr's Unique Views of the Covenant

Modern scholars have largely overlooked Peter Martyr Vermigli's significance for the development of the theology of the English and Reformed branches of the Reformation. With renewed attention being paid to his significant contributions, however, a substantial lacuna in our knowledge of the early reformation is finally being addressed.[50] As one considers Vermigli's view of the covenant in Genesis 17 and its relationship to the early Reformed covenantal paradigm, it should first be noted that his *Commentary on Genesis* did not appear until 1569, or seven years after his death.[51] Thus his published work could not have directly influenced the early paradigm since it appears thirty-five years after Bullinger's *De Testamento*. However, Frank James has shown that Martyr's *Genesis Commentary*

---

[48] Cf. Bullinger, De Testamento, "The Sacrament of the Covenant" in *Fountainhead of Federalism*, 131.

[49] At this point Bullinger and Calvin do not follow Augustine's understanding of the pre-fall covenant. For a consideration of Augustine's view of the pre-fall covenant, see *The Binding of God*, 41–45.

[50] Reformation scholars owe a hearty thanks to Philip M. J. McNair for his seminal biographical research on Martyr, PMI. That same gratitude must be extended to others as well, especially to CAS; VWG; and PPRED, not only for these studies of Martyr, but for the English translation and publication of Martyr's collected works entitled, The Peter Martyr Library, the first such literary attempt since they were written in the 1500's. Other significant Vermigli bibliography includes: PMRE; S. Corda, *Veritas Sacramenti: A Study in Vermigli's Doctrine of the Lord's Supper* (Zurich, 1975); R. M. Kingdon, *The Political Thought of Peter Martyr Vermigli: Selected Texts and Commentary* (Geneva, 1980); PMIR.

[51] *In Primum Librum Mosis Qui Vulgo Genesis Dicitur Commentarii* . . . Zurich: C. Froschoverus, 1569.

was based directly on his 1543–44 lectures at Strasbourg[52] and therefore Martyr had opportunity to interact with the developing covenantal views of his fellow reformers. If such discussions of the covenant
in Genesis 17 indeed took place, it would perhaps explain the emerging consensus regarding the early Reformed covenant paradigm.

There are several significant ways in which Martyr's exposition
reflects the same emphases of the early Reformed covenant thinkers.
His vocabulary is consistent with the early Reformed discussion of the
covenant: *pactum, testamentum* and *foedus* are used interchangeably.[53] Like
the other reformers, there is a commitment to the historic Augustinian
understanding of the unity of the Old and New Covenants.[54] Thus,
the Christian and the Old Testament believer are seen as one family of faith in the same covenant.[55] Furthermore, Vermigli and the
other reformers see Christ as the heart or substance of the covenant,
although the administrative circumstances of the covenants vary.[56]
Like the other reformers, Vermigli recognizes the mutuality of the
covenant as reflected in the formula, "I will be your God, and you
will be my people."[57] Even when Martyr does not use the terminology

---

[52] See PPRED, 44–50.

[53] "Notabis circumcisionem hic apellari pactum & testamentum, quod scilicet
foederis vel testamenti signum esset. . . ." 66. All of the subsequent Latin citations
are from Peter Martyr's *Commentarii* on Genesis 17. This is consistent with Zwingli,
Bullinger, and Calvin's covenantal vocabulary. See my, "Ursinus' Development of
the Covenant of Creation: A Debt to Melanchthon or Calvin?" *Westminster Theological
Journal* XLIII (1981): 247–88 and *The Binding of God*, 65–68, 83, 110, 128–134.
Luther's use of these terms is different, since he develops in the direction of a unilateral testament as opposed to a mutual covenant. See Kenneth Hagen, "From
Testament to Covenant in the Early Sixteenth Century" in *Sixteenth Century Journal*
3 (1972): 1–20; and *The Binding of God*, 65 ff.

[54] "Augustinus 2. Cap. 16. De Civitate Dei inquit, novum testamentum non esse
aliud quam vetus revelatum, & vetus novum occultatum." 67.

[55] "Qui sunt ex fide hi filii sunt Abrahae. Ad Romanos demum dicuntur Iudaei
excisi, ut nos qui eramus in oleastro, insereremur in bonam olivam, cum ergo simus
adoptati & adsciti in illorum familiam, idem cum illis habemus foedus." 67.

[56] "Utrobique summa res praecipuaque substantia, sive fundamentum foederis,
est Christus, quamvis quaedam circumstantiae ut ceremoniae & sacrificia sint immu-
tata." 67.

[57] "Agitur iam de circuncisione suscipienda, qua incorporabantur credentes famil-
iae Domini, idque in eis efficlebatur, ut Deus illis esset in Deum & ipsi ei in populum." "Sed quodnam est illud foedus cuius circuncisio est signum? Illius summa
est, quod Deus sit recipientibus in Deum, & illi sint ei vicissim in populum. Non
hoc leve est Deum habere pro Deo, imo Psalmus praedicat illos quibus id contigit,
beatos. Quid enim prodesset Deum esse Deum si mihi non sit Deus, id est, si non
me iuuaret, si mihi non benefaceret? Rursusque si talis in me esset, id autem ego

of "conditions of the covenant," he does recognize that faith and obedience are dual features of the Christian's covenant walk with God.[58] Thus, Martyr affirms the two benefits of grace that are emphasized by covenant theology: justification and regeneration (or sanctification).[59] In accord with the other reformers, the Old Testament sacrament of circumcision is seen as a picture of Christ's redeeming work to save sinners.[60] Perhaps one of the more significant aspects of this continuity, is seen in Vermigli's recognition that Old Covenant circumcision has implications for adults and their children, including infant baptism,[61] dedication to God, profession of faith, obedience and the education of children in the church in the fear of the Lord.[62] Thus, in many respects, Martyr stands in continuity with the general schema of the early reformed covenant paradigm.

---

non animadverterem, non sentirem? Mea proculdubio esset non vulgaris calamitas. Et arguitur insignis illiu in nos beneficentia, ut talis ac tantus qui coelum & terram condidit, infiniti pretii, omnia excedens, homuncionum tamen peculiariter velit appellari Deus." 67.

[58] For the necessity of faith consider, "Quia in patrem multarum gentium dedi te. Hoc & si Iudaei intelligunt propter Israelitarum regnum; Iudae & Edomaeorum, tamen rectius & luculentius a Paulo exprimitur, eum scribat & asseueret cum ad Romanos, tum ad Galatas Abrahae semen esse omnes vere credentes in Christum, qui cum in omnes nationes dispersi sint, omnium quodammodo gentium iam factus est pater Abrahamus." 66. "Primo, quod primus ita perhibetur credidisse ut fides illi ad justitiam sit imputata: quare ordine primus est in hac genealogia spirituali. Deinde imitatione, quotquot enim fideles sunt, illius insistunt vestigiis." 66. For the necessity of obedience consider: "Erat adhae ista nota quodammodo perpetua filiis Israel admonitio officii & vitae, quam praestare debebant, ut gentibus impuris & impiis non conformarentur, sed ut signo tam praeclaro ab illis discreti erant, ita sancta conversatione eos antecellerent." 66.

[59] ". . . cui non est aliquo pacto tribuendum, ut iustificet aut regeneret. . . . Ita Dominus iam Abramum possederat, iustificaverat ac regeneraverat fide, nunc notam circunciionis illi addit, & nomen imponit." 67.

[60] "Fuit etiam signum quo discernebantur fideles a caeteris nationibus. Certa corporis pars, id est, membrum generation: deputatum hoc sacramento insigniebatur, duplici de cause: Primo, qui Christus ibi repraesentandus erat ex sancto semine Abrahae oriturus. Praeterea cum peccatum ibi deleretur, cuius radix est originalis labes, quea cum traducantur in filios parentum semine, optime hoc signum ostendebata userendum illud peccatum." 66.

[61] "Ut sim tibi in Deum & semini tuo post te.) Quia ex hoc loco nos concludimus pueros quoque Christianorum in foedere Domini nasci, & idcirco baptizandos uti illi erant circuncidendi. Nam baptismus ut antea probavi circuncisioni succedit, ut idem nobis sit quod veteribus fuit circuncisio. Deinde illa quae Abramo Dominus pollicetur nobis etiam promissa sunt, cum nostrum eiusque foedus idem prorsus esse multa testentur." 67.

[62] At si me roges, quid nunc ad nos attintet circuncisio quando abolita est per Christum? Respondeo non parum, quia in illa sicut in omnibus aliis ceremoniis legis, imprimis debemus consyderare id quod nucleus est, summa & substantia rei,

Martyr's exposition of the covenant in Genesis 17 also has some unique insights that are not found in the other reformers. His emphasis on the sacraments is remarkable.[63] While Luther worries about circumcision, and Zwingli, Bullinger and Calvin discuss infant baptism in Genesis 17, Martyr discusses the concept of the sacraments in general including the Lord's Supper, baptism and circumcision.[64] In Martyr's exposition, it is as if the sacrament has a covenant rather than the covenant having a sacrament. This emphasis on sacrament seems to be the inverse of the other Reformed who accent the covenant.[65]

In this context, Martyr defines a sacrament as an instrument and makes the following points: that it is a sign instituted by God, designating and exhibiting grace in Christ; that it is intended for the ones who receive the sign and the offered grace in faith. Moreover, it exists not by nature, but by will; and that will is the will of God, and not the will of man. Also, it is instituted by God, and cannot be instituted by man. The sacraments have a double emphasis: first,

---

removendo circunstantias temporis, actionis & huiusmodi omnium quae ad ceremoniae rationem faciunt, ac ista omnia relinquentes Iudaeis ut temporarie instituta, quod in eis est praecipuum retineamus tanquam aeternum & impermutablie, ut in ista circuncisione erat dedicatio Deo; professio fide, obedientia, & puerorum qui susciperentur in ecclesia educatio sancta in timore Domini: ista inquam perpetua retineri debent." 69.

[63] This is perhaps not unexpected since Peter Martyr is known as a sacramental theologian. Cf. S. Corda, *Veritas Sacramenti*; VWG.

[64] Consider for example, "Notabis circuncisionem hic appellari pactum & testamentum, quod scilicet foederis vel testamenti signum esset, non quidem vacuum, sed illud asserens & exhibens quod in testamento continetur. Ut in coena dominica panis & vinum symbola sunt corporis & sanguinis Domini, non quidem incassum, sed ita ut illa sumendo corpus & Sanguinem Domini percipiamus. In circuncisione adhuc denotatur carnis mortificatio: nam cupiditates, affectiones & quae contra voluntatem Dei fiunt abesse oportet a populo Dei.... Quemadmodum in baptismo denotamur immersione aquae mortui & consepulti domino: ita hic significabantur patribus ablata esse peccata, & ideo ita vivendum, ut ulterius non admitterentur." p. 66. He also introduces a major heading called De Sacramentis before he treats the questions surrounding circumcision. His definition of a sacrament given in this section is "Imprimis ita definio Sacramentum, quod est signum a Deo institutum, ad gratiam per Chrstum designandam & exhibendam recipientibus ex fide. Signum est non naturale, sed ex voluntate, non quidem hominum sed Dei, ideo scribitur a Deo insitutum, quia non hominum est instituere Sacramenta." 68.

[65] "Notabis circuncisionem hic appellari pactum & testamentum, quod scilicet foederis vel testamenti signum esset, non quidem vacuum, sed illud afferens & exhibens quod in testamento continetur." 66.

they are apt likenesses and comparisons that represent what they signify; second, they exhibit what they signify. Hence, Martyr rejects
the medieval sophists' claim found in the *Sentences* to the effect that
the OT sacraments and the NT sacraments are fundamentally different.
The *Sententiarios* asserted that the OT sacraments only signified and
promised grace while offering no grace, whereas the NT sacraments
signify, promise and in fact offer grace.[66] Martyr rejects this dichotomy
between the sacraments of the Old Covenant and the New, since
the very essence of a sacrament from Martyr's perspective, whether
in the Old Covenant or the New, is to represent, exhibit and offer
grace as the instruments of God received by faith.

Clearly, Martyr's view of the sacraments in general, and the sacrament of circumcision in particular, is in accord with the Reformed
perspective represented especially by Calvin. While rejecting the
Roman Church's *ex opere operato* conception of sacramental grace,
Martyr still avers that the sacraments are an authentic means of
grace.[67] Although taking a very different view of Genesis 17 than
Luther, it is yet evident that Martyr shares Luther's deep concern
that the Protestant rupture with Rome not result in the diminishing
of the importance of the sacramental life of the Church. Perhaps
the primacy and the importance of the sacraments in Martyr's thought,
in view of his substantial influence on early Protestant Britain, may
help to account for the pronounced emphasis of the sacramental life
in the Anglican tradition. This inference is strengthened, when one
considers that the historic Anglican Eucharistic theology also reflects
the Martyr-Calvin receptionistic view of the real, yet spiritual, presence of Christ in the Lord's Supper.[68]

---

[66] These summary statements are from 68. Of the sacramental view of the
Sentences, Martyr writes, "... ponunt illud inter alia discrimen inter sacramenta
veteris testamenti & novi, Vestera videlicet tantum significasse & promisisse gratiam,
sed non praestitisse, Nova & significasse & praestisse. Quod abunde falsum esse iam
nos scimus, cum Deus circuncisis esticeretur in Deum, & illi in eius populum cooptar-
entur, quod sine eius gratia quis fieri posse dicere audeat? Praeterea cum circuncisio idem quod Baptismus habeatur, utrobique donatur recipientibus gratia." 68.

[67] "Quibus addas, non hanc fuisse vim circuncisionis, ut ex opere operato rec-
onciliartentur Deo, quod neque ullis aliis tribuitur Sacramentis. Nam circuncionem
si ex se spectas, actio est humana, cui non est aliquo pacto tribuendum, ut justificet
aut regeneret. ..." 67.

[68] Philip Schaff writes, "But the peculiar views of Luther on the real presence
and the ubiquity of Christ's body found no congenial soil in England. Cranmer
himself abandoned them as early as Dec. 14, 1548, when a public discussion was
held in London on the eucharist; and he adopted, together with Ridley, the Calvinistic

Furthermore, Martyr discusses in depth the questions surrounding circumcision. This is unique among the Reformed expositors of the covenant in Genesis 17 considered here. Luther, of course, addressed circumcision and as a result rejected the use of this chapter for believers. It might be said, then, that Martyr does exactly the reverse and indirectly answers Luther's warnings about circumcision. He rehabilitates circumcision for the Christian, by answering the difficult questions that arise in regard to it in light of Reformed covenantal thinking. In a section entitled "*De Circmcisione*",[69] he addresses the many issues associated with the Old Covenant Abrahamic sacrament: for example, the medieval sophists claimed that sin could be remitted by OT sacraments, but grace was not granted. (Martyr finds this absurd since remission and grace are inseparable.) What is the status of children who died before they were circumcised on the eighth day? (He rejects Augustine's view of a judgment upon such children and insists that God is the God of believers and their children. Salvation is not based upon a human act, but divine grace.) What does circumcision have to do with Christians when Christ has abolished it? (One must find the eternal and unchangeable in circumcision, that includes dedication to God, faith and obedience, the admission of children into the teaching ministry of the church.) In addition, what about the status of women who were excluded from OT circumcision? (They participated with their fathers and husbands and were truly part of the covenant. This sacramental distinction between men and women is abolished in Christ.) Also, since the Apostle Paul downplays circumcision, what significance can it have for a believer? (Paul treats not of circumcision as a sacrament, but

---

doctrine of a virtual presence and communication of Christ's glorified humanity. . . . Cranmer wrote very extensively on the eucharist, and especially against the romish mass. . . . His change of view is due to the influence of the book of Ratramnus (Bertram) against transubstantiation, the tract of Bullinger on the eucharist and the personal influence of Ridley, Peter Martyr, and Bucer. Bishop Browne says (on Art. XXVIII. Sect. I. 711 of the Am ed.): 'Both Cranmer and Ridley, to whom we are chiefly indebted for our formularies, maintained the doctrine nearly identical with that maintained by Calvin, and before him by Bertram. . . . In the main, Calvin, Melanchthon in his later views, and the Anglican divines were at one.' John Knox entirely agreed with Cranmer in the Reformed doctrine of the eucharist and he objected only to the kneeling posture, which led to the insertion of a special rubric in the Prayer-Book." In *Creeds of Christendom* (Grand Rapids: Baker, 1977), I.601, n. 1. See also John W. Nevin, *The Mystical Presence and Other Writings on the Eucharist*, (Philadelphia: United Church Press, 1966).

[69] These questions are found in Peter Martyr's *Commentarii* on Genesis 68–71.

as an OT distinctive between peoples, which was incorrectly thought a necessity for salvation.) Why were Ishmael and Isaac circumcised at such different ages? (To emphasize God's choice of the child of promised grace over the child of human natural effort.) Moreover, is circumcision an *ex opere operato* sacrament? (No. Consider the case of Ishmael. Paul teaches effectual circumcision is of the heart by the Holy Spirit.) How can circumcision be called an eternal covenant, if it was abolished by Christ? (If the scope, sum and substance of circumcision are considered, it is perpetual—God is the God of Abraham and his seed. Moreover, the Hebrew word *Holam* means a "long duration" rather than "never ending.") Why did Paul circumcise Timothy since circumcision had been abolished? (This was due to Paul's concern to exercise the rule of charity toward those he ministered to.) How can circumcision oblige one to keep the whole law if the law had not even been given when circumcision was first established? (This is because the Law became a pedagogue to lead the people to Christ. It is in that role that the law requires those who seek circumcision to keep all of the law.) What about the issue of the power of the covenant? Can parents whose faith is not a justifying faith, that is, a faith that is in name only or a dead or temporal faith, can such as these have their children baptized (or circumcised in the OT)? (No. Such were not to be circumcised in the past, and should not be baptized today.)[70] If circumcision and baptism do not work *ex opere operato*, but become effective through

---

[70] This perspective clearly argues against the view that later New England Congregationalists would take in what has become known as "the half-way covenant". On its surface, it also seems to challenge what was then the emerging Reformed view of Roman Catholic baptism's validity for entrance into a Reformed communion. What is at stake here is the ideal of a Christian society that is coextensive in terms of church and state, established by a common baptism. Martyr states, "... dicimus Christianorum liberos sive Iudaeorum ex vi foederis ad Deum pertinere, at quid statuemus de eis, quando contigerit ut eorum pater nomine tenus solum fidem habeat, vel si quam habet, illa sit mortua aut temporaria, quae vim justificandi non habeat? Nam tunc sine controversia pater aut mater, vel utrique ut fieri postest, ad Deum non pertinent, ergo videtur quod infans etiam illo casu a Deo sit alienus, ergo non furat circuncidendus, neque nunc talis esset baptisandus, Verum nos hic mitius sentimus, ac iubemus hoc objicientes, meminisse illos paruulos & si non patrem aut matrem vel proprios parentes habuerint Deo coniunctos, forte habuisse aliquos ex suis maioribus, quod si minus satis facit, eo quod certis non dubiis sit innitendum, cogiemus filios illius potissimum esse communitatis & reipub. in qua nascuntur, quod si ibi sit verae fidei professio, & Christum ecclesia cui offeruntur consiteatur, iam ad Deum ut ipsa attinent." 70.

faith, then how can the children participate since they cannot exercise faith? (This is due to the mere mercy of God's election. God has decreed through the covenant, that the children of Christians are holy, the people of God, and that He would be their God.) Thus in Martyr's mind, circumcision provided a covenantal and sacramental grace for the hearts of Old Covenant believers directly, and for the New Covenant believers indirectly as it anticipated the similar covenantal character of Christian baptism.

Martyr's sacramental emphasis conjoined with his covenantal exposition of circumcision also provided a significant polemical tool for the nascent Reformed system. In addition to critiquing and correcting medieval abuses, his perspective served polemically against the Lutheran rejection of covenantal continuity as well as the Anabaptist denunciation of paedobaptism. Arguably, Martyr's rehabilitation of circumcision and its covenantal relationship to baptism not only undergirded the Reformed doctrine of infant baptism, further insuring its significance as an important theological concept for the Reformed tradition, but it helped to solidify the covenant idea and covenant continuity as central aspects of the Reformed system itself.

Another important distinctive, although minor in emphasis, is Martyr's belief that God's covenant with Abraham in Genesis 17 includes material blessings for both the Old Testament believer and the New Testament believer. These earthly promises are expressions of God's nature captured in His name *Shaddai*—the Sufficient One. The New Testament includes such ideas when the believer is promised his daily bread, and the things he needs as he seeks first God's kingdom.[71] While we cannot be sure, given Martyr's impact on English theology, this understanding of the reality of earthly benefits for the covenant believer in the New Testament era, may have been an encouragement for the development of subsequent Puritan millennial

---

[71] "Neq, sine ratione hic factu videas, ut huic divino foederi & spirituali promissioni Dei, quod velit esse noster Deus, admixtae sint interim terrenarum rerum promissiones, . . . quia Deus iste noster se nominavit SHDY, id est sufficiens quare cum nobis & ista necessaria sint, non vult ut aliunde quam a se pendeamus, ex omni parte sufficiente, volente, ac potente nobis hae praestare. Cui rei & Christus astipulatur cum dicit, Primum quaerite regnum Dei, & haec omnia adiicientur vobis. Atque in oratione ab ipso insituta vult ut quotidie petamus nostrum panem quotidianum." 70.

viewpoints, that anticipated this worldly benefits for the members of the Kingdom of God.[72]

Another distinctive of Martyr's approach to the covenant in Genesis 17 is the absence of language of conditionality with regard to the covenant. As we have observed above, he affirms the two traditional graces of the covenant (justification and regeneration or sanctification), and, he also emphasizes the importance of faith and obedience. Calvin describes these as the "*duplex gratiam.*"[73] Nevertheless, he seems not to refer to these as conditions of the covenant as did Calvin and Bullinger. Significantly, on the text "*Ambula coram me*" and "*Esto perfectus*" there is no reference to the conditions of the covenant as one finds in Bullinger and Calvin. Remarkably, on the second phrase, Martyr focuses the meaning of "*perfectus*" on a simple, non-curious obedience to God's commands, especially on Abraham's soon to come command to receive and administer circumcision.[74] This is far less demanding than Bullinger's and Calvin's understanding of God's call to be perfectly holy, as the condition of the covenant of grace.[75] This study cannot offer a definitive rationale for Martyr's different approach to the covenant at this point. But perhaps the following proposal has warrant: Martyr's emphasis upon the sacraments as the instruments of divine grace received through faith overshadows the earlier reformed emphasis upon covenantal conditions of faith and obedience. In this regard, Martyr seems closer to Luther, who clearly eschewed any notion of obedience as a covenantal condition.[76] Perhaps here, Martyr's distinctive silence concerning covenantal conditions anticipates those forms of Reformed and Puritan covenantal teaching that entirely disapprove of conditional language in the covenant of grace, or, limit the covenant's condition to only faith.[77] Is it pos-

---

[72] See Shute's article on this.

[73] See *The Binding of God*, 180–183.

[74] "... integer, quamvis nonulli ad simplicitatem quandam hoc referendum putent ac si dicatur, ne sis curioosus ad rationem indagandam earum rerum quas ego tibi praecipiam, puta, cum paul post audiet sibi circuncisionem impereari, ne quaerat cur aut quare id velit Deus, sed simpliciter pareat." 65.

[75] In IV. XIII. 6, 1259–60, CO, II, 928–29, Calvin writes, "And there is no obstacle in the fact that no one can maintain in this life the perfect obedience to the law which God requires of us. For inasmuch, as this stipulation is included in the covenant of grace under which are contained both forgiveness of sins and the spirit of sanctification, the promise which we make there is joined with a plea for pardon and a petition for help."

[76] See *The Binding of God*, 65–80.

[77] As can be seen in Stephen Strehle, *Calvinism, Federalism, and Scholasticism: A Study*

sible that Martyr's emphasis on the promised, exhibited and offered grace of the sacraments has softened the Zurich-Geneva Reformed consensus on a conditional covenant? Conjectures aside, there is no mistaking Martyr's sacramental emphasis in his commentary on Genesis 17. It seems fair to observe that Martyr stands somewhere in between the Zurich-Geneva Consensus and the Wittenburg viewpoint on the matter of covenant conditionality.

The last distinctive to be developed here, seems to set Vermigli apart from his fellow Reformed theologians. This matter is in regard to Martyr's understanding of the necessity of the parents' living faith for the baptism of their children. The significance of this issue is its potential to rend the union between the church and state that was such a part of the Medieval heritage and the magisterial reformers' program for reform. One way to ask the question is whether baptism provides a unifying basis for culture, so that a geo-political and spiritual-political entity called Christendom could exist? The Medieval tradition as well as the Swiss Reformed tradition represented by Zwingli, Bullinger and Calvin thought that baptism did exactly that.[78]

Must parents be regenerate and true believers in the eyes of the church before their children can be baptized? While Martyr asserts that children of Christians pertain to God by the power of the covenant, yet he also insists that should the parental faith be in name only, or a dead or temporary faith, the children of such parents, ought not to be baptized.[79] Martyr's answer here may be anticipatory of the views that some later Puritans would develop claiming that the Church consists of only the regenerate. To those who object to his position, Martyr shows that he is not indifferent to the plight of such children, since he urges that there be special remembrance of them, and especially for those who are self-supporting orphans

---

of the *Reformed Doctrine of Covenant* (Bern: Peter Lang, 1988) there is an intramural debate in the later federalism as to whether faith and obedience are conditions of the covenant; whether faith is the only condition of the covenant; or if the use of conditional language at all is inconsistent with divine grace.

[78] See *The Binding of God*, 29–37; 82–83; 142–43; 239–241.

[79] Martyr's states, "... dicimus Christianorum liberos sive Iudaeorum ex vi foederis ad Deum pertinere, at quid statuemus de eis, quando contigerit ut eorum pater nomine tenus solum fidem habeat, vel si quam habet, illa sit mortua aut temporaria, quae vim justificandi non habeat? Nam tunc sine controversia pater aut mater, vel utrique ut fieri postest, ad Deum non pertinent, ergo videtur quod infans etiam illo casu a Deo sit alienus, ergo non furat circuncidendus, neque nunc talis esset baptisandus." 70.

who in faith seek association with the Church of Christ.[80] Whether or not a historical connection exists here between Martyr and the subsequent Puritan viewpoint, Martyr's conception does argue against the position that many New England Congregationalists would later take in the 1650's, in what has become known as "the half-way covenant". Thus Martyr's perspective adumbrates a debate that would unfold in the Reformed tradition calling forth the theological acumen of luminaries from the various Calvinistic communions.[81]

On its surface, Martyr's understanding of the necessity of authentic parental faith as a prerequisite for valid paedobaptism (and thus entrance into the church) also seems to challenge what was the emerging Reformed view of the validity of Roman Catholic baptism for admission into a Reformed communion. Zwingli, Bullinger and Calvin all believed the baptismal covenant constituted a covenantal culture that could include the power of faith to a thousand generations, although the covenantal succession of faith might skip at times intervening unbelieving generations.[82] Given the close association of Martyr and Bullinger, it is clear that the seeds of this subsequent debate already present in Martyr's position never directly impacted their relationship. But after Martyr's death, and after his commentary on Genesis was published, the debate over the propriety of baptizing children of other than truly believing parents broke out in earnest, producing a number of distinctive theories to address the question.[83] Martyr's discussion of this issue in the context of Genesis

---

[80] Martyr explains, "Verum nos hic mitius sentimus, ac iubemus hoc obijcientes, meminisse illos paruulos & si non patrem aut matrem vel proprios parentes habuerint Deo coniunctos, forte habuisse aliquos ex suis maioribus, quod si minus satis facit, eo quod certis non dubiis sit innitendum, cogitemus filios illius potissimum esse communitatis & reipub. in qua nascuntur, quod si ibi sit verae fidei professio, & Christum ecclesia cui offeruntur confiteatur, iam ad Deum ut ipsa attinent." 70.

[81] For a discussion of the theology and history surrounding the various views of the Reformed churches on the baptism of infants in relationship to the faith of their parents, see Charles Hodge, *Systematic Theology* (Grand Rapids: Wm. B. Eerdmans Publishing Company, 1977), vol. III, 558–579. Among those named by Hodge are: Reformed, (Francis Gomarus, Martin Vitringa, Johannes Marckius, Bernhardino De Moor), Separatist (Robert Browne, John Robinson), Congregational (Cotton Mather, Solomon Stoddard, Jonathan Edwards), and Presbyterian (John Blair, Charles Hodge).

[82] See *The Binding of God*, 36–37; 81–98; 233–39; 248–49.

[83] Hodge explains the various theories concerning the propriety of extending baptism to children of other than believing parents. Of the Roman Catholic view, he says, "The Roman church, therefore, believing that baptism is essential to salvation, baptizes all children presented for that ordinance without regard to their immediate parentage or remote descent." Hodge, *Systematic Theology*, III.561.

17 may well have laid the groundwork for this later intramural dis-
agreement in covenant theology. The weighty nature of Martyr's
theological impact on Reformed, Anglican and Puritan theology at
least suggests the fascinating possibility of a causal relationship.

Concerning the Protestant and Reformed tradition, he explains the theory based
on God's promise and the reality of spiritual adoption, "There are two principles
on which the baptism of children whose parents are not members of the visible
church is defended. The first is, that the promise is to parents and their children,
and their children's children even to the thousandth generation. Children, therefore, whose immediate parents may have no connection with the Church have not
forfeited their privileges as children of the covenant. If the promise be to them, its
sign and seal belongs to them. The second principle is, that of spiritual adoption.
Children who are orphans, or whose parents are unfit or unwilling to bring them
up in a Christian manner, may be so far adopted by those willing and qualified
to assume the responsibility of their religious education as to become proper subjects of baptism." Ibid., III, 561.

Another Reformed view is the two covenant theory. "A second theory advanced
on this subject was that of a twofold covenant; one external, the other internal;
answering to the distinction between the Church visible and invisible. God, under
the old dispensation, entered into a covenant with the Hebrew nation constituting
them his visible Church, which covenant was distinct from that in which eternal
life was promised to those that truly believe in the Redeemer who was to come.
The conditions of admission into this external, visible society, were outward profession of the true religion, and external obedience. The condition of admission into
the invisible church, was true and saving faith. The sacraments were attached to
the external covenant. All who made this external profession and yielded this outward obedience to the mosaic law, were of right entitled to circumcision, to the
Passover, and to all the privileges of the theocracy. So it is now, according to the
theory in hand. Christ designed to form an external, visible Church, furnished with
a constitution, laws, and proper officers for their administration. The conditions of
admission into this visible society, were the profession of speculative, or historical
faith in his religion, and external conformity to its laws and the laws of his Church.
To this external body all the ordinances of his religion are attached. Those, therefore, who apply for baptism or the Lord's Supper, do not profess to be the regen-
erated children of God. They simply profess to be believers as distinguished from
infidels or scorners, and to be desirous to avail themselves of church privileges for
their own benefit and for the good of their children. From this body Christ gath-
ers the great majority of his own people, making them members of his mystical
body." Ibid., III, 562–63.

The view held by those who espouse the so-called "Half-Way Covenant" is defined
by Hodge as, "A third theory on which the baptism of children, whose parents are
not communicants, is contended for, makes a distinction between baptism and the
Lord's Supper. More is required for the latter than for the former; and therefore,
adults who are entitled to baptism for themselves and for their children, may not
be entitled to admission to the Lord's table.... this is also the theory which was
known in New England as the 'Half-Way covenant.'" Ibid., III, 566–67.

The Puritan view is summarized by Hodge, "The Puritans, in the restricted sense
of that word, held, (1.) That the Church consists of the regenerate. (2.) That a particular church consists of a number of true believers united together by mutual
covenant. (3.) That no one should be admitted to church-membership who did not

Two final observations are in order. There is a nuance that unites Zwingli, Calvin and Martyr *vis-à-vis* Bullinger. There is also a nuance that brings Zwingli and Bullinger together *vis-à-vis* Calvin and Martyr. The first of the two is the relationship between the covenant and election. Bullinger does not comment on election in the covenant context of *De Testamento*.[84] Zwingli and Calvin do inter-relate covenant and election. And so does Martyr. Since Martyr rejects the *ex opere operato* view of the sacraments, he must explain how they benefit children who cannot receive the sacraments in faith. His answer is God's covenantal grace flowing out of divine election.[85]

The second nuance is in regard to the view that Genesis 17 is the target chapter or the paradigm chapter of covenant theology. The Swiss-Germans Zwingli and Bullinger assert this.[86] While recognizing the central importance of Genesis 17 for covenant theology, the expatriates, French/French-Swiss Calvin and Italian/English/German-Swiss Martyr, make no pretense to interpret the entire Bible

---

give credible evidence of being a true child of God. (4.) They understood by credible evidence, not such as may be believed, but such as constrains belief. (5.) All such persons, and no others, were admitted to the Lord's Supper. They, therefore, constituted the Church, and to them exclusively belonged the privileges of church-membership, and consequently to them was confined the right of presenting their children for baptism. All other professors of the true religion, however correct in their deportment, were denied that privilege.... According to this theory, therefore, the Church consists of those who are 'judged' to be regenerate. None but those thus declared to be true believers are to be received as members of the church. They alone are entitled to the sacraments either for themselves or for their children, and consequently only the children of communicants are to be admitted to baptism." Ibid., III. 569, 571.

[84] The reason for this is a subject of debate. It ought not to be thought, however, that Bullinger did not teach a Reformed doctrine of predestination. Whatever reason one offers for his not including personal election in his discussion of the covenant, it cannot be that he did not believe in election. This is manifest in his Second Helvetic Confession, chapter X, entitled, "Of the Predestination of God and the Election of the Saints." He there speaks of election and reprobation. Cf. Schaff, *Creeds of Christendom*, III: 847–49.

[85] "... conferuntur non ex opere operato, non ex fide quam non habent, sed ex mera Dei misericordia, quae suis pactis stare decruit, ut Christianorum filii sancti sint, Dei populus, & ille vicissim illorum Deus. Est praetera attendendum nostram salutem revera non aliunde pendere, quam a divina electione cuius vigore infantes regenerantur, unde si illa non sint comprehensi, ibi in sacramento gratiam aut regenerationem non assequuntur. Si vero ex electorum numero illos esse contingit, non modo a Deo salutem habent, sed omnia illis cum sacramenta tum alia media ad illam sunt efficacia." 71.

[86] See *The Binding of God*, pp. 95–98; McCoy and Baker, *Fountainhead of Federalism*, 104.

through Genesis 17. In this, Luther is the odd man out since in his estimation Genesis 17 with its circumcision teaching is a dangerous and difficult chapter for the Christian.

Conclusion: The Significance of Martyr's Contributions to Covenant Theology

Peter Martyr Vermigli's contribution to the early Reformed understanding of the covenant of Genesis 17 is distinctive and significant. While standing in the covenantal consensus already developing from Zurich and Geneva, Martyr's exposition also offered new directions for subsequent Reformed theological reflection upon the covenant.

Given his towering contribution and erudition in the treatment of the Eucharist, it is not surprising that Martyr would also proffer a penetrating examination of the sacrament of circumcision in Genesis 17. Showing himself in extensive agreement with Calvin and Bullinger, Martyr expounds Old and New Testament continuity in the covenant of grace. Yet it was the sacramental significance of circumcision in Genesis 17 that captured Vermigli's attention. Casting the covenant in sacramental guise, and underscoring the sovereignty of grace, he declared circumcision to be a *"circuncisionis cordis:"*[87] a covenantal and sacramental grace for the hearts of both Old and New Covenant believers and their children. With this conception of the circumcision of the heart coupled with his commitment to divine election, Martyr reflected the Reformed understanding of the monergistic character of the redemptive work of God in Christ within the familial or corporate character of God's covenant. But in so doing, he also highlighted the hermeneutical division between Luther and the Swiss Reformers concerning Old Testament and New Testament law-gospel covenantal continuity. What was dangerous in Luther's estimation was essential for Martyr. Thus Martyr's exposition of Genesis 17 presents the divine covenant of a circumcised heart, with sacraments instituted by the will of God that designate, exhibit and offer by faith the grace of Christ to believers and their children.

---

[87] "Unde meminit Moses Deuteronomii 10 & Levitici 26 circuncisionis cordis: Ieremias 4 asserit aures impiorum esse incircunsas. Et Ezechiel 44 incircuncises corde & carne dicit. Actorum 7 Iudaeis exprobravit Stephanus, quod auribus & corde incircuncisi essent. Quemadmodum in baptismo denotamur immersione aquae mortui & consepulti Domino: ita hic significabantur patribus ablata esse peccata, & ideo ita vivendum, ut ulterius non admitterentur." 66.

Moreover, Martyr's sacramental emphasis, while correcting medieval abuses, and providing an answer to the Lutheran rejection of covenantal law-gospel continuity, served as a reinforcement of the Reformed polemic against the Anabaptist rejection of infant baptism. Martyr's understanding of the sacraments of the covenant affirms that the thing signified is also linked to the sign itself.[88] In this way Martyr defends the sacrament of infant baptism as an important instrument of grace.[89]

---

[88] "Notabis circuncisionem hic appellari pactum & testamentum, quod scilicet foederis vel testamenti signum esset, non quidem vacuum, sed illud afferens & exhibens quod in testamento continetur." 66.

[89] The Reformed tradition did not accept baptismal regeneration in the Roman Catholic sense. Yet, with Martyr, it insisted that baptism was not an empty sign, but a true means of grace. Note Calvin's remarks to Martyr in a letter affirming that baptism results in some sense in union with Christ, "Now I come to those passages about which you give me your advice. Though what you write about the first entering into communion with Christ, I confess to be true, in the same sense, however, in which Paul teaches that Christ is manifested to us in baptism, I have not hesitated to say that we are inserted into his body." *Selected Works of John Calvin: Tracts and Letters*, VI. 122.

Similarly, Griffith-Thomas sees Peter Martyr's theological hand at work where the Anglican "Baptismal Service has, 'Seeing now that this child is regenerate'; and the Catechism also speaks of, 'My Baptism, wherein I was made a member of Christ.'" *The Principles of Theology*, 380–81. In regard to Martyr's role and the meaning of this form of regeneration in baptism, Griffith-Thomas goes on to explain, "The views of the Reformers.—They undoubtedly held a doctrine of "Baptismal Regeneration," but it was not identical with that of Rome. The controversy which is now called "Baptismal Regeneration" they waged under the name of the "Opus Operatum Theory." They all believed Baptism to be the Sacrament of regeneration, but this was not so by the rite itself, but always as conditional and associated with the Gospel. . . . but the Reformers treated both Sacraments exactly in the same way. They used sacramental language, that is, they employed interchangeably the name of sign and thing, teaching that while all received blessing sacramentally, not all received it really. They thus distinguished between sacramental and spiritual regeneration. This is a well-known principle of Scripture which our Prayer Book follows in speaking of the sign and the thing signified in the same terms. St. Paul can speak of 'the laver of regeneration,' and St. Peter can say, 'Baptism doth now save us,' though both mean much more than the water. In illustration of this view it may be pointed out that the leading Puritans never objected to the words, 'Seeing now that this child is regenerate,' nor did Baxter later on, because Whitgift had said that the Reformers taught that Sacraments did not contain, but only sealed grace. . . . This view was approved of by English Reformers, by Foreign Reformers, by early Puritans, and was never questioned for fifty years after the Reformation. On 14th June 1552, just after the publication of the Second Prayer Book, Peter Martyr wrote to Bullinger that everything had been removed from the Prayer Book which could nourish superstition. This has an important bearing on the meaning of our baptismal Service as finally settled in 1552. It is, therefore, incorrect to say that our Service was imperfectly reformed, especially since the words, 'Seeing now that this child is regenerate' date from 1552, which is usually regarded as the high-water mark of English Protestantism." *The Principles of Theology*, 383–385.

Martyr does not employ the specific language of the conditional-ity and the mutuality of the covenant. He does affirm the *"duplex gratiam"* of justification and sanctification in the covenant. By assert-ing the two parts of the covenant, there is an implied, if not expressed, condition of responsibility. That is why Martyr expressed concern for "a faith in name only, or that was dead or temporary." Similarly sacramental union with Christ, while emphasizing grace, does not deny the necessity of exercising faith and obedience, nor of condi-tionality,[90] for ultimately regeneration does not literally flow from the sacraments, but from God's electing grace experienced in the covenant relationship.[91] Nevertheless, his stress on the sacraments and their

---

What then did Calvin, Martyr and the Anglican tradition mean by baptism as a means of grace? The Leiden Synopsis is cited in Heinrich Heppe's *Reformed Dogmatics* in a relevant passage, "(XLIV, 32): 'We agree that the sacrament, like everything else is also exhibitive of the thing promised, in respect that in the law-ful and worthy use of this sacrament the things promised are by the H. Spirit not only offered to believers but also actually exhibited and conferred; God is true in sealing His promises and our sacraments are not affixes of a dying letter but those of a quickening spirit. . . .'" Heppe adds a comment and then quotes The Leiden Synopsis again, "Meanwhile the receipt of grace, the imparting of which is attended and sealed by baptism, is not tied to the outward act and to the moment of the act of baptism. The efficacy of baptism rather presupposes the faith and conver-sion of a man—both at least at heart.—Leiden Synopsis (XLIV, 29): 'The efficacy of baptism we do not tie to the moment at which the body is wet with outward water, but in all who are to be baptized we require with Scripture faith and repen-tance, at least according to the judgment of love. And this as well in covenanted children, in whom, we maintain, must be placed, by the power of the divine bless-ing and the Gospel covenant, the seed and spirit of faith and repentance, as in adults in whom the profession of actual faith and repentance is necessary. Then, as seed cast upon the ground does not always germinate at the same moment, but when rain and warmth supervene from heaven, so neither word nor sign of sacra-ment is always effectual at its first moment, but only at the time when the bless-ing of the H. Spirit is added." Heinrich Heppe, *Reformed Dogmatics: Set Out and Illustrated from the Sources* (Grand Rapids: Baker, 1978), 617–619.

[90] Consider Griffith-Thomas' remark, "They all believed Baptism to be the Sacrament of regeneration, but this was not so by the rite itself, but always as con-ditional and associated with the Gospel. . . . but the Reformers treated both Sacraments exactly in the same way. They used sacramental language, that is, they employed interchangeably the name of sign and thing, teaching that while all received bless-ing sacramentally, not all received it really. They thus distinguished between sacra-mental and spiritual regeneration." In *The Principles of Theology*, 383.

[91] Martyr explains, "Altera est, cum ex opere operato haec sacramenta non afferant regeneratine vel gratia, sed fide tanumodo sint efficacia, pueri autem non sint illa praediti, quomod Christo dum illa suscipiunt, incorporantur aut Deo Conjunguntur? Respondeo, In illis ista conferuntur non ex opere operato, non ex fide quam non habent, sed ex mera Dei misericordia, quae suis pactis stare decruit, ut Christianorum filii sancti sint, Dei populus, & ille vicissim illorum Deus. Est praetera attendendum nostram salutem revera non aliunde pendere, quam a divina electione cuius vigore infantes regenerantur, unde si illa non sint comprehensi, ibi

gracious character, joined with this silence respecting the conditions of the covenant, may have provided a point of departure from the initial Zurich-Geneva consensus on the covenant for subsequent Reformed theological developments.

Martyr's influence on subsequent developments in covenant theology cannot be fully delineated here, nor be established with any degree of finality. However, interesting possibilities of etiological significance do emerge when Martyr's insights are viewed through the telescope of the history of Reformed theological development. In view of Martyr's substantial impact on Anglican sacramental theology, did his sacramental emphasis also present an opportunity for the intramural debates to begin in Reformed and Puritan contexts in regard to the conditionality versus the non-conditionality of the covenant? Did Martyr's notion of material blessings in the New Covenant age provide a hermeneutical inspiration for the development of Puritan millennial thought? Was Martyr's view of a prerequisite living faith for the propriety of infant baptism and the concomitant idea of a circumcised heart the harbinger of the New England Puritans' struggle with the notions of the half-way covenant, the theology of conversion and revivalism, and the possibility of a Christian commonwealth? However one answers these questions, it is clear that Peter Martyr Vermigli was far more than a theologian of the Eucharist. As a theologian of the covenant, Vermigli stands face to face as a theological peer with Zwingli, Bullinger, Luther and Calvin. As his very name suggests, Peter Martyr was both a witness of and a foundational stone for the early construction of the covenant theology erected from Genesis 17. In a long overdue and appropriately renewed place of honor, Peter Martyr Vermigli not only stands face to face, but side by side with these other founding fathers of the early Reformed covenant paradigm as it emerged from the mid-sixteenth century. Out of the ashes of lost reformational history, the phoenix of Peter Martyr rises once again.

---

in sacramento gratiam aut regenerationem non assequuntur. Si vero ex electorum numero illos esse contingit, non modo a Deo salutem habent, sed omnia illis cum sacramenta tum alia media ad illam sunt efficacia." 71.

SACRAMENTAL CONTINUITY AMONG REFORMED REFUGEES: PETER MARTYR VERMIGLI AND JOHN CALVIN

Richard Gamble

Introduction

The Italian Peter Martyr Vermigli and the Frenchman John Calvin had much in common, not the least of which was the fact that they were both reformers in exile. More particularly, both spent their formative years of exile in Strasbourg under the tutelage of the Alsatian reformer, Martin Bucer, whose theological impact upon both refugee reformers cannot be overestimated.[1] Previous studies have shown that the sacramental unity between the two exiles and their mentor was no mere "theological coincidence."[2] Indeed, there seems to be an extraordinary degree of sacramental coherence among these "codifiers" of reformed theology.[3] If these exiles were incubated in the stimulating and nurturing environment of Bucer's Strasbourg, then an

---

[1] Bucer wrote to Calvin, October 1542: "A man has arrived from Italy who knows his Greek, Hebrew and Latin, knows his Bible, is 44 years old and of sharpest judgment. His name is Peter Martyr . . ." in Herminjard, ed., *Correspondance des Réformateurs dans les pays de langue française* (Geneva, 1893), VIII, 169 ff. Cf. PPRED, 194–197. James traces three phases in Vermigli's theological development. After studying in Padua, the first phase, Vermigli moved to Bologna (1530–1533). While there, he studied Hebrew (he had already learned Greek) and dug deeply into the scriptures. The third phase took place in Naples, where he recognized errors in the church and read Zwingli and Bucer. Thus Bucer may be considered in some sense formative for Vermigli's theology. Bucer's pivotal role in Calvin's theological development has long been recognized. See August Lang, *Der Evangelienkommentar Martin Butzers und die Grundzüge seiner Theologie* (Leipzig, 1900), 185 ff., 365–370; Henri Strohl, "Bucer et Calvin," *Bulletin du Societé de l'Histoire du Protestantisme francais* 87 (1938): 354ff; and Francios Wendel, *Calvin: The Origins and Development of His Religious Thought*, trans. Philip Mairet (London, 1963), 138–149.

[2] VWG, 272.

[3] Richard A. Muller, *Christ and the Decree: Christology and Predestination in Reformed Theology from Calvin to Perkins* (Grand Rapids, 1988), 67.

examination of their respective sacramental theologies and the role
they later played in the development of the Reformed view of the
sacrament is amply warranted.

The focus of this essay is upon Bucer's two apprentice reformers,
Vermigli and Calvin. The Italian, Vermigli, was nearly ten years
older than his French counterpart, but has been somewhat neglected
by modern scholarship. This is due in part to the fact that Vermigli
was repeatedly exiled (three times) and never really found a home
until his last six years in Zurich (1556–1562).[4] Despite the dissimi-
lar circumstances and the age difference, each was theologically self-
confident enough to disagree with the other. Both theological refugees
belonged to and helped to shape the theological direction of the
Reformed branch of early Protestant thought, particularly on the
issues of predestination and Eucharistic theology.[5] Yet they seem to
have held differing views on political resistance. Vermigli's political
thought, Robert Kingdon argues, is perhaps more Lutheran than
Reformed.[6] To best explicate their relationship, the locus of attention will be upon their mutual activities concerning the Lord's Supper
debate.

One of the saddest segments of sixteenth-century history concerns
these heated debates between the Swiss Reformed and the German
Lutherans surrounding the nature of the Lord's Supper. The course
of that controversy, as it involved Calvin and Martyr, follows an
identifiable but painful historical vector. Ulrich Zwingli of Zurich
had produced in 1525 two tracts on his understanding of the Eucharist[7]
and a more definitive work in February 1526.[8] Johannes Oecolam-

---

[4] CAS, 3.

[5] While the doctrine of predestination is generally associated with Calvin's name,
it should not be forgotten that Vermigli developed a doctrine of predestination perhaps earlier and independent of Calvin. Furthermore, there are differences in their
articulations of the doctrine. See PPRED, 246–249 and 251–255.

[6] Robert M. Kingdon, *The Political Thought of Peter Martyr Vermigli*, (Geneva, 1980),
xvii–xviii.

[7] The two tracts of Zwingli were: *Subsidium sive coronis de eucharistia* (Zurich, 1525)
and *Responsio ad epistolam Joannis bugenhagii* (Zurich, 1525). *De Vera et Falsa Religione*
(Zurich, 1525) also has a statement that the verb "is" was equivalent to "signifies"
in the Supper.

[8] The full title is *Eine klare Unterrichtung vom Nachtmahl Christi* (Zurich, 1526). The
English translation is found in G. W. Bromiley, ed. *Zwingli and Bullinger: Selected translations with introduction and notes* (Philadelphia: Westminster Press, 1953), 176–238.

padius of Basel joined the fray with the publication in 1525 of his
Wahre und aechte Erklaerung der Worte des Herrn: das ist mein Lieb.[9] By
1528, Martin Bucer, Oecolampadius, and Zwingli together defended
the thesis: "That it may not be proved from Scripture that the body
and blood of Christ are actually bodily received in the bread of the
Eucharist."[10] Martin Luther profoundly disagreed with this interpretation of the Supper and a colloquy was held in 1529 to discuss the
issues. This colloquy, held at the castle of Marburg, produced no
harmony between the Protestants but left the Swiss Reformed theologians smarting from Luther's condemnation.[11] The confrontation
continued with the publication of Zwingli's *Fidei Ratio* in 1530.[12] This
hastily produced work was incomplete and not conciliatory in the
least, which of course only further alienated Luther as well as
Melanchthon. Luther's judgment concerning Zwingli at this time was
clear: "I am confident that Zwingli is not a Christian. In all of his
teaching there is not one part that can be squared with Christian
belief".[13]

Five years later, Bucer and Philip Melanchthon signed the so-
called "Cassel Formula" on the Lord's Supper. They agreed that:
"Christ was truly and really received; that the bread and wine were
signia exhibitiva with which were received at the same time the body
and blood of Christ . . . what is posited of the one may be posited
of the other."[14] The discussion on the Lord's Supper did not end

---

[9] Oecolampadius wrote an *Apologetica Joannis Oecolampadii* against Lutheran attacks
in 1526 as well as a specific work against Luther in the same year. See Walther
Köher, *Zwingli und Luther* (Leipzig, 1924), Bd. I, 234–241.

[10] This is the fourth thesis of the Disputation of Bern, held in January, 1528.
See K. R. Wagenbach, *Johann Oekolampad und Oswald Myconius die Reformation Basels*
(Elberfeld, 1862), 139. In the same year Bucer published his "Vergleichung
D. Luthers und seins gegentheyls vom Abendmal Christi Dialogus." See Gottfried
W. Locher, *Die Zwinglische Reformation im Rohmen der europäischen Kirchengeschichte*
(Göttingen: Vandenhock & Ruprecht, 1979), 300–317.

[11] Literature on the Marburg colloquy is vast. See especially Walther Köhler,
*Zwingli und Luther: Ihr Streit über das Abendmahl nach seinen politischen und religiösen
Bezeiehungen*, 2 vols. (Leipzig, 1924 & Gütersloh, 1953). Cf. Peter Buhler, "Der
Abendmahlsstreit der Reformatoren und seine aktuellen Implikationen" *Theologische
Zeitschrift* 35 (1979): 228–241. Hastings Eels, *Martin Bucer* (New York: Russell &
Russell, repr. 1971), lists literature on 452 n. 151.

[12] Zwingli, *Fidei Ratio* (Zurich, 1530).

[13] Luther's condemnation leaves no room for doubt: "Ich bekenne fur mich, das
ich den Zwingel fur einen unchristen halte mit aller seiner lere, denn er helt und
leret kein stück des Christilichen glaubens recht" *WA* 26, 342.

[14] 30 December 1534. See Eels, *Martin Bucer*, 173–182.

there, however. The Second Swiss Confession (1537) also known as the *Confessio fidei de eucharistia* bolstered what may be called the "Zwinglian" or "non-Lutheran" position.[15] These progressive and positive developments toward Swiss Reformed unity on the Supper were met with counter-attacks from Lutheran Germany.

I. *Intensification of the Eucharistic Debates before 1555*

The *Confessio fidei de eucharistia* was answered by Martin Luther with the *Kurzes Bekenntnis vom heiligen Sakrament wider Schwenckfeld und die Schweizer* in 1544. As expected, a Zurich response appeared swiftly— the *Wahrhaftes Bekenntnis der Diener der Kirche zu Zurich* in 1545. Peter Martyr found himself inadvertently drawn into the dispute when Calvin appropriated Vermigli's opinions in his *De vitandis superstitionibus* in 1549.[16]

As one might expect in the turbulence of the sixteenth century, politics played a role even in what appears to be a purely theological debate. In 1547, Emperor Charles V had successfully attacked south Germany which then came under his political control. Concerned about the situation, Geneva sent Calvin to the other Swiss cities, including Zurich, to confer on the political conditions. While at Zurich, Heinrich Bullinger gave Calvin his treatise on the Lord's Supper, *Absoluta de Christi Domini et catholicae ecclesiae sacramentis tractatio*.[17] After several exchanges between the two Swiss reformers, unity was reached a few years later with the Zurich Agreement or *Consensus Tigurinus* of 1549.[18] The Consensus was ratified in May 1549 but not

---

[15] Eels, *Martin Bucer*, 214. An English translation is found in J. K. S. Reid, *Calvin: Theological Treatises* (London, 1954), 167–69.

[16] Calvin, *De vitandis superstitionibus . . . excusatio ad Pseudonicodemos . . .* (Geneva: J. Girard, 1549), 110–111. Calvin also cited Melanchthon and Bucer. Apparently, Calvin was drawing from Vermigli's earlier letters of 24 August 1542 and 25 December 1543, which explained his reasons for fleeing Italy. See LLS, 65–101. Cf. Klaus Sturm, *Die Theologie Peter Martyr Vermiglis waehrend seines ersten Aufenthalts in Strassburg 1542–1547.* (Neukirchen, 1971), 38, n. 127.

[17] W. de Greef, *The Writings of John Calvin.*, trans. L. Bierma, (Grand Rapids: Baker Book House, 1993), 190–193.

[18] Text is found in B. J. Kidd, *Documents of the Continental Reformation*, (Oxford, 1911). "The Consensus Tigurinus," (May 1549), 652–656 (no. 319). An English translation by Ian D. Bunting is in *JPH* 44 (1966): 45–61. See also P. Schaff, *The*

published until 1551. After the Latin original, a German translation (by Bullinger) and a French translation (by Calvin) followed.

For his part, Peter Martyr was also affected by the political upheaval of the First Schmalkaldic War—1546–47. With the victory of Emperor Charles V over the Lutherans at Mühlberg, Vermigli was in no position to decline Archbishop Cranmer's invitation to come to England and assume responsibilities as Regius Professor of Divinity at Oxford.[19] England proved to be a safe haven for the continental reformers, that is, until the English throne fell again into Catholic hands. The ascension of Queen Mary Tudor wrought havoc for the foreign theologians. Martyr was not the only continental divine forced to deal with a Catholic queen. Already in 1550 John Laski, the Polish reformer, had served the refugee churches in London. But when Mary Tudor came to power in 1553, Laski and his congregation had to take flight from England. Finding asylum, they assumed, in Denmark, they were quickly disappointed when they were informed by King Christian III that they would either have to confess Lutheranism or depart. By the end of the year the congregation was dispersed and Laski was back in Germany.[20]

Vermigli too had to flee England and returned to Strasbourg in 1553. Much to his consternation, the chief minister in Strasbourg at that time was Johann Marbach, who rigorously followed the Lutheran interpretation of the Supper. Vermigli was forced to take a stand against the Lutheran view and did so publicly in 1556. But the Lutheran contingent in Strasbourg was too entrenched and so to avoid further controversy, Martyr gladly accepted an invitation from Zurich the same year.

It was in the midst of this turmoil that Joachim Westphal, a

Creeds of Christendom, With a History and Critical Notes (Grand Rapids, Mich., reprint. 1983), I, 471–473.

[19] Diarmaid MacCulloch, *Thomas Cranmer: A Life* (New Haven, 1996), 379–383. Cf. Lorna Jane Abray, *The People's Reformation: Magistrates, Clergy and Commons in Strasbourg, 1500–1598* (Ithaca, New York, 1985), and Thomas A. Brady, Jr., *Ruling Class, Regime and Reformation at Strasbourg, 1520–1555*, Studies in Medieval and Reformation Thought, XXII, (Leiden, 1978).

[20] Schaff, *The Creeds of Christendom*, I, 281, relates the moving account. One hundred seventy-five Protestants were driven from England, and during a very cold winter were refused refuge in Denmark, also in Germany and finally found a place to stay in East Friesland. The refusal was at the insistence of Westphal who "denounced them as martyrs of the devil, enraged the people against them, and gloried in this cruelty as an act of faith."

Lutheran pastor in Hamburg, published the *Farrago of Confused and Divergent opinions on the Lord's supper...* in 1552 against the "Zurich Consensus" of 1549.[21] "Westphal lumped the teachings of Zwingli and Calvin together", says Donnelly, "and condemned as heretics those who denied a corporeal presence of Christ in the Eucharist and a literal eating of Christ's body."[22] The debate continued when Westphal launched yet another harpoon in 1553.

II. *John Calvin's* Defensio sanae et orthodoxae doctrinae de Sacramentis *(1555)*[23] *and responses to Joachim Westphal*

Laski had informed Calvin that he was going to respond to Westphal's *Farrago*. Bullinger thought that would be a good idea and had hoped that Calvin would respond to Wesphal's *Right Belief*. Pierre Viret of Lausanne thought that he too would respond and Calvin wrote to encourage him to take up the pen. Yet Calvin, like the others, was busy and by 15 August no one had responded. In September, however, Calvin found time to follow through with his earlier promise and informed Bullinger that he would write a response. Three weeks later the draft was sent to Zurich. Calvin said, "I am submitting this defense to your judgment. If it meets with your approval, take it up with the other churches. I shall calmly wait until you write what I should do."[24]

The Zurichers responded with many suggestions and Calvin submitted yet another draft to them within the week. More give and

---

[21] Westphal, *Farrago confusanearum et inter se dissiduntium opinoinum de Coena Domini, ex Sacramentariorium libris congesta* (Magdeburg, 1552). Cf. Karl Moenckeberg, *Ioachim Westphal und Iohannes Calvin* (Hamburg, 1865). Cf. Joseph N. Tylenda, "The Calvin-Westphal Exchange: The Genesis of Calvin's treatises against Westphal," *Calvin Theological Journal* 9, no. 2 (1974): 182–209.

[22] DIAL, xiii.

[23] John Calvin, *Johannis Calvini Opera Selecta*, P. Barth, W. Niesel and D. Scheuner, eds., (Munich, 1927–1952) II: 263–87. (Hereafter *OS*) A French translation was made by Calvin in 1555. Cf. Uwe Plath *Calvin und Basel in den Jahren 1552–1556* (Zürich, 1974), 174–192. Cf. Bernard Cottret, "Une semiotique de la Reforme: Le consensus Tigurinus et La Breve Resolution ... (1555) de Calvin" *AESC* 39 (1984): 265–85. Cf. Kilian McDonnell, *John Calvin, the Church, and the Eucharist*, 177.

[24] Cited in J. Tylenda, "The Calvin-Westphal Exchange," 192.

take occurred and final approval was given in the name of the Zurich church. The *Defensio sanae et orthodoxae doctrinae de Sacramentis* was published in Zurich in 1555. In the *Defensio* Calvin did not mention Westphal by name, with the hope that the controversy would now grind to a close. Peter Martyr thought that the booklet would prove to be "beneficial to the weak and a consolation to the learned".[25] Calvin was convinced that he had Philip Melanchthon's support on the nature of the Lord's Supper and therefore had reason to think peace was possible—although the debate did not turn out as he thought.[26] His theological defense did not satisfy the Germans, nor stop their attacks. Peter Martyr noted to Calvin that the Lutheran attacks were being published in Frankfort "perhaps to unsettle the French and English churches there."[27] And so Calvin published a second defense, in 1556: *Secunda defensio piae et orthodoxae de sacramentis fidei contra Ioachimi Westphali calumnias.*[28]

Calvin's *Defensio sanae et orthodoxae doctrinae de Sacramentis* "consisted of three parts: a letter of dedication to the other churches, a defense of the *Consensus Tigurinus*, and the text of the Consensus."[29] The *Secunda defensio* (1556)[30] reminds the reader that the *Consensus Tigurinus* had been published five years earlier and that no contrary (read Lutheran) position on the Lord's Supper had been attacked by name. The peace that had been hoped for by the *Consensus Tigurinus* was, said Calvin, used "as a kind of Furies' torch to rekindle the flame."[31]

The main issues, as Calvin saw them, were threefold: whether the

---

[25] Ibid., 195.

[26] Ibid., 197. Tylenda comments: "How lamentably Calvin had misjudged the strength of the Westphal party, and how incautiously he had overestimated Melanchthon's popularity!" (204).

[27] Cited in Tylenda, "The Calvin-Westphal Exchange," 200.

[28] John Calvin, *Ioannis Calvini Opera Quae Supersunt Omnia*, vol. IX, eds. G. Baum, E. Cunitz and E. Reuss, in *Corpus Reformatorum*, vol. XXXXIII (Brunsvigae: C. A. Schwetschke et Filium, 1876), 41–120. (Hereafter cited as *CO*). English translation is found in J. K. S. Reid, *Calvin: Theological Treatises* 258–324. Cf. Henry Beveridge and Jules Bonnet, eds., *Selected Works of John Calvin: Tracts and Letters*, (Grand Rapids, Mich., 1983) II: 245 ff.

[29] W. de Greef, *The Writings of John Calvin: An Introductory Guide*, (Grand Rapids, Mich., 1993), 192.

[30] *Secunda defensio piae et orthodoxae* . . . (Geneva: Jean Crispin, 1556). Text citations are from John Calvin, *Tractatus Theologici Omnes* Tom. VII (Amstelodami, Apud J. Schipper, 1667). Hereafter, *Secunda defensio*.

[31] Calvin, *Secunda defensio*, 659. ". . . ut nomen Consensus instar furialis tedae, ad renovandum incendium arripuerit." Calvin repeats the theme a little later, 661: "nisi a pestiferis facibis suggestus fuisset tantur ardor."

bread of the Supper is substantially the body of Christ, whether the
body of Christ is so immense that it exists everywhere and whether
there may be a figure of speech in Christ's words as he instituted
the Supper.[32] The Swiss maintained that the flesh of Christ gives
life, and that believers are truly made partakers of it in the Supper
but would not affirm that the bread is substantially the body. The
Swiss also held that the Holy Spirit transfuses life into partakers from
the flesh of Christ but would not agree that "the body of Christ is
actually placed before us."[33] They also believed that there was sufficient
warrant from scripture in regard to the sacraments that "an analogy is drawn between the sign and the visible action and the spiritual reality."[34] It would appear that the real heart of the debate
centered on the crucial question of whether or not unbelievers received
the substance of the flesh of Christ without the Holy Spirit.

Calvin's second defense against Westphal was presented in the
"calm and cool" style typical of sixteenth-century theological polemic:

> Let his mixed trifle be read. The reader will discover that he is not
> proposing to oppose the teaching found in our consensus formula, but
> rather consensus itself.[35]
>
> If someone like Eck or Cochlaeus were to blab such silliness, unre-
> gretably he could be turned over to boy's abuse. But when someone
> who professes the gospel so flagrantly prostitutes himself, the reader
> will pardon me in my method of refutation when what he has done
> is so disgraceful that it pains me.[36]

---

[32] Calvin, *Secunda defensio*, 659–660. "De tribus ergo capitibus residuum illi est
certamen quia panem Coenae vult substantialiter esse corpus Christi; deinde ut
Christus praesentem se fidelibus in Coena exhibeat, vult immensum esse ejus corpus, & ubique esse extra locum; tertio nullam in verbis Christi figuram vult admitti,
quamvis de re conveniat."

[33] Calvin, *Secunda defensio*, 660. "Nos carnem Christi & sanguinem vere nobis in
Coena offeri asserimus, ut animas nostras vivificent." Westphal was "hac simplici-
tate non contentus, urget ac contendit panem substantialiter corpus esse." "Quae
Dei verbo minime consentanea est, ut pani Christus carnem suam substantialiter
affigat." Strongly against the notion of actually consuming the body of Christ, Calvin
said: "Jam si non alia lege Westphalum placare licet, quam si fateamur dentibus
sensualiter Christum atteri: nonne centum potius mortes praeoptandae sunt, quam
ut se quispiam tanti sacrilegii monstro implicet?"

[34] Calvin, *Secunda defensio*, 660. "Itaque non modo totum Christi ordinem per-
vertunt, sed Spiritui Dei suum eripiunt loquendi morem, qui negant sub panis sym-
bolo repraesentari nobis Christi corpus."

[35] Calvin, *Secunda defensio*, 661. "Legatur ejus Farrago: reperient lectores, non tam
ei fuisse propositum, doctrinam, quae in formula Consensus a nobis comprehensa
est, quam consensum ipsum oppugnare."

[36] Calvin, *Secunda defensio*, 662. "Si quis Eccius vel Cocleus has naenias effutiret,

If he is to be believed, [asserted Calvin, then] I exhibit canine eloquence. Although I do not long for the praise of eloquence, nevertheless I am not so devoid of the gift of speaking as to oblige to be
eloquent by barking."

From the withered flowers which he sheds over his discourse, it is
plain how feeble he is as rhetorician, while his intemperance sounds
more of the Cyclops than anything human. I will not deny one thing:
I am not less alert pursuing the sacrilegious, than is the faithful dog
in hunting off thieves.[37]

In the *Seconda defensio*, Calvin explicitly points to Westphal's attack
on the reputations of such distinguished theologians as Oecolampadius,
Zwingli, Bucer, Peter Martyr, Bullinger, and John Laski, which to
the Frenchman, was nothing more than an "evil detraction."[38] Calvin
then explicitly defers to Vermigli, who is composing his own response to
Westphal. Calvin writes: "Furthermore, concerning the discussions
which have taken place in England, I would rather leave it to the faithful teacher of the church of Strassbourg, Peter Martyr, to give the
answer. I trust that he is now preparing such an answer."[39] Calvin's
rather long treatise (172 pages) did not end his conflict with Westphal,
nor was he alone in crossing swords with him. Besides Martyr,
Theodore Beza[40] and Heinrich Bullinger[41] also joined in the battle.[42]

---

minore cum molestia pueris ridendos traderem. Nunc quod se tam flagitiose pros-
tituit qualiscunque Euangelii professor, ignoscant lectores si in refutatione modicus
sim, quia dedecoris me pudet ac piget."

[37] Calvin, *Secunda defensio*, 676. "Jam Westphalus acsi his partibus probe defunc-
tus foret, ad subeundam aliam molestiam descendere se dicit, nempe ut crimina
depellat, in quibus caninam eloquentiam, si ei creditur, exerceo. Ego vero etsi elo-
quntiae laudem non appeto, non tamen mediocri dicendi gratia sic destituor, ut
latrando facundus esse cogar." "Nam & ex marcidis flosculis, quibus orationem
suam aspergit, quam jejunus sit facundiae captator palam est: & eius intemperies
cyclopicum nescio qud magis quam humanum ubique sonat. Unum quidem non
inficior, mihi ad sacrilegos insectando non minus esse animi, quam fidis canibus est
ad profligandos fures."

[38] Calvin, *Secunda defensio*, 663. "Sed dum tibi propositum esse vident omnes,
Oecolampadium, Zuinglium, Bucerum, Petrum Martyrem, Bulingerum, Joannem a
Lasco labefactare, ut tota eorum existimatio concidat, quem omnino pium & aequum
hominem in mundo esse putas, cujus stomachum in te non provocet tam maligna
obtrectatio?"

[39] Calvin, *Secunda defensio*, 677. "Porro, de habitis in Anglia disputationibus malo
respondeat fidelis ecclesia Argentinensis doctor Petrus Maryr, quod nunc fieri consido."

[40] *De Coena Domini plana et perspicua tractatio in qua Iohachimi Wesphali calumniae refel-
luntur.* (September 1559).

[41] *Tractatio verborum Domini, in domo Patris mei mansiones multae sunt . . .* (Zurich
Froshauer: 1561). Donnelly says that "Bullinger and Vermigli clearly concerted their
refutation." See his *Dialogue on the Two Natures*, xiv.

[42] Nor was Westphal the only Lutheran polemicist. Mathaesus Judex and Paul

The *Last Admonition to Westphal*, with this subtitle: *Who if he heeds it not, must henceforth be treated in the way which Paul prescribes for obstinate heretics*,[43] contains quite a bit of French heat. Calvin's methodological approach in the treatise hinges upon a few presuppositions. Calvin accused Westphal of three crimes. First, charges of heresy against the Swiss were unwarranted.[44] Second, Westphal unfairly slandered both the living and the dead, even when Westphal's own name was never mentioned in public.[45] Finally, Westphal's debating presupposition, that heretics should be treated harshly and be silent when proven wrong, was true in principle but applied to Westphal and not to the Swiss![46]

Given these "rules of debate" Calvin decided "to sharpen his pen"—and pointed it was! Indeed, Westphal protested such piercing words. There was no denying Westphal's charge that Calvin's response was "full of sting and virulence." As a matter of fact, "I am not surprised by the former epithet," said Calvin, "nor am I troubled that men so stupid have, at least, felt some pricks."[47] The charge that

---

von Eitzen also were involved in the debate. Donnelly notes (from Helmut Gollwitzer) that there are 190 titles published in the Lords Supper dispute between 1560–1600. See his *Dialogue on the Two Natures*, xiv, n. 11. See also Tylenda, "The Calvin-Westphal Exchange," 203.

[43] *Ultimo admonitio Ioannis Calvini ad Ioachimum Westphalum, cui nisi obtemperet, eo loco posthac habendus erit, quo pertinaces haereticos haberit iubet Paulus.* (Jean Crispin, Geneva). Cf. *CO* IX, 137–252. An English translation is found in *Calvin's Selected Works*, II, 346–494.

[44] Calvin, *Ultimo admonitio*, 685. "Cur Joachimus tam blande rogatus, haereticum clamitare maluit, quam errorem, si quis esset, monstrare?"

[45] Calvin's ire against having "Zwinglians" lumped together with all heretics first appeared in the second defense: Calvin, *Secunda defensio*, 664. "Nam Anabaptistas, Davidianos, & fanaticos fere omnes nobis permiscens, Sectam unam instar Hydrae conflat: quia omnes Zuinglii dogma profitentur." "Sed quibus tandem vinculis nos in unum fascem colligat?" Calvin, *Ultimo admonitio*, 686. "Quum prodiisset in lucem Consensus noster, ac Westphalo integrum foret corrigere si quid illic putabat esse vitiosum, speciem repugnantiae calumniose undique accersens, vivos & mortuos immani modo laceravit. Ego importunam hanc feritatem refutans, nomini tamen peperci, ut si forte sanabili esset ingenio, tacite sepeliretur ejus ignominia."

[46] Calvin, *Ultimo admonitio*, 686. "Sibi quidvis in nos licere vult Joachimus, quia veram doctrinam, ut ipse ait, contra impium errorem defendat. Si autem quod falso sibi arrogat vere in me competere doceo & ostendo, nempe fidelem me purae sanctaeque doctrinae patronum esse, & fidelem operam impendere, non modo refutando impio errori, sed etiam diluendis atrocibus maledictis: cur non eadem mihi dabitur libertas?"

[47] Calvin, *Ultimo admonitio*, 685. "Ac de priore quidem epitheto non ita miror, neque etiam moleste fero homines plus satis bardos punctiones saltem aliquas sensisse."

Calvin threw every possible insult at Westphal was countered: "When he says in another place that I have anxiously strived not to omit any kind of insult, how much he is mistaken will best appear from the fact."[48] Perhaps with a silent sigh, Calvin noted: "Just as in comedies desperate slaves throw everything into confusion, so he intermingles light and darkness. Why shouldn't I call this insanity by its proper name?"[49]

Westphal would not be silenced. After Calvin's final reply he published *Some apologetic writings* (1558), and against Calvin personally, Westphal wrote his *Answer to some of the outrageous lies of John Calvin.* Having suffered from the attacks of Joachim Westphal,[50] Calvin welcomed the scholarly defense of his position on the sacrament by his fellow exile, Peter Martyr Vermigli.

III. *Peter Martyr's* Defensio *(1559) and* Dialogue on the two natures of Christ *(1561)*[51]

Peter Martyr Vermigli was well aware of Genevan life and theology at the time of Calvin's *Defensio* of 1555. The two exiled reformers had been in contact earlier and had corresponded on a number of topics, including the Lord's Supper.[52] Calvin obviously knew Martyr's earlier writings on the Eucharist—*Tractatio de sacramento Eucharistiae* (1549) and his *Disputatio de eodem Eucharistia sacramento habita* (1552).[53]

---

[48] Calvin, *Ultimo admonitio,* 685 "Nam quod alicuubi dicit, anxie me affectasse ne quod probri genus omitterem, quam longe fallatur, ex reipsa optime liquebit."

[49] Calvin, *Ultimo admonitio,* 685. "Imo sicuti in comoediis servos nequam ad omnia turbana impellit despertio, ita hic suis clamoribus lucem tenebris permiscet. Hanc ego insaniam cur non suo nomine notarem?" Cf. Calvin, *Ultimo admonitio,* 686. "Ergo quum intractabilis fuerit ejus ferocia, quam tota ejus declamatio frivola sit & puerilis, facile apparet." Cf. Calvin, *Ultimo admonitio,* 686. "Quanquam hic quoque obiter hominis socordiam cum pari impudentia notare operae pretium est." Cf. Calvin, *Ultimo admonitio,* 685. "Dicas hic Julianuj apostateam, dum crudeliter saevit in totum Christianum nomen, de crucis tolerantia per ludibrium concionari."

[50] *Farrago . . . de coena Domini.* Et alia!!

[51] For more information, see McLelland, *The Visible Words of God* and Salvatore Corda, *Veritas Sacramenti: A Study in Vermigli's Doctrine of the Lord's Supper* (Zurich: Theologischer Verlag Zurich, 1975).

[52] Marvin W. Anderson, "Peter Martyr, Reformed Theologian (1542–1562): His Letters to Bullinger and Calvin," *Sixteenth Century Journal* 4 (1973): 41–65.

[53] English translations by Joseph C. McLelland and G. Duffield, eds., *The Life, Early Letters and Eucharistic Writings of Peter Martyr* (Appleford, Oxford: Sutton Courtenay Press, 1989), 173–289.

Calvin also knew about Martyr's views on union with Christ, which proved so important to Calvin's doctrine of the Lord's Supper.

In 1555, Calvin and Martyr exchanged some very important correspondence.[54] Two letters in particular concerned the doctrine of union with Christ.[55] Calvin was convinced that the two of them agreed on this central teaching, which included the importance of a mystical communion as well as a spiritual union with Christ. For them, only the regenerate enjoy mystical union with Christ. Both employ the same imagery for this union, that is, the Johannine vine and branches. By this mystical union or communion, believers enjoy Christ who comes "to dwell in us, to sustain us, to quicken us, and to fulfill all the offices of the Head."[56] Of signal importance is the role of the Holy Spirit in this mystical union. The Holy Spirit overcomes the physical distance between the heavenly Christ and his people.[57]

Necessarily connected to mystical union is spiritual communion with Christ, which both men agreed that only Christians enjoy. Spiritual communion is particularly important because of the gifts believers receive from it. This spiritual union is connected with the Christian walk, by which the life of Christ increases in the believer, and it is this spiritual communion with Christ that finds a specific connection to the Lord's Supper.[58] The mystical union provides the

---

[54] In that year Calvin also invited Martyr by letter to come to Geneva to pastor the Italian speaking congregation and help combat anti-Trinitarianism.

[55] Martyr wrote to Calvin on 8 March, 1555. Vermigli, *Loci Communes . . . ex variis ipsius authoris scriptis, in unum librum collecti et in quatuor Classes distributi* (Geneva: Pierre Aubert, 1627), 767–769. An English translation of Vermigli's letter is found in G. C. Gorham, ed, *Gleanings of a Few Scattered Ears* (London, 1857), 340–344. Calvin's letter to Martyr on 8 August, 1555, cf. *CO* XV, 722–725. An English translation is in Gorham, *Gleanings*. In this same letter Martyr declines Calvin's offer to come to Geneva.

[56] Gorham, *Gleanings*, 350 (Calvin to Martyr), cf. *CO* XV, 723.

[57] See William Duncan Rankin, "Carnal Union with Christ in the Theology of T. F. Torrance" (Ph.D. dissertation, University of Edinburgh, 1997), 178–181.

[58] Gorham, *Gleanings*, 351 (Calvin to Martyr), cf. *CO* XV, 723. There Calvin writes: "That we are strong in hope and patience, that we soberly and temperately keep ourselves from worldly snare, that we strenuously bestir ourselves to the subjugation of carnal affections, that the love of righteousness and piety flourishes in us, that we are earnest in prayer, that mediation on the life to come draws us upward, this, I maintain, flows from that second Communion, by which Christ, dwelling in us not ineffectually, brings forth the influence of His Spirit in His manifest gifts."

basis for the daily experience of spiritual communion. Mystical communion is definitive while spiritual communion is progressive. Mystical communion grounds the believer's justification. On the other hand, spiritual communion grounds their sanctification. For Calvin, as seen in his letter to Martyr, these are distinct concepts that the Holy Spirit brings about and each is inseparable from the other.[59]

As is evident from their correspondence, Calvin held the theological abilities of Vermigli in high regard. So high was Calvin's esteem for the Italian, that he wrote to Martyr in 1557 to ask him to pastor the Italian language congregation in Geneva and later that year informed the Senate of Zurich that Martyr's presence in Geneva would be of great help.[60] Alas, the two exiles would never reside in the same city. Vermigli had already settled in the calmer confines of Zurich.

Peter Martyr Vermigli's *Defense of the ancient and Apostolic Doctrine concerning the most holy Sacrament of the Eucharist* against Bishop Stephen Gardiner (1559)[61] was so highly valued by Calvin that he concluded "The whole was crowned by Peter Martyr, who has left nothing more to be done" on the subject of the local presence of Christ's body.[62] Such high praise did not come often from the Genevan.[63]

---

[59] Rankin, "Carnal Union," 184.

[60] PMRE, 170, 186–199, 217; Cf. Sturm, *Die Theologie Peter Martyr Vermiglis*, 18.

[61] Vermilgi, *Defensio Doctrinae veteris & Aposolicae. de sacrsancto Eucharistiae. Sacramento . . . Adersus Stephani Gardineri*. Vermigli is responding to Bishop Stephen Gardiner's *Confutatio Cavillationum, quibus sacrosanctum* (Paris, 1551) among other writings. Thomas Cranmer was also engaged against Gardiner with his *Defense of the True and Catholike Doctrine of the Sacrament* (London, 1550) and *Answer to a Craftie and Sophisticall Cavillation* (London, 1553). For Vermigli's mature reflection on the Lord's Supper see his *Brevis Epitome (sive Analysis) disputationis de Eucharistia in Gardinerum* (Zurich, 1561) which is found in his *Locorum Communium Theologicorum . . .* (Basel, 1580). There is an English translation of Martyr's Epitome in PMRD, 151–160.

[62] Henry Beverage and Jules Bonnet, eds. *Selected Works of John Calvin: Tracts and Treatises*, II, 535. According to Mariano Di Gangi, Vermigli's *Defensio* was ". . . probably the greatest single work on the Eucharist in the Reformation." See his *Peter Martyr Vermigli, 1499–1562: Renaissance Man, Reformation Master* (Lanham, Maryland, 1993), 169. A shorter version of Vermigli's *Defensio* is partially translated in McLelland and Duffield, The *Life, Early Letters and Eucharistic Writings*, 286–318.

[63] *Farrago . . . de coena Domini*. Vermigli's *Dialogue on the two natures of Christ* (Zürich 1561) was probably a response to Johannes Brenz's *De personali unione duarum naturarum in Christo, . . . Patris* (Tübingen 1561). cf. P. Schaff, *The Creeds of Christendom*, I, 279–294.

Earlier in 1557 Vermigli described to Calvin yet another sacramental dispute between Brenz and John Laski, calling Brenz's arguments for ubiquity "weak and sophistical."[64] It was this controversy that called for Vermigli's powerful response. His *Dialogue on the two natures of Christ*[65] (1561) was in many ways a response to Johannes Brenz's *De personali unione duarum naturarum in Christo, . . . Patris*.[66] There also is a brief critical mention of Tileman Hesshusen who would become one of Calvin's main Eucharistic opponents.[67] The political/ecclesiastical situation in the city of Strasbourg, with the rise of a Lutheran view of the Lord's Supper, and Martyr's subsequent departure to Zurich, is well spelled out in Martyr's, "Address to the Strasbourg Senate".[68]

Somewhat unusual was Vermigli's decision to employ the literary medium of a dialogue to refute Brenz. The genre of a dialogue is fairly uncommon in sixteenth-century polemical writings, but of course has a long and illustrious history among patristic and classical authors, with which Vermigli was very familiar. In his *Dialogue on the two natures of Christ*, he gives the debaters fictitious names, with *Pantachus* ("Everywhere") representing the Lutheran Brenz and *Orothetes* ("Boundary Setter") representing Vermigli. Brenz's name was not mentioned but his identity was clear to any discerning reader. Orothetes was not brutal in dealing with Pantachus, but Pantachus never won a single argument! After arguing that Christ's humanity is "immediately present to all things, but in a heavenly and not in a human way,"[69] and also in a certain place like the outer heaven, Orothetes counters that for his theory to be true then Christ's body must be

---

[64] DIAL, xvi.

[65] Ibid., xi. Vermigli was later joined by Bucer, who served at Cambridge University as Regius Professor of Divinity.

[66] Brenz had instructed Bucer at Heidelberg. As early as 1525 Bucer had written to Brenz asking him not to attack Zwingli and Oecolampad. See H. Eels, *Martin Bucer*, 75.

[67] Hesshusen wrote *De praesentia Corporis Christi in Coena Domini contra Sacramentarious* (Jena, 1560). Calvin responded to him with *Dilucida explicatio sanae doctrinae de vera participatione carnis et sanguinis Christi in sacra coena ad discutiendas Hehusii nebulas* (Geneva, 1561). There is an English translation in J. K. S. Reid, *Theological Treatises*, 258–324.

[68] See the English translation in PMRD, 160 ff.

[69] Vermigli, *Dialogus de utraque in Christo natura* (Zurich, 1561), 73r. A recent English translation is found in DIAL, 114.

carried around the daily orbit every day; being "whipped around daily from east to west".[70] And "if this strikes you as showing you up as silly, why do you leave the opportunity for this open?"[71]

Brenz did not let the challenge go unheeded and shot back with *De divina maiestate Christi et de vera presentia corporis et sanguinis eius in Coena* (1562). There Martyr is charged with being more capable of "showing the weakness of his mind than in attacking the truth." He is motivated by a "singular lust to criticize" and has "great rashness". Perhaps most biting was the charge that "Martyr is accustomed to cut things out of various authors [church fathers] to suit his own purpose and to twist them to his own fantasies."[72] The *De maiestate* appeared in September and before he could pen a reply Martyr died in November. Consoled at the close of his days with the words of the book of *Hebrews* that the Christian's citizenship is in heaven, nevertheless Vermigli was sure that "I know it is, but not in Brenz's heaven, which is nowhere."[73]

Conclusion

John Calvin and Peter Martyr remained good friends throughout these turbulent sacramental debates. This sense of camaraderie is evident in a letter to Calvin in 1561: "I was desirous in my return to see you . . . Herewithall I considered, that it should make but small if we were asunder in body sith [since] we have our minds and judgments most nearly joined together."[74] It seems apparent that Peter Martyr's words concerning their theological solidarity were not empty.

In his analysis of Martyr's scholia, *De Schismate* (or *Whether Evangelicals are Schismatics for having separated from the Papists*) from his commentary on Kings (published posthumously in 1566), Joseph McClelland

---

[70] Ibid., 73v. English translation: DIAL, 115.

[71] Ibid.

[72] Josiah Simler, *Oratio de vita et obitu viri optimi, praestantissmi Theologi D. Petri Martyris Vermilii, Sacrarum literarum in schola Tigurina Professsoris* (Zurich, 1563), 7. The funeral oration was often reprinted in the many editions of the *Loci Communes* beginning with the Basel edition of 1580. English translation in LLS, 60.

[73] DIAL, xviii.

[74] PMRE, 246.

demonstrates the similarities between Martyr's very last work and Calvin's *Institutes*.[75] Heinrich Bullinger, who years earlier had worked with Calvin on the *Consensus Tigurinus*, wrote to Calvin at Peter Martyr's death, that "He was an incomparable man and of all mortals the most dear to me". Calvin could not claim that closeness, but would have agreed with Bullinger that certainly in Peter Martyr there was "an incomparable man."[76]

---

[75] EW, 163–66. The scholia is titled *An Evangelici sint Schismatici, quod se alienauerint a Papists . . . de schismate*, was originally published in Vermigli's *Melachim id est, Regum Libri Duo posteriores cum Commentarijs* (Zuirch, 1566), fols. 102r–113v. McLelland isolates particularly noteworthy similarities as "the desire to distance their movement from that of Anabaptists" and solidarity noteworthy through the lenses of the Sadoleto affair (165).

[76] Bullinger to Calvin, 22 November 1562, cited in PMRE, 250.

PART II

BIBLICAL AND THEOLOGICAL REFLECTIONS

VERMIGLI ON TRADITION AND THE FATHERS: PATRISTIC PERSPECTIVES FROM HIS COMMENTARY ON I CORINTHIANS

Douglas H. Shantz

I. *Introduction: Previous Historiography and the Thesis of this Study*

The genre of this paper is that of a "modest proposal" which, it is hoped, may serve as a stimulus to future study of Vermigli and his views on tradition and the Fathers. The paper is suggestive, not conclusive, given its limited parameters, and the limited sample of primary sources it has been able to explore. The proposal is simply that future Vermigli research on this subject should make greater use of a comparative method, examining Vermigli's Patristic thought in relation to that of his contemporaries; that is, Vermigli research should integrate itself with paths already explored in the scholarship on Philip Melanchthon, Martin Bucer and John Calvin.

This paper seeks to make a start in the direction of this proposal, examining Vermigli's patristic thought in relation to Melanchthon, and applying to the Vermigli sources some interpretive questions and concerns that have already been applied to the study of Melanchthon as a patristic scholar.

1. *Previous Historiography on Vermigli's Patristic Learning*

Recent scholarship has recognized Peter Martyr Vermigli (1499–1562) as "*the* theologian of the Elizabethan Puritans."[1] "Expert in the three classical languages of Latin, Greek and Hebrew, he so excelled in biblical exegesis and patristic learning that his commentaries on various books of Scripture ... remained standard works of Protestant

---

[1] See Patrick Collinson, "England and International Calvinism, 1558–1640," in *International Calvinism, 1541–1715*, ed. Menna Prestwich (Oxford: Clarendon, 1985), 214.

reference for generations after his death."[2] On the second point of excellence, his knowledge of the Church Fathers and catholic tradition, Peter Martyr Vermigli has been counted among the most competent of 16th C. Protestant scholars. Yet there has been little comparative study of Vermigli that focuses directly on this aspect of his scholarship in terms of distinctive features of his use of the Fathers, the care and accuracy of his citations, influences on his thinking, changes and developments, and the impact of his thought on this issue upon English reformers such as John Jewel. A brief overview of pertinent Vermigli historiography should make this situation clear.

Joseph McLelland's 1957 book, *The Visible Words of God*, examined Vermigli's "Sacramental Theology," highlighting his Patristic understanding of the Pauline "union with Christ."[3] In a five page Appendix McLelland discussed "Peter Martyr's Patristic Sources," and suggested that Vermigli's thought was "Patristic in a profound sense."[4] McLelland discerned two principles that guided Vermigli's use of the Fathers. *First*, "theology has as its subject matter" the Bible, not the writings of the Fathers. First we should define doctrines soundly out of Scripture itself. Then afterwards the Fathers may be read with judgment.[5] The Fathers should be interpreted and corrected according to Scripture, and not vice versa as was the practice among his Catholic opponents. *Secondly*, McLelland noted that Vermigli recognized "degrees" of usefulness within the Patristic corpus, distinguishing fathers "of greater antiquity and the purer age" from "the latter writers of the Church." "Later Fathers speak less prudently."[6]

McLelland observed that "Peter Martyr's remarkable knowledge of the Fathers is evident throughout his whole life, and soon became known among his contemporaries as worthy of their notice."[7] One

---

[2] Philip McNair, "Biographical Introduction," in EW, 13.

[3] VWG. See Marvin Anderson, "Vermigli, Peter Martyr," in *The Oxford Encyclopedia of the Reformation* (New York: Oxford University Press, 1996), 231.

[4] VWG, 267.

[5] Ibid.

[6] Ibid., 268.

[7] Ibid.

sees this patristic knowledge in Vermigli's discussion of Purgatory while he was still in Naples; in his Strasbourg lectures on Scripture; in his lectures in England on I Corinthians and in his disputation in Oxford on the eucharist. McLelland argues that Martyr came to England as both a Patristic scholar and a Protestant, refuting Strype's suggestion that Cranmer's influence and patristic theology were decisive in winning Vermigli to the Protestant cause. The influence was more the other way around; Martyr's use of Gelasius and Theodoret to refute transubstantiation had a "profound influence" on the English church.[8]

Using statistical evidence, McLelland noted Martyr's "profound reliance upon Augustine's works"; indeed, "Augustine was his chief Patristic source." In the *Defensio* one finds approximately *sixty-four places* of Augustine quoted over one hundred times, as opposed to *thirty-four places* from Chrysostom, *twenty* from Ambrose, and so on, with a descending order of citation. "Such quantitative incidence reflects the profound reliance of Martyr upon Augustine's works." Martyr particularly drew upon Augustine for support in understanding the sacraments as the visible words of God and in seeing union with Christ as necessary for true eating.[9]

Marvin Anderson has also discussed Patristic influence on Vermigli's doctrine of the eucharist, and Vermigli's influence on Cranmer on this issue. Anderson stated that "The positive side of Martyr's theology rests on Pauline and Patristic reflection."[10] Specifically, Martyr used Augustine, Hillary, Irenaeus, Chrysostom and Theodoret to "drive a patristic stake into the heart of the late medieval argument for transubstantiation."[11] Cranmer's true presence views were influenced at a critical stage by Martyr's Patristic witness. Anderson noted the way in which "Peter Martyr led Archbishop Cranmer to adopt his patristic defense of union with Christ" in his debates of 1548.[12]

Frank A. James, III argues that the warm welcome Vermigli received in Zurich and Strasbourg can be attributed to his "profound

---

[8] Ibid., 271.

[9] Ibid., 269.

[10] Marvin Anderson, "Rhetoric and Reality: Peter Martyr and the English Reformation," *Sixteenth Century Journal* 19, no. 3 (1988): 461.

[11] Ibid., 463, 466.

[12] Ibid., 468.

Augustinianism."[13] More specifically, Vermigli is placed within the *schola Augustiniana moderna*, the Augustinian revival associated with Gregory of Rimini. James argues for Vermigli's "early absorption" of this school's ideals. More specifically, James elaborates upon the structural parallel between the predestination doctrines of Gregory and Vermigli.[14] James concludes that Gregory and Vermigli demonstrate a "remarkable parallel" in their soteriology, teaching that divine reprobation and predestination issue from the *propositum Dei*, the sovereign will of God. God's predestination does not depend upon foreseen works; God's reprobation does not depend upon foreseen sins.[15] Most importantly from the perspective of patristic scholarship, James' argument establishes only that Vermigli was a careful student of Gregory; there is no convincing evidence that Vermigli was an equally careful student and follower of Augustine and Augustine's interpretation of Paul.[16] Indeed, in a recent study James admits that Vermigli "diverges" from Augustine's doctrine at crucial points. At these points, James suggests, Vermigli came to Augustine with a "predestinarian agenda" derived from Gregory. Gregory "guided Vermigli's reading of Augustine."[17]

2. *Recent Scholarship on Patristic Thought in Bucer, Calvin and Melanchthon*

Left largely out of the above discussion is where Vermigli fits within the spectrum of continental Reformed thought and Protestant thinking generally on the use of the Fathers. Does Vermigli's use of

---

[13] Frank A. James, "A Late Medieval Parallel in Reformation Thought: *Gemina Praedestinatio* in Gregory of Rimini and Peter Martyr Vermigli," in *Via Augustini: Augustine in the Later Middle Ages, Renaissance and Reformation*, ed. Heiko A. Oberman and Frank A. James (Leiden: Brill, 1991), 157 f.

[14] Ibid., 162. "*Praedestinatio* is for both Gregory and Vermigli the positive soteric expression of the *propositum Dei*, which is portrayed within a causal nexus and revolves around a Christological axis." (174) Furthermore, both Gregory and Vermigli asserted that "the sovereign will of God is the ultimate and exclusive cause of reprobation." (175)

[15] James, "Gregory of Rimini and Peter Martyr Vermigli," 176, 185.

[16] PPRED, 94. James notes that Vermigli owned the ten volume Froben edition of Augustine's works. Vermigli appealed primarily to two works by Augustine: *De dono perseverantiae* and *De correptione et gratia*.

[17] Ibid., 104. Vermigli's predestinarianism is "a significant intensification of Augustine." (105)

Patristic authority differ in any way from that of Bucer, Melanchthon, Calvin or other contemporary Protestants, or were the Reformers pretty much alike in their regard for tradition and the Fathers, as William Haaugaard has argued?[18] A final question to be asked is whether the Reformers' interest in the Fathers extended to the point of careful study of Patristic writings in their own context, or whether the Reformers simply "dipped" into these writings to make points of their own with little regard for the original intent of the writings.

The assumption of broad similarity in the Reformers' Patristic usage has recently been challenged. Irena Backus, while observing "similarities" in Zwingli's and Martin Bucer's use of the Fathers, insists that "it would be difficult to speak of the Zurich-Strasbourg School of Patristic Theology."[19] Backus further observed that Bucer's "attitude towards the History of the Early Church as a model is much more positive than Calvin's."[20] For present purposes one must ask, Was Vermigli closer to Bucer or Calvin on this point?

Scholars have become more nuanced in their appreciation of change and development in the Reformers' use of tradition and the Fathers. James R. Payton has argued that between 1523 and 1536 Martin Bucer's appreciation for the value of the patristic tradition changed significantly. Earlier in his career he viewed the Fathers as fellow interpreters of Scripture deserving some deference, but he placed a chasm between their authority and that of the inspired Bible.[21] By 1536 Bucer could argue that the Fathers possessed an "unrivalled" hermeneutical authority in the interpretation of Scripture; later interpreters must follow the patristic lead if they would teach

---

[18] William P. Haaugaard, "Renaissance Patristic Scholarship and Theology in Sixteenth-Century England," *The Sixteenth Century Journal* 10, no. 3 (1979): 53 and 53 n. 55. Haaugaard, for example, found broad agreement between John Jewel and Lutheran Patristic scholars such as Melanchthon, Flacius Illyricus, and Chemnitz in "insisting that the fathers' statements be weighed by scriptural doctrine." A possible point of difference was that Jewel "does not apply the yardstick of justification by faith in the rigorous fashion of the Lutherans" as a basis for ranking the fathers.

[19] Irena Backus, "Ulrich Zwingli, Martin Bucer and the Church Fathers," in *The Reception of the Church Fathers in the West*, ed. Backus (Leiden: Brill, 1997), 627.

[20] Irena Backus, "Martin Bucer and the Patristic Tradition," in *Martin Bucer and Sixteenth Century Europe*, ed. Christian Krieger and Marc Lienhard (Leiden: E. J. Brill, 1993), 69. See also Irena Backus, "Calvin's judgment of Eusebius of Caesarea: an Analysis," *Sixteenth Century Journal* 22, no. 3 (1991): 419–437.

[21] James R. Payton, "Bucer and the Church Fathers," (Unpublished Manuscript, 1991): 3. I am grateful to Dr. Payton for providing me with a copy of his study.

rightly.[22] Bucer found the Fathers' lead especially helpful in negotiating his way through sixteenth century eucharistic controversies.

David Steinmetz has discovered significant development and change within Calvin's attitude toward the Fathers in the period between his early and later works.[23] Using Calvin's exegesis of Romans 8:1–11 as a test case for Patristic influence on Calvin, Steinmetz found that between his 1540 commentary on Romans 8, where no Fathers were cited, and the 1556 commentary, where four Fathers were cited, Calvin came to accept the Fathers as "commentators whose views must be taken into account as he writes his own exegesis." Calvin came to see the task of interpreting Paul as "a work carried on ... in conversation with the greatest interpreters of Christian antiquity."[24] However, the later Calvin did not treat the Fathers as authorities "in the medieval sense of the term." "They stimulate Calvin in his reflections on the text ... they do not have the last word." Indeed, in the 1556 commentary, "In every case, explicit and anonymous, in which Calvin has referred to Patristic exegesis, he has quarreled with it."[25] Calvin, one might suggest, is always the superior partner in his conversation with the Fathers; *he* has the last word.

In a similar vein, Johannes van Oort has recently argued that Calvin's use of the Fathers was "primarily polemical." Calvin cited primarily the early western Fathers, those writing from 325 to 451 AD, when they supported his own teaching and he used them to undermine Roman Catholic and Lutheran doctrines.[26]

On the question of whether the Reformers sought careful, "contextual understanding" of the Fathers, E.P. Meijering's 1983 study *Melanchthon and Patristic Thought*[27] represents a significantly new depar-

---

[22] James R. Payton, "Bucer and the Church Fathers," 9.

[23] David Steinmetz, *Calvin in Context* (New York: Oxford University, 1995), 136. Calvin and Vermigli were in frequent correspondence between 1553 and 1562, leaving one to wonder about possible influence on Calvin on this issue by Vermigli. See Marvin W. Anderson, "Peter Martyr, Reformed Theologian (1542–1562): His letters to Heinrich Bullinger and John Calvin," *Sixteenth Century Journal* 4, no. 1 (April 1973): 42. "Calvin and Martyr wrote each other a total of forty-five letters between 3 November 1553 and 16 March 1562."

[24] Ibid., 136 f.

[25] Steinmetz, 136.

[26] Johannes van Oort, "John Calvin and the Church Fathers," in *The Reception of the Church Fathers in the West*, ed. Irena Backus (Leiden: Brill, 1997), 698.

[27] E. P. Meijering, *Melanchthon and Patristic Thought* (Leiden: Brill, 1983).

ture. In comparing his method with the one used by Peter Fraenkel, Meijering claimed to have brought a new point of view and a new set of questions to the analysis of the Reformers' use of the Fathers:

> Melanchthon's relation to Patristic theology can be described primarily from the point of view of a Reformation scholar and primarily from the point of view of a Patristic scholar. The former is done in [Peter] Fraenkel's book,[28] the latter is attempted in the present study . . . We want to ask . . . what he wants to prove with these [Patristic] quotations . . . [and] how precisely he quotes his sources.[29]

Meijering's study yielded the following conclusion:

> If one asks whether the Fathers really influenced Melanchthon or whether he used the Fathers as supporters of views which he already held, there can be little doubt that the latter was the case. He had a number of quotations from the Fathers in store which he had either found himself in their writings or to which contemporaries drew his attention, and he used these quotations wherever it suited him, and he merely ignored what did not suit him . . . In Melanchthon we find two somewhat contradictory positions: on the one hand he claimed to reproduce the *consensus* of the Fathers and on the other hand he picked from the Fathers what seemed attractive to him. Usually he gives his quotations in such a way that the readers must get the impression that he does the former, only occasionally he admits . . . that he does the latter. In all his writings he shows that the latter is true.[30]

Meijering further noted that Melanchthon's Patristic citations "are not really interpreted from a historical context." Such selective engagement is a very different thing than open discussion with those "who can enrich our minds, who can open perspectives which we on our own would not have seen."[31] Despite all these qualifications, Meijering nevertheless found a greater degree of "continuity" between the theology of the Fathers and the thought of Melanchthon than he did in the case of John Calvin.[32] Meijering calls Melanchthon a "Biblicist traditionalist" who opposed in principle any doctrine that would add something new to the Bible.[33]

---

[28] Peter Fraenkel, *Testimonia Patrum: The Function of the Patristic Argument in the Theology of Philip Melanchthon* (Geneva: Librairie E. Droz, 1961).
[29] E. P. Meijering, *Melanchthon and Patristic Thought*, 2.
[30] Ibid., 139.
[31] Ibid., 144.
[32] Ibid., 139.
[33] Ibid., 11.

It is surely significant that many of the Reformers derived their Patristic citations primarily from medieval collections of Patristic citations, such as *The Decree of Gratian*, rather than from recent editions of their writings, such as those of Erasmus. "[This] tendency to use early Christian writers as precursors to the Reformation or to the doctrines of the Roman church without paying much attention to their historical contexts became a widespread phenomenon in the later sixteenth century."[34] Both Bucer and Calvin made extensive use of the *Decree of Gratian* as a handy textbook of patristic quotations.[35]

This historiographical survey has pointed to development and diversity among the Reformers as patristic scholars, and invites Vermigli scholars to pursue a more nuanced, comparative appreciation of Vermigli's use of tradition and the Fathers within the spectrum of sixteenth century Protestant opinion. More specifically, we shall pursue *two key questions*: did Vermigli follow a model of openness in reading the patristic writings, allowing them to really influence his thinking, or did he engage in selective, largely polemical use of the Fathers? Secondly, did the early church and its creeds represent some kind of standard of appeal for Vermigli, or not?

3. *Purpose and Thesis of this Study*

This study investigates these two key questions by appealing to Vermigli's explicit principles for using creeds, tradition and the Fathers, as found in two of his Latin writings: the Preface to his 1551 *Commentary on I Corinthians* and his 1562 treatise, *Schism and the True Church*. We will then compare these views with similarly focused discussions of the Fathers in Melanchthon's 1539 treatise *De Ecclesia et Autoritate Verbi Dei*. Although representing somewhat different genres and contexts, all these works discuss in principle the importance of "the

---

[34] Irena Backus, "Patristics," in *the Oxford Encyclopedia of the Reformation* (New York: Oxford University Press, 1996), 224 f. For example, "Calvin is both critical and cavalier in his use of patristic writings and occasionally 'adjusts' them to suit his own teaching."

[35] See Irena Backus, "Ulrich Zwingli, Martin Bucer and the Church Fathers," in *The Reception of the Church Fathers in the West*, ed. Irena Backus (Leiden: Brill, 1997), 657; Johannes van Oort, 698. Van Oort notes that after 1543 Calvin relied less upon the *Decretum Gratiani*.

primitive church of the ancient fathers and apostles . . ." for Protestant theology.[36]

Following the lead of Meijering and Backus, this paper suggests that while *quantitative* study points to Vermigli's wide and appreciative reading and use of patristic citations, when the impressive *quantitative* evidence for Vermigli's patristic usage is interpreted in light of *qualitative* evidence, namely Vermigli's *explicit methodological statements* of his guiding principles in making use of the Fathers, a somewhat different picture emerges. Like, Melanchthon, Vermigli relied on the Fathers primarily to make his *own* points; the Fathers were unequal partners in the hermeneutical discussion. Vermigli, too, had a ready store of stock phrases and examples from which he repeatedly drew over a ten year period.

II. *Vermigli's Early Study and Reading of Tradition and the Fathers*

This study of Vermigli's Views on Tradition and the Fathers first examines Vermigli's early education and reading in order to determine the basis and depth of his acquaintance with the Fathers of the early church. Philip McNair's 1967 biography offered some insight into Vermigli's early life and education up to 1542.[37] Vermigli learned Latin at his mother's knee and was already reading Terence with her as a child before her death in his twelfth year.[38] In July, 1514 Vermigli entered the religious life, joining the Canons Regular of St. Augustine of the Lateran Congregation in their monastery of S. Bartolomeo at Fiesole, known as the Badia Fiesolana.[39] His first biographer Josiah Simler tells us that Peter Martyr was attracted to the religious life by the "great abundance of excellent books" found

---

[36] John Jewel, *An Apology of the Church of England*, tr. J. E. Booty (Ithaca: Cornell University Press, 1963), 135.

[37] McNair notes that Vermigli's first biographer was his former student, Josiah Simler, whose *Oratio de vita & obitu viri optimi, praestantissimi Theologi D. Petri Martyris Vermilii* . . . was published in Zurich in 1563. Simler's work relied largely on Vermigli's memory for the first 37 years of his life. As a result, "Not only in chronology, but also in other details of Martyr's early life is Simler sometimes mistaken." PMI, xvii.

[38] Ibid., 59 f.

[39] Ibid., 76.

in religious houses.[40] This may also have guided the choice of
S. Bartolomeo di Fiesole. "Partly because of the excellence of its
library, partly because of the amenity of its situation, but mostly
because of the reputation of one outstanding Abbot, the Badia became
a centre of humanism during the last decade of the fifteenth century."
Here in summer 1489 Giovanni Pico della Mirandola finished the
Heptaplus, his sevenfold commentary on the first chapter of Genesis.[41]
Simler records that, "In those days Vermigli exercised himself not
only in the precepts of learning the arts which were diligently taught
to the younger fellows in this fellowship, but also in the reading of
holy scriptures." He was among those novices who were encouraged
to commit large portions of the Vulgate Bible to memory.[42]

Vermigli spent the years 1518–1526 in the monastery of S. Giovanni
di Verdara in Padua.[43] It was here Vermigli reached "intellectual
maturity."[44] There is hardly an Italian reformer not connected in
some way with Padua.[45] Padua remained a stronghold of Averroist
Aristotelianism.[46] Here in Padua, the Lateran congregation owned a
house with a small study centre connected with the larger Padua
University. The center offered a School of Natural Philosophy based
on the writings of Aristotle. McNair notes that, "Peter Martyr was
a Thomist before he became a patrist[ic scholar]."[47] In Padua Martyr
received a thorough training in Thomistic scholasticism.

Padua was also a center of both Patristic and classical learning,
and by 1521 the University had become "one of the most distinguished centers of humanism in Europe."[48] The library probably represents "one of the great formative influences on Martyr's early
years."[49]

> The manuscript collection was rich in the poets, philosophers, and his-
> torians of classical antiquity; it was profuse in the Schoolmen; and it

---

[40] Ibid., 78.
[41] Ibid., 77.
[42] Ibid., 82 f.
[43] Irena Backus, "Patristics," in *The Oxford Encyclopedia of the Reformation*, 223. There
was another monastic community in Padua that became a notable center for patristic learning; it was the Benedictine Congregation of Santa Giustina of Padua.
[44] Philip McNair, *Peter Martyr in Italy*, 86.
[45] Ibid., 86.
[46] Ibid., 107, 110.
[47] Ibid., 106.
[48] Ibid., 88.
[49] Ibid., 93.

was particularly abundant in the Fathers of the Christian Church, both Greek and Latin. Given . . . a retentive memory, seven years of hard work in such a library might well produce a formidable patrist[ic scholar]. In Martyr's case it certainly did.[50]

Here he taught himself Greek so that he could read Aristotle, as well as the ancient orators and poets.[51] This facility with languages Vermigli at some point directed to study of the Church Fathers as well. "Of the three A's who contended for the mastery of his mind, Aristotle outrivaled Averroës, but Augustine outclassed them both: in the life of this Augustinian, Augustine was to remain to the end his favourite reading after the Bible."[52]

Years later, when abbot in Naples, and the "light of God's truth began to dawn on him," "Martyr was already far advanced in Augustinianism and patristic studies."[53] Frank James likewise uses Simler to argue that Vermigli studied two chief traditions at the University of Padua: the theology of Thomas Aquinas and the Augustinianism of Gregory of Rimini.[54]

We gain some insight into the patristic reading of Vermigli from the extant book list of his "rich library." "Vermigli succeeded, despite his numerous travels, in amassing a personal library of great scholarly and commercial value."[55] In his library, patristic holdings clearly took priority of place. It included editions of the writings of twelve Greek Fathers, including Chrysostom, Clement of Alexandria, Justin Martyr, Origen, Basil, and Gregory of Nazianzus. There were also editions of the writings of eight Latin Fathers, including Tertullian, Ambrose, Jerome and a ten volume collection of Augustine's writings.[56] We know that upon Vermigli's arrival in England at Cranmer's invitation, Vermigli purchased books of the Fathers "at English expense." The chance survival of an expense account shows that

---

[50] Ibid., 95.
[51] Ibid., 114. In Bologna he learned Hebrew by studying with a Jewish physician. See Philip McNair, "Biographical Introduction," 5.
[52] Ibid., 94.
[53] Ibid., "Biographical Introduction," 6.
[54] James, "Gregory of Rimini and Peter Martyr Vermigli," 160.
[55] Alexandre Ganoczy, *La Bibliotheque de l'Academie de Calvin: Le Catalogue de 1572 et ses Enseignements* (Geneve: librairie Droz, 1969), 19. See also Patrick Donnelly, "Peter Martyr's Library," in CAS, 208–217.
[56] Alexandre Ganoczy, *La Bibliotheque de l'Academie de Calvin*, 22.

Abell the archbishop's agent "paid some 13 gulden in Basle for Martyr's three sets,"[57] of works by Augustine, Cyprian and Epiphanius. After the writings of the Fathers, in second place, were the literary works of Greek and Latin antiquity. In third place come works of Biblical scholarship, mainly relating to the Old Testament and Hebrew language. The almost complete lack of medieval scholastic writers in the list can be accounted for by the weaning out of less valuable works by the Genevan Academy.[58]

We conclude that there can be little question of Vermigli's reading and knowledge of patristics. It seems unlikely that he relied primarily upon collections of patristic citations such as *The Decree of Gratian*, although he did make some use of the latter.[59] We investigate now the role patristic writings played in Vermigli's Protestant reflection.

III. *Vermigli's Views on Tradition and the Fathers in the "Preface" of his* Commentary on I Corinthians *(1551), Compared with* Schism and the True Church *(1562)*

"Martyr lived in Italy until 1542, in Strasbourg with Bucer to 1547, in England (mainly Oxford) with Cranmer from 1547 to 1553, back at Strasbourg with the Marian exiles to 1556 when he left to spend his final six years with Bullinger at Zurich." Peter Martyr died in Zurich on 12 November 1562.[60]

"Martyr arrived in England on December 20, 1547 and made his way to Lambeth on December 21 where he stayed with Archbishop Cranmer and did not reside in Oxford until February/March 1548 . . ."[61]

---

[57] Haaugaard, 50 n. 41.

[58] Alexandre Ganoczy, *La Bibliotheque de l'Academie de Calvin*, 23. Donnelly notes that thanks to the efforts of Theodore Beza, the city of Geneva bought the library from Zurich in March 1566 to enhance the library of the Genevan Academy. The Genevans economized by returning to Zurich those books they considered less valuable for their Academy. Donnelly suggests, "Probably the toll was especially high in rabbinic commentaries and scholastic works." See Donnelly, 209.

[59] See the index to the recently published *The Peter Martyr Reader*, eds. John Patrick Donnelly, Frank A. James, Joseph C. McLelland (Kirksville: Truman State University Press, 1999), 254.

[60] Marvin Anderson, "Rhetoric and Reality: Peter Martyr and the English Reformation," *Sixteenth Century Journal* 19, no. 3 (1988): 452.

[61] Ibid., 455.

During the first ten months in Oxford he held private lectures and sermons in his house. Martyr began his Oxford lectures on I Corinthians in January of 1549, making his Protestantism public at this time in 1549. He relied on Erasmus' Greek *Novum Instrumentum* as the basis for these lectures.[62] In June, 1549 he began preparing his lectures for publication, and "as early as November 11, 1550 Martyr told Bucer that the Commentary was ready for publication."[63] The speed of publication leads some scholars to think that Martyr wrote his Corinthian lectures prior to his arrival in Oxford, at most making revisions to them while in Oxford.

1. *Noteworthy Features of Vermigli's Views on Tradition and the Fathers in the Preface to his 1551 Commentary*

This *Preface* represents Vermigli's programmatic statement of his views on theological method in a polemical context. In three equal sections, Vermigli discussed first the nature and "dignity of Scripture," secondly where to find competent "judges" and resources for determining the meaning of Scripture, and finally the method of self-preparation by which Christian readers might effectively appropriate these resources for themselves. Under the first two sections, Vermigli offered pointed comments about the value of Church councils, traditions and the Fathers.

Under the dignity of Scripture, Vermigli affirmed that all truths necessary for salvation were to be found there; no traditions were necessary for salvation which were not also to be found in Scripture. This was true in Christian experience, where the Scriptures served as the "seed" by which regeneration was experienced. Augustine's *Confessions* illustrated this in Augustine's own life. "Augustine extricated himself from the errors in which he was entangled when he began to read the Scriptures."[64]

---

[62] PMRE, 318. Salvatore Corda speaks of "the hour of truth," to describe Vermigli's situation as he prepared to deliver public lectures at Oxford University. See Salvatore Corda, *Veritas Sacramenti: A Study in Vermigli's Doctrine of the Lord's Supper* (Zurich: Theologischer Verlag, 1975).

[63] Marvin Anderson, "Rhetoric and Reality," 455.

[64] Vermigli, "Praefatio," *In Selectissimam S. Pauli Priorem Ad Corinth. Epistolam D. Petri Martyris, Florentini, ad Sereniss. regem Angliae, &c. Edvardvm VI. Commentarii doctissimi*

This principle also held true in theology. The singular authority and clarity of the Bible were seen in that, "the first principle according to which all true theological truths are determined should be considered this: 'the Lord has spoken.'"[65] "It is not possible that the dogmas of the Christian faith be established by any other means than by the authority of the Scriptures."[66] The church was the "pillar and foundation of the truth" not in a way that allowed it to pronounce new truths, but solely because it "has the Word of God [the Bible] and makes constant use of it in its teachings and definitions." Vermigli drew on statements from Augustine and the example of Constantine to reinforce the clear supremacy of Scripture. "Augustine says in reply to the Epistle of Fundamentus that things defined in the sacred writings should be preferred to all others."[67] "Constantine the Great encouraged the fathers of the Nicene Council that they should reconcile [their differences] by the oracles of the divine Scriptures."[68]

In the second section, under resources for determining the meaning of Scripture, Vermigli affirmed two—the Spirit of Christ who taught within the believer, and the Word of God itself which offered clear passages with which to interpret the unclear ones.[69] He cited Chrysostom in support of the first, Augustine in support of the second.[70] In *De Doctrina Christiana* Augustine "teaches that [the questioner] should compare passages of Scripture among themselves, and not resign [himself] to investigating the ideas of the Fathers, or seeking out the definitions of the Church, or the canons or traditions of men."[71]

(Zurich: Froschauer, 1551), 2v: "Et Augustinus tunc ex erroribus quibus impediebatur emersit, cum coepit legere scripturas."

[65] Vermigli, "Praefatio," 2r: "Ita ut primum principium ad quod omnina vera theological resoluuntur hoc haberi debeat, DOMINUS DIXIT."

[66] Vermigli, "Praefatio," 2v–3r: "Addis his, non posse christianae fidei dogmata confirmari alia ratione, quam authoritate scriptoraum idcirco . . ."

[67] Vermigli, "Praefatio," 2v: "Augustinus contra Epistolam Fundamenti ait, definite in sacris literis omnibus alijs debere praeferi."

[68] Vermigli, "Praefatio," 3r: "Constantinus Magnus, patres Concilij Niceri adhortatus est, ut oraculis divinarum scripturarum controversias de religione ortas componerent."

[69] Vermigli, "Praefatio," 3r.

[70] Vermigli, "Praefatio," 3v–4r.

[71] Vermigli, "Praefatio," 4r: "Et Augustinus de doctrina Christiana, suum concionatorem format, docetque ut loca scripturae inter sese conferat, neque illum remittit ad patrum sententias investigandus, quaerendas ecclesiae definitiones, aut canones, vel traditiones hominum."

There is a certain ironic inconsistency in Vermigli's appeal to the Fathers in order to discourage reliance on the Fathers.

Vermigli acknowledged one other resource for determining the meaning of Scripture: "the consensus and constant authority of the Catholic Church."[72] He insisted that this third criterion must ever be subservient to the first two, and not made into the supreme judge. Augustine's famous statement, "I would not have believed the Gospel unless the authority of the church had moved me," Vermigli interpreted as meaning: "unless the Church together with the two signs which we have just mentioned had moved me." Vermigli noted that the latin word for "move" was *commovisset* implying "helped to move," rather than *movisset* meaning simply "to move" or cause something independently.[73] The authority of the Church was certainly not great enough to accomplish this grace on its own.

Vermigli reflected upon the proper designation of the term "Church" in light of those who wished to attribute to it "supreme criticism of the Scriptures." He dismissed identifying it with the Bishops, many of whom were noteworthy for their impure lives; he also dismissed identifying it with the "holy Fathers," since "they disagree among themselves, they change their mind, they revise, and sometimes one of them contends against the other." Nor could Church Councils be relied upon "as if they would never err." Vermigli provided a catalogue of five errant Councils, including the Council of Ariminum which took sides with the Arians, the Council of Ephesus which sided with Eutychus, the Council at Chalcedon which wished to confer on Pope Leo the honour of "universal Bishop" and which he himself spurned, and the Synod of Constance which "agreed that a defective form of the sacrament of the Eucharist should be administered to the laity." Vermigli added: "And a good many other errors could be brought to public attention, which were introduced by the Councils." Vermigli offered a summary reflection that applied generally to the use of human traditions, including the Fathers and Councils and early church. "Everything should be immediately referred to the testing of the Scriptures . . . For as the Word of God is trust-

---

[72] Vermigli, "Praefatio," 4r: ". . . consensum authoritatemque constantem ecclesiae catholicae . . ."

[73] Vermigli, "Praefatio," 4r: ". . . authoritas ecclesiae movisset, verum significanter scriptit, commovisset."

worthy and abides forever, so the beliefs of men are uncertain and are always untrustworthy."[74]

Having offered these many qualifications and warnings about the Fathers and Councils, Vermigli concluded the section in moderate tones:

> These comments should not be interpreted as though we do not want pious brothers in holy assemblies to be heeded patiently, or would not wish in any way to elevate the authority of the Fathers and Councils. We do not bring forward these things in this spirit. We would grant to everyone the honour due to them, but it is right that that which belongs to the one true God should not be ascribed to men.[75]

In the end, what kind of a role do the Councils and Fathers and early Church play for Vermigli? It is somewhat surprising that in this methodological statement on Biblical interpretation found in the Preface, Vermigli had so little positive to say about the general value of the Fathers. Having clearly established theology's subject matter as the Bible, one might think the Fathers would figure prominently as a check upon private interpretation of the Bible. But no. Vermigli noted Augustine's recommendation that Bible readers "compare passages of Scripture among themselves, and *not* investigate the ideas of the Fathers." When Vermigli did introduce the "consensus of the Catholic church" as a resource, it was clearly in a subsidiary role.

But what exactly was this subsidiary role of the Fathers in Vermigli? Were the Fathers equal dialogue partners or inferior partners or in some sense superior? The answer would seem to be, with some exceptions, inferior partners. Four lines of evidence support this conclusion. *First,* Vermigli's explicit statements and implicit practice suggest a certain redundancy in the role of Patristic citations. Their place in Vermigli's theology was often to provide illustration for what Vermigli had already found in his own reading of Scripture. This redundancy is also suggested by the fact that when his reading of

---

[74] Vermigli, "Praefatio," 4v: ". . . omnia sine cunctatione ad scripturarum examen . . . Ut enim verbum dei solidum est, et aeternum manet, sic hominum placita incerta sunt, et perpetuo vacillant."

[75] Vermigli, "Praefatio," 4v–5r: "Nec ista eo trahenda sunt, quasi non velimus pios fraters in sacris conventibus patienter audiri, aut quaramus authoritatem patrum et conciliorum omnino elevare. Non hoc animo ista proferimus. Cuique suum honorem saluium expimus modo non tribuntia hominibus, quod unius dei esse convenit . . ."

Scripture found no precedent in the Fathers, it seemed to cause him little concern. For example, in his discussion of the *locus* of justification at the end of his commentary on I Corinthians, chapter one, one finds no Patristic references at all. He replied to Catholic critics, who cited the Fathers to oppose justification by faith, by simply observing, "the holy Fathers, in order to encourage people to righteous living, attributed many things to works and virtually justification, salvation and eternal life."

Secondly, while acknowledging the Fathers as his Christian brothers, Vermigli could make global, unqualified statements of condemnation of their thinking on certain issues. He could write that, "The excessive speech of the Fathers . . . wonderfully obscured the Sacraments . . . [They] leave no divine thing not attributed to this sacrament, by which they impudently take a step into horrible idolatry."[76] This language suggests that on some issues Vermigli thought that many of the Fathers simply taught error—were inferior dialogue partners. However, Vermigli identified a favoured few figures from whom he regularly culled passages with which he agreed. McLelland pointed to this somewhat self-serving use of the Fathers when he observed "the profound reliance of Martyr upon Augustine's works, and in particular certain passages which are foundational for his sacramental teaching . . . the sacrament as *verbum visibilis*, the necessity of abiding in Christ to eat His Body, etc."[77]

Thirdly, Vermigli's discussion of the role of the Fathers was often polemical, part of a strategy to refute those who would exalt the church's authority over that of Scripture.

Finally, in the texts examined for this paper, one does *not* find in Vermigli the language that one finds in Erasmus, of honouring the Fathers as superior dialogue partners because they were closer to the Biblical age and language, and so can be relied upon to provide useful guidance in approaching Scripture. Nor does one find a sense that the Early Church of the first five centuries represents some kind of standard for later Christian practice and thought.

Here are the preliminary answers to the two key questions posed at the beginning of our study. The study offers a modest proposal in favour of Vermigli as a selective, polemical reader of the Fathers,

---

[76] VWG, 284.
[77] VWG, 267–269.

with Vermigli as the superior dialogue partner. The early church and creeds do not represent a court of appeal. These features in Vermigli's perspective will be compared first, to his own later thinking on the Fathers, then to Philip Melanchthon's views.

2. Comparing the "Preface" with Vermigli's Views on Tradition and the Fathers as found in Schism and the True Church *(1562)*

Comparison of the Preface with Vermigli's later writing on *Schism and the True Church* makes clear that Vermigli continued to use the same store of "stock arguments" to establish the limits of Church authority and tradition when debating the subject with Catholic controversialists. In fact, one can find six identical arguments and references to Fathers and Councils that duplicate the arguments found in the Preface.

First, there is a similar listing of erring Fathers, Synods and Councils, including Cyprian, Nicea, Ephesus, Chalcedon and Ariminum, with the same failings specifically attributed to each.[78] *Secondly*, there is a similar discussion of Augustine's statement, "I would not believe the Gospel if the authority of the Church had not helped to move me." Vermigli again clarified the meaning of the Latin terms, and insisted, "the Church is not the whole cause of our faith . . ."[79] *Thirdly*, Vermigli made the same reference to Augustine's *On Christian Doctrine* and its advice to interpret unclear passages of Scripture in light of clear passages, not to turn to popes or Fathers.[80] *Fourthly*, Augustine was once again the most cited Father by far on disputed matters. *Fifthly*, one finds the same reference to Constantine's advice at the Nicene Council, calling upon the assembled Fathers to settle their differences by appeal to the prophetic and apostolic Scriptures, not by appeal to the superior authority of the church itself.[81] *Finally*, the notion was expressed

---

[78] Martyr *I. Librum Regum*, chap. 12 of *Melachim id est, Regum Libri Duo posteriores cum Commentariis, Petri Martyris Vermilii*, fol. 103r. Vermigli, "Schism and the True Church," in EW, 180 f., 187.

[79] Martyr *I. Librum Regum*, chap. 12 of *Melachim id est, Regum Libri Duo posteriores cum Commentariis, Petri Martyris Vermilii*, fol. 103r. "Schism and the True Church," 182.

[80] Martyr *I. Librum Regum*, chap. 12 of *Melachim id est, Regum Libri Duo posteriores cum Commentariis, Petri Martyris Vermilii*, fol. 103v. "Schism and the True Church," 185.

[81] Martyr *I. Librum Regum*, chap. 12 of *Melachim id est, Regum Libri Duo posteriores*

of "more reputable" synods and Fathers.[82] This use of "stock arguments" tends to confirm the impression, noted above, that both in
1551 and in 1562 Vermigli's use of the Fathers was largely polemical.

When Vermigli introduced the consensus of the Catholic church
as a resource, it was clearly in a subsidiary role. But what exactly
was this subsidiary role of the Fathers in Vermigli? Were the Fathers
equal dialogue partners or inferior partners or in some sense superior? The answer would seem to be, with some exceptions, "inferior
partners" who served to substantiate Vermigli's own points and
insights. Vermigli often relied on certain stock arguments on the limits of tradition that he used repeatedly. These included examples of
certain errors made by the Fathers and Councils, and appeals for
support in Augustine in challenging the idea that the Church was
always a reliable interpreter and judge of Scripture.

IV. *Vermigli's Views Compared to Melanchthon's Views on the Authority of
Tradition as seen in "The Church and the Authority of the Word" (1539)*

Scholarly attention has been drawn to the common rhetorical methods of Melanchthon and Vermigli as part of a common "Protestant
culture" and academic path. Vermigli followed the example of
Melanchthon in his methodical presentation in exegesis and teaching. Melanchthon's *Loci Communes* serve "as an essential point of
comparison for an understanding of the development and the reor-
ganization . . . of Vermigli's theological doctrine."[83] Comparison of
Vermigli's views on the Fathers with Melanchthon should illumine
how close Vermigli's polemical discussion of the Fathers was to that
of the influential Melanchthon.

In 1539 Melanchthon composed a treatise entitled, *De Ecclesia et
de Autoritate Verbi Dei (Concerning the Church and the Authority of the Word)*.
The work was devoted to reflecting on the authority of the church

---

cum Commentariis, Petri Martyris Vermilii, fol. 103v. "Schism and the True Church,"
185.
    [82] Martyr *I. Librum Regum*, chap. 12 of *Melachim id est, Regum Libri Duo posteriores
cum Commentariis, Petri Martyris Vermilii*, fol. 103r. "Schism and the True Church,"
183.
    [83] Cesare Vasoli, "*Loci Communes* and the Rhetorical and Dialectical Traditions,"
PMIR, 18 f., 26.

past and present in relation to biblical authority, a concern closely
related to Vermigli's purpose in his Preface. On the one hand
Melanchthon addressed "more moderate" Catholics who reproached
the Reformers for introducing novel doctrines, and for forsaking the
traditions taught by the authority of the Church and Fathers.[84]
Melanchthon likely composed the work in preparation for the anticipated national colloquy at Nürnberg to begin on 1 August 1539
where he expected to discuss the issue of tradition with moderate
Erasmian humanists.[85] On the other hand, Melanchthon was also
mindful of "some rather impudent characters," such as Servetus, who
"reject the unanimity of the true church and all of the synods without discrimination."[86] In both cases, Melanchthon was concerned to
defend Protestant understandings of Scripture in a way consistent
with the wisdom of the early Church. Melanchthon's work discussed
what the church is, what authority it possesses, and how its testimonies should be used.

For Melanchthon the Church was the assembly of true believers
which possess the gospel and sacraments and "who are being sanctified
by the Holy Spirit."[87] As Vermigli would later do, Melanchthon
emphasized that even the true Church was only comprised of humans,
and so could err. Melanchthon moved chronologically through some
of the great Fathers and synods of antiquity, frankly condemning
them where they were unscriptural. Much of the treatise consisted
of his "Catalogus" of the errors of ancient synods, writers and of

---

[84] "De Ecclesia et de Autoritate Verbi Dei Philippo Melanthone Auctore," in
H. E. Bindseil, ed., *Corpus Reformatorum*, vol. 23 (Halis Saxonum: C. A. Schwetscke
et Filium, 1855), col. 634. "Haec respondi moderatioribus, qui autoritatem Ecclesiae
aut Patrum nobis opponunt." James R. Payton has argued that one of Melanchthon's
goals for his *De ecclesia et autoritate verbi Dei* was "to divide the moderates . . . from
papal subservience and thus open them up to serious discussion for the reform and
reunion of the Church." See James R. Payton, Jr., "*Sola Scriptura* and Church History:
The Views of Martin Bucer and Melanchthon on Religious Authority in 1539"
(Ph.D. diss., University of Waterloo, 1982), 129.

[85] James R. Payton, "*Sola Scriptura* and Church History," 108–110, 130 f.

[86] "De Ecclesia et de Autoritate Verbi Dei Philippo Melanthone Auctore," col.
595. "Rursus etiam quaedam petulantiora ingenia, cum fingunt ex dictis scripturae
male detortis novas opiniones, prorsus aspernantur consensum verae Ecclesiae et
omnes Synodos sine discrimine . . ."

[87] "De Ecclesia et de Autoritate Verbi Dei Philippo Melanthone Auctore," col.
597. "Sed voco Ecclesiam, coetum vere credentium, qui habent Evangelium et
Sacramenta, et sanctificantur Spiritu sancto, sicut Ephes. 5 describitur Ecclesia, et
Iohan. 10."

the wickedness of many bishops.[88] Many of these were the same as those later noted by Vermigli, such as the unwise canons of penance added by the Council of Nicea, the human traditions introduced at Chalcedon that prohibited the marriage of monks and virgins, and many others.[89] Melanchthon also noted the errors of the Fathers, including Origen's misuse of Paul, Tertullian's condemnation of second marriages, Cyprian's call for rebaptism of heretics, and Gregory's approval of the sacrament for the dead.[90]

> I have wished only to enumerate these errors to show that they are mistaken who admire the fathers as though they have never erred and as if they nowhere disagree with divine Scriptures. Therefore, although the more enlightened fathers do at times admonish us in some matter, yet we must judge them in accordance with the Word of God.[91]

Melanchthon had harsh words for the Bishops and synods of Pontiffs as contemporary authorities within the Church.

> They are not bishops or members of the church, but the enemies of Christ who are being driven on by violent passions. They do not think about the harmony and peace of the church, but about strengthening the cause of tyranny.[92]

Melanchthon concluded that, "We should not so admire antiquity that we free it from all vices."[93]

For Melanchthon the Word of God was the only sure authority and rule of doctrine; the Church should only be heeded when it was faithful to Scripture. The Church must be judged "according to

---

[88] "De Ecclesia et de Autoritate Verbi Dei Philippo Melanthone Auctore," col. 604–640

[89] "De Ecclesia et de Autoritate Verbi Dei Philippo Melanthone Auctore," col. 605, 606, 607.

[90] "De Ecclesia et de Autoritate Verbi Dei Philippo Melanthone Auctore," col. 610, 611, 613, 614, 628.

[91] "De Ecclesia et de Autoritate Verbi Dei Philippo Melanthone Auctore," col. 629. " . . . tantum recensere errata volui, ut appareat falli eos, qui sic admirantur Patres, tanquam fuerint [anamartetoi], et nusquam dissentiant a scripturis divinis manifestis. Etsi igitur aliquid monent interdum eruditiores Patres, tamen de eis iudicandum est ex verbo Dei."

[92] "De Ecclesia et de Autoritate Verbi Dei Philippo Melanthone Auctore," col. 640. "Non sunt Episcopi, non sunt Ecclesiae membra, sed hostes Christi, qui cum furiis agitentur, non de Ecclesiae concordia et pace cogitant, sed de Tyrannide stabilienda."

[93] "De Ecclesia et de Autoritate Verbi Dei Philippo Melanthone Auctore," col. 609. "Hoc exemplum monet, ne ita miremur antiquitatem, ut eam omnibus vitiis liberemus."

the Word of God which abides always as the rule of doctrine."[94] He gave a subsidiary authority to those Fathers who were "more skillful in spiritual matters." "I do not appeal to all the authors but only to the better ones like Ambrose, Augustine, and others insofar as they agree with them." These figures deserved great honour, "even the highest praise."[95] Likewise, "devout synods" were well deserving if they preserved articles of Christian teaching.[96]

> The synods of the Church are to be heard. But let judgment be used, and when they yield us things that are true, let us believe them because of the Word of God. For example, the Synod of Nicea piously and usefully taught and admonished all posterity about the Son of God, but we believe the article, not because of the synod but because we see it has been so transmitted in the Word of God . . . We must look around to see . . . which assembly of the Fathers and of the synods is purer . . . The Fathers who have fought in the most bitter controversies and have retained pious dogmas are well-deserving of posterity.[97]

Melanchthon spoke forcefully about the value and use of the Creeds and "better Councils" and the consensus of the true Church. On the doctrines of the Trinity, the natures of Christ, infant Baptism, the Lord's Supper, ordination of ministers, marriage of ministers, the use of adiaphora, the repentance of the fallen, he wrote that "they confirm our position by their testimony."[98] Melanchthon insisted that

---

[94] "De Ecclesia et de Autoritate Verbi Dei Philippo Melanthone Auctore," col. 604. "Sed addendum est, ut auditi iudicentur ex verbo Dei, quod semper manet Regula doctrinae."

[95] "De Ecclesia et de Autoritate Verbi Dei Philippo Melanthone Auctore," col. 633, 634. "Non provoco ad omnes Scriptores, sed ad meliores, Ambrosium, Augustinum, et quatenus alii cum his consentiant, qui cum ipsi interdum pugnanti dixerint, veniam nobis dabunt, si quaedam reprehendemus, modo ut manifestam et certam scripturae divinae sententiam sequamur."

[96] "De Ecclesia et de Autoritate Verbi Dei Philippo Melanthone Auctore," col. 609. " . . . et tamen fatendum est, pias Synodos bene meritas esse, quia aliquos doctrinae Christianae articulos conservaverunt, et de his prodest tenere Synodorum et antiquitatis testimonium."

[97] "De Ecclesia et de Autoritate Verbi Dei Philippo Melanthone Auctore," col. 604, 605. "Audiendas esse Ecclesiae Synodos, quae, cum de verbo Dei disputant, docent et monent nos, sed iudicium accedat, et cum vera tradunt, credamus propter verbum Dei, ut Nicena Synodus pie et utiliter docuit, et admonuit omnem posteritatem de Filio Dei, Sed Articulum credimus non propter Synodum, sed quia videmus sic traditum esse in verbo Dei."

[98] "De Ecclesia et de Autoritate Verbi Dei Philippo Melanthone Auctore," col. 610. "Confirmant enim nos suo testimonio, De Trinitate, De naturis in Christo, De baptismo infantum, De usu coenae Domini, De ordinatione ministrorum, De coniugio ministrorum, De usu indifferentium, De poenitentia lapsorum."

it was his Catholic opponents who had forsaken the true Church with their errant teaching; it was the Reformers whose teaching expressed "the very consensus of the catholic church of Christ, as indicated by the confessions, the saner synods and more learned Fathers."[99]

Melanchthon clearly provides a precedent for the notion in Vermigli of "purer" Fathers and Councils, and for the undisputed priority assigned to St. Augustine. Among other commonalities between Melanchthon and Vermigli, one observes that for both scholars the Bible served as the highest authority, and was employed to determine the "purer" Fathers and Councils. Both men provided a similar catalog of errors committed by the ancients. Both Melanchthon and Vermigli made selective use of the Fathers to "confirm" their position by their testimony. These subsidiary authorities possessed a kind of "polemical authority," nothing more. Both Melanchthon and Vermigli had harsh words for the Bishops as contemporary authorities within the Church. We conclude that Vermigli's views closely reflect arguments found in Melanchthon's 1539 *De Ecclesia et Autoritate Verbi Dei*, and that they point to Vermigli's indebtedness to Melanchthon. We know that the works of Luther, Melanchthon, Oecolampadius, Zwingli and Bucer made their way to Italy in the 1520s and 1530s, and spread throughout the Italian peninsula.[100] They would have been available to Vermigli even before he traveled to England.

V. *Conclusion*

Without denying Vermigli's wide reading in the Fathers, is it entirely appropriate to say, "Peter Martyr's theology is Patristic in a profound sense"? This paper suggests that when the *quantitative* evidence for Vermigli's appreciative Patristic reading and use of citations is interpreted in light of Vermigli's explicit guiding principles in making use of the Fathers, a different picture emerges. Like Melanchthon,

---

[99] "De Ecclesia et de Autoritate Verbi Dei Philippo Melanthone Auctore," col. 634. "Nihil enim dubium est, hoc doctrinae genus, quod profitemur, vere esse ipsum consensum Catholicae Ecclesiae Christi, ut ostendunt Symbola, saniores Synodi, et eruditiores Patres."

[100] PPRED, 192 f. "On the whole, during the 1520s and 1530s, the works of northern reformers entered Italy with relative impunity." Venice served as the major printing and distribution center.

Vermigli relied on the Fathers primarily to make his own points; the Fathers were unequal partners in the hermeneutical discussion. Vermigli, too, had his ready store of stock phrases and examples from which he drew in writings separated by a span of over ten years.

PATRIARCHY AND PROPHETESSES: TRADITION AND INNOVATION IN VERMIGLI'S DOCTRINE OF WOMAN

John L. Thompson

Introduction

"For the most part, things which are done by women are usually credited to men."[1] So remarked Peter Martyr Vermigli in 1554, describing a well-known scene in the book of Judges, chapter four. There, the approach of Barak and his troops is reported to Sisera, the Canaanite commander, but without any mention of the battlefield presence of Deborah, the prophetess and judge—"not that pagans would have had any regard for Deborah's prophetic gift!" For Sisera, the oversight was costly and mortal. For Vermigli, however, lecturing in Strasbourg shortly after his eviction from Oxford by England's new Catholic queen, these calm observations betoken not only his keen regard for Deborah's gifts and leadership but also his nuanced appreciation for the difficulties faced by any woman called forth to public office.

Not that public office was commonly the lot of any woman, of course. Peter Martyr was very much at home among the Protestant writers of the sixteenth century, espousing mostly the traditional patriarchal values of the day. Indeed, in his earlier studies of Vermigli's teachings on marriage and related issues, John Patrick Donnelly has characterized him as "a theologian consciously working within an already established tradition" and hence as one whose influence was thoroughly diffused with that of his Reformed contemporaries, including Calvin, Beza, Viret, and Bullinger.[2] Nonetheless, however much he swam in the Protestant mainstream, Vermigli was also capable

---

[1] Vermigli, *Comm. Jud.* 4:11 (70r; ET 98r); the 1564 English translation, *Most fruitfull & learned Commentaries* . . . (London: John Day, [1564]) will be cited simply as ET. For the date of these lectures, see PMRE, 175–77, 383, 395.

[2] John Patrick Donnelly, "The Social and Ethical Thought of Peter Martyr Vermigli," PMIR, 118–19; see also idem, "Marriage from Renaissance to Reformation: Two Florentine Moralists," *Studies in Medieval Culture* 9 (1977): 161–71.

of serious and original reflection on gender issues as they arose from
his exegesis and also as they confronted him in the events and issues
of the day. Vermigli's thought may be summarized under three head-
ings, moving roughly from theory to practice. In the first place, drawing largely on Vermigli's early lectures on Genesis and his 1551
commentary on 1 Corinthians, we will examine what he had to say
about women and men as they were designed by their creator, and
how that design has been complicated or obscured by sin. Next,
drawing mostly on these exegetical writings and various common
places, we will consider his account of what might be called woman's
place—the usual and private role he envisioned for Christian women
in the domestic sphere. Last, and perhaps the best test case for
Vermigli's theology and exegesis, we will see how he interacted with
women who stepped out of their private roles to exert leadership in
the public forum, both in biblical history and in the sixteenth century.

Women and Men in Creation and the Fall

For biblical expositors of the sixteenth century, it would have been
impossible—and irresponsible—to read the Old or New Testament,
and particularly the weighty first three chapters of Genesis, without
taking account of the traditional glosses and questions that had accu-
mulated over the centuries. Many of these questions have been forgotten by modern commentators. Of perennial interest, however, and
often seen as crucial for understanding the nature of men and women,
is the question of what it means to bear the image of God. Like
most of his sixteenth-century colleagues, Vermigli knew both the traditional view of Augustine that the divine image lay in various trinitarian resemblances to be found in men and women (such as our
threefold faculties of memory/intellect/will), and also the medieval
predilection for expounding *imago* and *similitudo* disjunctively, as constituting a rational or essential image of God that is distinguishable
from the moral likeness and properties that sin displaces. Like most
Protestant interpreters, however, he tended to discount both views.
Augustine erred by locating the divine image in the bare faculties,
as if it could be possessed without regard to one's virtue or vice.[3]

---

[3] LC 2.1.14 (130; CP II, 223). All references to LC cite the 1583 Vautrollerius
pagination.

And, as a competent Hebraist, Vermigli knew that "image and like-ness" in Gen. 1:27 is a parallelism, describing not two things but the whole entity.[4]

At the same time, Vermigli liked much of what these traditional views were trying to say. His recognition of the synonymity of image and likeness in 1:27 actually follows a page-long discussion in which he plainly enjoyed building on the distinction, including an exposition of how Christ is himself God's image according to his divinity and God's likeness according to his humanity. Human beings, on the other hand, image God when they know God aright and are disposed to obey him, while the divine likeness or similitude consists more in their godly activities, characterized here as the exercise of dominion. Also, while Augustine's trinitarian distinction may not have adequately defined the image of God, it delineates the basis of the image: only because we have such faculties can we know God aright and bear dominion over creation.[5]

In all respects save one, then, Vermigli conforms to the Protestant pattern. Like his colleagues, he avoids defining the image of God in terms of an abstract human faculty and focuses instead on the relationship with God that such a faculty was designed to facilitate. The image of God thus consists largely in the righteousness that our first parents possessed and lost—a righteousness that has been re-imprinted on the "new man" by Jesus Christ, "who is the very image of God." Where Vermigli differs at least marginally from many other Protestants, however, is in the prominence he gives to dominion as a manifestation of the image of God—a reading advocated long before by John Chrysostom, but largely downplayed by almost all of his successors, who prefer to leave aside dominion as at best an effect of the image of God or as a sort of "secondary" definition.[6]

The prominence of dominion in Vermigli's general definition becomes even more determinative when he considers the most problematic of all the biblical references to the image of God—1 Cor. 11:7, where Paul writes that "a man ought not to cover his head, since he is the image and glory of God; but woman is the glory of

---

[4] *Comm. Gen.* 1:27 (7v).

[5] *Comm. Gen.* 1:26 (7r–v); *Comm. 1 Cor.* 11:7 (286r).

[6] Of Vermigli's Protestant contemporaries, only Wolfgang Musculus has a stronger advocacy of dominion in his commentary on this verse; see *In Mosis Genesim . . . Commentarii* (Basel: Johann Herwagen, 1554), 41–42.

man." Here is a truly cryptic statement. When the apostle describes woman as (only?) the glory of man, his truncated parallelism seems to deny that woman is the image or glory of God. Among patristic commentators, some were bold enough to fill in the awkward silence by arguing that women are not, in fact, made in the divine image; others worked hard to affirm that, somehow, women do bear the image of God.[7] The usual sixteenth-century solution almost always falls back on that "secondary" definition of which Vermigli was so fond. While righteousness is truly a quality with which both men and women may be graced and thereby image God, dominion naturally pertains more to men than to women. Vermigli thus resolves the scandal of the Pauline text by linking the woman's limited dominion to her limited role as a bearer of the divine image. Compared with lower creatures, woman is the image of God, for she has dominion over them. Compared with man, she is not said to be the image of God, "because she has no dominion over him but rather obeys him."[8]

Vermigli's patriarchal resolution of the problem of women as the image of God reliably forecasts other exegetical and theological moves that bear on the nature of women as created. Many of his views emerge in the course of addressing traditional exegetical questions, of which we may note four. First, when was the woman created? The question is occasioned by the discrepancy between Gen. 1:27, where the first man and woman seem created simultaneously, and 2:18, where the woman is created after the man as a helper for him. Vermigli harmonizes the chronology by asserting that the first account was written as an "anticipation" of the woman's actual formation in Genesis 2, prior to which time she existed "virtually" in him.[9] There are several implications of the woman's later arrival, the most momen-

---

[7] The two extremes are represented, respectively, by Ambrosiaster and Augustine. For further discussion, see John Lee Thompson, *John Calvin and the Daughters of Sarah: Women in Regular and Exceptional Roles in the Exegesis of Calvin, His Predecessors, and His Contemporaries* (Geneva: Librairie Droz, 1992), chapter two.

[8] *Comm. 1 Cor.* 11:7 (286r): "Dicimus: Si eam cum caeteris creaturis contuleris imago dei est, nam illis dominatur, & earum usum habet. Sed hic oportet ut eam compares uiro, & tunc imago dei non dicitur, quia uiro non dominatur sed potius ei paret." See also *Comm. Gen.* 1:26 (7r).

[9] *Comm. Gen.* 1:27 (7v): "virtute itaque & mulier quodammodo in eo fuit." He goes on to repudiate "the fables of the Jews" that imitate Plato by positing a "primal androgyne."

tous of which is that the prohibition against eating of the tree of the knowledge of good and evil was given to Adam in Gen. 2:16–17, apparently *before* his wife existed. For Vermigli, the lesson is plain: "women should be instructed in divine things by a man."[10] Still, such a lesson could be carried too far. Vermigli knows that God sometimes gives men wise counsel through women, and he is surprisingly unconvinced by the argument for male dominion that looks to the order of the creation of men and women, even when it carries an apostolic warrant. When Paul argued for male headship in 1 Cor. 11:8 by alluding to Genesis 2, that "man was not made from woman, but woman from man," Vermigli judged the argument from sequence to be "not strong enough in itself," which is why the next verse adds another argument, one from the purpose of woman's creation.[11]

A second traditional question addressed to the woman's creation in Genesis 2 pertains to the form of her creation. Why did God form her from the side of Adam? Peter Lombard is often credited with the commonplace that woman was not created from man's head, lest she be his ruler, nor from his feet, lest she be his slave, but from his side, so that she might be his companion.[12] Vermigli draws a similar moral. Woman's formation from the side of the man was to foster love and charity, he says, and men should exercise a dominion over their wives that is tactful and gentle (*politicum & mite*) rather than marked by power (*robustum*).[13] Clearly, Vermigli sees himself on a middle path of sorts, mixing male headship with compassion. To that end he rejects as unworthy the rabbinic notion that Adam was created first and alone so as to avoid contention, insisting instead that the woman was given to be cherished by the man; yet he can also invoke a Hebrew numerological argument whereby the name that Adam bestowed on the woman—*isha*—signals her

---

[10] *Comm. Gen.* 2:18 (11v). The point is one of Vermigli's "probable" (!) propositions for debate; see 4.P.6 on Genesis 2, EW, 96 (LC, 1002; CP supp., 145).

[11] *Comm. 1 Cor.* 11:8–10 (287r). In the *querelle des femmes*, woman's later creation was sometimes taken to prove her superiority, as in Agrippa von Nettesheim's "Declamatio de nobilitate et praecellentia foeminei sexus" of 1509/1529 (*Opera* [reprint ed.; Hildesheim: Georg Olms, 1970], II, 506–7). The passage has been translated by Albert Rabil, Jr., in *Declamation on the Nobility and Preeminence of the Female Sex* (Chicago: University of Chicago Press, 1996), 48.

[12] The apothegm appears twice in Lombard, in 2 *Sent.* 18.2 and 4 *Sent.* 28.4, but there are earlier parallels.

[13] *Comm. Gen.* 2:21 (12r).

imperfection.[14] Lest the point be missed, Vermigli would later take Chrysostom explicitly to task for asserting the equality of men and women in unfallen paradise. On the contrary, Vermigli demanded, one of the lessons of the woman's status as man's "helper" (*adiutorium*) is that even in the state of natural integrity, she was less perfect than the man and was to be ruled by him even then.[15]

If we turn now from the second chapter of Genesis to its sequel and from the woman's creation to her fall, a third question may be posed. Who sinned more, the man or the woman? The question is less a contest over Genesis 3 than a referendum on an altogether different text, 1 Tim. 2:14, which enjoins women's silence and submissiveness on the grounds that "Adam was not deceived, but the woman was deceived and became a transgressor." Once again, the argument from silence is weighty and awkward, for the verse could be taken to imply not only that Adam was not deceived, but also that he did not become a transgressor. However, virtually no one ever read the verse with such wooden literalism, for there are other scripture texts that blame Adam, as in Romans 5. So the usual procedure is to add some sort of gloss, as Vermigli does: Adam was not deceived, at least not by external persuasion of the sort that misled his wife, but he certainly did commit a deadly transgression of his own.[16] But whose was the worse transgression? The spectrum of opinion was nicely mapped between Ambrose, who took 1 Tim. 2:14 as evincing the woman's greater *liability* to sin, and Augustine, who thought that the man's greater intellect made him more *responsible*. Writing in rebuttal of Lombard, who argued for the greater culpability of the woman, Vermigli prefers to say that the man's sin was more grievous, as was his punishment, owing to his "perfection and excellence." The conclusion, of course, is double-edged: the woman is partly exonerated, but only as an adjunct of her inferiority. Still, he concedes, the punishments of Adam and Eve may well have been equivalent, and even if they were not, the circumstances remain complex and not easily compared.[17]

---

[14] *Comm. Gen.* 2:23–24 (12).
[15] *Comm. 1 Cor.* 11:3 (283r); translated in CP 2.8.4 (II, 379).
[16] *Comm. Gen.* 3:6 (14r–v).
[17] LC 2.11.31 (325–26), CP 2.11.34 (II, 493). Vermigli's consideration of whether Adam or Eve sinned more is actually a subsection of a much longer section on who sins more in adultery, to be considered below.

A fourth and final question of these narratives will serve nicely also to summarize Vermigli's understanding of the nature of women and of the relationship between the sexes. What were the effects of the Fall and the ensuing "curse"? In Gen. 3:16, two punishments are imposed on Eve and on all women: pain in childbirth and subjection to the rule of one's husband. Vermigli does his best to interpret this punishment persuasively, arguing that the penalty of birth pain is really a *lex talionis* (that is, Eve was tempted by her belly in desiring fruit, and so she is punished by her belly or womb) and urging both men and women to perceive that these "punishments" are also salutary: they are remedies, bridles against sin, laws for living well, healthful counsels, and declarations of duty.[18] Nonetheless, Vermigli stands with the majority of Protestant commentators in insisting that the subjection imposed on women by the Fall was not a loss of equality but an intensification or worsening of a prevailing condition. "The plan for the relationship of male and female was instituted by God so that the man ought to preside over the woman, but with a gentle hand (*placido regimine*). But when she sinned, the man was obliged to treat her more severely, so that one might say he came to dominate her."[19] Stark as that may sound, Vermigli would prefer to leave his readers pondering something else, namely, the salutary dimension of these punishments, as mentioned above. Indeed, there is a further amelioration for Christian women and men, for while the whole of the curse remains to be borne by the impious, Christ has lightened these punishments for the faithful, and at his second coming he will take them away altogether.[20]

Almost nothing in Vermigli's exposition and understanding of man, woman, or the relationship between them before and after the Fall departs from the prevailing norms established by patristic and medieval theologians. Woman was created and divinely designed to be helper to the man, and while sin damaged that relationship, some of the original order has been restored by Christ so that Christian women

---

[18] *Comm. Gen.* 3:16 (16v, 17r); see also Proposition 6.N.4 on Genesis 3–4, EW, 98 (LC, 1002; CP supp., 145).

[19] *Comm. Gen.* 3:16 (17r): "ita erat instituta ratio coniunctionis maris & foeminae a Deo, vt vir mulieri debuerit praeesse, sed placido regimine, cum vero lapsa est, debet vir in illam seuerius agere, ita vt dicatur illi dominari." Similar phrasing is used in *Comm. 1 Cor.* 11:3 (283r); translated in CP 2.8.4 (II, 379).

[20] *Comm. Gen.* 3:19 (17v); see also Proposition 6.N.7 Genesis 3–4, EW, 98 (LC, 1003; CP supp., 146).

and men are able to regain some of what was intended from the beginning. In the following sections, however, we will see how Vermigli contended for some distinctively Protestant viewpoints and added stronger personal marks as well.

Women in Private: Marriage, Family, and Everyday Life

Peter Martyr Vermigli was an Augustinian canon for a quarter of a century and intimately familiar with celibacy and the monastic life. However, after his conversion to Protestantism and flight to Zurich, then Strasbourg, he married Catherine Dampmartin, evidently a former nun from Metz, who accompanied him to Oxford. There, after eight childless years of marriage, she left him a widower. And although he once opined that he would not marry again, in his sixtieth year he did just that.[21] Back in Zurich, following his flight from Mary Tudor and his subsequent happy departure from the uncongenial Lutherans of Strasbourg, he married Catherina Merenda, an Italian refugee living in Geneva. She bore him a son and a daughter, both of whom died in infancy, and was pregnant with a daughter when Vermigli died in 1562. In short, Vermigli lived to experience firsthand not only consecrated celibacy as a Catholic, but also all the Protestant variations as single, married, a widower, then married again. And if he lacked direct experience of raising children of his own, he surely had some vicarious exposure through the person of his household servant of two decades, Julius Santerenziano, whose wife apparently bore a son named, or nicknamed, "little Martyr."[22]

Unfortunately, while Vermigli's experience may have been wide-ranging, his literary remains on the subject of marriage and family are less so, and his personal and pastoral disclosures are even more

---

[21] Vermigli to Jan Utenhove (Letter 80, 9 May 1553); translated in George Cornelius Gorham, *Gleanings of a Few Scattered Ears, During the Period of the Reformation in England and of the Times Immediately Succeeding* (London: Bell and Daldy, 1857), 294. Simler's biography says Vermigli remarried out of a desire to have children; see LLS, 45.

[22] On Julius Santerenziano, see PMI, 271–74. The supposition that *Martyrillus* was the son of Julius and his wife Anna was advanced by Gorham (*Gleanings*, 295 note n) and is based on the eponym's appearance in the letters of Vermigli's close friend, John Jewel, from March of 1559.

rare. His letters make regular and congenial references to his wife, passing on her greetings to Vermigli's correspondents, but neither of his wives is especially featured, except briefly when his first wife was ill. His corpus of letters is significant, but not huge, reflecting both his limited years as a Reformer and the niche he filled. As Donnelly writes, "Calvin and Bullinger were pastors directing model churches that found imitators in many countries. Vermigli was a professor with only a minor involvement in direct pastoral work and no responsibility for running the ecclesiastical life of a city."[23] One might add, too, that nearly all Vermigli's teaching and ministry would have had to be conducted in Latin, for there are few signs that he was able to master German, French, or English sufficiently to preach or pastor in these local vernaculars.[24] Finally, it is also the opinion of Donnelly that Vermigli never found the occasion to expound a positive theology of marriage at any length—which is not to say, of course, that he did not have one.[25] Instead, his most pertinent writings on such subjects are all of a polemical nature, arguing against Roman Catholic opponents on matters such as celibacy, marriage, divorce, and vows.

Despite these handicaps, it is possible to utilize various passing remarks and common places in his commentaries to reconstruct how Vermigli's general teachings on marriage (including divorce and adultery) reflect his understanding of the nature and role of women. It should be clear from his exegesis of the creation and fall narratives that he believes categorically in woman's submission to the headship or leadership of the man, and that he writes from his own male perspective. Indeed, he proclaims at 1 Cor. 11:3 that *all* women are subject to *some* man or another—whether daughters to fathers, wives to husbands, or widows to brothers—but men are *in no way* subjected

---

[23] Donnelly, Introduction to LLS, 3.

[24] His ignorance of English and German is implied by Simler, who also calls attention to his limitations in French; see LLS, 34, 45, 50, 52.

[25] Donnelly, "Two Florentine Moralists," 169; "Social and Ethical Thought," PMIR, 116. While one must interpret such apparent silences with great care, it is true that the modern reader will find notable missed opportunities in Vermigli's incidental writings. Roland Bainton, for example, found it ironic that Vermigli could lavish extensive praise upon Bucer for the piety of his household yet spare not a word for the obvious contributions of his wife, Wibrandis Rosenblatt; see *Women of the Reformation in Germany and Italy* (Minneapolis: Augsburg, 1971), 88.

to their wives.[26] "The gospel," he writes, "does not overthrow social order (*politiam*), but rather commends it."[27] What this general policy of women's submission means is not often illustrated by Vermigli in terms of actual cases, and he probably thinks his readers know what he means without being led by the hand. One example, however, can be derived from a letter he wrote on the subject of flight during persecution. There, he stresses that it is normally the duty of a wife to accompany her husband if he should flee from persecution. Here, Vermigli is concerned to preserve not only the wife's submission to her husband's leadership, but also the chastity of each, which a separation would surely put at risk. In a similar fashion, Vermigli presumes that women should stay at home, protecting their reputation and chastity—a point he derives as the moral of various biblical stories, including the unhappy outcome of Dinah's wandering about the countryside and the similar fate of the daughters of Shiloh, who were foolishly dancing when they should have been under closer watch.[28] Like so many of his contemporaries, Vermigli was by no means above the usual stereotypes by which women were typified as weak, or quarrelsome, or impetuous and timid.[29]

Even in this context, however, Vermigli is aware both that men's leadership needs to be tempered, not absolute, and that theories do not always perfectly describe practice. As Aristotle observed, a wife is not to be a servant. Moreover, what rulership the man has is based on his greater virtue and dignity. As stated, that is the theory, but Vermigli is obviously enough of a pastor to know that he must write this in an optative mood: "The man is the head of woman because in virtues and wisdom he ought [*sic*] to excel her—even if this does not always come to be the case."[30] Vermigli goes on to

---

[26] *Comm. 1 Cor.* 11:3 (284v): "Mulieri profitenda est habito suo subiectio erga uirum, quia nunquam mulieres liberae sunt a uiris.... Sed uir nullo pacto uxori subiicitur."

[27] *Comm. 1 Cor.* 11:3 (282r). Vermigli amplifies the point a few pages later (283v): "God bestows many things on women by the hands and works of men, on account of their status and natural dignity. But if it sometimes happens otherwise, so that men should be instructed for the better or receive any of God's gifts by means of women, it happens but rarely and does not prejudice the order established by God."

[28] *Comm. Gen.* 34:1 (139v), *Comm. Jud.* 21:20–23 (205v, 208r; ET 285v, 288r).

[29] These stereotypes commonly emerge from his comments on the actions of various biblical women, such as Sarah and Hagar. One should note, however, that Vermigli is equally capable of transcending his stereotypes to find truly heroic deeds and piety in these same women. Hagar is a case in point, as is Rebecca, below.

[30] *Comm. 1 Cor.* 11:3 (283r): "Vnde liquet uirum caput esse uxoris, quod uir-

plead for patience in husband-wife relations, not violence or tyranny—
not so that men fail to reform and constrain their offending wives,
but so that it be done with charity.[31]

Having argued for this basic submission of women to men as manifested in the restriction of women's activities to the home, to the
private sphere, under the protection and supervision of men, there
remains a collateral case to make for women's equality both in the
spiritual and in the domestic realm. In his own way, Vermigli
embraced the doctrine of the priesthood of all believers, male and
female. Women were expected to learn Christian doctrine from both
pastors and husbands; they might teach other women, privately; and
they should be active in prayer and service.[32] Vermigli's first wife,
Catherine Dampmartin, seems to have modeled most of these traits:
Simler commemorated her as a "mother to the poor" in Oxford,
and Thomas Harding recalled her regular presence among the small
company who enjoyed Vermigli's private sermons in Italian, delivered at home during those Oxford years.[33] But Vermigli's argument
for the spiritual equality of women arises in other contexts, too. In
his comparison of New Testament baptism to the rite of circumcision in the Old Testament, Vermigli considers another traditional
exegetical question, namely, why only men were circumcised and
not women, even though women were certainly included in the
Abrahamic covenant. His solution is indirect but revealing, for he
argues that this is precisely what makes baptism a better sacrament
than circumcision, that in baptism the covenant sign is applied equally
to men and women, just as is the covenant itself.[34]

---

tutibus & sapientia debeat ei antecellere. Idque etsi non semper usu ueniat, tamen
ratio exigit ut frequentißime sic habeat."

[31] *Comm. 1 Cor.* 11:3 (283r–v): "caput in membra tyrannidem non exercet: ita
inter uirum & uxorem uiolentia non deberet opus esse. Quod non idcirco dixerim,
quasi uiri non teneantur peccantes uxores emendare & coercere. Nam Christus
ecclesiam suam interdum & castigat & uerberat, sed hoc ut melior fiat: ita uiri si
uxores interdum corripiant aut castigent, id oportet ut eadem charitate faciant, qua
Christus ecclesiam emendat."

[32] *Comm. 1 Cor.* 14:34–35 (393v–394r).

[33] For Simler's account, see LLS, 31. Harding's recollection survives in his polemic,
A Reiondre to M. Iewels Replie (Antwerp: Ioannis Fouleri, 1566), sig. CCC 3; cited by
Jennifer Loach, "Reformation Controversies," in *The Collegiate University*, ed. James
McConica, vol. III of *The History of the University of Oxford*, ed. T. H. Aston (Oxford:
Oxford University Press, 1986), 369.

[34] *Comm. Gen.* 17, "De circuncisione" (69v): "Nunc vero in Christo sublatum cum
sit omne discrimen, vt non in illo sit masculus aut foemina, seruus aut liber, ideo

Vermigli could also argue for a woman's equality (or, better, for her equal rights and responsibilities) in the domestic sphere, with respect to the integrity of marriage. The studies by Donnelly and Olsen have amply documented that Vermigli's doctrine of divorce is in the mainstream of sixteenth-century Protestant thought. Accordingly, against the insistence of canon law that the sacramental status of marriage allows merely separation from bed and board, without the right of either partner to remarry another, Vermigli argued that scripture allows divorce in the case of adultery and also (he later added) in the case of a spouse who lapses into heresy or converts to Catholicism.[35] Of special interest, however, is Vermigli's tremendous opposition to the double standard, both with respect to divorce and adultery. What this means is that Vermigli argued strongly for the right of women to initiate divorce proceedings against an unfaithful husband, even though such a right is expressly denied to wives in the Old Testament. Vermigli, however, appeals rather to St. Paul, who insists that both spouses are equally bound by their marriage vows.[36] To be sure, like Calvin and most other Protestants, Vermigli was by no means quick to encourage divorce; on the contrary, he urged the wounded spouse to forbearance and forgiveness in the hope of eventual reconciliation.[37]

Vermigli took a similar position with respect to the crime of adultery—a question traditionally argued with a view to establishing whether adultery and infidelity is a greater crime for a man or for a woman. Here, too, Vermigli proved to be a foe of the double standard in civil laws by which women were held more accountable for

---

merito habuimus regenerationis sacramentum mitius, baptismum inquam, cuius merito cum mares tum foeminae sunt capaces, neque amplius cogimur sanguinem effundere, cum Christi sanguis quem in cruce fudit tanti momenti fuerit, vt omnem potuerit sanguinem sistere."

[35] Donnelly, "Two Florentine Moralists," 166–67; "Social and Ethical Thought," PMIR, 113–14. V. Norskov Olsen, *The New Testament Logia on Divorce: A Study in Their Interpretation from Erasmus to Milton* (Tübingen: J. C. B. Mohr, 1971), 88–94.

[36] Donnelly, "Social and Ethical Thought," PMIR, 114 n. 30, citing LC 2.10.58–71.

[37] One should note Vermigli's commonplace at *Comm. Jud.* 19:1–10 (179r–v; ET 249r–250r), "De reconcilatione coniugum post adulterium admissum." On opposition to the double standard among the Reformers, see Cornelia Seeger, *Nullité de mariage, divorce et séparation de corps a Genève, au temps de Calvin: Fondements doctrinaux, loi et jurisprudence* (Lausanne: Société d'Histoire de la Suisse Romande, 1989), 403–4 and studies cited there; more generally, see Keith V. Thomas, "The Double Standard," *Journal of the History of Ideas* 20 (1959): 195–216.

this crime and were more liable to be punished. Vermigli refutes those who would excuse the man, considering some two dozen arguments.[38] He is not unique in opposing the double standard in adultery,[39] but his argument should be credited for a unique degree of acuity. One of the arguments for the greater culpability of adulteresses is that their crime and guilt are more apparent than in the case of a man—meaning that their shame is as obvious as their pregnancy. Vermigli dismisses this with contempt: a woman's shame may be more manifest, but it is not more real! He goes on to add a stunningly modern insight, and a bit of discernment shared by few of his theological contemporaries: it is of no weight, Vermigli writes, that so many laws regard adultery as more "infamous" for a woman, for if this is so, it is only because *men* have written these laws and generated such a prejudicial sentiment! Regardless of what the laws may say in their imperfections, Christians should demand equal treatment for men and women—a position that takes on grave significance when one notices that Vermigli also believed in reinstating the traditional Old Testament punishment of death for adultery.[40]

Like other Reformers, Vermigli's interest lay not in developing new ideas about marriage but in restoring biblical practices. If his views are rarely original, they still testify to his desire for justice in society, order in the church, and mutual respect, fidelity, and friendship in marriage. It is fitting to recall Vermigli's vision of marriage as the pinnacle of human friendship—another traditional Christian insight, but a fervent one! Writing to Bucer's widow in 1551, he praised matrimony with this solitary but telling sentence: "No bond can be closer than that of husband and wife; among true friends everything is shared with candor and sincerity so that whoever is human would wish these friendships to be indissoluble and everlasting."[41]

---

[38] Vermigli's long discussion is reproduced in LC 2.11.27–35 (II, 323–27) and CP 2.11.30–38 (II, 489–95); he cites a variety of classical examples, including some from the Theodosian Code, but he takes issue most often with Roman law.

[39] See esp. LC 2.11.29 (324), CP 2.11.32 (II, 491), where Vermigli credits Jerome with a similar opinion.

[40] LC 2.11.33 (II, 326), CP 2.11.36 (II, 491). The position is helpfully illuminated by Robert M. Kingdon's chapter, "Death for Adultery," in *Adultery and Divorce in Calvin's Geneva* (Cambridge: Harvard University Press, 1995).

[41] Vermigli to Wibrandis Rosenblatt (Letter 59, March 1551), LLS, 115.

Women in Public: Prophetesses, Judges, and Queens

To this point we have seen that if Vermigli derives from scripture an unshakable commitment to the rule of men in public and private, he also knows from the Bible that there are areas in which men and women must be considered as equals, and he knows just as well that—again, from scripture but also from his own experience—there are exceptions even to the ostensibly divine rules for governing home, church, and society. Vermigli's refusal to bind God to these rules emerges nowhere so clearly as it does in his appreciation for the biblical office of prophetess, as well as for the surprising correlates he found in his own day.

One may begin by noting that the issue of women prophets was moderately divisive among early Protestants. None disputed that a few women once prophesied, especially in the Old Testament, but the examples of women prophesying in the New Testament—whether the fulfillment of Joel 2 when the Spirit is poured out in Acts 2, or Philip's four daughters, or the passing reference to the women who publicly prophesied in 1 Corinthians 11—lodged closer to home and were therefore all the more threatening, particularly when women of the sixteenth century might be tempted to appropriate such a role for themselves. Consequently, there were some among Vermigli's colleagues who essentially redefined "prophesying" in these texts (though, significantly, not in biblical texts that did not have women specifically in view) so that it consisted either of merely "listening to" prophecy, or of an activity that occurred only in private, or even of an activity simply forbidden to women.[42] Although Vermigli says it is of no importance which definition is correct, his words must be taken as a politic cover for his actual dissent from some of his Reformed colleagues, for even a cursory reading makes plain that his own sentiments lie elsewhere, with a fourth definition that he lists. For Vermigli, the gift of prophecy confers on a woman not an ordinary office, but

---

[42] These are three of the four exegetical positions listed by Vermigli in the common place on prophecy attached to his 1556 lecture on 1 Sam. 19:23–24 (*Comm. 1 Sam.* 112r)—in Zurich, significantly. While he does not name the advocates of these various views, the first seems to have been the party line in Zurich, held by Zwingli, Bullinger, and Pellican; the second was articulated by Calvin (*inter alia*), in his commentary on Acts 21:9; and the third view was voiced also by Calvin, albeit with less conviction, in his commentary on 1 Cor. 11:5–6. Details in Thompson, *Calvin and the Daughters of Sarah*, 187–226.

an extraordinary one. That view was not unknown in Christian theology, but Vermigli stands out among his predecessors and his contemporaries for the sanguinity with which he not only articulates this interpretation but also seems to expect and even regularize the phenomenon of women prophets. The details are worth reviewing.

What may be termed Vermigli's "openness" to women in exceptional roles emerges both from his consideration of Old Testament women and from his discussion of the pertinent New Testament texts. While the most obvious examples of Old Testament prophetesses are those of Deborah and Huldah, some equally striking observations are occasioned by the prophetic office Vermigli discerns in the figure of Rebecca, who received an oracle of how Jacob would supplant his brother Esau and who may also have been divinely warned that Esau, robbed of his father's best blessing, was planning to kill Jacob. Vermigli's observations are impressive particularly because they are apparently fully original to him. In Gen. 27:42–46, where Rebecca directs Jacob to flee his vengeful brother, Vermigli goes out of his way to find in Rebecca's actions "an ordination to the ministry of the Church and a promotion to sacred function, in which she was obligated to exercise the greatest care . . . lest a scornful and unworthy person [sc. Esau] be obtruded upon the Church."[43] Although he claims to be following an argument of Ambrose in *De beata vita*, Vermigli has vastly upgraded whatever he found there, and although he does not explicitly label Rebecca as a prophetess here, his references to her participation in this "ordination" and "sacred function" faintly echo Ambrose, who earlier had praised Rebecca's "prophetic and apostolic soul."[44]

Not surprisingly, Vermigli is quick to craft an encomium also for the judge Deborah, albeit with the customary admixture of stereotyping: "Because Deborah was of the weaker sex, when [God] chose her for this ministry he immediately made her conspicuous and

---

[43] *Comm. Gen.* 27:43 (112r): "ista fuerit ordinatio ministri Ecclesiae & promotio ad sacram functionem, in qua illa summopere cauere debuit, vt dignior sumeretur & ex quo fructus vberior posset prouenire, auertere autem tenebatur, ne contemptor aut indignus Ecclesiae obtruderetur."

[44] The phrase occurs in Ambrose's earlier treatise, *De Isaac et anima* 4.18 (PL XIV, 510): "prophetica atque apostolica anima." In *De Jacob et vita beata* 2.5–7 (PL XIV, 617), Ambrose does speak of Rebecca as moved (and excused) by her love for Jacob, as does Vermigli, but none of Vermigli's allusions to ministerial ordination are traceable to this treatise.

famous for her prophetic powers. By this gift and perhaps by many other miracles, she was divinely inaugurated and miraculously confirmed as the one who had been chosen for such a great office."[45] Remarkably, Vermigli found fewer problems in Deborah's prophetic office than in her civic leadership, particularly because she commanded a private person, Barak, to rebel against a tyrant.[46] But Deborah's divine office was not otherwise troubling to Vermigli, and—perhaps more than some of his Reformed colleagues—he was quick to welcome Queen Elizabeth as a new Deborah, urging her upon her accession in 1558 to "find a Barak" upon whom she might rely.[47] (Indeed, Vermigli offered Elizabeth a host of biblical role models, not only women but also men, ranging from Jael and Esther to David, Hezekiah, and Josiah.)

Vermigli's repeated considerations of 1 Corinthians 11 and the possibility that women could be raised up to fill the prophetic office thus represent a more than passing interest in an issue that bore more than theoretical ramifications.[48] In brief, 1 Cor. 11:3–16 is a difficult passage that forces the interpreter to address not only whether

---

[45] *Comm. Jud.* 4:4 (66v; ET 92v): "Deboram itaque sexu debilem, cum ad hoc ministerium delegisset, facultate prophetandi statim conspicuam & illustrem reddidit. Quo charismate atque aliis fortasse compluribus miraculis diuinitus inaugurata est, & miraculis confirmata, ut quae ad tantum munus electa fuerit."

[46] *Comm. Jud.* 4:6 (69r; ET 96v). Vermigli's prose thus implies that the poignant controversy over resistance to religious tyranny felt far more urgent than the question of prophetesses per se. Curiously, he also found Deborah's example useful to prove the legitimacy of clergy marriage, thereby underscoring her *clerical* status; see *Comm. Jud.* 4:5 (67r; ET 93v).

[47] Vermigli to Queen Elizabeth (Letter 200, 22 Dec. 1558), LLS, 170–77. Calvin drew a similar comparison between Deborah and women rulers of his own day, but his remarks were far more tepid than Vermigli's—an understandable coolness, since Mary Tudor was on the throne when he first wrote, and his later letter recalled the first. See Calvin's letters to Bullinger (28 Apr. 1554) and William Cecil (May 1559); CO XV, 125; XVII, 491. Elizabeth herself could play both ends against the middle: not only was she fully willing to exploit the conceit of womanly weakness (see e.g. Allison Heisch, "Queen Elizabeth I: Parliamentary Rhetoric and the Exercise of Power," *Signs* 1 [1975]: 31–55), but she could also style herself as a new Deborah, as one of the pageants depicted her on the day of her coronation (see Robert M. Healey, "Waiting for Deborah: John Knox and Four Ruling Queens," *Sixteenth Century Journal* 25 [1994]: 381). Elizabeth likened herself to Deborah also in a collection of her prayers published in 1569; see Leah S. Marcus, Janel Mueller, and Mary Beth Rose, eds., *Elizabeth I: Collected Works* (Chicago: University of Chicago Press, 2000), 157, cf. 424.

[48] While Vermigli's commentaries address only nine biblical books, he found occasion to address this text and issue on three separate occasions, during his lectures on 1 Corinthians (1548–49), Judges (1555), and 1 Samuel (1556).

women may prophesy, but also a host of related problems, including whether such prophecy constitutes a public ministry, whether and how women and men should adorn their heads in worship, whether Paul's remarks about "custom" diminish the urgency of his advice, and how the apparently public actions of women in this passage are to be reconciled with Paul's command for women's silence in church in 1 Cor. 14:34. Vermigli integrated all these problems with his characteristic clarity. First of all, the principle of man's preeminence and woman's submission is firm, and Paul's prohibition against women teaching men or even speaking in church is simply an application of this principle. Nonetheless, even if women's silence represents their ordinary function in ordinary situations, that is not the whole picture, for there are also extraordinary arrangements for extraordinary circumstances, as was evidently the case in Corinth. Accordingly, women may indeed be called to the office of prophet, teacher, or minister—albeit as an extraordinary call and office. Moreover, it is *only* to prophetesses that the matter of headcoverings pertains: "Women are not forbidden to prophesy for the edification of the whole Church; but they are commanded to cover their heads while doing so, lest they become proud on account of their extraordinary office, having forgotten their proper state [as subject to men]."[49] Vermigli thus understands all of Paul's instructions concerning veils, hair, and other "customary" or "natural" headcoverings as *adiaphora*, as indifferent matters. They are all merely symbolic expressions of an abiding principle, and as symbols they are relative to a particular time and a particular church.[50]

Vermigli's account of the problem of headcoverings in 1 Cor. 11:3–16 displays a sophisticated appreciation, unusual for his day, of the cultural relativity of at least some apostolic precepts. Still more

---

[49] *Comm. Jud.* 4:4 (66v; ET 93r): "Illae sane prophetare non uetantur, ad Ecclesiae communem aedificationem: sed ut ne ob munus extra ordinem sibi commissum propriae conditionis oblitae superbiant, ut contecto capite sint praecipitur."

[50] *Comm. 1 Cor.* 11:3 (284v). Modern practice, Vermigli observed, is just the opposite of what prevailed in Corinth: men today remove a hat in the presence of higher authority, so that an uncovered head now denotes submission. Still, Vermigli did not feel that a man should preach with a cap on during cold weather unless—as Bullinger, Pellican, Calvin, and Musculus likewise urged—he were to remove the cap, briefly, at the beginning and end of the service. Vermigli's remarks about the indifferent character of signs and symbols were reiterated in his advice to Bishop Hooper during the vestarian controversy; see Letter 48 (4 Nov 1550), LC supp. 1088, translated in Gorham, *Gleanings*, 194.

unusual, however, is his further development of a theory to account for the manifestation of prophetic gifts and callings among women. As he stated in his 1555 lectures in Strasbourg, "In a church newly planted, when there are no men present to preach the gospel, it is possible for a woman to serve at the outset, but in such a way that when she has taught for a while, some man from among the faithful should be ordained who will from then on minister the sacraments, teach, and pastor faithfully."[51] These remarks actually constitute the "lessons" to be drawn from Deborah's example, and it is revealing that Vermigli's generalized account of women's extraordinary public ministry makes no demand that the woman be supernaturally called or gifted, nor that there be the miraculous confirmation that Deborah enjoyed.

Was Vermigli wholly original in his advocacy for a theory of the emergency ministry of women? Technically, no. A familiar precedent might be found in the medieval practice of emergency baptism, in which a sickly newborn might be baptized by the midwife without waiting for a priest to arrive—though Reformed theologians, unlike their Lutheran counterparts, were utterly hostile to this practice. The notion of women as emergency preachers, however, can be traced back before Vermigli, to brief remarks made by Jacques Lefevre d'Etaples in 1512, by Martin Luther as early as 1521, and more laconically still by John Calvin in 1535 and 1546.[52] None of these three offers anything as systematic as the treatment of Vermigli, however, whose earliest account (c. 1549) was framed in response to "Anabaptist" claims that women may preach even if never instructed.[53] While Vermigli was willing to grant that women were sometimes sent by God to preach under emergency circumstances, he insisted that their calling and office were extraordinary, having come to pass "either because the church was not yet constituted or else it was so collapsed as to be otherwise beyond repair"—a description (we may observe) that uncannily resembles the state of the church, in Protestant

---

[51] *Comm. Jud.* 4:5 (67r; ET 93v): "in Ecclesiis de nouo plantandis, cum uiri qui praedicent Euangelium desunt, mulierem id posse ab initio praestare, sed ita ut cum aliquot edocuerit, uir quispiam ex fidelibus ordinetur, qui deinceps ministret sacramenta, doceat, & pastorem fideliter agat."

[52] Details regarding Lefevre, Luther, and Calvin may be found in Thompson, *Calvin and the Daughters of Sarah*, 196–205.

[53] *Comm. 1 Cor.* 16:15 (452r); translated in CP 4.1.15 (IV, 11). The Anabaptists are also in view, for Vermigli, at *Comm. 1 Cor.* 11:16.

eyes, not only on the eve of the Reformation but even after the work of reform had been underway for some time.[54]

As a matter of fact, Strasbourg would have been an ideal setting for the development of Vermigli's mediating views on women as extraordinary ministers. Throughout the 1520s and 1530s, Strasbourg experienced considerable lay involvement and activism. Some of this activity smacked of Anabaptism, including the visionary prophesies of women such as Ursula Jost and Barbara Rebstock that came to shape the apocalypticism of Melchior Hoffman—himself an "Anabaptist" provocateur in Strasbourg until his death, imprisoned, in 1543, about a year after Vermigli's arrival.[55] However, as early as 1526, François Lambert—an advocate of lay piety, but by no means an Anabaptist—had argued for the fitness of lay men and women to proclaim the gospel. Significantly, Lambert saw such activity as an exception to the rule, by which preachers were normally trained pastors. And although Bucer and Capito distanced themselves from Lambert and his views, the arrival of Hoffman ensured that the discussion would not go away.[56]

There is little doubt, then, that Vermigli's own approval of women as emergency preachers was developed not merely on paper but in full awareness of other views advocated in Strasbourg, both on the right and on the left. That Vermigli could respond to his unnamed Anabaptist opponents without overreacting seems to signal at least a guarded appreciation for the rare but real contribution of women to the public ministry of the church, both in biblical times and his own. As one might discern also from his letters of praise for Queen Elizabeth, Vermigli clearly knows that many good things have come

---

[54] *Comm. 1 Cor.* 16:15 (453v); translated in CP 4.1.18 (IV, 12).

[55] On Jost, Rebstock, and Hoffman, see Klaus Deppermann, *Melchior Hoffman: Social Unrest and Apocalyptic Visions in the Age of Reformation* (Edinburgh: T. & T. Clark, 1987), 203–13, 349–58, 361–69.

[56] Lambert, *Commentarii de prophetia, eruditione atque linguis, deque litera et spiritu* (Strasbourg, [1526]); note how he glosses 1 Cor. 14:34, where women are commanded to be silent in church (111r–v): "Quod intellige, nisi non eßet uir qui loqui poßet." For a fuller discussion of the work and the responses of Capito and Bucer, see R. Gerald Hobbs, "François Lambert sur les langues et la prophétie," in *Pour retrouver François Lambert: Bio-bibliographie et études*, ed. Pierre Fraenkel (Baden-Baden and Bouxwiller: Valentin Koerner, 1987), 273–301. Of special interest is Hobbs's suggestion (289) that Lambert's views were shaped by his perception of the "missionary situation" of the reform in Alsace—the same sort of perception that moved Vermigli to allow that women might teach and pastor in churches newly established (above, n. 51).

to pass in the course of the Reformation that, strictly speaking, did not follow the rules.

Conclusion

Peter Martyr Vermigli was in most respects a traditionalist on matters of gender and gender relations. He was a rigorous exegete, concerned to be true to the teachings of scripture even when such teachings might be unpopular, even at the risk of dissenting from his Reformed colleagues. But Vermigli was also a keen enough observer of both scripture and the church of his day that he could be unusually flexible when it came to apply his exegesis, for he knew that if scripture itself could cast women in surprising and exceptional roles, so also might contemporary circumstances. Vermigli's fundamental respect for women and for the spiritual equality of men and women is evidenced not only by his occasional outspokenness regarding the way human customs and prejudices can disadvantage women, but also by his willingness to see God work through women in the highest possible public offices, whether sacred or secular. Vermigli's commitment to the word of God thus shaped both his traditionalism and his moderate openness to women's public leadership—so much so, that in some cases his fidelity to scripture actually enabled him to set aside the strictures and stereotypes that the Bible itself elsewhere reinforced.[57]

---

[57] In researching this essay, I am happy to acknowledge the contribution of my graduate assistant, Mr. Brian Ebersole, as well as of R. Gerald Hobbs, who kindly called my attention to the activities of the Strasbourg prophetesses and to the exchange between François Lambert and Martin Bucer.

AND ALL ISRAEL SHALL BE SAVED: PETER MARTYR AND JOHN CALVIN ON THE JEWS ACCORDING TO ROMANS, CHAPTERS 9, 10 AND 11

Dan Shute

Introduction

The Protestant Reformers were not of one mind on the proper interpretation of Romans, chapters nine through eleven, where Paul seems to affirm the Jews' continuing place in the economy of salvation.[1] John Calvin and Peter Martyr are a case in point. Calvin published his Romans commentary in 1539. That same year Martyr was completing his work as abbot of S. Pietro ad Aram in Naples, and it was during his term there that his convictions became decidedly evangelical.[2] Martyr expounded Romans in 1550 during his stay at

---

[1] In fact, Paul's teaching on this point puzzled interpreters before the Reformation and continues to do so today. Cf. John Calvin, *Commentarius in epistolam Pauli ad Romanos*, ed. T. H. L. Parker, D. C. Parker (Geneva: Droz, 1999), 186; ET *The Epistles of Paul the Apostle to the Romans and to the Thessalonians*, trans. Ross Mackenzie, eds. David W. Torrance, Thomas F. Torrance (Edinburgh: Oliver and Boyd, 1961), 190: "But he passes to a discussion of the present subject so abruptly that there appears to be no connection in his discourse, and yet he commences his new exposition as if he had already touched on it previously." Gerald Bray, ed., *Romans, Ancient Christian Commentary on Scripture, New Testament, VI* (Downers Grove, Ill.: InterVarsity Press, 1998), 244: "Paul's detailed listing of Jewish privileges was respected by the Fathers, but they did not elaborate on them much. It was clear to them that the apostle was referring to the Jews of the Old Testament, not to their own contemporaries, who had rejected Christ." C. E. B. Cranfield, *A Critical and Exegetical Commentary on the Epistle to the Romans* (Edinburgh: T. & T. Clark, 1975–1979), 445: "The difficulties which this division of the epistle presents are notorious. . . . A superficial reading of the epistle might easily leave one with the impression that chapters 9 to 11 are simply an excursus which Paul has included under the pressure of his own deep personal involvement in the matter of Israel's destiny but which is without any real inner relatedness to the main argument of Romans."

[2] Josiah Simler, *Oratio de vita & obitu . . . Petri Martyris Vermilii*, LC 1583 (no pagination); ET "Oration on the Life and Death of the Good Man and Outstanding Theologian, Doctor Peter Martyr Vermigli," in LLS, 19–20.

Oxford University as Regis Professor of Theology, though he may
have also begun to lecture on Romans at his first Protestant teaching position in Bucer's Strasbourg academy in 1545–1546.[3] He was
more Calvinian than Calvin was "Vermiglian." Peter Martyr was
nonetheless capable of arriving at exegetical and dogmatic conclusions independent of the acknowledged leader of the Reformed
churches. As we shall see, Calvin managed to avoid any meaning-
ful notion of the Jews' continuing special status,[4] while Martyr made
statements that were harbingers of a philo-Semitism that was to fas-
cinate some Reformed students of scripture in the next generation.
Philo-Semitism never completely died away in the evangelical churches,
and with the revival of millennialism among dispensationalists, Romans
9, 10, and 11 again has currency.

Comparing Martyr and Calvin's commentaries is a bit like comparing apples and oranges. Calvin was clear and consistently precise. Martyr was discursive and at times pedantic. Calvin writes for
a busy but well-educated Reformed pastor or layman, while Martyr's
work more resembles an academic commentary with the footnotes
included in the text. Martyr will digress at the best of times and will
occasionally include in his commentaries loci (also called scholia or
excursus) pages in length. Martyr will name other commentators and
provide synopses of their views. By contrast the work of others usually disappears into the seamless fabric of Calvin's commentary.

---

[3] Simler ("Life of Martyr," 33) says he began his stay in England by lecturing
on 1 Corinthians. PPRED, 48 n. 49, mentions possible Romans lectures in Strasbourg;
but we know from a 25 March 1550 letter of John ab Ulmis to Henry Bullinger
that Martyr, in England, began lecturing on Romans at the time of that letter: see
Peter Martyr Vermigli, *The Oxford Treatise and Disputation on the Eucharist*, trans. and
ed. Joseph C. McLelland, Peter Martyr Library, vol. 7 (Kirksville, Mo.: Truman
State University Press, 2000), xix; Hastings Robinson, ed., *Original Letters Relative to
the English Reformation* (Cambridge: University Press, 1847), 401. Could Martyr have
started lecturing on Romans in his first Strasbourg period and then begun all over
again in England?

[4] Even though the literature on Calvin and the Jews is extensive (Is not literature on topics relating to Calvin always extensive?), it is not helpful for the present
inquiry. See Jack Hughes Robinson, *John Calvin and the Jews* (New York: Peter Lang,
1992), 70–83, "The Jews in Calvin's Interpretation of Romans 9–11"; Mary Sweetland
Laver, "Calvin, Jews, and Intra-Christian Polemics," (Ph.D. diss., Temple University,
1988), 16–35, "Literature on Calvin and the Jews."

Martyr's commentary on Romans is much longer than Calvin's and far more detailed. Part of the reason for the length of Martyr's exposition is the two long scholia embedded in it. One is on predestination and is found at the end of his comments on Romans 9; the other is on justification and is at the end of Romans 11.[5] Because of these two scholia, Martyr's commentary on Romans 9, 10, and 11 is twice the relative length of Calvin's. The extent to which Martyr wrestled with the profound mysteries in Romans 9, 10, and 11 reminds one of Karl Barth's *Church Dogmatics* §34, which Barth himself termed "minute exegesis" and of which he seemed so proud.[6] To my knowledge, among the Reformers only Martin Bucer's exegesis of Romans 9, 10, and 11 approaches the length of Martyr's.[7]

The matter of the continuing special status of the Jews has generated a vast and disparate literature, scholarly as well as popular. The bibliography represented in what follows is only a hesitant sounding of a nearly unfathomable sea. I shall be limiting my remarks to three areas: the eventual conversion of the Jews to Christ, the Jews' return to the land of Israel, and finally, the advantages of being a Jew even after Judaism has rejected Jesus as Messiah.

The Eventual Conversion of the Jews to Christ

The climax of Paul's argument in Romans 9, 10, and 11 is thus:

> So I ask, have [the Jews] stumbled so as to fall? By no means! But through their trespass salvation has come to the Gentiles, so as to make Israel jealous. Now if their trespass means riches for the world, and if their failure means riches for the Gentiles, how much more will their full inclusion mean! . . . [I]f their rejection means the reconciliation of the world, what will their acceptance mean but life from the dead? . . . [A] hardening has come upon Israel, until the full number of the Gentiles come in, and so all Israel will be saved. . . .[8]

---

[5] These two scholia have been published as: JAP.

[6] KD § 34; CD II/2. Karl Barth, *Briefe, 1961–1968*, ed. J. Fangmeier and H. Stoevesandt (Zürich: Theologischer Verlag, 1975), 34–35, ET *Letters 1961–1968*, trans. and ed. G. W. Bromiley (Grand Rapids, Mich.: Eerdmans, 1981), "Letter 18, to Pastor H. Poms," 25–26.

[7] *Enarrationes Epistolae D. Pauli ad Romanos* (Basil, 1562).

[8] Rom. 11:11–12, 15, 25b–26a.

Most of the church fathers believed that Paul referred to a mass
conversion of the Jews as a prelude to the return of Christ.[9] There
is an apparent allusion to the general conversion of the Jews in the
Christian Jewish work, *The Testaments of the Twelve Patriarchs*.[10] Tertullian
explicitly refers to the conversion of the Jews in his treatise *De
Pudicitia*,[11] as does Cyril of Alexandria (*Explanatio in Epistolam ad
Romanos*).[12] Theodore of Mopsuestia (*In Epistolam Pauli ad Romanos*)
understands Paul to be saying that the Jews "will not always remain
outsiders to true religion: there will be a time when they will also
know the truth, as soon as people everywhere may receive knowledge of true religion."[13] According to Theodoret of Cyrhus (*Interpretatio
epistolae ad Romanos*) Romans 11:25 teaches that Jews who did not
believe the first time will do so when Elijah returns to preach to
them.[14] According to Augustine's *Questiones XVII in Evangelium*, the
prodigal son is to be understood allegorically:

> But for the moment he is angry, and up to that point does not want
> to go in. When therefore the fullness of the Gentiles have come in,
> his father at an opportune time will go out, so that all Israel might
> be saved at that time also: he had partial blindness as if away in the
> field, until the fullness of the younger son, for a long time set in idol-
> atry of the Gentiles, enters to eat the calf. For at some point there is
> to be an open call of the Jews to the salvation of the gospel.[15]

---

[9] Henry Hammond, *Paraphrase and Annotations upon All the Books of the New Testament,
Briefly Explaining all the Difficult Places Thereof* (Oxford: University Press, 1845),
4:71; Karl Hermann Schelke, *Paulus lehrer der väter: altkirchlich auslegung von Römer 1–11*
(Düsseldorf: Patmos, 1959), 380 ff.

[10] PG 2:1104; ET *The Ante-Nicene Fathers*, 8:26, "For [Satan] knows that in the
day on which Israel shall believe, the kingdom of the enemy shall be brought to
an end. . . ."

[11] PL 2:1048; ET *The Ante-Nicene Fathers*, 4:82, ". . . for it is fitting for the Christian
to rejoice, and not to grieve, at the restoration of Israel, if it be true, (as it is), that
the whole of our hope is intimately united with the remaining expectation of Israel."

[12] PG 74:849; ET *Romans*, ed. Bray, 297–299: "Although it was rejected, Israel
will also be saved eventually, a hope which Paul confirms by quoting this text of
scripture. For indeed, Israel will be saved in its own time and will be called at the
end, after the calling of the Gentiles."

[13] PG 66:857; ET *Theodore of Mopsuestia's Commentary on Romans: An Annotated
Translation*, ed. and trans. Charles David Gregory, (Ph.D. diss., The Southern Baptist
Theological Seminary, 1992), 109; Gregory used the Greek text in K. Staab, "Paulus
kommentare aus der griechischen Kirche," *Neutestamentlich Abhuandlungen*, 15 (Münster,
1933).

[14] PG 82:180.

[15] PL 35:1347. Martyr cites this, not in his *Romans* commentary but in his *In
librum Iudicum* (Zurich, 1569), 40–41, in a scholium entitled "Should Christians live

An apparently separate issue in the mind of several of the Fathers was the identity of "all Israel" in "and thus all Israel will be saved." Several of them claimed that "all Israel" was the Israel of God, both Jews and Gentiles.[16] Clement said that "all Israel" is to be allegorically understood as the spiritual Israel—implicitly including Gentiles. Theodore of Mopsuestia claimed that "all Israel" includes Jews by nature as well as Gentiles.[17] Augustine, in *Letters* 149, wrote, "not all the Jews were blind; some of them recognized Christ. But the fullness of the Gentiles has come in among those who have been called according to the plan, and there arises a truer Israel of God . . . the elect from both Jews and the Gentiles."[18]

To sum up, then, the church fathers took as a received Christian teaching that the Jews would eventually be converted to Christ; at the same time, some hesitated to identify "all Israel" with Jews only.

Medieval interpreters continued to teach the Jews' return to Christ. Thomas Aquinas, for example, in his commentary on Romans, interprets both Romans 11:15 ("life from the dead") and 11:25–26 ("And so all Israel will be saved") as references to the conversion of the Jews in the latter days.[19]

---

with unbelievers?," the section on Jews (ET *Judges* 57A–58A). Martyr expresses some doubt as to its authenticity, but Oliver Jean-Baptist Du Roy de Blicquy (*The New Catholic Encyclopedia* 1:1051) includes it among the genuine works, and so will we. It is also called *Questiones XVI in Matthaeum*. For the debate on its authenticity see *Augustine through the Ages: an Encyclopedia*, s.v. "Questiones." Elsewhere Augustine affirms the Jews' eventual conversion in *Enarrationes in Psalmos* 58.2–10 and in *Adversus Judaeos*: see *Augustine through the Ages*, s.v. "Jews and Judaism." Augustine further seems to affirm the Jews' conversion in *De civitate Dei* 20.29. On the subject of Augustine's ambiguous interpretation of Romans 11, see Joseph A. Fitzmyer, *Romans: A New Translation with Introduction and Commentary*; Anchor Bible vol. 33 (New York: Doubleday, 1933), 624.

[16] Fitzmyer, *Romans*, 623–4, lists them: "Irenaeus, *Adversus haereses* 4.2.7 (SC 100.2.410–11); Clement of Alexandria, *Excepta ex Theodoto* 56.4–5 (GCS 17.2.126; SC 23.174); Theodore of Mopsuestia, *In ep. ad Romanos* 11.26 (PG 66.857); Theodoret of Cyrrhus, *Interpretatio ep. ad Romanos* 11.26–27 (PG 82.180)." See also K. H. Schelkle, *Paulus Lehrer der Väter: Die altkirchliche Auslegung von Römer 1–11* (Dütmos-Verlag, 1956), 400–401. Irenaeus does not belong in this list, in the sense that Irenaeus believes that Paul refers to converted Jews, not Jews and Gentiles together (PG 7:978–979, ET *Ante-Nicene Fathers* 1:463; see also Schelkle, *Paulus Lehrer*, 400). I cannot find evidence in Theodoret of Cyrhus' commentary on Rom. 11:25 that he thought "all Israel" included Gentiles.

[17] Theodore of Mopsuestia *In ep. ad Romanos* 11.26 (PG 66.857), ET *Romans*, ed. Gregory, 109.

[18] PL 33:638; ET *Romans*, ed. Bray, 297–299.

[19] *Expositio in Onmes S. Pauli Epistolas*, "Ad Romanos" Section 2 and 4, *Opera Omnia* (New York: Musurgia, 1949), 13:112, 115.

As far as I have been able to determine, most Reformation exegetes followed the majority opinion among early and medieval interpreters. They affirmed an eventual mass conversion of the Jews. Luther, near the beginning of his public career, did so reluctantly:

> On the basis of this text it is commonly accepted that the Jews at the end of the world will return to the faith, although the text is so obscure that unless one is willing to follow the authority of the fathers who explain the apostle in this way, no one would seem to be convinced of this purely on the basis of the text. But the Lord also agrees with this idea of the apostle in Luke 21:23–24. . . .[20]

Luther delivered these lectures in 1515–1516, before he had taken the virulent anti-Jewish attitudes associated with the 1542 pamphlet, "On the Jews and their Lies." Zwingli in his Romans commentary also affirms a future for Israel in his comment on 11:25:

> They indeed are enemies of God for your sakes who believe the gospel: but as regards election, they are those whom God elected from eternity, and he loved them more than others: thus for the sake of the fathers they are elect until now. . . . The fact that they are indeed the people of God for the sake of the fathers is plain. Nor does God repent of his promise. He called Israel to be his people: therefore that people will not be damned but will return to faith and will be saved, even though they have been rejected for a time.[21]

Martin Bucer similarly affirms:

> The mystery which Paul proclaims and the prophecy is that the blindness of Israel happened only in part, temporarily, until the destined and prescribed multitude of Gentiles enter into Christ, and thus all

---

[20] *WA* 61:436, esp. n. 25; ET *LW*, 25:429, n. 8. Luke 21:24: ". . . and Jerusalem will be trodden down by the Gentiles, until the times of the Gentiles are fulfilled." *Contra* I. John Hesselink, "The Millennium and the Reformed Tradition," *Reformed Review* 52:2 (Winter 1998–1999), 101.

[21] *In Epistolam ad Romanos Annotationes* in *Opera . . . Latinorum Scriptorum* (Zurich: Schulthess, 1838), 6.2:119; n.b., this work is not in *CR*. By contrast, Zwingli sees no end-times conversion alluded to in 11:15 ("If their rejection means the reconciliation of the world, what will their acceptance mean but life from the dead"): "If their rejection was so useful for your salvation, what do you think will be if they would be received again, be one people, one church with you? This would be so great a miracle as if they were raised from the dead. Now they have plainly died, been indeed unfaithful, deprived of Christ. This Paul says to tame the ferocity of the Gentiles and to exhort them to bear the Jews with equanimity, lest they reject and despise them. This teaches us to be neither harsh nor impatient toward the infirm (*Ad Romanos*, 117).

Israel will become saved. He speaks of the people of the Jews. . . .
They are now indeed blinded, but by a blindness which is temporary
(i.e. "partial"), not to last forever. For when the fullness of the Gentiles
has come to Christ, that is, the full number of the elect, all Israel also,
that is, the entire nation, will be saved, and the kingdom of God will
flourish publicly once again among them. . . .[22]

In general, then, the Reformers affirmed (however hesitantly) that
Paul predicted a future conversion of the Jews. Calvin is a notable
exception. In his *Romans* commentary he toils to avoid the trend of
Paul's argument. With reference to Paul's statement "If their rejection means the reconciliation of the world what will their acceptance
mean but life from the dead?" he maintains that "reconciliation"
and "life from the dead" are synonymous: "There is no difficulty,
as some maintain, that reconciliation is no different from resurrection."[23]
With reference to Paul's words, "A hardening in part has befallen
Israel until the full number . . ." Calvin writes:

> The words *in part* do not, I believe, refer simply to time or number,
> but have been used, as I interpret it, to mean in a measure. Paul
> wanted, I think, merely to qualify a word which in itself was other-
> wise harsh. *Until* does not suggest the course or order of time, but
> means rather, "*In order that* the fullness of the Gentiles. . . ." The mean-
> ing, therefore, will be that God in some measure has blinded Israel
> in such a way that while they reject the light of the Gospel, it is trans-
> ferred to the Gentiles, and these may seize the vacant possession. And
> so this blindness of the Jews serves the providence of God in accom-
> plishing the salvation of the Gentiles, which He had ordained. *The full-
> ness of the Gentiles* means a great number, for proselytes did not then,
> as they had done before, connect themselves with the Jews in small
> numbers, but there was such a change that the Gentiles formed almost
> the entire body of the Church. *26* "And so all Israel shall be saved."
> Many understand this of the Jewish people, as if Paul were saying that
> religion was to be restored to them again as before. But I extend the
> word Israel to include all the people of God . . .[24]

Calvin's language is by no means unambiguous, and he so hedges
his argument that he seems unsure whether or not he might be
"twisting" this scripture a bit. However that may be, he appears to

---

[22] *Ennarrationes in Epistolam D. Pauli ad Romanos* (Basil, 1562), 442.
[23] *Ad Romanos*, ed. T. H. L. Parker, 241, ET *Romans*, trans. Ross MacKenzie,
248.
[24] *Romans*, 255. Bucer, if I understand him correctly, criticizes Calvin's argument
(*Ennarrationes ad Romanos*, 444–445).

be trying to avoid any notion that Paul promises that religion will be "restored to them again as before." This is not Calvin's finest hour as exegete—his most ingenious maybe, but not his finest. I have found no other Christian exegete before Calvin's time who interpreted Romans 9, 10, and 11 in such a way that a future conversion of the Jews was excluded. The Calvin Translation Society's editor of Calvin's *Romans* commentary, John Owen (English vicar, d. 1867) notes:

> The explanation of this verse is by no means satisfactory. It does not correspond at all with what the Apostle has already declared in verses 11, 12, and 15; where the restoration of the Jews to the faith is most clearly set forth. Besides, by making Israel, in the next verse, to mean generally the people of God, the contrast, observable through the whole argument, is completely destroyed . . . *Hammond* tells us, that many of the Fathers wholly denied the future restoration of the Jews; and we are told by *Pareus*, who mentions some of the same Fathers, that they maintained it. But it appears from the quotations made by the first, that the restoration disallowed was that to their own land, and that the restoration referred to by the latter was restoration to the faith; two things wholly distinct. That "Israel" means exclusively the Jewish nation, was almost the unanimous opinion of the Fathers, according to *Estius*; and their future restoration to the faith as here foretold was the sentiment held by *Beza, Willet, Mede*, and others, and is generally held by modern divines.[25]

Owen does not hazard a source for Calvin's eccentric interpretation, but it seems to me that Calvin could in part justify his stance by alluding to the church fathers' allegorical interpretation of "all Israel."

Peter Martyr reverts back to the traditional Christian interpretation of the eventual conversion of the Jews. He introduces Romans 11 with the following summary of Paul's argument:

> The sum of this chapter's teaching can be briefly reviewed in the following way: the Jews have not so perished without exception that no hope remains for their salvation. To this day remnants are preserved who are saved, now to be sure in a small number (even so they are the salt of the earth), but one day they will become a mighty band in full view.[26]

---

[25] *Commentaries on the Epistle of Paul to the Romans*, ed. John Owen (Edinburgh: Calvin Translation Society, 1848), 436–437, n. 1.

[26] *In Epistolam S. Pauli Apostoli ad Romanos*, 3d ed. (Basil, 1568), 488. "Salt of the earth": Matt. 5:13.

Further, Martyr makes it plain that "one day" means "towards the end of the world."[27] He freely criticizes those who try to escape Paul's meaning by claiming that "all Israel" does not refer to the Jews only, but to the elect of the Jews and the Gentiles. Such an interpretation does violence to the context.[28]

As I noted above, the Calvin translator and editor John Owen showed that Calvin's spiritual descendents were not prone to follow Calvin's interpretation of Romans 11. This has been my conclusion as well. Jean Alphonse Turretini, for example, held that Paul envisaged a future conversion of the Jews. How or when "God alone knows."[29]

The debate as to what Paul meant by "all Israel shall be saved" has continued. Calvin's attempt to avoid any notion of an eventual conversion of the Jews has found few takers.[30] The attempt to limit "all Israel" to the elect remnant of Israel converted ever since the beginning of the Gentile mission and similarly avoid a mass conversion of the Jews also has had few supporters.[31] Recent interpreters have conceded that "all Israel" means the Jews, but have placed this mass turning to Christ outside history. Cranfield is representative when he states: "Paul was thinking of a restoration of the nation of Israel as a whole to God *at the end*, an eschatological event in the strict sense."[32] But Jürgen Becker is surely right when he points out that making the final salvation of Israel "a last offering of salvation independent of the gospel" is wrong-headed. Rather:

---

[27] *Ad Romanos*, 496: "He adds TO THIS DAY, since towards the end of the world they will believe."

[28] *Ad Romanos*, 531–532.

[29] *In Pauli Apostoli ad Romanos epistolae capita XI Praelectiones . . .* (Lausanne: Marc-Michel Bousquet, 1791), 365.

[30] Douglas J. Moo, *Epistle to the Romans* (Grand Rapids, Mich.: W. B. Eerdmans Publishing Co., 1996), 720–21 n. 45, says that Calvin's interpretation "became especially widespread among Protestant Continental theologians in the late sixteenth and seventeenth centuries" but he cites no examples. I find J. A. Bengel's interpretation of Romans 11:15, 25–26 impossibly subtle: see *Gnomon Novi Testamenti*, 3rd ed. (Tubingen: Ludov. Frid. Fues., 1855), 586, 588, ET *Gnomon of the New Testament*, trans. James Bryce (Edinburgh: T. & T. Clark, 1858), 3:151, 156–57. He seems to me to be trying to restate Calvin's argument.

[31] William Henriksen, *Israel in Prophecy* (Grand Rapids, Mich.: Baker Book House, 1968), 40–52. Similarly the solution that François Refoulé presented in 1984 is too clever by half: ". . . *Et ainsi tout Israël sera sauvé": Romains 11, 25–26* (Paris: Iditions du Cerf, 1984), 179–189.

[32] Cranfield, *Romans*, 576–577.

When Paul wrote the letter to the Romans, he had just closed his mission in the East and was now turning to the West (15:23–24). Following this mission and before the end of all things, he expected one last proclamation of the gospel to Israel which clearly has more success than the present one, which is already leading a few Jewish Christians to the church of God.[33]

We are, I believe, left with the uncomfortable option that Paul envisaged a general conversion of ethnic Israel in this world of time and space. Whether or not Paul was correct, or, to put it more positively, whether or not we are required to receive his opinion as gospel truth, is another question entirely.

A short survey of the history of Christian interpretation of Romans 11 reveals that Martyr, far from being a voice crying in the wilderness of anti-Semitism, conforms to the majority opinion from the church fathers onward. To sum up, then, Martyr upholds the traditional Christian interpretation of Romans 11; this interpretation continues to hold its own until the present day. While an eventual general conversion of the Jews had traditional and strong support in Latin Christendom, any notion of the Jews' final return to the land of Israel did not.

The Jews' Return to the Land of Israel

Nowhere in the extant writings of the Apostle Paul is the final return of the Jews to the land of Israel mentioned. At the same time, this was part of the messianic expectation of the Jews, even after the partial return of the Babylonian exiles.[34] Nor in the extant writings

---

[33] Jürgen Becker, *Paul, Apostle to the Gentile*, trans. O. C. Dean, Jr. (Louisville, Ky.: Westminster/John Knox Press, 1993), 472; Douglas J. Moo, *The Epistle to the Romans*, 724–725: "The OT quotation that Paul cites in v. 26b–27 to confirm the truth that 'all Israel will be saved' probably refers to the second coming of Christ. . . . Nor is it possible to be precise about the exact timing of the conversion of Israel in comparison with other events of the end times, although the fact that it will take place only after the salvation of all elect Gentiles suggest that it will be closely associated with the return of Christ in glory." Moo can affirm this, yet still contend Israel's acceptance will not be independent of the gospel, since with millenarians, he holds to an "interim stage of eschatological fulfillment" (695, n. 67).

[34] Zech. 2:6–12.

of the church fathers is such a final return affirmed. At the same time, many of the early fathers predicted a millennial reign of Christ before the last judgment. Tertullian is a case in point. In *Against Marcion* he insisted that references in scripture to the Jews' return to Israel were to be interpreted allegorically, yet he was equally firm that the reference in Rev. 20:5 was to be taken literally.[35] As far as I have been able to determine, Christian belief in the restoration of the Jews to the land of Israel had to wait for the fringes of the reform movements of the sixteenth century. Such an advocacy was not shared by the magisterial Reformers. The exception that tests this rule is Martyr's predecessor at Bucer's Strasbourg College, Wolfgang Capito, who taught the return of the Jews to their own land.[36]

In his Romans commentary Calvin does not mention any promised restoration of the Jews to the land of Israel. We must look elsewhere to discover how Calvin interpreted statements in the Old Testament prophets which might be interpreted as referring to an end-times return. One of the sources for such prophecies is the second half of Zechariah. Calvin says concerning Zech. 10:8 ("I will whistle for them and I will gather them for I have redeemed them, and they will be many as they were many"):

> It is indeed true that this had not been fulfilled as to all the Israelites: but we must ever remember, that gratuitous election so existed as to the whole people, that God had notwithstanding but a small flock, as

---

[35] David Brown, *The Restoration of the Jews: The History, Principles, and Bearings of the Question* (Edinburgh: Alexander Straham & Co.; London: Hamilton, Adams, & Co., 1861), 29–33; Hammond, *Paraphrase of the New Testament*, 4:71; Tertullian *Adv. Marc.* 3:24 (PL 2:384–386), ET *Ante-Nicene Fathers* 3:342; *Dictionary of the Later New Testament & its Developments*, s.v. "millennium"; J. Massyngbaerde Ford implies a complete dominance of millenarian views in the early Church (*Anchor Bible Dictionary*, s.v. "millennium"), but this is an exaggeration; see *Cyclopedia of Biblical, Theological, and Ecclesiastical Literature*, s.v. "millennium"; Ford also states that Tertullian in *Adv. Marc.* 3:24 taught that "the Jews will be restored to Palestine", but this is not the case, for Tertullian writes, "As for the restoration of Judaea, however, which even the Jews themselves, induced by the names of places and countries, hope for just as it is described, it would be tedious to state at length how the figurative (*allegorica*) interpretation is spiritually applicable to Christ and his church." (See David Brown's correct interpretation of this passage in the reference above.)

[36] Brown, *Restoration of the Jews*, 38–39; *In Hoseam Prophetam V. F. Capitonis commentarius* (Argentorati: Apud Ioannem Hervagium, 1528), 72r, as cited in R. Gerald Hobbs, "*Monito Amica*: Pellican à Capiton sur le Danger des Lectures rabbiniques," in *Horizons européens de la Réforme en Alsace* (Strasbourg: Librairie Istra, 1980), 83–84.

Paul teaches us. (Rom. 9.5.) The Prophet at the same time intimates that Christ would be the head of the Church, and would gather from all parts of the earth the Jews who had been before scattered; and thus the promised restoration is to be extended to all the tribes.[37]

As to the millennial kingdom, Calvin did not venture a commentary on Revelation, nor does he mention the millennium in his Romans commentary. We must turn to his curt, dismissive remarks in the *Institutes* 3.25.5.[38]

Martyr takes the traditional Christian approach to this matter. He begins, in effect, his exposition of Romans 9, 10, and 11 by an anti-millenarian scholium on Rom. 4:13, where Paul teaches, "The promise to Abraham and his seed, that they should inherit the world, did not come through the law but through the righteousness of faith." Martyr identifies Christ as the one to whom this promise truly applies. This is nonetheless problematic, since inheriting the world appears to be a very materialistic promise. As Martyr notes:

> The prophets have more often expressed this promise of Christ's kingdom by the properties and condition of a worldly dominion and carnal happiness. For there is no other way in which spiritual things can be understood by crass intellects. Sometimes they say that it shall one day come to pass that the dispersed and exiled children of Israel will be born back in ships to their own place by the Gentiles. . . . But all these things are principally to be attributed to our great king Jesus Christ. . . .[39]

The elect in Christ are also heirs of all things; even so their present material circumstances do not reflect this. This observation leads Martyr to say:

> And since the faithful understand all things to be theirs, they are content with food and clothing—other things they take advantage of as is suitable for their calling. There is nothing in the world which cannot but turn out to be advantageous for them. The "chiliasts," whom in Latin we call "millenarians," suppose that this inheritance of the whole world is to be declared before the end of this world, when

---

[37] *CR* 72:295, ET *Commentaries on the Twelve Minor Prophets*, trans. [and ed.] John Owen, *V, Zechariah and Malachi* (Edinburgh: Calvin Translation Society, 1846–1849), 295.

[38] See also Heinrich Quistorp, *Calvin's Doctrine of the Last Things* (Richmond, Va.: John Knox Press, 1955), 116 and 158–162, "The Question of the Millennium."

[39] *In Epistolam S. Pauli Apostoli Ad Romanos*, 3d ed. (Basil, 1568), 129.

Christ, as they suppose, will reign a thousand years in this world with his saints, after all wicked and profligate people have been destroyed.[40]

There follows a fine discussion of the history and doctrine of millennialism. Martyr tells who of the early church fathers (as well as the heretics against whom they strove) believed in a millennium. Then he explains the impossibility of interpreting Paul's teaching on the return of Christ in a millennialist fashion. Finally he exposes the doctrinal difficulties of trying to square millennialism with the notion that "flesh and blood shall not inherit the Kingdom of God."[41] On this latter point Martyr's arguments are telling. Less convincing is his assumption that all Old Testament prophecies that purport to proclaim a return of the Jews to the land of Israel actually refer to the spiritual realities of Jesus Christ and his kingdom that is not of this world. Martyr had expounded the minor prophets at the beginning of his Protestant teaching career, and evidently not even such prophecies as Zechariah chapters nine to fourteen convinced him otherwise.

With the rise of philo-Semitism in the seventeenth century, Protestant interpreters, Puritans among them, boldly announced the return of the Jews to the land of Israel as a prelude to the Millennium.[42] Enthusiasm for a millennium proved in time to be no more than a marginal, passing phenomenon among Puritans. The Presbyterianism which the seventeenth century passed on was destined to be amillennialist.[43] At the same time the notion of the restoration of the Jews to Israel endured. For example, the nineteenth-century American Presbyterian T. V. Moore, concerning Zech. 10:6–12, says:

Henderson follows Grotius in supposing that this restoration took place before the coming of Christ, but the terms in which it is described

---

[40] *Ad Romanos*, 130.

[41] 1 Cor. 15:50.

[42] Brown, *Restoration of the* Jews, 38–64; David S. Katz, *Philo-Semitism and the Readmission of the Jews to England 1603–1655* (Oxford: Clarendon Press, 1982), 94, 98, 123–124. Philo-Semitism may be best understood as a Christian appreciation of Jews and Judaism during a time of eschatological speculation. It would therefore be misleading to define philo-Semitism as the opposite of anti-Semitism. Nor were most seventeenth-century philo-Semites rationalist: they did not believe that Judaism was an equally valid path to salvation, or even that Judaism was no better or no worse than any other religion. This mix of eschatological expectation and interest in things Jewish is present today in the grass-roots evangelicalism of North America and beyond.

[43] Hesselink, "The Millennium," 102.

can hardly be restricted to any return that took place during that period. Calvin refers it entire to a spiritual restoration. But the most natural interpretation seems to be that which predicts a future return to their own land, and a spiritual return to God, which is predicted as a separate and ultimate result in v. 12.[44]

Millennialism and the return of the Jews to Israel received a new lease on life in the ministry of John Nelson Darby and the Plymouth Brethren. The whole matter has become enormously important in the mind of popular evangelicalism, since many Jews have, in fact, returned to the modern state of Israel. In the twentieth century this has led to an unwavering support of Zionism in the North American Evangelical-Pentecostal axis; by contrast, there has been much uncritical support for the Palestinian cause by mainline Protestant leadership.[45] There is much wisdom, as I see it, in trying to take an honest look at scriptural passages that presage a final return of the Jews. I am inclined to agree with David Brown that denying that such a return as envisaged creates more problems than affirming it.[46] It is, of course, another matter to determine the status of such a return as an article of faith, or to reckon the present resettlement of Jews in their ancestral homeland to be a fulfillment of Old Testament prophecy.

The Advantages of Being a Jew

It has been relatively easy to track what Christian interpreters have said about the Jews' return to their homeland and about their end-times conversion. It is more difficult to compare how these same interpreters assess the continuing advantages of being a Jew according to Paul in Romans. It is often a question of the tone of their exegesis. Gerald Bray in an essay on the church fathers' attitudes to the Jews as reflected in their Romans commentary demonstrates that the fathers were at worst enemies of Judaism but that the label of

---

[44] Thomas V. Moore, *The Prophets of the Restoration* (New York: Robert Carter, 1856), reprinted (Carlisle, Pa.: The Banner of Truth Trust, 1979), 245.

[45] See, for example: Hall Lindsey, *The Road to Holocaust* (New York: Bantam Books, 1989); Naim Ateek, Marc H. Ellis, Rosemary Ruether, eds., *Faith and the Intifada: Palestinian Christian Voices* (Maryknoll, N.Y.: Orbis Books, 1992).

[46] Brown, *Restoration*, 67–68.

anti-Semitism simply will not stick.[47] While this is certainly true, the fathers missed many opportunities to say positive things about being Jewish, things which would have been well within the parameters of Paul's argument in Romans. Chrysostom is a case in point. While he affirms an end-times conversion of the Jews, he tries to mitigate the force of Paul's statement "beloved for the sakes of their ancestors;" Martyr criticizes Chrysostom in this regard.[48] It is a tribute to the exegetical honesty of the church fathers that they interpreted Paul on the Jews in Romans 9, 10, and 11 in a straightforward manner, especially considering the superior position of Judaism in the Roman *imperium* before Constantine. What Christian exegetes were tempted to do was this: affirm the inescapable (the Jews' eventual conversion) but sidestep other positive things Paul has to say about being a Jew.

Christian scriptural interpretation emphasizing the importance of being Jewish is scarce before the modern era and appears in unexpected places. The Luther that would pen his notoriously vile pamphlet, "On the Jews and their Lies," had earlier written the surprisingly sympathetic tract, "That Jesus Christ Was Born a Jew."[49] Martin Bucer was in practice no friend of the Jews yet was moved by Romans 11 to give a remarkably frank analysis of the origin of the Jews' troubles in Europe. According to Bucer, we are commanded by the Apostle Paul to cherish the Jews and to deal kindly with them; harsh treatment of them was responsible for the degradation into which Bucer believed they had sunk.[50]

Calvin's exegesis of Romans 9, 10, and 11 is hostile to the Jews in a subtle sort of way. Though Calvin does not indulge in stridently anti-Jewish rhetoric in his comments, he evades parts of Paul's argument. The desire for consistency seems to be behind Calvin's aim in denying the end-times conversion of the Jews. When Paul says

---

[47] "Attitudes Towards Jews in Patristic Commentaries on Romans," in *Interpreting the Bible: Historical and Theological Studies in Honour of David F. Wright*, ed. A. N. S. Lane (Leicester: Apollos, 1997). See also Bray's collection of patristic quotations in *Ancient Christian Commentary on Scripture: Romans*, 244–304.

[48] *In epist. ad Rom. homil.*, PG 60:585, 591–592, ET, *Nicene and Post-Nicene Fathers of the Christian Church* 11:488, 493. Martyr, *Ad Romanos*, 536.

[49] *WA* 53:417–552, 11:314–336; *LW* 47:121–306; 45:199–229.

[50] R. Gerald Hobbs, "Martin Bucer et les Juifs," in *Martin Bucer and Sixteenth Century Europe: Actes du Colloque de Strasbourg (28–31 août 1991)*, ed. C. Krieger and M. Leinhard (Leiden: Brill, 1993), 681 n. 1.; Bucer, *Enarrationes in Romanos*, 448.

"all Israel will be saved," Calvin wanted Paul to be saying that it was still possible for individual Jews to be converted to Christ even though the nation as a whole rejected him. Thus Calvin could maintain that the Church had permanently superceded the Synagogue and that the elect of the Gentiles (and Jews) were the people of God. Paul's argument is not, of course, so consistent. Paul maintains the continuing normative election of the Jews, even though they do not now believe. This is plainly a contradiction of sorts, and Calvin's interpretation gets rid of it.

Martyr, on the other hand, tries to follow Paul's tortuous argument. He vigorously maintains the contradiction. The Jews are enemies as well as friends. On the latter he is persuasive:

> [God] who was formerly well-disposed to the Jews has not become hateful to them, and what was in time past by nature a grace, namely to be born a Jew, is hardly disdainful now. Nor are the Jews odious to God for the very reason that they are Jews; for how could this have happened since they were embellished with so many great gifts....[51]

That is the nub of the matter, isn't it? "The Jews are not odious to God for the very reason that they are Jews." This is the distinction between anti-Judaism (which all the Reformers shared, as did all Catholics of the era) and anti-Semitism (with which the Reformers and unofficially the Catholics at points flirted).

Further into his exposition Martyr expressly declares the essential "nobility" of the Jewish people, drawing (in typical Martyr-fashion) upon Aristotle's definition of nobility. The Jews are noble because: 1. They have the covenant made with the patriarchs; 2. They were free and lived under the best laws; 3. They are the most ancient of peoples; 4. They had great leaders among their prophets, judges and kings.[52] Martyr is forthright in criticizing such church fathers as Chrysostom and Ambrose for trying to interpret away Paul's statement that the Jews are beloved for the sake of their fathers. When they disobey the gospel, they, like the rest of humanity, are condemned; yet they still remain beloved in a way that is not true of the rest of disobedient humanity.[53] Martyr offers as proof of their continuing place in the economy of God their indestructibility. Other

---

[51] *Ad Romanos*, 488–489.
[52] *Ad Romanos*, 518.
[53] *Ad Romanos*, 536.

nations—in fact, all other nations of the ancient world—have ceased to exist. Not the Jews.[54] This is an argument that was received from Augustine, repeated in the Middle Ages, and again taken up even by such a theological giant as Karl Barth.[55]

The uniqueness of Martyr's exposition of Romans 9, 10, and 11 as it concerns the continuing place of the Jews is not in his disavowal of a millennium, or his espousal of an end-times conversion of the Jews, but rather in his emphasis on the continuing benefits of being Jewish. He expounds the place of the Jews in Romans *in bonam partem*. He casts the Jews in as favorable a light as an honest exegesis of Romans will allow. Thus Martyr's treatment is unusual only when set against the often reluctant or non-existent affirmations of such previous interpreters as Calvin.

The question remains as to whether or not Martyr's exposition of Romans 9, 10, and 11 had any lasting influence. In a recent article, "The Millennium and the Reformed Tradition," I. John Hesselink connected Peter Martyr's commentary on Romans with the rise of premillennialism in England.[56] Hesselink is making reference to a claim made by Iain Murray:

> The first volume in English to expound at some length [the conviction of a future general conversion of the Jews] was the translation of Peter Martyr's *Commentary upon Romans*, published in London in 1568. The probability is strong that Martyr's careful exposition of the eleventh chapter prepared the way for a general adoption amongst the English

---

[54] *Ad Romanos*, 538.

[55] *Augustine through the Ages*, s.v. "Jews and Judaism"; Barth, KD § 34, e.g. ET II/2.263: "the personification of a half-venerable, half-gruesome relic, of a miraculously preserved antique, of human whimsicality." Outside the context of the exegesis of Romans 11, the Martyr corpus which survives has another section which, in a rather backhanded sort of way, lauds the Jews; this is in a *scholium* entitled "Whether it be lawful for Christians to dwell with infidels" in his *Judges* lectures. As was the case in his *Romans* exegesis, Martyr says nothing startlingly new. He misses a golden opportunity to advocate expulsion of the Jews from Christian territory. The bulk of his comments have to do with the authenticity of the Hebrew Old Testament: it, not the Vulgate or the Septuagint, is the final authority. What makes his defense of the Hebrew Old Testament arresting is the vigor with which he pursues his argument. Apart from Martyr's explicit statements on the Jews, we can also indirectly gather something of his attitude toward things Jewish by the fact that Martyr makes no secret of his dependence on the philological Jewish commentators of the Middle Ages, such as Ibn Ezra; he cites them explicitly hundreds of times in his lectures on Scripture. Also, his first Hebrew teacher was a Jew, and Martyr was responsible for winning the Jew-turned-Catholic, Emmanuel Tremellius, to the cause of evangelical reform.

[56] *Reformed Review* 52:2 (Winter 1998–1999), 101–102.

Puritans of [this] belief. . . . Closely linked as English Puritanism was
to John Calvin, it was the view contained in Martyr's commentary
which was received by the rising generation of students at Cambridge.[57]

In actual fact, it is not surprising that Calvin's spiritual descendants
ignored Calvin's eccentric interpretation of Rom. 11:15, 25–26 and
held to the main stream of exegetical opinion up to that point. Does
this mean that Martyr's exegesis did not contribute to philo-Semitism
and its often concomitant millennialism? Not necessarily. When Martyr
presented the Jews in a *relatively* favorable light in his widely disseminated Romans commentary, this was potentially one factor in
the development of philo-Semitism and its often concomitant millennialism among English Puritans. That this was in fact the case,
will have to be the subject of another inquiry.[58] Until the rise of
Protestant modernism, there was a continuing legacy of philo-Semitism
in the sense that many Protestant Churches held to a continuing
expectation of an eventual conversion of the Jews and took a lively
interest in proselytizing them. For example, the remarkable career
of Leon Levison, the Jewish-Christian turned Scottish Presbyterian
minister, was a product of a Presbyterian Jewish mission.[59] Peter
Martyr Vermigli's exposition of Romans 9, 10, and 11 was one factor, however small, in the establishment of these missions.

---

[57] Iain H. Murray, *The Puritan Hope: A Study in Revival and the Interpretation of Prophecy*
(Carlisle, Pa.: The Banner of Truth Trust, 1971), 42. Neither Hesselink nor Murray
present hard data to back up their contention.

[58] I have reason to suspect that Martyr was, in fact, cited frequently by millen-
nialists. For example, Henry Jessey (1601–1663), one of the more moderate members of the millennialist sect, the Fifth Monarchy Men, cites Martyr. See "A
Philo-Semitic Millenarian on the Reconciliation of Jews and Christians: Henry Jesse
and his *The Glory and Salvation of Jehudah and Israel (1650)*," in *Sceptics, Millenarians
and Jews*, eds. David S. Katz and Jonathan I. Israel (Leiden: Brill, 1990), 180.
Another millennialist, Nathan Homes, also cites Martyr in *A Brief Chronicle Concerning
the Jews*, a work which is contained in *Two Journeys to Jerusalem*: see Katz, *Philo-
Semitism*, 99.

[59] Frederick Levison, *Christian and Jew: the Life of Leon Levison, 1881–1936* (Edinburgh:
Pentland Press, 1989), 14–15.

CHRISTOLOGICAL CURRENTS IN VERMIGLI'S THOUGHT

John Patrick Donnelly, S.J.[1]

Research on Peter Martyr Vermigli as theologian usually begins with the selections of his writings that Robert Masson gathered and published at London as the *Loci Communes* in 1576, but a student searching there for his teaching on christology will be somewhat disappointed. The subject is treated in Book II, chapter 17, and contains a scattering of passages taken from Martyr's commentaries on Romans, I Corinthians, and I Samuel.[2] Masson was well aware that these passages were thin on major aspects of christology, so he pointed readers to Martyr's *Dialogus de utraque in Christo natura* for a treatment of the hypostatic union.[3] He also printed at the end of his treatment of christology a fresh Latin translation of Martyr's *Una semplice dichiaratione sopra gli XII articoli della fede christiana*, most of which deals with Christ.[4]

The vast majority of Martyr's works were either biblical commentaries or polemics against Roman Catholics, but Martyr generally agreed with Catholics about christology. Christological questions were not likely to arise in his Old Testament commentaries, and at Oxford he chose to lecture on I Corinthians and Romans so that he could defend doctrines over which he and the numerous Catholics at Oxford were at odds. Martyr's christological controversies were with Protestants and, with one exception, are found in his letters. Fortunately all editions of the *Loci* after the first added a selection of his letters. Four

---

[1] I wish to thank Dr. Frank A. James, III for suggestions that have improved this essay.

[2] LC, 411–420.

[3] Ibid., 415.

[4] Ibid., 421–442. There are fifty-one sections in the *Dichiaratione*; Martyr, following the trinitarian structure of the creed, devotes sections 5 to 31 to Christ and his work. The tone is popular and pastoral, a far cry from the learned and systematic approach in Martyr's *loci* on justification and predestination in his commentary on Romans.

letters, two of which are printed in the *Loci*, deal with christology and are the main source for this essay. With the exception of one letter to the Polish Lords (14 February 1556), all of Martyr's writings on christology date from 1560 and 1561. He died in 1562.

Martyr's Dialogue against Brenz

Martyr's longest writing on christology was his *Dialogus de utraque in Christo natura*, directed against Johannes Brenz, who was arguably the premier Lutheran theologian after Melanchthon's death in 1560. Vermigli's book never names Brenz but quotes extensively from Brenz's *De personali unione duarum naturarum in Christo . . .*, so many readers would have known that his target was Brenz.[5] Of all his opponents in polemics, Vermigli seems to have respected Brenz the most. Brenz was determined to ground his defense of Christ's real physical presence in the eucharist in a christology of the human and divine natures in the one person of Christ. Luther had developed these ideas, but Brenz carried them considerably further, and in attacking Brenz Vermigli was careful not to attack Luther himself. The controversy between Lutherans and Reformed on how Christ is really present in the eucharist spilled over into christology and produced more than 190 books and pamphlets which are listed by Helmut Gollwitzer, who also lists 184 modern studies of this controversy.[6] Two recent studies have looked into the Vermigli-Brenz confrontation, so the treatment here will be brief, even though the *Dialogus* is Vermigli's longest and most important work on christology.[7] The work is a dialogue between Pantachus (for Brenz) and Orothetes (for Vermgili). The *Dialogus* follows Brenz's work closely, putting quotations from the *De personali unione* in the mouth of Pantachus so that Orothetes can refute them point by point. Although

---

[5] Johannes Brenz, *De personali unione duarum naturaum in Christo . . .* (Tubingen: Marhard, 1561).

[6] Helmut Gollwitzer, *Coena Domini: Die altlutherische Abendmahlslehre in ihrer Auseinandersetzung mit dem Calvinismus, dargestellt an der lutherische Frühorthodoxie* (Munich: Kaiser, 1988), 312–328.

[7] DIAL, ix–xxv; Hans Christian Brandy, *Die späte Christologie des Johannes Brenz* (Tübingen: J. C. B. Mohr, 1991), 54–90.

it provides no synthetic treatment of christology, the main lines of Martyr's teaching are clear enough. Both Brenz and Martyr saw themselves as upholding the christology of the early Church as formulated at the Councils of Ephesus and Chalcedon and explained in the writings of the Church Fathers. Their differences arose over how these teachings applied to Christ's presence in the eucharist, Brenz defending Luther's insistence on the real, physical presence of Christ's body in, under, and with the bread and wine, and Vermigli arguing for Christ being symbolically and spiritually present for believers when they partook of the eucharistic bread and wine since Christ's body and soul remains at the right hand of the Father in heaven. Although their controversy was really about the eucharist, Martyr seldom refers to the institution narratives in Matthew, Mark, Luke and I Corinthians or to the discourse on the bread of life in John's sixth chapter.[8]

Most of the *Dialogus* explores how the communication of idioms between the divine and human nature in the person of the Word made flesh plays out: does the ubiquity of Christ's divine nature mean that his human nature, including his body, can be present in more places than one? Since neither the scriptures nor Ephesus and Chalcedon get into this arcane question, both Brenz and Vermigli lined up citations from the Church Fathers that seemed to defend their different positions. Most of Vermigli's *Dialogus* is spent in refuting Brenz's use of the Fathers and citing their support for the Reformed teaching.[9] Toward the end of the *Dialogus* Martyr lines up a supporter for his teaching who must have been especially painful for Brenz: Philip Melanchthon in his later years.[10] Rarely did Reformation era polemicists raise the white flag. Brenz replied to the *Dialogus* with his *De divina maiestate Christi et de vera praesentia corporis et sanguinis eius in Coena*.[11] Despite his failing health Martyr was

---

[8] For such references see DIAL, 193, 200–202.

[9] The following writers of the early Church are quoted or cited in the *Dialogus*: Ambrose, Athanasius, Augustine, Basil, Bede, Bernard, Chrysostom, Clement of Alexandria, Cyprian, Cyril of Alexandria, Didymus, Dionysius, Eustatius, Fulgentius, Gelasius, Gregory of Nazianzen, Gregory of Nyssa, Hippolytus, Irenaeus, Jerome, John of Antioch, John of Damascus, Photinus, Prosper of Aquitaine, Ruffinus, Severian of Gabala, Tertullian, Theodoret, and Vigilius. Less numerous are references to medieval theologians and Martyr's own contemporaries.

[10] Ibid., 164–170.

[11] Frankfurt, 1562.

preparing notes toward refuting it when his death cut short the project.[12] Martyr's *Dialogus* is an erudite and effective polemic and proved
surprisingly popular, five Latin editions plus translations into German
and French. It is his longest work on christology, but it does not
attempt a systematic statement of Martyr's christology or soteriology
and thus can leave modern readers somewhat disappointed.

Martyr's four other writings on christology have not been subjected to study, so they deserve more careful examination here than
the *Dialogus*. They share several characteristics. All were written
against theological tendencies related to the Radical Reformation.
Vermigli was less charitable toward these opponents to traditional
christology than he was toward Brenz. The four works are all letters written to Reformed churches that lacked major theologians of
their own. They all deal with larger christological issues than did
the *Dialogus*, and they have a greater pastoral concern. All have been
recently translated in my edition of Peter Martyr Vermigli's *Life,
Letters, and Sermons* [henceforward LLS], volume V in *The Peter Martyr
Library*.[13] References to the *Loci Communes* [henceforward LC] in this
essay are from the London 1583 edition.

The Haemstede Controversy over Christ's Heavenly Flesh

On 15 February 1561 Martyr wrote a long letter to the Dutch
Strangers' Church in London.[14] There were two strangers' churches
for foreign Protestants living in London; most of their parishioners
were refugees fleeing persecutions on the Continent or the families
of merchants. The French community used the former Chapel of
St. Anthony on Threadneedle Street and was not involved in this
controversy. The Dutch community occupied the nearby former

---

[12] For Martyr's projected refutation, see Erland Herkenrath, "Peter Martyr
Vermiglis Vorarbeit zu einer zweiten christologischen Schrift gegen Johannes Brenz
1562," *Blätter für württembergische Kirchengeschichte* 75 (1975): 23–31.

[13] LLS.

[14] There is a summary of Martyr's letter with background in John Strype's *The
History of the Life and Acts of the Most Reverend Father in God, Edmund Grindal....* (Oxford:
Clarendon Press, 1821; reprinted edition: New York: Burt Franklin Reprints, 1974),
63–66.

church of the Augustinian Friars.[15] This Dutch church was rather large: in 1561, the year of Martyr's letter, it registered 429 male and 257 female communicants.[16] Both of these churches had been established under Edward VI, were dissolved under Mary Tudor, and were re-established when Elizabeth I came to power in 1558.

The christological controversy at the Dutch Strangers' Church centered on Adriaan van Haemstede (c. 1525–1562), who is best remembered for his *Historie de Martelaren* (1559), a history of the Dutch Protestant martyrs only slightly less important for the Dutch Reformed church than the martyrologies of John Foxe and Jean Crespin were for English and French Protestants.[17] For several years he served as minister in Antwerp, but his public preaching brought down greater persecution on Protestants and his abrasive personality led to disputes with other ministers and with his congregation. He fled to London in 1559 where he served as minister at the Strangers' church. Soon Peter Delenus [Deleen] took over as minister with Haemstede as his assistant, but after a short period of co-operation their relationship soured. Delenus had been raised in London under Edward VI and had served as a minister in Emden, where there was a significant English refugee community during Mary Tudor's reign. On 3 July 1560 the parish Consistory heard a report about a meeting between Haemstede and some Dutch Anabaptists in which, it was claimed, he had shaken their hands in brotherhood. The next day Haemstede was summoned before the Consistory where he defended himself by saying that he had done so not because he agreed with their teachings but as a sign of friendship. When the Consistory demanded that he confess his fault openly, he stalked out of the meeting.[18] In subsequent negotiations he refused to condemn

---

[15] The history of these two churches is studied in detail by Andrew Pettegree, *Foreign Protestant Communities in Sixteenth Century London* (Oxford: Oxford University Press, 1986). On the location and founding of the two churches, 36–37.

[16] Ibid., 182.

[17] My account of the Haemstede affair draws on Pettegree, 164–181, the article on Haemstede in the *Oxford Encyclopedia of the Reformation* (New York: Oxford University Press, 1996) II, 207–208, and Patrick Collinson, *Archbishop Grindal, 1519–1583: The Struggle for a Reformed Church* (Berkeley: University of California Press, 1979), 134–140. None of these works discusses Martyr's role in the affair.

[18] Pettegree, 168–169. Haemstede did not profess Anabaptist doctrines, and his martyrology pointedly did not contain accounts of the many Dutch Anabaptist martyrs; several of his parishioners testified that he had attacked Anabaptist teaching in his sermons.

Anabaptists for errors on some doctrinal points that he considered unimportant or anaphora, especially since they were pious, peaceful and law-abiding, unlike the Münsterites. His defense of his position evoked considerable sympathy among members of the church and resentment toward the Consistory. When the Consistory put before him a statement condemning Anabaptist teaching, he refused to sign it without making unacceptable additions. When he was criticized for failing to attend several Consistory meetings, he threw on the table the fines for missing meetings. His truculence led to his being dismissed from the Consistory.[19] The whole case was referred to Edmund Grindal, then Bishop of London, who lectured Haemstede about doctrinal heterodoxy on 9 September. After more hearings Haemstede challenged the Consistory to a disputation. Grindal issued a statement of excommunication on 14 November, which was read in the Dutch church three days later. Still many of the congregation sympathized with Haemstede, and several of his supporters were hailed before the Consistory.[20] The most important of his supporters was the Italian philosopher-scientist Jacobo Acontius (c. 1520–1567), whose 1565 *Satanae Stragemata*, probably influenced by the Haemstede affair, argued for toleration of all who did not deny a small number of fundamental doctrines. In May 1561 Acontius and nine other of Haemstede's supporters were excommunicated. On 31 August 1561 Grindal presented Haemstede with a long formula of recantation and when he refused to sign it, he was deported to East Friesland.[21]

Peter Martyr wrote his letter of 15 February 1561 attacking Haemstede at the request of the Strangers' Church, presumably made by the Consistory.[22] Why did the Church ask Martyr to intervene?

---

[19] Ibid., 170.

[20] Ibid., 171–172; Collinson, 134–138.

[21] Collinson, 138–140. Strype prints the formula of recantation, 67–69. On his refusal to sign it: Strype, 69. Acontius argued that Satan's strategy was to set Christian against Christian over peripheral theological issues. The Haemstede affair, which sprang from whether a christological teaching of the Anabaptists could be tolerated, may have influenced Acontius's thinking on toleration, but it seems more likely that Acontius influenced Haemstede to regard the disputed Anabaptist christological teachings as anaphora.

[22] Martyr's letter is printed in LLS, 184–197; Latin text of the letter cited in this essay are from the 1583 London edition of the LC, 1128–1133. Strype [64] says of Martyr's letter, "And the said reverend man wrote back a very large and learned answer to the church, strengthening that article of faith, and confuting Adrian's paper and arguments. . . . He shewed how very unseasonably Adrian had

In 1561 he was at the height of his career as a Reformed theologian. Like the members of the Strangers' Church, Martyr had been a foreigner when he served as Regius Professor of Theology at Oxford under Edward VI.

Martyr never referred to Brenz by name in his *Dialogus*, but the very first word of his letter to the Strangers' Church is *Hadrianus* [for Adriaan van Haemstede], and the name recurs frequently. The Anabaptist teaching at the center of the controversy was the teaching of Menno Simons (*c.* 1496–1561) that Christ's flesh was not taken from the Virgin Mary but was a heavenly flesh.[23] Martyr's letter develops three main arguments: that this teaching should not be tolerated because toleration would have serious consequences for the Dutch community, that the teaching could not be classified among anaphora or peripheral questions, and that it was heretical.

Martyr begins by attacking Haemstede's claim that the Anabaptists' opinion that Christ's flesh was brought down from heaven did not prevent their salvation, even if they clung to it obstinately. Supporting them encouraged the Anabaptists in their error and was discouraging other Christians from avoiding it.[24] Martyr admits that Haemstede himself had opposed the Anabaptists on other points and has a reputation for a holy life, but his teaching causes much harm.[25]

Martyr then attacks the Anabaptist teaching itself. He questions their claim that Christ can be a true mediator if his flesh was not taken from the Virgin. "[H]ence those who paste a heavenly flesh on [Christ] do not have the mediator proposed by God but one they have dreamed up. . . ."[26] He condemns the Anabaptist teaching

---

disturbed the church, by moving a controversy in it, of which they at Zurick had been consulted; that he was not to be approved in defending that opinion, whereby the people were rather destroyed, than edified in true orthodox doctrine."

[23] Martyr had attacked the doctrine of heavenly flesh much earlier while lecturing at Oxford on I Cor. 15:47; the lectures were published in 1551 and the passage was reprinted in the LC, 2, ch. 17, 413–415. There Martyr attributes the doctrine of heavenly flesh to two ancient heretics, Valentinus and Marcion, and to one contemporary, Kaspar von Schwenckfeld (1489–1561). Martyr refutes ten arguments supporting the heavenly flesh doctrine and gives twelve arguments of his own why Christ had a human body. Officials at the Strangers' Church probably knew how Martyr stood on the issue, and this most likely influenced their request for his intervention in the Haemstede affair.

[24] LLS 184; LC 1128.

[25] LLS 184–185; LC 1128–1129.

[26] LLS 186; LC 1129: Quocirca illi qui ei carnem coelestem affigunt, non a Deo propositum mediatorem habent, sed illum quem sibi ex invento et cerebro suo confinxerunt.

as having no foundation in scripture and claims that those who hold such a position are deprived of eternal salvation, for their blindness to what the scriptures teach about the mediator will result in their damnation. Ignorance about the articles of faith entails extreme consequences; it is not so much ignorance as disbelief.[27] Martyr insists that Christ's birth from Mary "pertains to the most important articles of faith."[28] Being born of Mary means that Christ did not just pass through her uterus; he took his flesh from her. To deny this is to destroy Christ as our mediator, even if the Anabaptists verbally profess faith in him. Martyr argues, "[T]hey are going to perish forever since they do not have a true mediator but one they have manufactured for themselves."[29] In passing, he notes that the papists are not freed from eternal destruction just because they think they are preaching the true gospel.[30]

For Martyr the key scripture text is 1 John 4:2–3: "By this you know the Spirit of God: every spirit which confesses that Jesus Christ has come in the flesh is of God, and every spirit which does not confess Jesus is not of God." Martyr exclaims, "We know that according to you, O Adriaan, the Christ who comes in the flesh and who took flesh from the Virgin are two, and two in such a way that one can be believed in without the other, just as we today see has become the practice of the Anabaptists."[31] The Anabaptists' failure to believe that the Lord's flesh was taken from the Virgin was not a trivial error that the Reformed could ignore because that very flesh belonged to Christ's substance [ousia] as regards his humanity and hence his

---

[27] Ibid.

[28] Ibid.: Christum auten ex Maria virgine natum esse ad summa fidei capita pertinere nemo sanae religionis ambigit.

[29] LLS 187; LC 1129: . . . aeternum sint perituri, cum verum mediatorem non habeant, sed illum quem ipsi fabricarunt.

[30] LLS 187; LC 1129. It seems that the question of Martin Luther's salvation had also been brought up by Haemstede or his supporters. Luther's teaching on the ubiquity of Christ's human body in the eucharist was opposed to Reformed Christology, and was similar to that of Brenz. Martyr answered that the Reformed should not stir up hostility toward Luther and should hope that God may have enlightened him at the moment of death since God's mercy is abundant and he helps his own at the point of death even when they seem forsaken. Lutheran readers would have drawn cold comfort from this!

[31] LLS 189; LC 1130: Nos scimus juxta te, O Hadriane, Christum in carne venissse, ac illam ex virgine sumpsisse, duo esse, ac ita duo, ut possit unum credi absque altero, ut hodie cernimus Anabaptistis usu venire.

role as mediator. It is not merely a minor circumstance of Christ's birth.[32]

Martyr claims to be astonished that Haemstede on the one hand maintains that Christ's taking flesh from the Virgin is necessary for our salvation and then is willing to admit that those who deny this can attain salvation. "We confess that we believe in Jesus Christ, the Son of God, conceived and born of the Virgin Mary, not in him who went through her as through a canal."[33] Those who deny this are worthy of condemnation just as the early church condemned Arians, Nestorians, Eutychians and others. Martyr brushes aside Adriaan's argument that the church allows the salvation of children and the mentally defective, therefore it should allow that the Anabaptists can be saved. The Anabaptists are adults and mentally competent; they can read the scriptures and hear sermons and thereby correct their errors. Adriaan urges that it is absurd to deny salvation to somebody who rejects only this one doctrine about Christ's flesh. Martyr replies: "All of God's words, inasmuch as they flow out from him, carry equal weight and authority, and therefore it is not right for a person by private judgment to accept this one and to refute and reject that one as false." If that were so, Arius himself would have to be accepted as a member of Christ.[34]

Moreover the error about Christ's heavenly flesh brought with it many other errors. If his flesh was brought down from heaven, Christ was not the seed of Eve or Abraham or David nor even of Mary—all things stated clearly in scripture. Indeed, how can he be called Son of Man? If the teaching about heavenly flesh is accepted, then Christ cannot be a true mediator for the human race. When his opponents proposed this last argument, Haemstede dismissed it as a sophistical quibble; Martyr replied that the Church Fathers and Aristotle had used the same method of argument against opponents.[35] Martyr also refuted Haemstede's argument that his opponents must

---

[32] LLS 190–191; LC 1131.

[33] LLS 191; LC 1131: Fatemur quippe nos credere in Iesum Christum Dei filium, conceptum et natum ex Maria virgine, non in eum qui per eam ceu per canalem transierit.

[34] LLS 193; LC 1132: Omnia verba Dei quatenus ab eo fluxerunt, paris esse ponderis atque authoritatis, atque idcirco nemini fas est pro suo arbitrio istud recipere, aliud vero confutare, atque ut falsum aspernari.

[35] LLS 193–194; LC 1132.

produce an explicit statement from scripture that those not believing that Christ took his flesh from the Virgin are damned and beyond
salvation. God made no effort to list in scripture all the errors which
heretics might hatch; rather the scriptures provide what we must
believe. For instance some heretics in the early church rejected the
books of the Old Testament, but the Bible never says that such persons are condemned.[36] Toward the end of his letter Martyr crafted
his arguments so that the majority of the congregation at the Strangers'
church could understand them: Christians should celebrate God's
mercies, but not in a way that overthrows God's judgment against
heretics, as Haemstede was doing. Martyr then attacks Origen and
those urging universal salvation. He concludes with a plea that the
Dutch church work for peace. Indeed, he urges those who have
defended the truth against Haemstede welcome him back as a minister of God and beloved colleague *if he agrees with those who have
admonished him.*[37]

Christological heresies usually fit nicely into one of three camps:
the Arians, the Nestorians, and the Monophysites/Eutychians. Martyr
in his *Dialogus* classifies Brenz's teaching on the ubiquity of Christ's
body as Monophysite because it misuses the communication of idioms;
by attributing divine ubiquity to Christ's human body Brenz was
destroying the integrity of his human nature. The Anabaptist teaching about Christ's heavenly flesh seems at first sight Nestorian.
Nestorius first came under fire for denying that Mary was the mother
or bearer of God. The Anabaptist teaching about heavenly flesh
seems an emphatic denial that Mary was the mother of God. Yet
on a deeper level the doctrine has Monophysite roots: the divine
nature by providing heavenly flesh destroys the integrity of Christ's
human nature even more fundamentally than does extending the
divine ubiquity to Christ's body.

Martyr, Stancaro and Christ as Mediator

Last we need to examine three letters in which Martyr replied to
requests for theological guidance from pastors and noblemen in the

---

[36] LLS 194–195; LC 1132.
[37] LLS 196–198; LC 1133.

Polish Reformed church, which was far more beset by attacks on the Trinity and christology and the teachings of the first four ecumenical councils than were the churches of western Europe. Roman Catholics, Lutherans and the Reformed all accepted these teachings, but no country of Europe allowed so much religious toleration as Poland. Religious radicals, especially Italians, drifted there where they often found support from Polish noblemen on whose estates they could live, preach and write in safety.

Martyr's first letter was written from Strasbourg on 14 February 1556 and was reprinted in all editions of the *Loci Communes* except the first. The second (27 May 1560) and third letter (March 1561) were not published in the *Loci* and hence are less well known. They were published in *Epistolae duae, ad Ecclesias Polonicas, Iesu Christ . . . de negotio Stancario*,[38] [henceforward ED], but only two copies of this are known to exist, one in Geneva, one in Warsaw.[39] I have recently published an English translation of all three letters.[40] The second and third letters are directed against Francesco Stancaro, as the title page of the published edition makes clear.[41]

Stancaro (*c.* 1501–1572) was a Mantuan trained in classical languages who had taught at the universities in Padua, Vienna, and Kraków; later he went to Prussia and he became engaged in controversies with Andreas Osiander, Wolfgang Musculus and Melanchthon. As a theologian he was both abrasive and prolific, writing more than fifty treatises. After a turbulent stay in Hungary he returned to Poland Minor in 1559, attacked Jan Laski and built up a following among the Polish nobility. By 1561 he headed a school and seminary which

---

[38] Vermigli, *Epistolae duae, ad Ecclesias Polonicas, Iesu Christ . . . de negotio Stancario* (Zurich: C. Froschauer, March, 1561). Henceforward ED.

[39] Donnelly et al., *A Bibliography of the Works of Peter Martyr Vermigli* (Kirksville, Mo.: Sixteenth Century Journal Publishers, 1990), 140.

[40] LLS 142–154, 178–183, 198–220. The second letter is also printed in PMRD, 127–131.

[41] On the Stancaro controversy see Theodor Wotschke, *Geschichte der Reformation in Polen* (Leipzig: Rudolf Haupt, 1911; New York: Johnson Reprint Corporation, 1971), 179–193; Waclaw Urban, "Die großen Jahre der stancarianischen 'Häresie' (1559–1563)" *Archiv für Reformationsgeschichte*, 81 (1990): 309–318; Marvin Anderson devotes a section to Vermigli's role in the controversy in his PMRE, 439–455. More scattered in its treatment of the Stancaro affair but richer in background is George H. Williams, *The Radical Reformation*, 3rd ed. (Kirksville, Mo.: Sixteenth Century Journal Publishers, 1992).

had three hundred students and five teachers and served as head-quarters for his own Reformed synod.[42] Martyr's first letter is more far ranging and devotes only a paragraph to Stancaro's teaching. He begins by rejoicing in the recent spread of the gospel to Poland but then bewails Mary Tudor's persecution in England and the spread of the teaching of Arius and Michael Servetus. He also attacks those who teach that Christ's body is everywhere and that his flesh was not taken from the Virgin Mary. Here he assigns no names, but he may have already had Brenz, Menno Simons, and Karlstadt in mind. His language is more violent than that found in his later polemics against Brenz and Haemstede: "Who except a fool and a madman would grant that these fellows confess and accept the true God and the true Christ as he is described in the sacred letters."[43] Such fellows adore a Christ whom they have fabricated for them-selves who is not found in the scriptures. After arguing that scrip-ture alone is the criterion of sound doctrine[44] he exhorts the Polish pastors to take action against the heretics: "Let the evil seeds and rotten roots be cut off right down to their beginnings, for if they are neglected at the start (I know what I am saying), they are much harder to pull out later."[45] Martyr next discusses the right under-standing and use of the sacraments and urges the pastors to intro-duce discipline. Seminaries should be set up and train the clergy in Greek and Hebrew; the clergy should teach upright morality and correct doctrine.[46]

Martyr closes by addressing five doctrinal questions, several deal-ing with christology, that Francesco Lismanino (1504–1566), the leader of the Reformed church in Poland, had put to him.[47] 1) Martyr denies that Christ suffered in his divinity. 2) Against Francesco Stancaro he argues that Christ is mediator in both his divine and

---

[42] Williams, 1035.

[43] LLS 142–144; LC 1110: Quis istos nisi desipiat ac deliret, verum Deum, verumque Christum, ut in sacris scripturis describitur, concesserit fateri atque suscipere?

[44] LLS 144–145; LC 1110.

[45] LLS 145; LC 1111: "... aurruncentur sub ipsis initiis mala semina et putres radices, nam si e principio negligantur (scio quid loquor) postea multo difficilius tolluntur."

[46] LLS 146–150; LC 1111–1114.

[47] Lismanino put several of the same five questions to Calvin in a letter of 15 September 1555: CR *Calvini Opera*, XV, 868–871.

human nature. This will be the central issue in Martyr's two later letters to the Polish church. Here he does not mention Stancaro by name, but he shows how Stancaro's favorite proof text (1 Tim. 2:5: "one mediator between God and man, the man Christ") does not support Stancaro's contention that Christ is mediator only in his human nature. 3) Christ is by nature the Son of God and by nature the son of man, but Christians must guard against mixing the two natures of Christ. 4) Martyr attacks by name Andreas Osiander (1496?–1552), who had taught that in addition to imputed right-eousness Christians possessed an essential justice.[48] 5) The Poles had asked about Martyr's reaction to the execution of Michael Servetus (1509?–1553) at Calvin's Geneva for denying the Trinity. Martyr justified the execution since Servetus was a son of the devil whose blasphemies were intolerable.[49]

Martyr's second letter to the Polish churches (27 May 1560) was written on behalf of the ministers at Zurich to answer a request of Felix Cruciger (d. 1563), who served as the first superintendent of the Reformed Churches of Lesser Poland, 1554 to 1560.[50] On 7 August 1559 a Polish Reformed synodal assembly had met at Pinczów and took up Stancaro's teaching that Christ is mediator only in his human nature; it excommunicated him and threatened pastors cling-ing to his teaching with removal from office. The meeting was so heated that Jan Laski threw a Bible at Stancaro's head. On 10 August Laski and his supporters issued their "*Confessio de Mediatore generis humani Jesu Christo Deo et homine.*"[51] Laski's death on 8 January 1560 deprived the churches of their best theologian. Stancaro was condemned again at another synod at Pinczów 5 May 1560,[52] but lacking a major theologian, the Polish churches wrote the ministers at Geneva and Zurich for guidance.

John Calvin replied for the Geneva church (thirteen pastors and doctors were co-signers of his letter, dated 9 June 1560). Martyr's letter, dated 27 May, was written on behalf of the pastors, preachers and ministers of the Zurich church.[53] The two letters make an inter-

---

[48] LLS 151–153; LC 1113–1114.
[49] LLS 154; LC 1114.
[50] For Martyr's letter, LLS 178–183; ED 1–10.
[51] Williams, 1028–1030; Williams prints an English translation of the "Confessio" on 1030–1031.
[52] Ibid., 1037.
[53] There were several reasons why Martyr was chosen to write on behalf of the

esting contrast. They are nearly identical in length. Both start by lamenting Laski's death. Calvin takes up the question of the priesthood of Christ, something Martyr does not treat. Calvin has fourteen scripture citations, Martyr only four, but curiously the two theologians never cite the same text. Martyr's letter impressed me as more theological, clear and profound than Calvin's.[54]

After paying tribute to Laski, Martyr takes up the Polish request that he explain how Christ is the one mediator between his Church and the Father so that the Polish churches can respond to Stancaro: "The two natures [of Christ] subsist in a way that they are joined with each other so that they cannot in any way be pulled apart from each other. Therefore all actions of Christ should be attributed to the hypostasis or person because the two natures do not subsist separately . . . so every work of Christ of any sort should be ascribed to the hypostasis or person itself. Meanwhile the properties of the two natures which are in Christ should be kept distinct, whole, and unmixed. . . ."[55] Hence in Christ's work as mediator one nature cannot be torn apart from the other. Christ's death, resurrection and ascension are his work as a mediator; these are the work of the person as a human, but not in a way that the divine nature is excluded. Indeed, the value of these works also depends on Christ's divinity, which gives them an excellence no human or angelic work could possess. Another work of the redeemer is to send the Holy Spirit to revivify humans and protect the Church, and this pertains to Christ

---

Zurich church. Along with Bullinger he was the most eminent theologian there, and Bullinger was far more burdened with pastoral duties and was sick of Polish controversies. Martyr may well have wanted to refute Stancaro because Italians were so prominent in Polish heterodoxy. Moreover Brenz's *De Personali unione* had just appeared and Martyr was either preparing or had started to write his dialogue on the two natures in Christ, which appeared in August 1561. His attack on Stancaro's Nestorian christology would implicitly shield him from accusations by Brenz that his teaching was Nestorian.

[54] Joseph Tylenda has studied and translated this letter in "Christ the Mediator: Calvin versus Stancaro," *Calvin Theological Journal*, 8 (1973): 5–16. For the translation, 11–16. For the Latin text, see CR *Opera Calvini*, IX, 337–342.

[55] LLS 179; ED 2–3: Christus Iesus est una persona, in qua duae naturae subsistunt, adeo inter sese coniunctae, ut nullo modo a se invicem sint divellendae. Omnes itaque Christi actiones hypostasi seu personae debent attribui: quia duae naturae non seorsim et per se subsistunt . . . ita omne opus Christi cuiuscunque generis fuerit, ipsi personae sive hypostasi ascribendum est. Interim duarum naturarum, quae in Christo sunt, proprietates, distinctas, integras et impermixtas conservare oportet. . . .

as divine. Martyr then develops briefly the doctrine of the communication of idioms. Another task of the mediator is to intercede for us with the Father; Christ does this as man, but the unique power of his intercession derives from his divine nature. Martyr then gives an explication of 1 Tim. 2:5 consistent with his and not Stancaro's doctrine of Christ as mediator. He closes by exhorting the Poles to preach and defend the true gospel and asks that they keep the Zurich church in their prayers.[56]

Martyr's third letter, addressed to the illustrious Polish noblemen, is much longer and is his best single statement on christology.[57] This time the pastors at Zurich in whose name Martyr wrote decided to publish the letter along with their second one of May 1560. It is dated March 1561 and was printed the same month. The printing is not up to the usually high standards of the Froschauer press, which suggests that the two letters were rushed into print. John Calvin also wrote a letter against Stancaro on behalf of the Geneva pastors, also dated March 1561. It too was published.[58]

The decision to publish the letters written by Calvin and Martyr on behalf of the Genevan and Zurich churches stemmed from new developments in Poland. On 16 September 1560 a synod held at Ksiaz condemned Stancaro unanimously, but the next day the nobleman Jerome Ossolinski defended Stancaro's contention that the previous letters of Calvin and Martyr were forgeries produced by the Polish ministers to support their case against him; therefore both sides should hold a truce while the confessions of Stancaro and of the ministers were sent to Geneva and Zurich for a decision on their doctrinal orthodoxy. Although the ministers opposed his proposal, the noblemen supported Ossolinski and the ministers yielded. On 2 October Lismanino wrote Bullinger and sent along several documents on the Stancaro affair, including Stancaro's 1559 treatise, "*De officiis Mediatoris, Pontificis et Sacerdotis Domini nostri Iesu Christi et secundum quam naturam haec officia exhibuerit et executus fuerit.*"[59] Stancaro him-

---

[56] LLS 180–183; ED 4–10.

[57] LLS 198–220; ED 11–52.

[58] Calvin's letter is printed in CR *Opera Calvini*, IX, 349–358. Joseph Tylenda has studied and translated this letter, as he did the Calvin's previous one: "The Controversy over Christ the Mediator: Calvin's Second Reply to Stancaro," *Calvin Theological Journal*, 8 (1973): 131–157.

[59] Joseph Tylenda, "The Controversy on Christ the Mediator: Calvin's Second Reply to Stancaro," *Calvin Theological Journal* 8 (1973): 134–135.

self wrote a letter jointly to Calvin, Martyr, Bullinger, Wolfgang Musculus and their colleagues, dated 4 December 1560, in which he claimed that certain rascals have been spreading Arianism and Monophysitism around Poland under their name. Stancaro also claimed that when he confronted these fellows they brought forward the letters purportedly written by Calvin and Martyr (obviously their letters of May 1560); Stancaro then "proved" that these letters did not agree with the real teaching of the Swiss theologians by pointing out how they agreed with him in their published works! These Arians had then urged that the confession condemning his teaching issued tyrannically by a synod in November 1559 at Pińczów had been approved by the Swiss theologians—something Stancaro claims he could not believe. He next argues that his doctrine that Christ is mediator only in his human nature is the Catholic faith received around the world. He ended by asking the Swiss theologians to write the Polish nobles and set them straight on his orthodoxy.[60] Write they did, but to condemn him. In addition to answering Stancaro's insulting letter, Martyr was also replying to some Polish noblemen who early in 1560 sent a legate to Zurich to request additional guidance on Christ as mediator.[61]

In the opening paragraph of his reply Martyr bristles that some people (obviously Stancaro and his disciples) have misconstrued his previous letter and pretended that it contained Arian and Monophysite doctrine.[62] Against Stancaro's accusations Martyr insisted that he teaches two natures in Christ, human and divine, tightly and inseparably conjoined to the person or hypostasis of the Word. The properties of the two natures are not abolished or confused for actions proceed from the person. He also rejects the teaching of the Monothelites and posits two wills and two actions in Christ while retaining the unity of the person. Martyr breaks his discussion into three sections: I. Christ as Mediator according to Both Natures;

---

[60] Stancaro's letter is printed in CR *Calvini Opera*, XVIII, 260–263. On 10 December 1560 Stanislaus Stadnicki, a Polish nobleman on whose estate Stancaro was staying, addressed a parallel letter to Calvin and Martyr defending Stancaro and developing similar arguments. Ibid., 263–267. The editors suggest that Stancaro may have ghost written the letter: Ibid., 264. Calvin replied on February 26 to Stadnicki and warned him to beware of Stancaro: Ibid., 378–380.

[61] See the preface opposite page 1 of ED.

[62] Ibid., 1; LLS 199–200.

II. No Heresy Flows from This; III. This was the Teaching of the Fathers and the Church.[63]

I. Christ as Mediator according to both Natures: Here Martyr does not dwell on how he is mediator in his human nature since Stancaro admits this. Both natures exist conjointly and do not act separately in the role of mediator. Martyr anticipates an objection from Stancaro: how can Christ before his incarnation be mediator according to his human nature? Martyr replies that all human events are present events for God the Father, so that in this respect Christ was mediator before his incarnation; in God's foreknowledge the two natures are joined and linked together.[64] The hypostatic union would have been without purpose if humanity by itself could have performed the task of redemption, but redemptive acts of the human nature performed by the divine person had much greater excellence. A creature can be sacrificed but sanctification requires God; the mediator must be both victim and sanctifier, so both natures must be conjoined. Just as both parties in a litigation are joined together by a mediator, so too the divine and the human should be conjoined in Christ the mediator.[65] Martyr points out that Stancaro paradoxically and without precedent assigns some mediatorial role to the Father and the Holy Spirit while denying it to the Son as God![66]

II. No Heresy Flows from This: Here Martyr shows that his position is consistent with the traditional doctrine of the Trinity. He does not teach that the divinity suffered or died, although the dignity and merit of Christ's suffering and death flowed from the divinity. The person who was born of the Virgin and died was God. The communication of idioms has its sole source in the fact that the two natures are tightly joined in one person. He then refutes arguments which Stancaro developed by distorting his statements in his previous letter and drawing false inferences. God as such cannot intercede or pray, but Christ could and did pray and suffer as regards to his humanity, but these placated the Father because they derive from the divine supposite.[67] Martyr also cites Heb. 7:3 to argue that Stancaro errs when he excludes the divine nature from the priesthood

---

[63] LLS 202–203; ED 17.
[64] LLS 208; ED 18–19.
[65] LLS 295; ED 22.
[66] LLS 206; ED 23–24.
[67] LLS 207–209; ED 26–30.

of Christ. Martyr concludes this section by showing how his teaching stands against that of Sabellius, Paul of Samosata, Arius and Eutyches. Stancaro, however, is virtually indistinguishable from Nestorius.[68]

III. This was the Teaching of the Fathers and the Church: Martyr shows how his teaching is consistent with Canon 10 of the Council of Ephesus which condemned Nestorius and asserted that the Word of God was made our High Priest when he was made flesh. Christ's priesthood pertains to both his natures. Martyr also cites Canon 13 as consonant with his position and claims that he could cite other decrees of Ephesus but he passes over them for the sake of brevity. Stancaro's teaching, in contrast, cannot be squared with the canons of the Council.[69] Martyr then quotes at length from Irenaeus, Chrysostom, Theophylact, Ambrose, Theodoret, Cyril of Alexandria, Dionysius the Areopagite, and Augustine to show that his teaching agrees with that of the Church Fathers.[70] Stancaro did have one medieval theologian whose support for his position he treasured: Peter Lombard.[71] Martyr dismissed the appeal to Lombard as insignificant compared to the Church Fathers who agreed with his own teaching.[72]

Martyr closes his letter to the Polish noblemen by urging them to unanimity and concord rather than the rancor stirred up by Stancaro's teaching. He then urges them to embrace Christ whole and complete as mediator. Stancaro had torn the Reformed community in Poland apart over an abstruse question, especially at a time when the Polish Reformed needed to bend their efforts against the new Arians. The Arians not only rejoice in the division Stancaro has caused but also can use his teaching to argue that the Son is less than the Father. Therefore Reformed pastors must preach frequently that there are three distinct persons, equal and consubstantial, in the one divine essence and that the two natures in Christ are both distinct in their properties but also united in the same hypostasis.[73]

Stancaro replied to Martyr and the Zurich ministers in his *Contro i ministri di Geneva e di Zurigo* (1562) and made his often quoted claimed

---

[68] LLS 209–210; ED 31–33.
[69] LLS 210–211; ED 33–35.
[70] LLS 212–217; ED 36–46.
[71] *Sentences*, III, 19.
[72] LLS 218; ED 48.
[73] LLS 218–220; ED 48–52. Martyr's claim that Stancaro's views were helping the Polish Arians was well founded: see Williams, 1029, 1043.

that Lombard was worth more than one hundred Luthers, two hundred Melanchthons, three hundred Bullingers, four hundred Peter Martyrs and five hundred Calvins.[74] The same year he gathered several of his treatises together and published them: *De Trinitate et Mediatore Domino nostro Iesu Christo, adversus Henr. Bullingerum, Petrum Martyrem, Ioh. Calvinum et reliquos Tigurinae et Genevensis Ecclesiae Ministros, Ecclesiae Dei perturbatores* (Kraków, 1562). Martyr died 12 November 1562 before he could reply. At the end of his life he was preparing notes for an answer to Brenz's new attack, *De Divina maiestate Christi* . . . . (Frankfort, September, 1562). Instead Josiah Simler, Martyr's biographer and successor to his chair at Zurich, published his *Responsio ad maledictum Francisci Stancari Mantuani Librum adversus Tigurinae ministros, de Trinitate et Mediatore domino nostro Jesu Christo* (Zurich, 1563), "by far the most skilled and most penetrating of the several responses to originate in Switzerland."[75]

The Reformed ministers at Geneva and Zurich tried to uphold the scripture-grounded christological teachings of the Councils of Ephesus and Chalcedon,[76] but doing so meant walking the thin line between Nestorianism and Monophysitism as questions arose over how precisely to deal with the communication of idioms. Martyr kept to that thin line, yielding neither to the Monophysite tendencies he saw in Brenz's eucharistic theology and in the heavenly flesh of the Anabaptists nor to the Nestorianism of Stancaro.

In the preface to the 1559 edition of the *Institutes of the Christian Religion* John Calvin tells readers that his purpose is "to prepare and instruct candidates in sacred theology for reading the divine work . . . without stumbling."[77] Readers then are warned to expect something less than a *summa theologiae*. Still less should readers of Martyr's *Loci Communes*. Its readers will usually know that it has been modeled on Calvin's *Institutes* in the arrangement of its subject matter, but Martyr never wrote a systematic treatise on theology. He wrote polemical works, theological letters dealing with specific problems, and biblical commentaries. His commentaries were rich in theological *loci*, most of them short but some major systematic treatises in themselves,

---

[74] Quoted by Anderson, 442; Williams, 1041; Tylenda, "Second Reply," 141.
[75] Tylenda, "Second Reply," 143.
[76] LLS 202; ED 15–16.
[77] John T. McNeill's translation (Philadelphia: Westminster Press, 1977), I, 4.

notably those on justification and predestination in his commentary on Romans. But Martyr never wrote that sort of treatise on christology. Students of Martyr have to patch together his scattered comments on christology, ever mindful of their original context, and accept the fact that there are lacunae in what he has written, even though a comprehensive vision and coherent theology lay behind his remarks. Martyr also seems to have been writing for a somewhat more advanced audience than did Calvin in his *Institutes*.

Richard A. Muller in his *Christ and the Decree: Christology and Predestination in Reformed Theology from Calvin to Perkins* made a considerable contribution with his comparative study of the christologies of Calvin, Bullinger, Musculus, Vermgili, Beza, Ursinus, Zanchi, Polanus and Perkins, but subtle differences and emphases in christology between Calvin and Vermigli tend to get lost in such a large crowd of theologians.[78] Moreover, his study examines their christology in the shadow of their teaching on predestination. Finally Muller draws exclusively on the *Loci Communes* for Martyr's teaching, but we have already noted the weakness of the *Loci* as a source for his christology.[79] Given the relative inaccessibility of Martyr's 1560 and 1561 letters to the Polish churches in 1986, it is hardly surprising that Muller did not consult them. The two letters of Calvin and the two of Martyr, all written at the requests of the Polish churches and dealing with the same problem, make a perfect subject for a detailed comparative study, for which there is no space here. My impression is that Vermigli's two letters are at least equal to Calvin's letters as theological treatises but are perhaps less effective rhetorically.[80]

---

[78] Richard A. Muller, *Christ and the Decree: Christology and Predestination in Reformed Theology from Calvin to Perkins* (Durham, N.C.: Labyrinth Press, 1986).

[79] Muller treats Vermigli on 56–67.

[80] Thus Vermigli's 1561 letter devotes four times more space than Calvin to marshalling patrisitic citation against Stancaro: For Vermigli, LLS 212–217, ED 36–46; for Calvin, CR *Calvini Opera*, IX, 357–358.

NATURE, VIRTUE, AND HUMANISM: CROSS-DISCIPLINARY REFLECTIONS ON VERMIGLI'S ROMANS COMMENTARY (10–16)

Norman Klassen

Introduction

There is evidently a longstanding and fascinating discussion of Peter Martyr Vermigli's relative scholasticism and humanism.[1] In this debate, Vermigli is thought to be scholastic in his methodology—for example, in his use of four-fold Aristotelian causality, the Aristotelian distinction between *substantia* and *accidentia*, and the *quaestio*. His humanism is associated with his emphasis on philology, patristics, and exegesis, especially the response to the call, *Ad fontes*. I have initial misgivings about this distinction because I do not know that it is desirable or even possible to separate form (here Aristotelian methodology) and content (here humanistic founts) as such an argument implies. I will argue for a more integrative understanding of Aristotelian (or Thomistic-Aristotelian) and humanistic elements in Martyr's thought. In order to achieve that, the key term of humanism needs reexamination, especially in connection with the name of Aristotle. I want to contribute to a discussion of Vermigli's humanism that tacitly challenges some conventional distinctions first by articulating the distinctions and showing how they do and do not obtain. Secondly, I also want to suggest that an ongoing interest in humanism in the work of Vermigli is timely, given recent trends in historiography and critical

---

[1] E.g. PPRED, 12–17; Marvin W. Anderson, "Peter Martyr Vermigli: Protestant Humanist," PMIR, 65–84; J. C. McLelland, "Peter Martyr Vermigli: Scholastic or Humanist?" in PMIR, 141–51; CAS, and also his "Calvinist Thomism," *Viator* 7 (1976): pp. 441–55. James offers a thorough set of references to this subject in the footnotes to his "Prolegomena."

discourse, where Aristotle's name again has prominence. Specifically, I want to draw to our attention Peter Martyr Vermigli's use of naturalistic metaphors in his commentary on Romans 10–16. These metaphors and allusions augment the suggestion that Vermigli holds an Aristotelian view of the world and confirm his humanism to the extent that they reveal both his delight in this world and his desire to associate learning with the affairs of the world and of human concerns.

Two Kinds of Humanism and the Use of Aristotle

There are two established views of humanism, one "scientific," one "literary"; in contemporary Cultural Studies, Aristotle's name has become associated with aspects of both of them, even while Cultural Studies has tried to distance itself from humanism altogether. R. W. Southern outlines the notions of "scientific" and "literary" humanism in his book *Medieval Humanism*.[2] In describing what he calls "scientific" humanism, he emphasizes the dignity of human nature and the dignity of nature itself. For Southern, "The two are linked together by indissoluble ties, and the power to recognize the grandeur and splendour of the universe is itself one of the greatest expressions of the grandeur and splendour of man."[3] The emphasis here is on the role of reason, the intelligibility of the universe, and the growing delight in the world in for its own sake.

In the debate on humanism in Vermigli studies, however, "humanism" conforms to Southern's definition of "literary" humanism. Here the emphasis is on the humane study of ancient literature, rhetoric, urbanity, and practical relevance as opposed to the self-contained formality and aridity of scholasticism: "the formal and systematic studies of the Middle Ages in scholastic theology, canon law and logic . . . were thought to have excluded humanity, destroyed style, and to have dissociated scholarship from the affairs of the world and man."[4] In this paradigm, Aristotle represents scholasticism, particu-

---

[2] R. W. Southern, *Medieval Humanism and Other Studies* (Oxford: Basil Blackwell, 1970), 29–32.
[3] Southern, 31.
[4] Southern, 30.

larly scholastic methodology, and is anti-humanistic.[5] Charles Nauert presents a nicely nuanced account of Aristotle and humanism. He points out that, in philosophy, scholasticism and Aristotle remained unchallenged until the Scientific Revolution.[6] Following Paul O. Kristeller's thesis, he contends that humanism was not a philosophy in the formal sense. Nonetheless, he contrasts humanistic education to Aristotelian science: "education in humanistic subjects appeared practical while education in logic and natural science, the dominant subjects in the medieval liberal-arts curriculum, seemed to breed idle debate about purely speculative issues that were totally useless for real life."[7] What matters is not mastery of absolute truth, "the metaphysical certitude exalted by medieval Aristotelian philosophy";[8] rather, what matters is preparation for participation in political life, the ability to make decisions in the course of daily life based on probability, not certainty.[9]

In medieval Cultural Studies, Aristotle often plays a role that combines elements of "scientific" and "literary" humanism. In accordance with an emphasis on nature, Aristotle is invoked as the arch-representative of the body and delight in the world for its own sake, which in turn buttresses a methodological commitment to particularity and specificity. At the same time, Aristotle connects readily with the political, with "the affairs of the world and man," not least through his abiding interest in phronesis (practical wisdom). Alasdair MacIntyre provides a useful summary of the Aristotelian emphasis, particularly in contrast to the Platonic tendency, which shows the crossover between what we have been referring to as "scientific" and "literary" humanistic elements: "For the Platonist, as

---

[5] Frank James, "At the Crossroads of Late Medieval Scholasticism, Christian Humanism and Resurgent Augustinianism," *Protestant Scholasticism: Essays in Reassessment*, ed. Carl R. Trueman and R. Scott Clark (Exeter: The Paternoster Press, 1999), 65–6; Nicholas Mann, "The Origins of Humanism," *The Cambridge Companion to Renaissance Humanism*, ed. Jill Kraye, Cambridge: CUP, 1996, 14 (on Petrarch and Aristotelians); Peter Mack, "Humanist rhetoric and dialectic," in Kraye, ed., 85–6 (on Valla and Aristotelian dialectics). For a dissenting view, expounding humanist Aristotelianism, see Jill Kraye, "Philologists and philosophers," in *The Cambridge Companion to Renaissance Humanism*, 142–53.

[6] Charles G. Nauert, *Humanism and the Culture of Renaissance Europe* (Cambridge: Cambridge University Press, 1995), 4.

[7] Nauert, 15.

[8] Nauert, 15.

[9] Nauert, 15–16.

later for the Cartesian, the soul, preceding all bodily and social existence, must indeed possess an identity prior to all social roles; but
for the Catholic Christian, as earlier for the Aristotelian, the body
and the soul are not two linked substances. I am my body and my
body is social, born to those parents in this community with a specific
social identity."[10] Rita Copeland traces the influence of Roman rhetorical theory into the Middle Ages, with Aristotle playing a prominent
role. He holds up the ideal of "practical wisdom" (*phronesis*), embodied especially in politics. Rhetoric relates directly: "its association
with the intellectual virtue of practical wisdom, *phronesis*, is clear.
Rhetoric calls for an ability to deliberate about the contingent and
the variable, about human actions and ethics, for which there are
no fixed, necessary principles."[11] This description fits almost exactly
Nauert's description of humanistic concerns *in contrast to* Aristotelian
philosophy. These are all humanistic ideals, partly in Southern's

---

[10] Alasdair MacIntyre, *After Virtue: A Study in Moral Theory* 2nd ed. (London:
Duckworth, 1985), 172. These emphases on nature and politics very often go together
in Cultural Studies. Hence titles such as Dolores Warwick Frese and Katherine
O'Brien O'Keeffe, eds., *The Book and the Body* (Notre Dame: U. of Notre Dame
Press, 1997); Miri Rubin, *Corpus Christi: The Eucharist in Late Medieval Culture* (Cambridge:
Cambridge University Press, 1991); and Elizabeth Alvilda Petroff, *Body and Soul:
Essays on Medieval Women and Mysticism* (New York and Oxford: Oxford University
Press, 1994). In their different ways and among many others, all of these strive for
a profoundly socio-political cultural situatedness.

[11] Rita Copeland, *Rhetoric, Hermeneutics, and Translation in the Middle Ages* (Cambridge:
Cambridge University Press, 1991), 15. To follow the implications of this deployment of Aristotle in medieval Cultural Studies further, for David Wallace the aim
in reading Chaucer is "to read the text as if it were its own politics." David Wallace,
Chaucerian Polity: Absolutist Lineages and Associational Forms in England and Italy (Stanford:
Stanford University Press, 1997), 3. This means resisting a gridwork, which "signals a basic failure to understand the nature of politics. Terms such as 'the common good' and 'common profit' resist stabilization, varying their meaning with each
instance of deployment." Ibid., 3. The source of this politics is principally Aristotle:
"the importance of Aristotle before and after William of Moerbeke's translation of
the *Politics* (c. 1260) can hardly be exaggerated." Ibid., 74, cf. 24, 44. In this environment the contrast is supplied not by humanism but by a certain conception of
Augustinianism, associated most readily with otherworldly Neoplatonism and Stoicism.
Ibid., 44, 74–5. Miri Rubin locates debates on the eucharist in the space between
"the breakdown of Augustinian symbolism and the emergence of Aristotelian real-
ism" (18) and the implications of his philosophy of matter (30). For a different perspective on the relative attitudes towards the body in Aristotelian and Thomistic
thought on the one hand and Platonic and Augustinian traditions on the other, see
Caroline Walker Bynum, *Fragmentation and Redemption: Essays on Gender and the Human
Body in Medieval Religion* (New York: Zone Books, 1992), 222–38, esp. 227–30.

"scientific sense" but also in the "literary" sense, embracing what Nauert calls "a degree of intellectual relativism."[12]

Peter Martyr and the Unity of Nature

Peter Martyr's references to nature and naturalistic metaphors support a case for his humanism in the twofold sense of evincing his Aristotelian delight in nature and contributing to his turn towards a concern with action. Although these metaphors are scattered throughout the material, I will concentrate on a portion at the beginning of this section of his commentary, where they are most prominent.

Aristotle cannot have all the credit for naturalistic elements in Vermigli's discussion, of course. The epistle to the Romans itself foregrounds natural theology. In the opening chapter, a discussion of the created order serves as one of Paul's most fundamental and introductory themes. In the latter portion of the epistle, Paul develops the metaphor of the branch grafted into the olive tree, a comparison Peter Martyr takes up in his extended discussion of the state of Jews and Gentiles in the divine scheme of things. Yet where Martyr's prose does not directly resonate with Paul's language, his occasional references to nature illustrate an attitude befitting his Aristotelian regard for the senses and hence for the natural world. John Patrick Donnelly has argued that, beyond the basic given for Martyr that God created the universe, Martyr locates man in an Aristotelian universe.[13] Martyr's attentiveness to nature, reflected in the literary texture of this portion of his commentary on Romans, further substantiates that claim.

As I am sure others have noticed elsewhere in Vermigli's writings, chapters 10–16 of his commentary on Romans contain many brief yet arresting allusions and references to nature and the physical world in all its particularity, as well as numerous metaphors drawn from nature. At the very outset of chapter 10, for example, he suggests the presence of the body with an allusion to doctors and medication.[14] The University of Padua, with its Aristotelian attention

---

[12] Nauert, 16.
[13] Donnelly, *Calvinism*, 71.
[14] Peter Martyr Vermigli, *In Epistolam S. Pauli Apostoli ad Romanos . . . Commentarii, 10–16* (Basel, 1558), 442.

to the body and the natural world, would inculcate such comparisons.[15] Shortly after the chapter summary, Martyr compares a rhetorician who offers gentle words before saying anything harsh to a scorpion that embraces with its foreclaws so that it might better strike with its tail, and both with our need to embrace our neighbour with good will and charity, so that we might heal him.[16] References to the body, the face, healing, and mind/body duality recur throughout these chapters—not insistently, but as gentle reminders of Martyr's interest in the natural world. These accord with what has come to be known as a "scientific" version of humanism.

Martyr's allusions to nature are often connected with the discourse of virtue. He refers to the similarity between sea water and rainwater in terms of their humour to make a point regarding virtue and vice coming from the same affect.[17] In chapter 12, he refers to the cyclical pattern of clouds and rain to elaborate upon the close relationship between good acts and virtues, citing the philosophical opinion that each is born of the other.[18] At the start of chapter 13, he demonstrates a cosmological understanding of the role of virtues as infused from the heavens, coming down to earth and resulting in fruits.[19] A great proportion of the references to nature in the com-

---

[15] On Padua as a centre of medical learning see Hastings Rashdall, *The Universities of Europe in the Middle Ages* Vol. 2 (1936), ed. F. M. Powicke and A. B. Emden (Oxford: OUP, 1997), 20–21.

[16] Vermigli, 442.

[17] Vermigli, 445.

[18] Vermigli, 594.

[19] Vermigli, 604. As a point of comparison, this understanding of virtue powerfully informs Dante's *Commedia*:

Dentro dal ciel della divina pace
    si gira un corpo nella cui virtute
    l'esser di tutto suo contento giace.
Lo ciel seguente, c' ha tante vedute,
    quell'esser parte per diverse essenze,
    da lui distinte e da lui contenute.
Li altri giron per varie differenze
    le distinzion che dentro da sè hanno
    dispongono a lor fini e lor semenze.
Questi organi del mondo così vanno,
    come tu vedi omai, di grado in grado,
    che di su prendono e di sotto fanno. (*Par.* 2.112–23)

"'Within the heaven of the divine peace spins a body in whose virtue lies the being of all that it contains; the next heaven, which has so many sights, distributes that being among different existences, distinct from it and contained in it; the other spheres, by various differences, direct the distinctive qualities which they have in

mentary on chapters 10–16 involve the concept of virtue. If the allusions to nature conform to a "scientific" conception of humanism, those that go on to make a connection between nature and virtue draw in a more literary and urbane version of humanism, one marked by concern with human affairs in the world.

Near the beginning of his commentary on Romans 10, Martyr makes a particularly interesting and sustained series of references to nature. These contribute to a shift in attention from doctrinal issues to matters of praxis. They help us to understand the fullness of Vermigli's humanism. Interpretation of Paul's Epistle to the Romans has often observed a basic division in the book between chapters 1–8, which represent a sustained exposition of theological doctrine, and what follows, either the entirety of Rom. 9–16 or, more specifically, 9–11. Wayne Meeks, who calls the section that includes chapter 10 "A Stumbling Block for the Reader," points out that "There is, as everyone notices, a sharp break between 8:39 and 9:1"[20] and he goes on to claim that "[t]he function of chaps 9–11 is . . . not to continue but to disrupt the smooth assurances of confidence that have capped the whole argument of chaps 1–8."[21] There is a break after chapter 8, but what follows cannot simply be lumped together as collectively being decisively different from Rom. 1–8; and of course, besides the complicated question of the relationship between chapters 1–8 and 9–11, one wants to bear in mind that with Rom. 12 we move into a section on application and exhortation.

Peter Martyr Vermigli's commentary on the epistle suggests a slight variation on the theme of the basic division in Romans which draws attention to a more complicated transition. In this way he anticipates Meeks. He includes a *locus de praedestinatione*, an excursus on

---

themselves to their ends and fruitful working. These organs of the universe proceed thus, as thou seest now, grade by grade, each receiving from above and operating below.'" Dante Alighieri, *The Divine Comedy*, ed. and trans. John D. Sinclair (Oxford: Oxford University Press, 1939). For a thorough introductory discussion of the range of meanings of *virtù* in Dante, which provides a good sense of the medieval Thomistic understanding of the term, see Philippe Delhaye and Giorgio Stabile, "Virtù," *Enciclopedia Dantesca*, ed. Antonietta Butano et al. (Rome, 1976).

[20] Wayne A. Meeks, "On Trusting an Unpredictable God: A Hermeneutical Meditation on Romans 9–11," *Faith and History: Essays in Honor of Paul W. Meyer*, ed. John T. Carroll et al. (Atlanta: Scholars Press, 1990), 107.

[21] Meeks, 108. While he makes this acknowledgement, in the article Meeks develops the point that "Recent critical discussion of Romans 9–11 has at length recognized that these chapters are not a mere 'appendix' or 'excursus'" (106).

the theme of predestination, after his explication of chapter 9. The stakes here are quite high. Joseph McLelland has written that "His treatise following chapter nine represents one of the important documents of the Reformation."[22] Frank James, with a view to articulating the importance of *gemina praedestinatio* or "double predestination" in Martyr's thought, points out that "Vermigli's most extensive treatment of predestination occurs in the *locus de praedestinatione* following his exegesis of chapter 9 of Romans."[23] James argues for the significance of the placement of this discussion: "The *locus* on predestination is strategically placed at the end of Romans 9. Vermigli is convinced that this doctrine derives directly from Romans 8 and 9."[24]

Another strategic reason for placing this locus here is that predestination represents both a difficult doctrine, perhaps a culminating argument, and a turn towards practical matters. For James, "according to Vermigli, replacing the doctrine of predestination with a non-predestinarian 'safe doctrine' is tantamount to removing the only real basis for *practical* benefit."[25] The end of chapter 9, then, including the locus on predestination, represents a natural turn in Martyr's commentary on Romans, the point after which he begins to turn his attention to matters of application and praxis.[26]

Martyr's respect for nature facilitates a movement towards the practical; the turn represents a combination of "scientific" and "literary" aspects of his humanism. Early in his commentary on chapter 10, Martyr develops a particularly striking and sustained appeal to nature that serves this purpose especially well. The immediate context is as follows: after a short summary of the chapter's contents, Martyr takes up Paul's concern to console the Jews and prove his good will towards them. He is, the commentator insists, eager for their salvation, doing such things as pouring out prayers to that end. Martyr discusses the contrast between reproofs and conciliatory words, and offers this explanation for the difference: "The reason for the difference is this: in chapter 9 [Paul] discussed election or

---

[22] J. C. McLelland, "Calvinism Perfecting Thomism? Peter Martyr Vermigli's Question," *Scottish Journal of Theology* 31 (1978), 575.

[23] PPRED, 62.

[24] PPRED, 68.

[25] PPRED, 66 (emphasis mine).

[26] All of this helps to explain why the translation of Vermigli's commentary on Romans has been divided into two volumes, with the break coming between chapters 9 and 10 (with the *locus* on predestination published separately).

predestination, which is not changed by prayers; therefore it would have been vain to mention them. In this place, however, the right-eousness of faith is considered, and since that faith is a gift of God, there is no doubt that it can be obtained for our neighbours through faithful prayers."[27] This distinction suggests Martyr's sensitivity to a change in emphasis: from the doctrine of predestination to things we can do, such as pray.

The next question Paul takes up, the zeal of the Jews, involves a similar nuanced distinction between knowledge and actions. The cli-mate in which Vermigli will develop an appeal to nature is one of close relationships and a subtle transition between these themes. On the question of zeal, Paul acknowledges that the Jews did in fact do things, but rues their lack of knowledge. Martyr defines zeal first and foremost as signifying love, and as "an affection, which subsists in the part of the soul that desires."[28] He distinguishes between good and bad forms of zeal on the basis of whether knowledge accom-panies it. For Martyr, this leads to a question: "whether any sins can please, that we should pluck the desire from them, or any good can be promoted?"[29] Some sins are very bad but can be spoken of as good, as it were *per accidens*, if one repents and the sins illustrate the truth that "where sin abounded, there also grace will abound."

This leaves another class of works, namely the moral works done by the unregenerate, which Martyr acknowledges we cannot but praise. And here he embarks on a long set of comparisons with nature:

> For even as it is a delight, and certainly not a small one, to contem-plate the characteristics of herbs, the properties of animals, of precious stones, and of stars, so also one enjoys seeing the acts of illustrious men, which God wishes to be in human nature, so that republics and civil discipline might be preserved. Who does not take delight to read about the honest life and worthy actions of Socrates? Or when he reflects upon the achievements of Scipio Africanus? Or when he sees

---

[27] Vermigli, 443. "Istius discriminis haec est ratio: In 9 capite egit de electione seu praedestinatione, quae precibus non muratur: ideo supervacanea fuisset earum mentio. Hoc vero loco agitur de iustitia fidei, quae fides cum sit donum Dei, non dubium est, quin promimis nostris impetrari possit fidelibus precibus."

[28] Vermigli, 443. "Est sane zelus affectio, quem in parte animi consistit concu-piscenti. . . ."

[29] Vermigli, 444. "An ulla peccata sic placere possint, ut ex illis voluptatem capi-amus, vel ulla benevolentia propterea concilietur."

those things which in our own times are often done by heroic men, even though they are outside the Christian religion?[30]

This appeal to the acts of moral but unregenerate men begins with an analogy from the delight found in nature. There is a hint of Aristotelian taxonomic methodology here, to be sure, with the list dividing into organic and inorganic examples. Besides this suggestion of attention to detail, the emphasis is on delight. Martyr finds pleasure virtually anywhere he looks in nature, from stones and stars, from plants and animals. This too indicates the influence of Aristotle: Martyr strongly suggests that the study of nature is pleasurable in and of itself. It establishes the viability of the comparison that follows. Martyr does not apologize for delight in nature; this delight here facilitates a new focus on actions in the scheme of salvation.

Martyr's discussion of the longstanding, vexed question of the status of the moral acts of the unregenerate continues with another extended appeal to nature:

Similarly, a skilful farmer, if by chance he should see a field overgrown with ferns and weeds, desires to work it. For he thinks, if the weeds were plucked out, and the fern tamed with the plough, good things would happily grow there. He acts in the same way if he sees wild grapes or olive trees spring up of their own accord in any place, for he judges the place to be fitting both for vines and olive trees if he undertakes cultivation.[31]

The picture of a farmer observing nature with a loving and knowing attentiveness not only serves as a model for our need to look discerningly at the lives of those around us, it also impresses upon us Martyr's understanding of husbandry and awareness of nature generally. The allusion at once foreshadows the discussion of graft-

---

[30] Vermigli, 444. "Quemadmodum enim voluptas est, & quidem non parva, contemplari herbarum vires, proprietates animalium, gemmarum, & astrorum, ita etiam delectat gesta videre illustrium virorum, quae Deus in natura humana extare voluit, ut Respublicae conservarentur, & disciplina civilis. Quis non capiat voluptatem Socratis legendo honestam vitam, & probas actiones? Vel secum repetendo Scipionis Africani res gestas? Nec non videndo quae nostra tempestate saepe fiunt ab heroicis viris, cum tamen a Christiana religione sint alieni?"

[31] Vermigli, 444. "Veluti peritus agricola si fortasse conspicatus fuerit locum filice ac malis herbis copiose luxuriantem, cupit illum emere. Nam cogitat, 'Si herbae vitiosae fuerint extirpatae, & filix aratro mansuerscat, fruges ibi felicissime proventuras. Idemque faciet si labruscas aut oleastros viderit sponte alicubi nasci, locum enim iudicabit aptum & vineis & pinguibus oleis, modo cultus accesserit."

ing in chapter 11 and shifts the ground of that later passage from a strictly Pauline comparison to suggest a larger awareness of and delight in the natural realm.

Such delight links crucially to virtue. For Martyr, the moral acts of the unregenerate are like the delights and the possibilities of nature. By collocating nature and positive moral actions, Martyr emphasizes in a positive way the shift from a discussion of doctrine to one of action. Consideration of the state of the unregenerate, particularly that of the Jews, will lead inexorably to reflections on the state of the Gentiles through Paul's organic metaphor, then into a discussion of the ethical implications of the gospel for the Christian. The number of references to nature in the later chapters actually tapers off. It is in the midst of the difficult task of linking Paul's understanding of God's purposes for the Jews and Gentiles with the status of their various actions that Vermigli appeals to nature. While he is following the development of Paul's argument, his own Aristotelian love of nature provides him with a helpful rhetorical strategy for advancing his discussion. Elements of a natural theology perhaps also help Vermigli negotiate the difficult questions arising out of Paul's treatment of predestination and the history of salvation.

Thomism, Protestantism, Humanism

Donnelly has discussed the Aristotelian features of Vermigli's thought in considerable detail. The features to which he draws attention reinforce both "scientific" and "literary" humanism. In spite of Vermigli's warning against reading into the Bible the philosophical principles of being, "his theological works are in fact shot through with the Aristotelian principles of being."[32] Martyr celebrates the role of the senses and sense appetites. Even though the first pre-reflective desire for the sensible good can often be contrary to God's law, the appetites are not wrong or injurious; rather, they constitute a real good. It is the Stoic doctrine, that man must root out his sense appetites, which Martyr opposes.[33] He follows Aristotle too in believing that the acquisition of virtues enables man to control his emotions. One acquires

---

[32] CAS, 72.
[33] Ibid., 82.

virtues through repeated acts and education and, according to Donnelly, like Aristotle, Vermigli views virtue as a mean between two extremes.

The presence of Aristotle suggests the influence of Thomas as well. Donnelly proposes that "Martyr's career shows clearly that a Protestant theology could rest on a Thomistic base."[34] So can humanism. The admiration Vermigli has for the moral works of the unregenerate is accounted for in Donnelly's account of his anthropology, in which Vermigli sees a fourfold division that applies to all men. There are those who lack both faith and moral virtues to keep emotions from running riot; those who lack faith but who possess moderation and can control passions; Christian believers who are led by passion into sin; and finally Christians who due to God's gift are free from passions and direct emotions to the good. The good acts of men described in the passage from chapter 10, whether Jews or virtuous pagans, require moderation and the control of the passions.

Both Thomas and Martyr stress the preeminence of the intellect. In the debate on scholastic and humanistic elements in Vermigli's thought, it might seem that a conception of the preeminence of the intellect goes hand in hand with the dry, cerebral systematising of the schools—a key feature opposed by "literary" humanism as described by Southern; by implication, then, one who sees profoundly humanistic elements in Vermigli would be inclined to qualify or to distance Vermigli from such a taint. But to draw the conclusion of aridity because of a stress on the intellect is to misunderstand the richness of the Thomistic understanding of the intellect. Rowan Williams provides a thumbnail sketch of the implications of this emphasis:

> *Intellectus* . . . means "understanding" in a very comprehensive sense; and it involves a genuine union of knower and known correlative to the union of lover and beloved. The life of the *intellectus* involves a transition of the object into the subject and is fulfilled and complemented by the life of the will (which is characterized at its summit by love) in which there is a kind of transition of subject into object. . . . The *intellectus* longs for truth exactly as the will longs for good; and . . . it is made very clear that will and understanding are inseparable.[35]

This explanation suggests a holistic emphasis in giving priority to the faculty of intellect. An interconnectedness among ways of know-

---

[34] Ibid., 27. See also his article "Calvinist Thomism."

[35] Rowan Williams, *The Wound of Knowledge: Christian Spirituality from the New Testament to St John of the Cross* 2nd ed. (London: Darton, Longman, and Todd, 1990), 125.

ing accompanies this focus on union. Knowledge of, as well as delight in, nature is related to the knowledge of God:

> Aquinas and those who in greater or lesser degree followed him accepted that the understanding operates eccentrically where God is concerned, but do not deny that there is some "family resemblance" between the knowing of God and other knowledge; and this allows us to maintain the importance of historical and contingent elements in the learning of faith.[36]

Far from embodying scholastic rigidity, such a formulation brings together the naturalistic, the contingent, and the learning of faith in a way that cuts across distinctions sometimes made between scholasticism and humanism.

While the natural theology articulated by Williams helps show the theological suppleness of a "scientific" humanism, a proper understanding of *intellectus* also has implications for an understanding of humanism that connects nature to the social and the political. Williams contrasts the Thomistic view, which helps us better to appreciate aspects of Peter Martyr's thought, with that of voluntarism, in which the preeminence of the will has led to an emphasis on an ultimately unconditioned decision. He cites Ockham as one for whom voluntarism is a matter of obedience to the propositions God chooses to make known. For Williams, Ockham evades the issue of "how, humanly, we *come* to know, how we learn, where God is concerned."[37] The isolation of the will leads to "a theology that privileges either authoritarian views of revelation or subjective and emotional accounts of religious knowing or both."[38] Williams is concerned to show how Christian theology at its best encourages both a profound awareness of the hidden God and a profound humanism: "The Word re-forms the possibilities of human existence and calls us to the creation of new humanity in the public, the social and historical, world."[39]

The Aristotelian-Thomistic elements in Peter Martyr's writings draw attention to a natural theology that in turn draws together scholastic and humanistic strands. Donnelly's work on Martyr's outlook as "Calvinist Thomism" has done much to encourage an ecumenical

---

[36] Ibid., 141–2.
[37] Ibid., 141.
[38] Ibid., 142.
[39] Ibid., 181.

approach to Martyr. For McLelland, "One of Donnelly's signal contributions . . . is to demand revision of the familiar Roman charge
that the Reformation was the child of nominalism."[40] With reference
to his evident love of nature and application of his "natural theology" to his commentary on Romans 10–16, Thomistic Aristotelianism
makes a contribution to Peter Martyr's thought beyond that of method
alone. The deep respect for nature fostered by Aristotelianism fuses
easily with important aspects of humanism. If humanism means a
turning towards and a love of this world for its own sake to the
exclusion of God, a self-contained naturalism, then it is probably not
possible to make this claim seriously, nor would I want to. The "family relationship" stressed by Williams means that, in Thomism, other
kinds of knowing cannot be divorced entirely from the knowledge
of God. But if we do not insist on such a separation, then Aristotelianism fosters delight in this world, as indeed it fosters other aspects
of life in this world as well, such as politics. Martyr's delight in the
good deeds of famous men for the sake of republics and civil discipline evinces a concern that is one of the hallmarks of humanism.
As McLelland writes, agreeing with Donnelly, Martyr's Aristotle
"shows the marks of the Renaissance concern for human values."[41]
A theology or spirituality that orients itself towards the body, towards
contingency, towards the public and social towards the moral and
relational world, in my opinion upholds what is best in the humanistic vision.

Conclusion

A theology that orients itself towards the public and social on the
basis of a "family relationship" in ways of knowing can renew itself
in the aftermath of the critique of humanism. It is very apparent
that sixteenth-century studies, like medieval studies, also wrestles with
questions raised by contemporary cultural and literary theory as

---

[40] McLelland, "Perfecting" 578. Williams too does not create a sharp divide. He
sees Luther as among the "literate 'primitivist' Catholic reformers" (145). Why?
Because for Luther, God makes himself a worldly reality, not a subject for speculative theology.
[41] McLelland, "Perfecting", 573.

informed by recent philosophical and hermeneutical developments.[42] These include a deep questioning of humanism in its various forms. I am hoping that a perspective informed by these rather varied emphases can contribute to an already rich discussion of the humanism of this sixteenth-century figure.

After Nietzsche, humanism became extremely vulnerable. Heidegger offered a devastating critique in his "Letter on Humanism."[43] This critique has informed much of the work in Cultural Studies and the unrelenting emphasis on politics there. It used to be the case in some religious quarters that the label of "humanism" itself caused deep suspicion on quite other grounds—too much involvement in the world. Some have attempted a rudimentary distinction between secular humanism and biblical humanism. It has not proved possible to shelter "humanism" simply by adding the modifier *biblical* in front of it. The movement was always susceptible to attacks on Greek conceptuality and revaluations of culture through the lens of politics and through careful engagement of the philosophical assumptions.[44]

Emmanuel Lévinas, who saw both the necessity of Heidegger's critique but was also unhappy with his alternative, lamented that "Humanism has to be denounced only because it is not sufficiently human."[45] His thought has initiated a renewed interest in ethical questions related to what one commentator calls "a humanism of the other human being."[46] For example, Rorty has recently derisively labeled Derrida a humanist in light of his latest, ethically oriented works.[47] As contemporary Cultural Studies, heavily influenced

---

[42] Such questions were in evidence in the opening plenary session of the Sixteenth-Century Studies conference in St Louis (October 1999), in which two young scholars defended quite different methodological assumptions.

[43] Martin Heidegger, "Letter on Humanism," *Basic Writings* (New York: Harper and Row, 1995), 193–242.

[44] The thinkers just cited, particularly Nietzsche, Heidegger, and Derrida, have exercised a profound influence in these regards. For a recent example of a sophisticated attack on early Italian humanism, see Wallace. Among other topics, his introduction is must reading for theorists of medieval/Renaissance periodization.

[45] Emmanuel Lévinas, *Otherwise than Being or Beyond Essence*, trans. A. Lingis (The Hague: Nijhoff, 1981), 128.

[46] Simon Critchley, *Ethics—Politics—Subjectivity: Essays on Derrida, Levinas, and Contemporary French Thought* (London: Verso, 1999), 67.

[47] Richard Rorty, "Remarks on Deconstruction and Pragmatism," *Deconstruction and Pragmatism*, ed. Chantal Mouffe (London: Routledge, 1996), 14. On humanism and deconstruction, see Bill Martin, *Humanism and Its Aftermath: The Shared Fate of Deconstruction and Politics* (New Jersey: Humanities Press, 1995), 47 ff. See also Michel

by critical theory, begins to incorporate current ethical thought and reconsider aspects of humanism, we need ecumenical, theologically oriented revaluations of the participation of historical figures such as Vermigli in larger cultural movements.

There are more local issues, such as the relationship between scholasticism and humanism. As McLelland in particular has suggested, it might not prove possible to find a comfortable niche for Martyr in the midst of the terms "scholasticism" and "humanism."[48] On the other hand, careful engagement with the language Vermigli employs, including metaphors as well as technical terminology, and sensitivity to the flow of the argument in which he uses language in subtle ways to specific ends, can contribute to a broader understanding of his indebtedness to Aristotle and his humanism. Further discussion of the character of Vermigli's outlook and further wrestling with various labels that are both necessary and yet run the risk of oversimplifying complexities should enrich ecumenical church historiography and have a positive impact on the broader philosophical issues in the academy which, after all, owe much to historical tensions and ambiguities related to the term "humanism."

Foucault, "What is Enlightenment?" *Ethics: Subjectivity and Truth*, trans. Catherine Porter (New York: The New Press, 1997), esp. 312–15; and Charles Taylor, "Overcoming Epistemology," *Philosophical Arguments* (Massachusetts: Harvard University Press, 1995), esp. 15.

[48] McLelland, "Scholastic" esp. 146–51.

PART III

CHURCH AND REFORM

SACRIFICE AND SACRAMENT: ANOTHER EUCHARISTIC CONTRIBUTION FROM PETER MARTYR VERMIGLI

Donald Fuller

Introduction

Peter Lombard's Eucharistic doctrine, adopted by the Fourth Lateran Council in 1215, codified the *elemental* conception of the *union* of sacrifice and sacrament in Christian worship, especially evident by his distinction *res et sacramentum*.[1] During the Reformation, Peter Martyr Vermigli sought to reform Lombard's conception of *union* by replacing the *elemental* understanding with one that was *Word*-centered. In many ways Vermigli's Supper doctrine is an extension of Aquinas's earlier *Word*-centered reform of Lombard's doctrine of God as found in *Summa Theologia* I, qq. 27–29, which refers particularly to the doctrine of Trinitarian procession.[2] Did Vermigli "complete" a reform agenda for Christian worship and piety in the 16th century that Aquinas began in the 13th century by extending Aquinas' *Word*-centered theological principle to the very words of God, Holy Scripture? If so, Vermigli's extension of Thomistic theology in this manner makes his Eucharistic reforms an interesting case of what J. P. Donnelly calls "Calvinism perfecting Thomism."[3]

Vermigli's *Word*-centered theology results in two principles that guide his reform of Christian worship: The first states that God communicates His salvific intent *intelligibly* by "the words of God" in each

---

[1] Peter Lombard, *Quatuor Libri Sententiarum* Bk. 4, dist. 8, pt. 7, 791. This section is entitled, "De Sacramento et re." Lombard writes, "Res contenta et significata est caro Christi, quam de Virgine traxit, et sanquis, quem pro nobis fudit; . . ." Bernard Leeming, S.J., *Principles of Sacramental Theology*. London: 1956. 251–52.

[2] Thomas Aquinas. *Summa theologia*. Blackfriars edition. (Macraw Hill Book Company, New York: 1963), vol. VI, see I qq. 27–29.

[3] J. P. Donnelly, "Calvinist Thomism," *Viator* 7 (1976), 441–55. Also see Joseph C. McLelland, "Calvinism Perfecting Thomism? Peter Martyr Vermigli's Question," in *Scottish Journal of Theology* (Edinburgh: 1978), 571–78, which is a favorable review of CAS.

and every aspect of the service of worship, including the rite of the
Lord's Supper. The second principle suggests that God's words are
communicated and received in worship by activities that encompass
the *whole* human person such as thinking, speaking, hearing, seeing,
and doing. Vermigli applies these principles—the *intelligibility* of God
and the *wholeness* of man—to the Sunday service of worship by making "the words of God", Holy Scripture, the mediating basis or foundation of Christian worship.[4] The storyline of God's words (in the
Bible) is communicated and received throughout the service of worship so that each participant *understands* God's salvific intent. The
means of grace (preaching, prayer, sacraments, singing, and reading
of the Word) correspond to and affect the *whole* person as she thinks,
gives, prays, sings and offers her whole self to God throughout the
service. Originating in Aquinas' doctrine of God, Vermigli conceives
the *union* of sacrifice and sacrament as one mediated by *verbum Dei*
not by the *elements* of bread and wine. Vermigli's principles of *intelligibility* and *wholeness* present a major challenge to the Lombardian
conception of union with Christ, whereby God's salvific intent is
communicated *elementally* by means of theurgic acts; acts which are
not attributable to human nature proper but rather are considered
activities *above* human understanding.

What are the sources of Lombard and Vermigli's understandings
of how God communicates His salvific intent within Christian worship? What are the implications of these principles on their views of
Christian worship? Answers to these questions will be sought by
examining Vermigli's understanding of mediation and union with
Christ as each relates to the Eucharist/Lord's Supper. Mediation
pertains to what governs the foundational framework of worship.
Union with Christ describes how the believer, in this earthly life, is
joined to Christ in the transformational process of her "return" to
God, or as Vermigli prefers to put it, in the process of her "resurrection life". He takes his cue on the *union* issue from Romans 8.[5]

---

[4] Vermigli, *In Epistolam S. Pauli Apostoli ad Romanos commentarii doctissimi* (Basel,
1558), dedicatory epistle to Sir Anthony Cooke, unpaginated. Vermigli describes
the scriptures as "oracles from heaven", "God's books" or simply "God's words."
At one point he writes, "We will speak to men, not with the words of men but
with the words of God."

[5] Vermigili, *Romanos*, 282. "Tradit his Paulus, principium nouae vitae esse, quod
habemus eundem spiritum, qui fuit in Christo: quae est tota, & integra causa resurrectionis nostrae." In contrast he writes, "Probatur manducationem reale carnus
Christi non esse causam resurrectionis" (*Romanos*, 283).

Finally, we examine Vermigli's definitions of sacrifice and sacrament, how he understands them to apply in Christian worship generally, and then how his re-union of sacrifice and sacrament may have contributed to the Supper rite contained in the 1552 English Book of Common Prayer. Throughout these sections, the *intelligibility* of God and the *wholeness* of man guide Vermigli's *Word*-centered reform of the Eucharist. We begin, however, with a brief historical excursus, which will shed light on why the marks of *intelligibility* and *wholeness* are so fundamental to Vermigli and why they contrast so sharply with those of the *elemental* and *theurgic*.

Historical Excursus

The doctrines of God and man were undergoing important revisions during the Renaissance due to the major shift in European culture from a Platonic world, defined broadly by the metaphysic of *divine things*, to one shaped by Aristotle's metaphysic of *being*.[6] Vermigli's reform of Christian worship addresses the fundamental nature of *intelligibility* and *wholeness* as each relates to these (important) doctrines and their philosophical underpinnings. While Renaissance Platonism may be found in a variety of forms, according to C. H. Lohr, it culminated in Nicholas of Cusa's *De docta ignorantia*, the doctrine of "learned ignorance."[7] The picture of God and man painted by this Neoplatonic metaphysic of divine things is one in which God is unintelligible (i.e., a non-being) and the goal of human knowledge is "a higher type of knowledge, an intellectual vision which transcends not only sense perception but also reason itself."[8] It was the *Parmenides* that had been the Platonist's chief witness to the esoteric doctrine of God as a non-being or, what may be referred to as, a *supersubstantial*

---

[6] *The Cambridge history of Renaissance Philosophy*, general editor, Charles B. Schmitt; editors, Quentin Skinner, Eckhard Kessler; associate editor, Jill Kraye (Cambridge and New York, Cambridge University Press: 1988) 582–3.

[7] E. R. Dodds, *Proclus: The Elements of Theology: A Revised Text with Translation, Introduction, and Commentary*. Oxford: Oxford University Press, 1963, xxxii. Proclus' works including the *Elements of Theology, Platonic Theology*, and the *in Parm.* formed the "favorite reading of Nicholas of Cusa, who derived from Proclus important elements of his own doctrine and often cites him as an authority." Also, see Schmitt, *Renaissance Philosophy*, 585.

[8] Schmitt, *Renaissance Philosophy*, 585.

substance.[9] And the "idea of man" to which it corresponded was an equally abstract theological anthropology intimately connected to the forms of divine procession which constituted its being.[10] The most systematic expression of this Parmenidian world-view, however, had been developed in the 5th century by Proclus and transmitted into the medieval schools primarily through the pseudo-Aristotelian and pseudo-Dionysian *corpora*.[11] It is a world-view in which the *truth* that "the many are united in the One" is resolved within medieval Christendom through the ideal of the church as a hierarchy of cre-

---

[9] Schmitt, *Renaissance Philosophy*, 582. Also, see Vivan Boland OP. Ideas in God according to Saint Thomas Aquinas: Sources and Synthesis. *Studies in the History of Christian Thought LXIX*. Leiden: E. J. Brill, 1996. 91–146. Boland summarizes well the structure of Dionysius' thought about God: "God is absolutely transcendent, beyond all things and separated from all things. God may be referred to as being but this does not explain his 'supersubstantial substance.' Likewise it is beyond our capacity to celebrate God's 'supersubstantial' goodness, being, life, and wisdom. God lives beyond all life and enjoys a wisdom beyond all wisdom. God's knowledge is removed from all things and his power is beyond all power. Things may be similar to God but God is not similar to things. To call God peace is to refer to the unity he enjoys far beyond all things. . . .This transcendent God is the cause and principle of all that is and of the qualities of all things" (98). For a brief historical overview of 'hen' or "One" as used before the medieval period see Peters, F. E. *Greek Philosophical Terms: A Historical Lexicon*. New York: New York University Press, 1967, 78–83 especially 5 and 14.

[10] Renaissance Platonism and medieval Christendom share a similar "view of man," one originating in Proclus and Pseudo-Dionysius, with the later borrowing much from the former (Boland, *Ideas in God* 115). With Proclus and P-D the relationship between divine procession and anthropology takes a peculiar turn toward the Parmenidian theoretical problem of "the One and the many". While neither Augustine nor Aristotle make this problem central to their intellectual programs, Proclus, and Pseudo-Dionysius do, offering a broadly encompassing solution and form of spirituality directly related to it. The purpose of P-D's *Divine Names*, for example, is to celebrate as far as possible the emanation of the absolute divine essence into the universe of things." (98–99)

[11] A comprehensive yet succinct summary of the influence of Proclus in medieval and renaissance thought is found in, Dodds, *Proclus: Elements of Theology*, xxvi–xxxiii. Dodds sees the influence Proclus as transmitted into the medieval schools primarily through the *De divinis nominibus* of Dionysius, the Aeropagite. It was the renaissance humanist Laurentius Valla who first questioned (and correctly so) the authenticity of this work. Proclan thought also reached the West through the influential *Liber de causii*, which circulated as a work of Aristotle though, in fact, it was a translation of an Arabic work based on Proclus' *Elements of Theology*. Dodds also observes that translations of Proclus' actual works "appeared at a time when Plotinus, and Plato himself (save for the *Phaedo*, the *Meno*, and part of the *Timaeus*), were still unknown in the West; and they played a decisive part in shaping the later medieval notion of 'Platonism'." (xxxi). For similar observations and comments see P. O. Kristeller, *Renaissance Thought and Its Sources*. (Columbia University Press, 1979), 53–54.

ated means objectively mediating and infusing supernatural grace by means of *theurgic* acts. These acts united sacrifice and sacrament in worship *elementally*, culminating liturgically in Lombard's Eucharistic formula *res et sacramentum*. During the Reformation, however, the metaphysic of divine things, which underlies the *un*intelligibility of God and abstract nature of the human being, was challenged by a fresh look at the Thomistic/Aristotelian idea of God as *being* or *spiritual substance*.[12] The principal impact of this intellectual transition on the doctrines of God and man is that God became *intelligible* by means of His Word, and man became distinct from God, a separate object for investigation. The human person, considered as a *whole*, is no longer conceived of merely as a composite of *divine things*, but rather man's faculties and activities are considered integral aspects of human nature proper. It was Thomas Aquinas, however, who first took up the challenge of explaining Christian doctrine in a *Word*-centered direction during the initial transformation of these metaphysical first principles during the 13th century.

After considering the Aristotelian world-view, Aquinas responded to Lombard's Neoplatonic view of Trinitarian procession by reformulating it in a more *intelligible* manner, that is, by reforming it in a *Word*-centered direction. In the *Summa*, Aquinas replaced Lombard's triadic procession of *memoria, intellegentia*, and *voluntas* with the Trinitarian procession of *principium verbi, verbum*, and *amor* based on the unity of God as pure act and the analogy of intelligible emanation.[13] Aquinas' *Word*-centered doctrine of God was primarily derived from Augustine's emphasis on *verbum Dei* as *singular* and *intelligible* and on Aristotle's

---

[12] Boland, *Ideas in God*, 147–192. Boland summarizes well the primary features of Aristotle's metaphysic: The notions of potentiality and actuality are fundamental to Aristotle's explanation of change and becoming. Logically and chronologically actuality must precede potentiality. Substance is the starting-point of all production, but production requires an actual substance to pre-exist. In seeking the cause or principle of things we are seeking a thing's substance or the primary cause of its being (156). Philosophy par excellence is "theology"; it apprehends what is "in itself" and knows all things in relation to the necessary Being which is the End of the universe. God is pure "spirit", that is, He is the eternal, necessary, *spiritual substance* distinct from the world and supreme intelligence (160).

[13] William B. Stevenson, "The Problem of Trinitarian Processions in Thomas's Roman Commentary," *The Thomist* 64 (2000), 620, 627–628. See also 625–26 for the discussion of what Stevenson views as Lombard's "mistaken" interpretation of Augustine on the triad of *memoria, intellgentia*, and *voluntas*. For Aquinas, generation in God is *secundum intellectualem emanationem*; the Word alone proceeds *per viam intellectus, quia procedit ab uno*. (Boland 236)

distinction between the *form* as both the 'principle' of knowledge and
the 'object' of knowledge.[14] Aquinas also distanced anthropology from
the topic of theology proper in the *Summa*, recognizing the need for
greater distinction between the nature of God and that of man.[15]
Trained *in via Thomae* at Padua, Vermigli was also convinced of the
principium verbi.[16] He insists, however—in line with the Augustinian
and Aristotelian aspects of Aquinas' thought—that the *intelligibility* of
God is founded on the very words of God in the Bible, which was
for him the chief *principium theologia* and *obiectum fidei*.[17] Vermigli's

---

[14] The distinction between *form* as 'principle' of knowledge and *form* as 'object'
of knowledge means that the intellect is capable of understanding forms, which are
both objects and principles of knowledge. For Vermigli and other Protestants this
means that the Word of God, Holy Scripture, is both the *principium theologia* and
the chief *object* of faith. For example, the Bible is the chief locus of the knowledge
of God accessible to finite human beings, especially in matters of salvation and
morals. This use of Aristotle is a significant departure from the un-differentiating
metaphysic of the Neoplatonic appropriation of Aristotle's categories that trans-
formed his apparatus of genus, species, and differentia into an objectively conceived
hierarchy of entities and forces where "the cause is but a reflection of the 'because'"
(Dodds, xxv), where the forms are not just *in things* but become *divine attributes*, that
is, God becomes the idea of every thing" (Boland, 93–146, 318–19.) With Augustine
and Aristotle "ideas are in the divine mind" but neither develops an ontology that
implies, "God is the idea of everything" as do Proclus and P-D. With Augustine
"the plurality of ideas is secondary to the single *verbum* which is produced by the
divine intellect." (235) Theologically, Augustine's primary concern is to protect the
Christian view of creation; Aristotle's concern is to make the locus of the ideas *in
things*.

[15] Stevenson, *The Thomist* 64 (2000), 621, 628–29. In Aquinas's *Roman Commentary*
on the *Sentences*, the prologue to his discussion of the Trinity is the *imago Dei*. In
the *Summa*, the prologue is *De Deo uno*, with the discussion of the *imago Dei* placed
later in the *ordo doctrina*.

[16] CAS, 13–41. Donnelly provides a comprehensive analysis and assessment of
the sources of Vermigli's thought. Peter Lombard and St. Thomas are Vermigli's
two most frequently cited medieval sources. Of the rival schools of Thomas, Scotist,
and Occam, Vermigli clearly prefers *in via Thomae* (24). While Augustine is Vermigli's
favorite theologian, he has a clear preference for Aristotle in matter philosophical
(34–35). Donnelly comments that Vermigli has little interest in the mystical element
of medieval theology and piety and of the half dozen citations of Dionysius, most
are hostile (24). Donnelly notes Vermigli's use of Aristotle's metaphysic "act and
potency" as a philosophical tool for his understanding of actual grace as a species
of divine concurrence from the prime mover and first act (199). In addition, grace
is a particular kind of concurrence that God sends to men that operates according
to man's intellectual and volitional nature by illuminating the intellect and strengthening the will so that man acts in accord with the divine will (160). Vermigli uses
Aristotle's "act and potency" against the medieval doctrine of the Eucharist (69–72).

[17] Richard A. Muller. *Dictionary of Latin and Greek Theological Terms: Drawn Principally*

Word-centered doctrine of God and Scripture leads him also to a renewed appreciation for Hebrew anthropology, the biblical idea of human *wholeness*. An Old Testament biblical scholar and lecturer, Vermigli insists, for example, that when St. Paul uses the term "soul" in his writings he means that term to "refer to the whole man, meaning all the powers and parts." Vermigli views this Hebrew or biblical anthropology as the alternative to the prevailing (and abstract) anthropology of the *platonici*.[18] Vermigli's use of Scripture in the formulation of anthropology is not surprising. Remarkable, however, is his heightened appreciation for the relevance and breadth of human capacities to genuinely participate in God's economy of salvation and worship that results from his anthropology. This appreciation will directly impact the role of the human agent in his vision for the reform of Christian worship.

Thus, in summary, with his starting place *in via Thomae*, Vermigli extends Aquinas' general notion of an *intelligible* doctrine of God, founded on the *principium verbi* and *verbum*, to the locus of that *intelligibility* in the words of God, Holy Scripture, thereby, making the Bible itself the foundation of Christian faith and worship. Aquinas, of course, did not take this step. Instead, he continued to support *theurgy* in such writings as *De occultis operibus naturae* and *De substantiis separatis*, as did other medieval philosopher/theologians such as Albertus in *De mineralibus* and William of Auvergne in *De universo*.[19] These

---

from Protestant Scholastic Theology. (Grand Rapids, MI, Baker Book House: 1985. 245–6 and 206, respectively.

[18] Vermigli, *Romanos*, 54. In chapter 2 where he defines the human soul, "Anima hominem significant", Vermigli writes, "Verum mihi videtur, simplicius dicendum, Hebraica phrasi per animam ipsum hominen significari: vel, ut rectius loquar, omnes facultates, & partes hominis." The significance of the Hebrew understanding of wholeness is shown later in chapter 12 (*Romanos* 582) where he speaks of the "error platonicus": "Si ita rem intelligamus, plenum erit sacrificium, Hoc enim pacto quemadmodum a Deo totum accepimus, ita Deo vicissim totum reddemus. Quod Platonici non recte videntur intellexisse. Illi enim, ut colligi potest ex Timaeo, senserunt, mentem tantum, & rationem immediate dari a Deo. Nam substantiam corporis ab elementis haustam esse statuerunt: temperamentum vero, quod appellant complexionem, a sphaeris coelestibus: affectus & crassiores animi partes a daemonibus. Atque id circo docebant, mentem, & rationem Deo rddendam esse. Nos autem scimus, totum hominem a Deo esse formatum: ideoque totum ili redid oportere. Quod si iam sumus insiti in Christum totique cessimus in possessionem Dei, illi debemus nos perpetuo totos exhibere."

[19] Schmitt, *Renaissance Philosophy*, 266. Dodds (xxxi) points out the significant parallels between and direct citations of Proclus' *Elements* and the teaching of Aquinas in *De substantiis separatis*, one of Aquinas' later writings.

works clearly illustrate the influence of Neoplatonism on the medieval church, especially that of Proclus and Pseudo-Dionysius (P-D). Vermigli, on the other hand, had the unique historical advantage of being a Thomistic theologian during the Italian Renaissance. The *Word*-centered nature of his reform was a by-product, on one hand, of Renaissance *humanism*, with its emphasis on evaluating texts, refreshing translations, and classical approaches to interpretation. On the other hand, it was consonant with the rich, intellectual history of the *scholastic* tradition in treating *verbum Dei* as a fundamental topic of philosophical theology.[20] Vermigli stood at an important cultural crossroad where the full bloom of late-Medieval *via ignorantia* was challenged by a budding, Reformation-inspired *via scriptura*; a crossroad where doctrinal collisions were inevitable.[21] Perhaps, no other theological topic during the Reformation displays the division between metaphysical and theological first principles more clearly than the Eucharistic controversy. Vermigli's thoughts on mediation and union with Christ adroitly address this topic.

Mediation in Worship: The Areopagite or the Bible?

In his major writings on the Eucharist, prominent theologians Richard Gardiner, William Tresham, and Johannes Brenz directly debate Vermigli. His principal protagonist in the Supper controversy, however, is the Parmenidian form of spirituality originating in the priestly school of 5th century Platonism. Proclus, the last head of the Platonic academy and a great synthesizer of Greek philosophy, attempted to create a single Hellenic philosophy while at the same time meeting the religious needs of his day.[22] Directly and indirectly, Proclan ide-

---

[20] For a balanced discussion of Vermigli as both a scholastic and humanist in theological method see Frank A. James, III. "Peter Martyr Vermigli: At the crossroads of late medieval Scholasticism, Christian Humanism, and resurgent Augustinianism," in Carl Trueman and R. Scott, *Protestant Scholasticism: Essays in Reassessment.* (Carlisle Cumbria: Paternoster Press, 1999), 62–78.

[21] *In via ignorantia* refers to Nicholas of Cusa's important work, *De docta ignorantia.* As Lohr observes (*op cite*, note 8), the Renaissance Platonism of Lull, Nicholas of Cusa, and Ficino found little they could use in Aristotle's approach. Their goal—consistent with that of the Neoplatonist *via negativa* that preceded them—was "a higher type of knowledge, an intellectual vision which transcended not only sense perception but also reason itself. Nicholas of Cusa went furthest in this regard."

[22] Dodds, *Proclus: Elements of Theology*, xviii.

ology was enormously influential in medieval thought: His *Elements of Theology*, a concise *summa* of the Neoplatonic system in its fully developed form, for example, is the actual underlying text of the influential pseudo-Aristotelian work, *Liber de causii*.[23] While Proclan in origin, the *Parmenidian* spirituality of that school was transmitted into medieval Christian theology primarily through P-D.[24]

The P-D form of spirituality had an enormous impact on medieval theologians including writers such as Maximus the Confessor, Erigena, Hugh of St. Victor, Robert Grosseteste, Peter Lombard, Albertus Magnus, Thomas Aquinas and others. As E. R. Dodds puts it, "Dionysius rapidly acquired an authority second only to Augustine."[25] Dodds observes two related but also divergent trends in the development of Platonism: "The fundamental change of outlook after Porphyry is clearly recognized and stated by Olympiodorus, who remarks that 'some put philosophy first, as Porphyry, Plotinus, etc.; others the priestly art, as Iamblichus, Syrianus, Proclus and all the priestly school.'"[26] In the words of Iamblichus, "It is not thought that links the theurgist to the gods: else what should hinder the theoretical philosopher from enjoying theurgic union with them? The case is not so. Theurgic union is attained only by the perfective operation of the unspeakable *acts* correctly performed, acts which are beyond all understanding; and by the power of the unutterable symbols which are intelligible only to the gods."[27] Proclus writes that *theurgia* is, "a power higher than all human wisdom, embracing the blessings of divination, the purifying powers of initiation, and in a word, all the operations of divine possession." Secondly, like Iamblichus, Proclus believes that "it is not by an act of discovery, nor by the activity proper to their being, that individual things are united to

---

[23] Dodds, *Proclus: Elements of Theology*, x.

[24] Schmitt, *Renaissance Philosophy*, 567. "Pseudo-Dionysius borrowed much from the *Parmenides*, especially in his *De divinis nominibus*." See also Kristeller, *Renaissance Thought*, 53: Proclus' "neat and scholastic system . . . supplied practically all later Greek Church Fathers and theologians with their philosophical terms and concepts, most of all that obscure father of most Christian mysticism who hides under the name of Dionysius the Areopagite, and whose writings owed a tremendous authority to the name of their supposed author, a direct disciple of St. Paul the Apostle."

[25] Dodds, *Proclus: Elements of Theology*. xxvii.

[26] Dodds, *Proclus: Elements of Theology*. xxiii.

[27] Dodds, *Proclus: Elements of Theology*. xx. For a general introduction to the technical aspects of *theurgia* see the Greek terms 'mantike' and 'dynamis' in Peters, *Greek Philosophical Terms*, 113–14, 42–45.

the One", but by the mysterious operation of the occult "symbols" which reside in certain stones, herbs and animals.[28] Finally, a point especially evident in the Proclan *kosmos noetos*—a unique blending of Neoplatonism and the Aristotelian categories devoid of their essential grounding in things[29]—is that the spiritual world is viewed as the same *type* of uninterrupted continuum as was concurrently being propagated for the physical world.[30] For Proclus and P-D, the distinction between the categories of "substance" and "quality" is blurred so that the power of the created thing and the thing itself are indistinguishable.[31] In the priestly act of uniting sacrifice and sacrament at the consecration in the Mass, this undifferentiating metaphysic lays behind Lombard's Eucharistic expression *res et sacramentum*.

It is precisely to this Neoplatonic metaphysic that Vermigli objects when he contests the requirement in the Eucharist that the *thing* must pass from "the substance into the accident. . . ." Vermigli writes, it "makes Quid" to be "Quale."[32] By requiring the *qualities* of flesh to be present in the elements, Lombard's view requires *totum Christi* offered on the cross and on the altar to be *of the same kind* or quality (i.e., *quale*). From a liturgical point of view, Vermigli is particularly concerned about this Proclan-inspired tendency to conflate physical and spiritual realities because the *elemental* reception of the Eucharistic rite had come to overshadow the *intelligible* reception of saving faith through the *Word*. Vermigli's conviction (in line with Augustine and Aristotle) is that the Word of God, Holy Scripture, is the principle, and object, the intelligible basis and single locus of the communication of God's salvific intent. He writes,

> Furthermore, we no less receive the body and blood of Christ in the word of God, than in this sacrament. For what else by the testimony

---

[28] Dodds, *Proclus: Elements of Theology*, xxii–xxiii.

[29] Kristeller, *Renaissance Thought*, 53. Kristeller observes that in Proclus' *Elements of Theology* and *Platonic Theology* "all things and their mutual relations are neatly defined and deduced in their proper place and order; and the concepts of Aristotle's logic and metaphysics, divested of their specific and concrete reference, are used as elements of a highly abstract and comprehensive ontology."

[30] Dodds, *Proclus: Elements of Theology*, 32–33, 216. This is especially evident in proposition 28 where to the laws of emanation and of undiminished giving, Proclus adds a third principle governing the procession, that of continuity.

[31] Peters, *Greek Philosophical Terms*, 198. Dodds, *Proclus: Elements of Theology*, xxv.

[32] Vermigli, *Disputatio*, 280. Nego argumentum, transis enim a substantia ad accidens et Quid facis, Quale. Illud ipsum corpus esse, quo ad naturam, fere centies conce[b]i: at non sequitur quo ad modum praesentiae corporalis, vel ibi esse, vel a nobis accipi.

of Augustine be sacraments, than visible words. . . . No less account is the word of God, than is the Eucharist. . . . Whatsoever fruit of grace the bread has in the sacrament, it has by the word. And besides this, the words do more plainly both express and signify the nature of a sacrament, than the signs do.[33]

While the *Word*-centered intellectual tradition of Augustine and Aquinas is evident here, the Proclan necessity of a real *elemental* presence is missing. The significance of the metaphysical aspects of the *elemental* and *Word*-centered approaches to sacramental theology is further highlighted in Vermigli's Oxford Disputation on the Lord's Supper where he connects "the words" of the sacraments to the meaning of *truth* and the nature of divine *presence*. He writes,

> . . . the words which we have in our sacraments [i.e., sacraments of the New Testament], be far more clear and plain than were the words of the old sacraments in the law [i.e., sacraments of the Old Testament]. But you [D. Chadse, a Roman Catholic opponent] understand the word, truth, as though it should signify real presence; and therefore you infer, that the body of Christ is present with us really, corporally, and substantially. But the fathers understand, truth, to be in our sacraments if they be compared to the sacraments of the old fathers; because they represent the thing that is now performed, even that the kingdom of heaven is opened, and that the benefit of our redemption is, with all evidence and assuredness, already finished and made perfect, and bestowed on us, as it were before the eyes of faith.[34]

Vermigli contrasts two views of *truth* in this quotation, each implying a different conception of Christ's *presence* in the Supper. The

---

[33] Vermigli, *Disputatio*, 225–26. Praeterea, non minus accipimus corpus & sanguinem Christi in verbo dei, quam in hoc sacrmento: Quid enim sunt aliud sacrmenta Aug. testimonio, quam verba visibilia? Imo idem Augu. Ut habetur de cosecr. Distinct. 2. cap. Interrogo vos ait: Non aliquid minus esse verbum Domini, quam Eucharistiam. Hieron. Item in ecclesiasten attestatus est, nos in sacris litteris carnum Domini manducare, & cruorem eius bibere. Orig. idem scripsit super Math. Tractat. 25. & in numeros homi. 26. Chrysost. Super Ioan. Ho. 45. & Basilius epi. 141. Quin et ipsa ratio fuadet: Nam quod havet panis in sacramento fructus aut gratiae, per verbum adipiscitur. Et ad haec, verba clarius quam symbola, & exprimunt & significant sacramenti rationem:

[34] Vermigli, *Disputatio* 288–89. Deinde verba quae habemus in sacramentis nostris, longe sunt clariora ac lucidiora, quam fuerint verba antiquorum sacramentiorum in lege. Sed tu accipis veritatem, quasi significet realem praesentiam, ideo infers nobis corporaliter et substantialiter adesse corpus Christi: at veritatem patres intelligent in nostris sacrmentis collatis ad vertera, eo quod repraesentent rem iam praes[t]itam, scilicet apertum regnum coelorum, & beneficium redemptionis nostrae, summa claritate & certitudne iam peractum atqua perfectum, & collatum in nos, veluti ob oculos fidei ponunt.

Roman view of truth, for example, implies the idea of *real* presence in the elements: The Christ on the altar must be the very same Christ of the cross; that is, the *truth* about Christ's presence in the Eucharist is that he is present *realiter*. To the concept of truth as *real* presence, Vermigli contrasts his own: the truth of the words of Scripture implies the idea of *completeness* or *fulfillment*.[35] His view that truth-equals-fulfillment suggests that the benefits of redemption were perfected and completed in the Person and work of Christ on the cross and are now bestowed upon believers by faith; the Christ at the table of the Lord's Supper is, indeed, the very same Christ present in the sacraments of the Old Testament.

As suggested by Fr. Francis Clark, the ecclesiastical implications of these alternative views of *truth* are quite significant. "The Reformers' basic protest [against the Roman sacramental system] can be summarized in the words of Adolf Harnack: rightly did they rebel against the Catholic sacramental system, he says, since 'it was rooted in the fundamental conception that religion is an antidote for the finiteness of man, in the sense that it deifies his nature.'"[36] In other words, the central *truth* of real presence—with its *elemental* form of union and *theurgic* form of mediation—is a solution directed primarily at the Parmenidian problem of the "One and the many" or human "finiteness." Vermigli, however, writes that the principal truth of the Word, Holy Scripture, is that, "Christ the Son of God suffered for us so that through him we might receive the forgiveness of our

---

[35] LC (1580), 197–212. Vermigli refers to the sacraments of the Old Testament as "shadow and figures" or "examples" of "God's promise to be our God" and of the mysteries of human salvation. Throughout the whole of this treatise, Vermigli links the nature of sacramental presence to the nature of the differences between the Old and New Testaments. In so doing, he uses the analogy of substance to accident. In addition, now that Christ has been revealed in the New Testament, Vermigli suggests that one must understand the "eternal" truth ("mento pertinent ad res aeternas") implicit in what may appear to be only temporal promises in the Old Testament. In this regard, Vermigli points to particular "kingdom" passages of the Old Testament, such as those referring to David, stating that, "Promisit olim Deus patriarchis, Davidi, & eius posteritati regnum tradendum, id autem non trantum est intelligendum de Solomone, verum etiam de Christuo." Other examples of this approach to interpretation of the Old Testament occur with the prophets such as Zachariah and Isaiah. In VWG, 86–119 considerable evidence of Vermigli's understanding of Christ in the Old Testament and New Testament signs is offered.

[36] Francis Clark. *Eucharistic Sacrifice and the Reformation.* (Westminster, Md., Newman Press: 1960), 105.

sins."[37] These different views of the primary human religious "problem"—finiteness or sin—and of God's salvific intent in relationship to them, mean that quite different views of *truth* are, in fact, guiding the foundational principles of *mediation* and *union with Christ* for which each party is contending in the Eucharistic debate. Neither Augustine nor Aristotle makes the Parmenidian problem of "the One and the many" central to their intellectual programs and Vermigli's appropriation of this line of Aquinas' thought for his purposes is not surprising. Aquinas himself inherited the issue from the Neoplatonic sources of his thought. The influence of the Parmenidian problem and its resolution by the medieval church, however, fundamentally altered sacramental theology and Christian piety, moving them away from the *Word*-centered tradition of Christian theology toward the *Mind*-centered and *elemental*.[38] It was not unexpected, therefore, as Fr. Francis Clark states, that the Protestant movement developed different conceptions of soteriology, the Church, even the very nature of the Christian dispensation.[39]

Vermigli's difficulty with real "flesh" in the Eucharistic elements is not only due to the un-intelligibility of that notion but also is a function of his concern for the biblical view of personhood. While sharing aspects of Aristotle's psychology, Vermigli's "idea of man" is derived more from the Hebrew idea of *wholeness* than from the abstract theological anthropology of the *platonici*.[40] In fact, the hallmarks of Vermigli's anthropology are concreteness and wholeness. These differences in anthropology between Vermigli and the *platonici*, however, do not play themselves out in the topic of Christology, but rather in Christian *pietas*. Vermigli's Hebrew anthropology has little

---

[37] Vermigli, *Romanos*, 565: "Christum filium Dei pro nobis passum esse ut per eum acciperemus condonationem peccatorum." CAS, 57. Donnelly states that this master truth of the Bible "was not controverted in the sixteenth century." While this may be true at face value, Vermigli's reclamation of an authentic *Word*-centered theology (*in via Thomae*) meant that its application to Christian *pietas* would profoundly alter the ecclesiastical landscape. What is central to Vermigli's intellectual program of theology is its *Word*-centered orientation; predestination is just one of several doctrinal emphases. Also, as Donnelly states, Vermigli's prolific writings on the Eucharist do not make it the center of his theology as a whole either, but rather suggests the need for a corrective of too much emphasis on it.

[38] Dodds, *Proclus: Elements of Theology*, 310. Boland, *Ideas in God*, 62–65.

[39] Clark, *Eucharistic Sacrifice and Reformation*, 176.

[40] *Op cite*, note 18.

impact on Christology per se: *Totum Christum* of history is a real *communicatio idiomata concreto*, fully in accord with Catholic Christology. On the other hand, the implication of his biblical anthropology for Christian *pietas* is ecclesiastically shattering: If the human nature of Christ is *whole* in the Incarnation, then the properties of Christ's ascended human nature can not be construed as existing *in abstracto* but must exist *in loco esse* if substantial continuity and integrity are to remain between the Christ of history, of resurrection, and of ascension.[41] If Christ's human nature is *whole*, then Christ's presence in the Supper cannot entail a procession of the *real* human qualities of the Incarnation.[42] But without an *elemental* real presence at the altar, the form of *pietas* characterized by "union with the One"—by the ascent of 'vision' and 'deification'—through theurgic union is radically challenged. According to Vermigli the unity of *res sacramenti* with the Christ-of-the-cross is found not in their common kind, that is, including the qualities of *real* flesh, but in their common *spiritual substance*. But if Vermigli rejects the Parmeniedian/P-D-inspired form of spirituality and the theurgic instrument at its foundation, then to what does he appeal as the mediatorial basis of Christian worship?

The mediatorial foundation of Christian worship is *verbum Dei*, Holy Scripture, whose word of promise is the very object of faith.[43]

---

[41] CAS, 199.

[42] Another way to think about this is from the point of view of the *ordo doctrina*: In Lombard the topic of the *imago dei* is positioned between *Uno Deo* and *Trinitas*. In other words, the topic of anthropology is a subject matter addressed within theology proper. The topic of Trinitarian procession is taken up *after* theological anthropology. Perhaps, this is the source of Lombard's procession of the qualities of real human nature? Does this choice of the *ordo doctrina* point to a Neoplatonic view of man in Lombard? Not surprisingly, in Aquinas' first two commentaries on the *Sentences*, he follows Lombard's *ordo*. When Aquinas constructs his own *ordo doctrina* in the *Summa*, he removes the *imago dei* topic from theology proper. He seems to have done this as a direct result of his "recovery" of a Word-centered approach to theology proper and to the Trinity specifically. His adoption of the Aristotelian psychology over the Platonic was undoubtedly influential.

[43] LC (1580), 251a. Vermigli writes that chief object of faith is the "promise of God . . . wherein He promises through Christ to be favorable and merciful to us." "Est ea in primis promissio, qua pollicetur, se nobis fore placatum atqua propitium per Christum. Et licet in Sacris literis permultae legantur, nobisque esserantur Dei promissiones, . . ." But beyond that Vermigli states that the Word of God, as set forth in Holy Scripture, is the chief object or common object of faith. He writes, "Hinc patet, quodnam sit objectum prae[cipaum] fidei. Commune autem obiectum, . . ., est verbum Dei, [eabis] in Sacris literis declaratum. Vitra hoc obiectum fides se non extendit: . . . Nos autem dicimus, fidem esse assentum, qui exhibetur Scripturae sanctae, . . ."

For, as he writes, "Faith is a firm and certain assent of the mind to God's words inspired by the Holy Spirit and leading to the salvation of believers."[44] Even in the Lord's Supper, Vermigli seems to have the objectivity of the Word in mind when he refers to the sacraments of the New Testament as "visible words of God." He writes that the sacramental signs are as "perspicuous" in what they offer as Holy Scripture is in what it offers and what both offer is Christ, who is the *truth*, and gospel of God.[45] The sacramental signs of the New Testament combine the *verba institutionis* (audible words of God) and *signa* (visible words of God) to offer Christ as objectively as the Word of God, that is, as clearly as Scripture and preaching.[46] Consistent with the Word-centered foundation of worship, Vermigli suggests that even with respect to the elements of the Eucharist "the perspicuity and plainness of the sacraments must chiefly be regarded in the words."[47] In so doing, the Word itself becomes the most crucial "element" of the rite of the Lord's Supper. Vermigli writes, "Whatsoever fruit of grace the bread has in the sacrament, it has by the word."[48] By attributing the "fruit of grace" to the Word in the sacraments, Vermigli ascribes to the Word the

---

[44] CAS, 150.

[45] *Op cite*, note 33.

[46] LC (1580), 465. Vermigli speaks of one's "conjunction" with Christ as threefold ("Tribus rebus per gradus coniungitur corpus Christi"): By Christ himself, words, and signs. The three together mean that in the Lord's Supper is found, perhaps, the most intimate spiritual feeding on Christ, though not inherently, but rather in view of the multiple forms of the Word of God provided in one rite.

The objectivity herein described seems primarily to connote the ideas of *clarity* or *trustworthiness*. Holy Scripture, as the testament of God's saving actions, is the *most trustworthy basis* for grasping those things pertaining to it. Secondly, while the Roman church has an equally "high view" of the inspiration of Holy Scripture, the Reformation emphasis on *sola Scriptura* brings to objectivity the added idea of *authoritative*. Thus, what is being emphasized here is that Holy Scripture is objective in the sense that it is more trustworthy and authoritative than, say, the liturgy of the Mass.

The point is sometimes made that the Reformers' rejection of the objectivity of the Church and Mass meant the resolution of Christianity into subjective inner feelings (see Clark, *Eucharistic Sacrifice and Reformation*, 105). However, in so far as the Reformers viewed Holy Scripture, the Word, as the objective basis for the promises of God, the object of faith regarding those promises, and thus the foundation of the service of worship, can such criticism be sustained? Said differently, are the words of Holy Scripture any less objective than the words and acts of the liturgy?

[47] Vermigli, *Disputatio* 292. "Respondeo: Euedemtiam & claritatem sacramentorum, praecipue spestandam esse in verbis:"

[48] *Op cite*, note 33.

objective basis of the *thing offered by God to us*—Vermigli's definition of *sacrament*—in worship.[49] When the believing communicant apprehends the visible words of God (i.e., the signs of bread and wine) in faith, she is joined with *spiritus Christi* or *totus Christi*, the true substance of the eternal Word of God, creating a real *manducatio spiritualis*.[50] Again, the ecclesiastical implications are striking: By adopting the Augustinian and Aristotelian aspects of Aquinas' theology, Vermigli's reform means that the *theurgic* mediation of the Proclan-inspired *opus operatum* must be exchanged for the salvific mediation of Word and Spirit, an *opus Trinitati*, as the chief instrument of Christian worship.[51] The Bible itself is now the *intelligible* foundation of the knowledge of God in Christian worship and, therefore, is the foundation for the believer's union with Christ, which begins with "the mind's" grasp of the truth of God's "words" but is not complete without the productive activity of Word and Spirit affecting the *whole* person.

Union with Christ: The Areopagite or Hebrew Wholeness?

Union with Christ describes how the believer, in this earthly life, is joined to Christ in the transformational process of her "return" to God, or as Vermigli prefers to put it, in the process of her "resur-

---

[49] LC (1580), 472: A sacrament "quod etiam voluntarium opus est & religio sum, necnon a Deo institutum, ut per illud promissa & data bona consignentur ac exhibeantur: quoniam ibi nos quippiam Deo ne quaquam offeramus, verum ipie profert signa & dona sua nobis amplificat, dum ea quae offeruntur, solida fide percipimus" Vermigl's distinction between a sacrament and sacrifice is indicated in *Loci*, 430a,b: "Natura enim sacrificii est, ut a nobis offeratur Deo: Sacramenti autem natura est, ut nobis offeratur a Deo.

[50] Vermigli, *Romanos*, 280. "Itaque si fide complectimur ea, quae commemorantur, affequimur spiritum Christi, & Christus ipse ist in nobis, ut Paulus hoc loco restatur. Corpus autem, & carnem Christi iuxta suam naturalem, & realem praesentiam, nihil opus est advocare: quae tamen spiritualiter satis habemus praesentia, quum illa fide comprehendimus." Respecting how the spirit of Christ works in the life of the believing communicant, Vermigli writes in *Romanos*, 278: "Christi ingenium, proprietas, indoles, sensus, motus, nobis inseruntur: ut, qui cofit potitus, dicere posit cum Paulo: Viuo ego, iam non ego, viuit vero in me Christus."

[51] Clark, *Eucharistic Sacrifice and Reformation*, 105 and VWG, 71–72. McLelland seems to make this point about the Trinitarian action of God as Father, Word, and Spirit wherein human beings are created by the Word of God in order to image His holiness, righteousness, and truth. Vermigli writes in LC (1850), 445a: "Id tantum dicam, non esse contemnenda Sacramenta, sed vicissim non esse eis tribuendem, quod unius est Dei."

rection life." Roman Catholic and Protestant theologians both refer to union with Christ as *spiritually feeding* on Christ. In Lombard's Eucharistic system spiritual eating involves the believing communicant feeding on the real flesh of Christ in the elements of bread and wine and, thereby, feeding on *res tantum*, the mystical flesh of Christ.[52] For Vermigli, spiritually feeding on Christ involves the believing communicant feeding on *spiritus Christi* or *totus Christus*, understood as the *whole* Person of the eternal Word of God.[53]

As with mediation, Vermigli's perspective on *union with Christ* is heavily influenced by the *intelligibility* of God in His Word and the *wholeness* of man. The *intelligible* communication of God's grace in Vermigli's conception of *union* begins with the "mind" or "soul's" apprehension (by faith) of the words of Scripture, whether read, spoken or sung. This intellectual phenomenon results in an *immediate* union of Christ with the soul of the communicant, so that Christ might *fulfill* His life-giving purpose within the individual believer on behalf of the community of faith. For in view of the principal *truth* of Scripture—"through Christ we have received the forgiveness of sins"—the salvific intent of Scripture is that Christ might fulfill the very same *type* of obedience in His body, the Church, which He fulfilled on behalf of the Father during His own earthly ministry. Vermigli, in fact, describes this goal of the Church as "the obedience of Christ" or "the obedience of faith."[54]

The intellectual nature by which union with Christ begins—through "the words of God"—does not mean that Christian *piety* ends with contemplation; union with Christ is a union of the *whole* person with

---

[52] Lombard, Peter. *Quatuor Libri Sententiarum* Bk. 4, dist. 8, pt. 7, 792 ". . . res et non Sacramentum mystica eius caro." In Dist. ix, Cap iii, 795, entitled, "De intelligentia quarundam verborum ambiguorum" Lombard writes, "Sacramentum hic dicit corpus Christi proprium, de Virgine ductum; rem vero, spiritualem Christi carnem."

[53] *Op cite*, note 18.

[54] VWG, 71. "Truly this Body is not destitute of its weapons: but they are spiritual, not carnal, namely the Word and the Spirit, through whom it overcomes human wisdom, casts it to the ground, and leads captive our mind and thought to the obedience of Christ." (*Catechimus* 39). Another term used by Vermigli to describe this goal of the Church is "obedientia fidei" which is found in Romans 1:5 and 16:26. (*Romanos* 7 and 643). He describes the obedience of faith as the "end" (finem) of both apostleship and the gospel itself. The equivalency of the "obedience of Christ" to the "obedience of faith" is apparently linked to his citation of 2 Corinthians 10:5 in the context of describing the obedience of faith in Romans 1:5.

the *whole* Christ. It is a union that has implications for all dimensions of human nature and existence. Vermigli writes that,

> a true conjunction between us and Christ [exists] whereby not only our mind is united with him but also our body and flesh hath his renewing from thence, and we are truly made the members of the Lord and do receive him to be our head, from whence we perpetually draw both spirit and life.[55]

And though he affirms the importance of the intellect (and faith) as prior and fundamental to *spiritual eating*, yet the spiritual eating proposed by him is of the "flesh" of Christ. Vermigli writes that,

> eating belongs unto the soul and to faith. For we grant that in the sacrament the flesh of Christ is eaten spiritually but yet truly. Neither do we at any time say such flesh is severed and divided from the divine person of the word.[56]

This presence of the *whole* Christ, *totus Christus*, to the *whole* person in communion, however, is immaterial and spiritual, affecting the believing communicant through the gracious movement of the soul by *spiritus Christi* through the words of Scripture, which are the very objects of faith.[57] Indeed, Vermigli believes that the *spiritual* substance of Christ is the *thing* eaten when a believing person partakes of the Supper. He writes,

---

[55] LC (1580), 457a: "...sed vera coniunctio inter nos & Christum, qua non solum noster animus cum ipso unitur, sed etiam corpus & caro nostra inde habet suam instauartionem, efficimurq, vere membra Domini, & ipsum nostrum caput suscripimus, ex quo perpetuo & spiritum & vitam haurimus.

[56] LC (1580), 461b. "Confitemur enim Christum nobis ad esse per naturam divinam, item per gratiam, & ulta dona quae nobis affert spiritus eius. Deinde si sanquinem & carnem illius cupimus, ea possumus complecti in hoc Sacramento fide, & spiritualiter manducare."

[57] LC (1580), 456a: Vermigli grants that the very body and very flesh are present in the sacrament but the manner of eating is not "carnally" but "spiritually." Also, Vermigli here speaks of faith and our mind as needing to move beyond the signs to the thing signified and of the efficacy of the Holy Spirit and faith: Adiicias istis, fidem tantae esse efficaciae, ut res praesentes faciat, non quidem realiter aut substantialiter, sed spiritualiter. Nam ellas vere complectitur." Again, Vermigli does not deny eating the flesh and blood of Christ but such eating must be construed as spiritual. *Loci*, 461b: "Confitemus enim Christium nobis ad esse per naturam divinam, item per gratiam, & multa dona quae nobis assert spiritus eius. Deinde se sanguinem & carnem illius cupimus, ea possumus complecti in hoc Sacramento fide, & spritualiter mandcare, ad quod postea consequitur, verissima, arcane tamen & ineffabilis nostra coniunctio cum Christo, quando in illum mutatmur."

> ... touching our cognitions of the mind and comprehension of faith, we confess that as touching the thing itself, the nature of bread and wine go away, and that our mind only cleaves to the things signified, to that which by the signs is offered unto us, that is, the body and blood of Christ.[58] ... in the sacrament the flesh of Christ is eaten spiritually but yet truly.

Vermigli's emphasis on the *whole* person in union with the *whole* Christ is a rejection of the anthropology of the *platonici*—whose pietistic goal was deification or vision—in which union with Christ was considered *above* human nature and *beyond* human understanding. Having rejected this Parmenidian form of spirituality and Eucharistic sacrifice as its instrument in favor of obedience to Christ through encounter with Word and Spirit, why does Vermigli continue to maintain the idea of sacrifice in the Supper? How do the principles of *intelligibility* and *wholeness* lead him to *re*-join sacrifice and sacrament in worship as a form of spirituality analogous to the *obedience of Christ*? Before addressing these questions in more detail, the following passage from a section on the Lord's Supper gives a hint of his constructive solution. Vermigli states,

> for the nature of a sacrifice is, to be offered of us unto God: but the nature of a sacrament is, to be offered of God unto us. I confess, indeed, that in the celebration of the Supper of the Lord, are contained thanksgiving, alms, praises, and other such things, which may have the consideration of a sacrifice. But we deny, that the very sacrament of the Eucharist may properly be called a sacrifice.[59]

The Biblical Shape of Sacrifice and Sacrament

For Vermigli, the central defining idea of sacrifice is *something we offer to God*, and the central characteristic of sacrament is *something God*

---

[58] LC (1580), 457b: "... totum hoc accipere quo ad nostras animi cogitations, & fidei complexum, & tibi fatebamur, quo ad issum naturam & panis & vini abire, animumq nostrum tantummodo inhaerere significatis, & rebusquae per symbola nobis offeruntur, id est, corpori & sanguini Christi."

[59] LC (1580), 430a, b: "Natura enim sacrificii est, ut a nobis offeratur Deo: Sacramenti autem natura est, ut nobis offeratur a Deo. Fateor equidem in actione coenae Dominica concludi gratiarum actions, eleemosinas, preces, & alia id genus, quae rationem sacrificii hibere possunt: Ipsum autem Eucharistiae sacrmentum, negamus proprie vocari posse sacrificium.

offers to us.[60] By drawing on a number of passages from Vermigli's writings on the subject of sacrament and sacrifice, the following table was composed to highlight the *thing* offered by God to us in sacrament and the responsive human offer and connection Vermigli creates through the liturgical re-union of sacrament and sacrifice:

The *thing* offered by God in sacrament is . . .	The *thing* offered by us in sacrifice is . . .
God	Thanksgiving
Christ	Alms
Reconciliation	Prayers
Grace	Singing
Remission of sin	Sermon
	Obedience to the Word of God
	Love of Neighbor

One first observes that the thing offered by God to believers (in the sacrament) is offered by God *alone*. The priestly or pastoral role is *not* construed as an *offerer* with respect to the *things* of God; the proximate offerer of the *things* of God in worship, as we have seen before, is *verbum Dei*, Holy Scripture. The priestly or pastoral role is similar *in kind*, if not in vocation, to that of the members of the congregation: The priestly or pastoral office is to lead the congregation in *sacrifices* of thanksgiving through the presence of the Word: preaching and administration of the sacrament. Even the sermon is viewed as a sacrifice of thanksgiving, specifically, the sacrifice of the Gospel.[61] Indeed, as Vermigli writes, the whole "work of faith is to give thanks."[62] Secondly, though the *offerer* and the *thing* offered in sacrament and sacrifice are different, nevertheless, they are parallel in

---

[60] *Op cite*, note 49.

[61] Vermigli, *Romanos* 632: "Collatio sacrificii Missae ac Euangelii." In the context of the consecrating role of the priestly office (Romans 15:15–16) Vermigli writes that the minister's sermon is a "sacrifice of the Gospel" in contrast to the Roman "sacrifice of the Mass."

[62] Peter Martyr Vermigli, *In Selectissimam S. Pauli Priorem Ad Corinthios Epistolam. Tiguri, 1551,* 442a. Commentating on 1 Corinthians 15.57, he writes, "Opus fidei est gratias agere." The whole context of this marginal note is, "Pro tanto Christi beneficio, deo gratias agit, quod opus est sincerae fidei: quia nec diligenier nec ex animo gratias agunt, nisi qui beneficium probe senserunt." VWG, 240.

purpose: coupling the communicant in holy society with God.[63] Vermigli's general rule of worship is that wherever in the service *God offers something to us* (through the Word preached, read, sung, prayed, or present as Jesus Christ Himself) and the Church responds with *offers of thanksgiving* (through confession, praise, alms, love, singing, prayer), a true and spiritual worship occurs.[64] By this general rule, we see Vermigli liturgically joining sacrament and sacrifice: on one hand, based on the *intelligibility* of God, His words (Holy Scripture) are the mediatorial foundation of worship, the very objects of faith. Based on the *wholeness* of persons, God is given thanks for the grace He first gives in worship as a genuine human response of words and deeds, thoughts and actions, in pursuit of the *obedience of Christ* in every aspect of life.

In the Lord's Supper, however, the believer's union with Christ is especially aroused by the multiplicity of the forms of the Word present: *spiritus Christi* (i.e, the eternal Word of God), *verba institutionis* (i.e., audible Word of God) and *signa* (i.e., visible words of God). This dynamic offer of the Word, facilitated by the Holy Spirit, is a true and present reality for the believing communicant, a *manducatio spiritualis* of Christ, the Word, in the fullest sense possible from Vermigli's perspective.[65] The receiving communicant, in response to God's offer of grace in the Supper, offers her whole self to God as a sacrifice of thanksgiving; first, *internally* from the heart and then with *external* activities and signs corresponding to the tangible gifts and duties of love for God and neighbor: enacting the *obedience of Christ*.[66] An example of this *type* of joining of sacrament and sacrifice in the Lord's Supper is seen in the Post-Communion Prayer of the

---

[63] LC (1580), 472–473. It appears that Vermigli's reference to "holy society" also has a parallel in the Lombardian sacramental system in that what is signified but non-contained in the sacrament of the Eucharist is the mystical body of Christ, the unity of the church. See note above.

[64] This point, also, follows from McLelland's insights on the fundamental role of Word and Spirit operative in Vermigli's theology. See VWG, 71–79. *D. Petri Martyris comment. In librum Iudicum.* 149. "Nos Christianorum sacrificia esse statuimus, cor contritum, preces, gratiarum actions, elecmosinas, affectuum & carnes mortificatione, atque alia huiusmodi. Haec nobis relicta sunt post abrogatas carnales victimas, ut ea offeramus, ut fidei nostrae fructus, & grati animi testimonia."

[65] Corda, Salvatore: *Veritas Sacramenti: A Study of Vermigli's Doctrine of Lord's Supper,* Zurich: Theologischer Verlag, 1975. 138–141 and summarized on 148–49.

[66] *Op cite,* note 54.

1552 English Book of Common Prayer ("BCP"). After the delivery of the cup in the sacrament of Lord's Supper:

> *Then shall the Priest say the Lord's prayer, the people repeating after him every petition.*
> *After shall be said the following.*

> O Lord and heavenly father, we thy humble servants entirely desire thy fatherly goodness, mercifully to accept this our Sacrifice of praise and thanks giving: most humbly beseeching thee to grant, that by the merits and death of thy son Jesus Christ, and through faith in his blood, we and all thy whole church may obtain remission of our sins, and all other benefits of his Passion. And here we offer and present unto thee, O lord, our selves, our souls, and bodies, to be a reasonable, holy, and lively Sacrifice unto thee: humbly beseeching thee, that all we which be partakers of this holy Communion, may be fulfilled with thy grace and heavenly benediction. And although we be unworthy through our manifold sins to offer unto thee any Sacrifice: yet we beseech thee to accept this our bounden duty and service, not weighing our merits, but pardoning our offences, through Jesus Christ our Lord; by whom and with whom, in the unity of the holy ghost, all honor and glory be unto thee, O father almighty, world without end. Amen.[67]

The language of this prayer certainly contains the idea of sacrifice: Such sacrifice is one of thanksgiving but also it is one offered by the *whole* person (i.e., "our selves, our souls, and bodies") as her immediate response to the grace of God offered in the sacrament. The prayer includes the *living sacrifice* language from Romans 12.1–2 as the *intelligible* basis for the New Testament understanding of sacrifice, resulting in the tangible "duty and service" that is our obedience to Christ. In this case the response of obedience comes not only from the grace offered by the visible word of God in the sign of the cup but also by the grace of the word of God spoken in the Lord's Prayer. This Word-centered *union* of sacrament and sacrifice, however, is viewed as a "holy Communion." This particular post-communion prayer is not found in BCP (1549) prior to Vermigli's arrival and consultations with Cranmer. This 1552 prayer, however, is retained in Elizabeth's revision of 1558. Might Vermigli have contributed this language or the concepts behind it to the BCP through Cranmer?

---

[67] The Second Prayer Book of King Edward VI, 1552. *The Ancient and Modern Library of Theological Literature.* (Griffith, Farran, Okedent, Welsh, London: 1891) 169–170. The Prayer-Book of Queen Elizabeth, 1559. *The Ancient and Modern Library of Theological Literature.* (Griffith, Farran, Okedent, Welsh, London: 1890) 103–104.

Conclusion

The *intelligibility* of God through the words of Scripture and the *wholeness* of persons in their response to God's Word are the distinguishing principles of Vermigli's reform of Christian worship, especially his reform of the Eucharist. Originating in Aquinas' *Word*-centered reform of Lombard's doctrine of God, Vermigli "completes" what Aquinas began for Protestant worship and piety by replacing Lombard's *elemental* conception of the *union* of sacrifice and sacrament with one that is *Word*-centered. This reform was in line with Augustine's emphasis on *verbum Dei* as *singular* and *intelligible* and on Aristotle's distinction between the *form* as both the 'principle' of knowledge and the 'object' of knowledge, but represented a clear challenge to the Neoplatonic-inspired aspects of Lombard's Eucharistic theology and the prevailing Platonic "view of man." The 5th century, Proclan origins of Lombard's Eucharistic formula *res et sacramentum*, the Parmeniedian "problem" that guides the Pseudo-Dionysian form of spirituality of the medieval church, and the *theurgic* aspects of Lombard's Eucharistic rite were highlighted. Vermigli's solution to *union* with Christ in worship is a *Word*-centered joining of sacrifice and sacrament whose form of spirituality—the *obedience of Christ*—is one mediated by Scripture alone and a work of the Trinity alone. While it is difficult to attach Vermigli's hand to any particular liturgical reform, the Supper rite of the 1552 BCP is a good example of his key reform principles at work. In accord with the assessment of Frank A. James, "Vermigli was one of the most remarkable men of his age, "for his religious career spanned the ecclesiastical horizon from prominence as a Roman Catholic theologian to one of the formative theologians of sixteenth century Reformed Protestantism. No other theologian was so distinguished in both camps."[68]

---

[68] PPRED, inside jacket cover.

VALDÉS AND VERMIGLI: SPIRITUALITY AND THE DEGREES OF REFORM

Joseph C. McLelland

Introduction

Juan de Valdés (1498?–1541) and Pietro Martire Vermigli feature prominently in much of the current debate on the nature of "Italian Evangelism".[1] They symbolize a dimension of reform largely neglected in the shadow of the "magisterial" reformation. There was a thrust toward a spirituality and theology of radical revision informed by currents both mystical and practical. Questions of the nature and extent of reform in Spain and Italy, the definition of Evangelism and its relationship to the *spirituali* and the influence of northern Reformers on these southern movements—are legitimate issues that arise from our title. But there are three particular items that occupy our interest: spirituality and mysticism, degrees of reform, and Nicodemism.

---

[1] There is a growing body of literature on Italian Evangelism. Some of the more important writings include: E.-M. Jung, "On the Nature of Evangelism in Sixteenth-Century Italy," *Journal of the History of Ideas* 14 (1953): 511–527; Delio Cantimori, *Eretici italiani del Cinquecento: Ricerche storiche* (Florence: G. C. Sansoni, 1939); Elisabeth G. Gleason, "On the Nature of Italian Evangelism: Scholarship, 1953–1978," *Sixteenth Century Journal* 9 (1978): 3–25; Silvana Seidel Menchi, "Lo stato degli studi sulla Riforma in Italia," *Wolfenbütteler Renaissance Mitteilungen* 5 (1981): 35–42, 89–92 and *Erasmo in Italia,* 1520–1580 (Turin: Bollati Boringhieri, 1987); Anne Jacobson Shutte, "Periodization of Sixteenth-Century Italian Religious History: The Post-Cantimori Paradigm Shift," *Journal of Modern History* 61 (1989): 269–284; John Martin, "Salvation and Society in Sixteenth-Century Venice: Popular Evangelism in a Renaissance City," *Journal of Modern History* 60 (1988): 205–233 and *Venice's hidden Enemies: Italian Heretics in a Renaissance City* (Berkeley: University of California Press, 1993). Salvatore Camponetto, trans. Anne and John Tedeschi, *The Protestant Reformation in Sixteenth Century Italy* (Kirksville: Thomas Jefferson University Press, 1999); Massimo Firpo, *Riforma protestante ed eresie nell'Italia del Cinquecento: Un profilo storico* (Rome-Bari: Laterza, 1993); and Manfred Welti, *Breve storia della Riforma italiana* (Casale Monferrato: Marietti, 1985).

Spirituality and Mysticism

The Spanish reform movement began with mysticism and ended with Inquisition. It provides the context for the Valdésian spirituality crucial for Italian Evangelism. The spectrum from humanism to intolerance is symbolized by Francis Ximénes and Thomas Torquemada—both Grand Inquisitors. The former combined Franciscan spirituality and power politics; he tried to coax Erasmus to join his new university at Alcalá (opened in 1508). Torquemada continued the tragic tradition of Spain, including massacres of Jews in 1491 and their expulsion in 1492. The earlier pogrom involved forced and often hypocritical conversions, producing the *Conversos* (or *Marranos*) of Spanish society. In one sense this represents a Spanish form of "religious deception" which in Italy is known as Nicodemism.

Ironically, it is the Spanish Juan de Valdés who offers perhaps the best example of the origins and development of "Italian Evangelism." This phenomenon is now termed by some scholars more simply and correctly that of "*spirituali*".[2] It describes what Eva-Maria Jung called "the last Catholic reform movement before the Council of Trent and the first ecumenical movement after the schism of the Reformation".[3] Jung regards it as tending towards the undogmatic, aristocratic and transitory. This thesis has been challenged. Cantimori relates the movement to an indifference to theological speculation and ecclesiastical forms. Bouwsma views it more in terms of Renaissance republicanism. McNair argues the influence of northern Reformers.[4] He states emphatically: "The main implication of these scholars [de la Tour, Jedin, Jung, Cantimori] is that Evangelism was an indigenous Catholic phenomenon independent of Lutheranism. This I believe to be demonstrably false." His demonstration proceeds: "Wherever the doctrine of Justification by Faith took root in

---

[2] Dermot Fenlon, *Heresy and Obedience in Tridentine Italy: Cardinal Pole and the Counter Reformation* (Cambridge: Cambridge University Press, 1972), pp. 21–23.

[3] E.-M. Jung, "On the Nature of Evangelism," 512.

[4] See E. G. Gleason, "Italian Evangelism," 3–25; she cites D. Cantimori, 'La riforma in Italia' in *Problemi storici e orientamenti storiografici*, ed. E. Rota (Como, 1942) 6 f.; William Bouwsma, *Venice and the Defense of Republican Liberty* (Berkeley and Los Angeles: University of California, 1968).

pre-Tridentine Italy—whether in Lucca, Modena, Naples, Padua, Venice, or Viterbo—it was preceded by Lutheran, Zwinglian, or Calvinist tracts which the timely invention of printing had disseminated far and wide."[5] He thus redefines Italian Evangelism as: "the positive reaction of certain spiritually minded Catholics to the challenge of Protestantism, and in particular to the crucial doctrine of Justification by Faith."[6] One can gain no better insight into Italian Evangelism than to consider the case of Juan de Valdés himself.

The research of Marcel Bataillon on Valdés' *Diálogo* accepted his ostensive Erasmianism.[7] José Nieto challenged Bataillon's thesis arguing for an indigenous explanation, namely, that the *Diálogo* was an Erasmian mask or "contrived device". He notes the influence of Los Alumbrados, particularly Pedro Ruiz de Alcaraz, a son of *Conversos*, representing "the dexado type of alumbrado spirituality."[8] Alcaraz joined the household of the Marqués de Villena at Escalona, which included a young Juan de Valdés, and was arrested by the Inquisition in 1524 (fingered by the Franciscans who represented the recogido type of spirituality). Nieto discounts Northern influence, a position now challenged, particularly by Carlos Gilly who claims that Valdés appreciated Luther's teaching even in the 1520's. His close analysis of the *Diálogo* shows a debt to Luther and also Oecolampadius.[9] Support for the latter position is afforded by the famous work of Benedetto da Mantova, *Beneficio di Cristo* (1543), which also seems to have been inspired by the Valdésian circle and to embody substantial teaching of Calvin.[10]

---

[5] Cf. Paul Grendler, "The Circulation of Protestant Books in Italy," in *Peter Martyr Vermigli and Italian Reform*, ed. McLelland (Waterloo ON: Wilfrid Laurier University Press, 1980), 5–16.

[6] PMI, 7 f.

[7] M. Bataillon: "Juan de Valdés Nicodemite?" in *Aspects du Libertinisme au XVIe Siecle* (Paris: Vrin, 1974), 93–103.

[8] José. Nieto, ed., *Valdés' Two Catechisms: The Dialogue on Christian Doctrine and the Christian Instruction for Children* (Lawrence, Kansas: Coronado Press, 1981), 5 ff.

[9] José Nieto, *Juan de Valdés & the Origins of the Spanish & Italian Reformation* (Geneva: Droz, 1978); C. Gilly, "Juan de Valdés: Ubersetzer und Bearbeiter von Luthers Schriften in seinem *Diàlogo de Doctrina*" in *Archiv für Reformationsgeschichte* 74 (1983): 257–305.

[10] Tomasso Bozza, *Il Beneficio di Cristo e la Istituzione della religione cristiana di Calvino* (rome 1961); his *Introduzione al'Beneficio di Cristo* (Rome, 1963) and *Il Benificio di Cristo, Nuovi studi sulla Riforma in Italia*, vol. 1 (Rome, 1976). See also McNair, *Peter Martyr in Italy*, 41 ff.; S. Caponetto, *Benedetto da Mantova. Marcantonio Flaminio: Il*

The question of mysticism in relation to such spirituality is a thorny one. The three religions of medieval Spain shared the Neoplatonic heritage of Mediterranean countries. The love imagery of that *arabicus christianus*, Ramon Lull (1232–1316), in his theory of the three degrees of ascent towards the optimum/maximum, expresses the familiar unitive mysticism of the Pseudo-Denis.[11] But the Golden Age of mysticism in the sixteenth century shows the complexity of the subject. It began with Garcia de Cisneros (1455–1510), a Benedictine, and Franciscans such as Bernardino de Laredo and Francisco de Osuna. It has been argued that Muslim mysticism of the Shadhîlî kind of renunciation entered Christian devotion with the *Conversos* and continued its influence even in Teresa of Avila and John of the Cross, *Doctor universalis*.[12] Themes of abandonment and love for God (*dejamiento al amor de Dios*) led to the goal of perfection (*dexamiento*). One observes here the influence of Illuminism, and the sufficiency of the *luz interna* to explain Scripture and to inspire loving behaviour. It was a religion of the heart, its inward piety and passive abandonment free from the outward means of grace.[13] Just what sort of "mysticism" is this?

While Nieto denies mystical influence on Valdés, a more nuanced view of the phenomenon allows a different conclusion. There exists a helpful typology of mysticism, identifying the "numinous feeling" or "mystical consciousness" and distinguishing numinous/mystical (Smart) or extrovertive/introvertive (Stace) or monistic/theistic (Zaehner).[14] The exuberant language of love-mysticism expresses an affective spirituality; Francis above all was consumed with the affective life of the Crucified. The stigmata betoken not a pathological but a unitive state. Ecstasy (as Tillich's "ecstatic reason" illustrates) may mean

Beneficio di Cristo (Torino: Claudiana, 1975); Barry Collett, *Italian Benedictine Scholars and the Reformation: The congregation of Santa Giustina of Padua* (Oxford, Oxford University Press, 1985) and Leon Morris, *The Benefit of Christ, Valdés and Don Benedetto*, trans and intro. (Portland, Oregon, 1984).

[11] See C. H. Lohr, "Metaphysics as the Science of God" in *The Cambridge History of Renaissance Philosophy*, ed. C. Schmitt and Q. Skinner (Cambridge University Press, 1988) 539 ff. His influence carries on at Padua in the early fifteenth century as "a permanent Lullism" (545).

[12] M. A. Palacios, *Saint John of the Cross and Islam*, ET by E. H. Douglas and H. W. Yoder (NY: Vantage, 1981).

[13] L. Dupré and D. E. Saliers, *Christian Spirituality III: Post-Reformation and Modern*, (NY: Crossroads), 72 ff.

[14] Summarized in Rowe & Wainwright, *Philosophy of Religion: Selected Readings* (NY: Harcourt Brace Jovanovich, 1973), 252 ff.

either "standing outside" one's self, or a "heightening" of the self
with its mental and affective powers. For the Alumbrados, mental
prayer—described as "this quietistic prayer of nothingness"[15]—is
affective rather than intellectual, breaking with the Aristotelian-
Thomistic epistemology of mental images or phantasmata. Yet its
reliance on the "beneficial" Christ suggests its affinity with the doctrine of *unio Christi*.

The point at issue is how to classify the Reformation concept of
faith as "union with Christ". This connotation is prominent in the
Reformers. Luther's edition of the *Theologica Germanica* suggests a
dimension to his original formulation of justification often missed by
historians. In that text union means deification (*Vereinigung, Vergottung*).
Luther agrees that only by identification with the new humanity of
Christ is the alien righteousness truly ours.[16] As for that cold fish,
John Calvin, his opening gambit in book three of the *Institutes* on
the mode of receiving grace and its benefits provides a context of
mystical spirituality: "as long as there is a separation between Christ
and us, all that he suffered and performed for the salvation of
mankind is useless and unavailing to us. To communicate to us what
he received from his Father, he must, therefore, become ours, and
dwell within us."[17]

The same is found in Valdés and Vermigli, but the latter attempted
to develop it further with Calvin and Beza. Vermigli suggested that
there are "three degrees of our communion with Christ, . . . the middle, secret and mystical degree [which] is expressed in Holy Scripture
under the metaphor of members and head, and of husband and
wife."[18] Beza and Calvin agreed with Vermigli, but cut him short,

---

[15] *New Catholic Encyclopedia* (Washington DC: The Catholic University of America, 1967) vol. 1, 356.
[16] Martin Luther, *Luther's Works*, trans. J. Pelikan (St Louis: Concordia Publishing House, 1963) vol. 26, 6. In the "Argument" to the 1535 Lectures on Galatians Luther states: "first put on the new man by faith in Christ," that is the "passive righteousness . . . the righteousness of Christ and of the Holy Spirit, which we do not perform but receive, which we do not have but accept, when God the Father grants it to us through Jesus Christ."
[17] John Calvin, *Institutio Christianae Religionis* (Geneva, 1559), III.1.1: "nostrum fieri et in nobis habitare oportet."
[18] LC, Appendix, (letter to Calvin on 8 March 1555), 1094 ff. See VWG, 142 ff.

presumably considering it a true but dangerous doctrine. As for Valdés, we note simply the initial place of the "image and likeness" in both the *110 Considerazioni* (110 Considerations) and the *Diálogo*. By opening with this theme, the unitive nature of justifying faith is made clear, and provides the context for his treatment of Christian perfection. One also finds further evidence of this in his *Alfabeto christiano* where Giulia Gonzaga's guide to perfection tells her to "enamor yourself with Christ".[19]

It was with this idea in mind that Karl Barth remarked: "In emphasizing this more than mystical and more than speculative statement, that faith means unity with the thing believed in, i.e. with Jesus Christ, Calvin did not in the least lag behind a Luther, or either of them behind an Augustine, an Anselm, a Bernard of Clairvaux."[20] His corollary is decisive for our understanding of that central concept of Italian Evangelism: "Without this statement the Reformed doctrine of justification and faith is impossible to understand."[21]

We belabor this point to underline the complexity of the subject. The relation between nominalism and mysticism is one that Oberman has explored in Jean Gerson, distinguishing "penitential" and "transformative" mysticism.[22] One might put the question this way: if Occam was unable to say enough, Eckhart tried to say too much. Is this a polarity similar to Italy's Paduan scepticism and Florentine Platonism?

The *devotio moderna*, typical of reform (as Gabriel Biel understood it) "through an active life of simple piety", stressed interiority without the *unio mystica* of late medieval mysticism.[23] Instead of an ascetic discipline as preparation for negative theology, it offered a spiritual training (*exercitium*) making for progress in virtue (*profectus virtutum*). It was this style of spirituality combined with Spanish humanism and

---

[19] Massimo Firpo, ed. *Alfabeto cristiano* (Torino: Giulio Eionaudi editore, 1994), 30–31.

[20] Karl Barth, *Church Dogmatics*, trans. G. T. Thomson, T. F. Torrance and G. W. Bromiley (Grand Rapids, Michigan: Eerdmans Publishing, 1936) I.1, 275. The context is Barth's definition of faith as "conformity with God," drawing on texts from Luther: *per fidem fit homo similis verbo Dei ... fide homo fit Deus* (274). For Bernard's influence on Calvin, see D. Tamburello, *John Calvin and the Mysticism of St. Bernard* (Louisville, KY: Westminster/John Knox Press, 1994). Tamburello deals briefly with Calvin's correspondence with Martyr (86 f.) but does not develop the matter.

[21] Ibid.

[22] H. Oberman, *The Harvest of Medieval Theology* (Grand Rapids MI: Eerdmans, 1967), 323 ff.

[23] Oberman, *Harvest*, 344 f.

Erasmus's program of biblical studies aiming at moral improvement, that informs the thought of the young Valdés in Spain as well as his circle in Naples. It reinforced the program of reformation without schism, and qualified the sort of mystical influence of Alcaraz.[24]

Thus Juan de Valdés represents a type of Spanish evangelicalism which emphasized biblical authority, personal piety, and informality in church ordinances. In his *Diálogo de Doctrina Cristiana* (1529) the prayer for daily bread includes a petition "that God send us true and holy doctors that may distribute among the Christian people the bread of evangelical doctrine, clean and clear and not soiled and dirty with human opinions and affects."[25] His few later works, reflecting the Valdésian Sunday discussions and gathered in the *110 Consideraziones*,[26] reveal the ideal of contemplation, moving from Erasmianism to otherworldly spirituality.

The dichotomy attending this otherworldly spirituality is striking. The means of grace are diminished along with means of nature. Bodily health, for instance, belongs to the divine will in an "all or nothing" theology reminiscent of Camus's Father Paneloux.[27] Valdés says that the sons of God differ from the sons of Adam in that they "equally renounce the utility of medicine ... accepting God alone as their physician."[28] The Holy Spirit has direct access so that personal experience assures salvation, not ecclesiastical ordinances. Whether his stress on the Spirit came close to anti-trinitarianism remains doubtful[29]—we are "incapable of comprehending the divine generation of the Son of God, and the spiritual generation of the children of God."[30] What is clear, as Benedetto Croce put it, is that his doctrine of faith "implied a negation of the papal church, of its

---

[24] J. Van Engen, *Devotio Moderna: Basic Writings*, trans. and Intro. (NY: Paulist, 1988), 25 ff.

[25] A. M. Mergal, "Evangelical Catholicism as Represented by Juan de Valdes", *Spiritual and Anabaptist Writers*, Library of Christian Classics XXV (Louisville, KY: John Knox, 1967), 321.

[26] Luis de Usoz i Rio, ed., *Ziento I diez consideraziones de Juan de Valdés* (Madrid, 1863); ET by John T. Betts in *Life and Writings of Juian de Valdés, Otherwise Valdesso, Spanish Reformers in the Sixteenth Century*, by Benjamin B. Wiffen (London, 1865).

[27] In *The Plague*, Paneloux dies—without benefit of physician—while preparing a pamphlet entitled "Is a Priest Justified in Consulting a Doctor?"

[28] Ibid., *Cons.* III.

[29] Contra the contention of Massimo Firpo, "The Italian Reformation and Juan de Valdés," *Sixteenth Century Journal*, 27 (1996), 353–364.

[30] Luis de Usoz i Rio, ed., *Ziento I diez consideraziones*, *Cons.* XCV.

juridical decisions in things pertaining to moral conscience, of its sacramental system, of indulgences, and of everything else."[31]

Degrees of Reform

Such "evangelism" lays the groundwork for a counter-reformation. It is still part of a reform movement, but remains unacceptable to the northern Reformers. Delio Cantimori is helpful here when he declares that Italian evangelism is heretical but not schismatic.[32] In the terms of *reformatio in capite et in membris* it agrees with the ecclesiastical Orders, particularly the Franciscan, that the key to reform lies in personal renewal. Philip McNair distinguishes "six degrees of reformation in Western Europe" exemplified by Ximénes, Erasmus, Zwingli, Luther, Calvin and Lelio Sozzini.[33] Our analysis thus far suggests that the first two degrees account for the phenomenon of "Evangelism" in Spain and Italy, until the Inquisition expelled those of more advanced reform convictions in 1531 and 1542 respectively. But in fact the situation in both Spain and Italy appears too fluid and compromised by the Inquisition to establish its "degree" of Reform. One might say that Valdés advanced from "Catholic reform" to Nicodemism, while Vermigli and other Valdésians went further, crossing the ecclesiastical Rubicon into northern Protestantism.[34]

In Naples a quasi-ecclesiastical congregation formed around Juan de Valdés, from his arrival in 1535 to his death in 1541. Pietro Carnessechi, Papal Protonotary, called these gatherings a "*regno di Dio*" (kingdom of God)[35] while Celio Secondo Curione termed Valdés "Doctor and Pastor of noble and illustrious persons."[36] The group included Bernardino Ochino, General of the Capuchins and the most famous preacher in Italy, Peter Martyr Vermigli, abbot of the influential

---

[31] Cited by Mergal, "Evangelical Catholicism," 318, 339.

[32] D. Cantimori, *Prospettive di Storia ereticale italiana del Cinquecento* (Bari: Laferza, 1960).

[33] PMI, 2 ff.

[34] Cf. J. C. McLelland, "McLelland on Six Degrees of Reform," *Peter Martyr Newsletter* 10 (Reformed Theological Seminary, Oviedo FL, October 1999), 4, suggests that in view of the significance of the *Schola Tigurina*, a new category should be interposed between Calvin and Sozzini, namely "Bullinger-Martyr."

[35] Nieto, *Juan de Valdés*, 148.

[36] Capponetto, *Protestant Reformation*, 64.

monastery of S. Pietro ad Aram from 1537–40, and the Countess of Fondi, Giulia da Gonzaga.[37]

During Vermigli's Neapolitan triennium and membership in the Valdésian circle, a mutual influence between the two is clear. Frank James has argued the "probability that Valdés introduced Vermigli to a Lutheran doctrine of justification", and has documented the approximation of Valdés' doctrine of predestination to that of Vermigli, and of both to Gregory of Rimini.[38] Valdés took up the study of Paul's Romans in the privacy of this small group, followed by First Corinthians, while at the same time Vermigli preached publicly from the prestigious pulpit of S. Pietro ad Aram. His audience was large and included the elite of church and state. One was Galeazzo Caracciolo, later to leave home and family for the sake of reform, becoming chief founder of the Italian Church in Calvin's Geneva. A more sinister hearer was Gaetano da Thiene (1480–1547), cofounder with Gian Pietro Caraffa of the Order of Theatines.[39] Dedicated as they were to a reform of morals through a renewed clergy, they disliked Vermigli's exegesis and were suspicious of his orthodoxy. The result was a suspension of his preaching office by Rome, to be loosened only with further intervention, particularly from Reginald Pole.

Martyr's mature position reflects much of his earlier Valdésian spirituality. Caught between the polemics of sacramental means as either absolutely necessary or else indifferent, he attempted a compromise that often suited neither side. Bucer suspected him of being soft on Zwinglianism, Bullinger on Calvinism. But his voluminous writings on the sacraments profile the man, for they reflect the spirit of Plato, the categories of Aristotle, the piety of Valdés, and the biblical narrative he expounded so well. Such was the dense web of his discourse about God's visible words.

---

[37] PMI, 39–40. Valdés' *Alfabeto cristiano* is his dialogue with this "Nuova Helena" following a sermon by Ochino.

[38] PPRED, 151–187; "Juan de Valdés before and after Peter Martyr Vermigli: The Reception of *Gemina Praedestinatio* in Valdés' later thought," *Archiv für Reformationsgeschichte* 83 (1992), 180–208 and "*De Iustificatione*: the Evolution of Peter Martyr Vermigli's Doctrine of Justification," (Ph.D. diss., Westminster Theological Seminary, Philadelphia, Pennsylvania, 2000), 93–139.

[39] See J. C. Olin, *The Catholic Reformation: Savonarola to Ignatius Loyola* (NY: Harper & Row, 1969), 128 ff.

The Valdésian circle scattered after the master's death. Some gathered in that other remarkable circle at Viterbo, headed by Reginald Pole.[40] The *chiesa viterbinense* included Marcantonio Flaminio and Vittoria Colonna (recovering from the flight of her hero, Ochino, from Italy and from Orthodoxy);[41] they read pseudonymous works of the northern Reformers. The Inquisition established in 1542 took careful note, summoning Ochino and Vermigli, both of whom chose exile northward. In due time "Valdésianism" was declared a distinct heresy; Carnesecchi was questioned about *Valdesii de justificatione et certitudine gratiae* and at last, he was executed in 1567.[42] Gaetano, meanwhile, went on to canonization. In the list of his credits as Saint Cajetan in 1671 was his uncovering of "the heresy of Juan de Valdés and Bernardino Ochino."[43]

Here are the chief elements in the sort of moderate reform typified by Erasmus. The fact that the Inquisition was unable to distinguish it from advanced degrees of Reformation should not blind us to the complexity of the phenomenon. The question is whether at Naples Valdés went beyond "Catholic Reform" to become a Protestant Nicodemite.[44] Philip McNair thinks so, taking issue as we have seen, with those historians who restrict the term Evangelism to denote "an indigenous Catholic phenomenon independent of Lutheranism". He claims that this has proved "a useful device for explaining away an embarrassing phase of Catholic history when what looks suspiciously like crypto-Lutheranism invaded the very College of Cardinals."[45] Thus between 1517 (Luther's year of grace) and 1547 (The Council of Trent's *Decretum de iustificatione*) there was room for harder as well as softer kinds of Reform, and in this mix Northern ideas circulated as catalyst.

---

[40] Camponetto, *The Protestant Reformation in Italy*, 96–100.
[41] Cf. E. Campi, *Michelangelo e Vittoria Colonna: un dialogo artistico-teologico ispirato da Bernardino Ochino* (Torino: Claudiana Editrice, 1994).
[42] Camponetto, *The Protestant Reformation in Italy*, 311–312.
[43] PMI, 160.
[44] M. Bataillon, *Introduction au Diálogo de Doctrina Cristiana de Juan de Valdés* (Paris: Vrin, 1974).
[45] PMI, 5 ff.

Nicodemism

"When the blow fell in 1542 the reformers of the earlier period were divided into three groups. Some went to the stake, some went into exile, both men and women, and others lapsed into silence and made cloisters of their own hearts."[46] The Inquisition forced the hands (or feet) of Ochino and Vermigli in 1542; they chose exile rather than persist in Nicodemism. Soon after leaving Naples Martyr concludes that reformation must be not only *in membris* but also *in capite*. His writings on "flight in persecution" show a rejection of Nicodemism and acceptance of the break with Rome as necessary.

Once settled in Strasbourg, Vermigli wrote to his former congregation in Lucca, describing his journey through Basel and Zurich (Ochino had proceeded to Geneva), until Bucer offered him a position. In justifying his flight to his congregation at Lucca, he explained:

> Here is the whole hinge on which the whole controversy turns so that we can understand when the need was pressing. . . . Besides, you are hardly unaware of the tortures which tormented my conscience because of the way of life which I was following. I had to live with countless superstitions every day; not only did I have to perform superstitious rites, but also I had to demand harshly that others do many things which were contrary to what I was thinking and teaching.[47]

In his letter *De Fuga in Persecutione*, he regards fear of death as not sinful in itself, if it aims at God's glory. There is for Vermigli a role for "prudence", and "degrees of fortitude." But featuring Matthew 10:23 as his text, he makes it clear that he regards dissimulation as deceit. In particular, "the Nicodemites should not compare the ceremonies of the old law with human inventions" in apology for their continuance in the Church of Rome visible. The Mass above all is a case of "unlawful rites . . . ceremonies lacking the Word of God", "a public profession of popery". Therefore all participation in the Mass is idolatry, so that not only priests but the laity also are obliged to choose exile.[48]

---

[46] R. Bainton, *Women of the Reformation in Germany and Italy* (Minn., MI: Augsburg, 1971), 167. See C. Ginzburg, *Il nicodemismo—Simulazione e dissimulazione religiosa nell' Europa dell'500* (Turin, 1970).

[47] LC, Appendix, 1072. English translation is found in LLS, 100.

[48] LC, Appendix, 1073–1085. English translation is found in LLS, 67–95.

Such a strongly structural view of the church interprets Nicodemism, as does Calvin in the heat of their struggle, as the mere dissimulation of "Pseudonicodemites." That is to say, it is a failure of nerve or a stance of cowardice. But there are other options. One is the sort of "deceit" recommended by Machievelli's *Discorsi* or that practised by the *prudente* of Carli Piccolomini's Trattati Nove Della Prudenza, springing from an ethic for which religion is not so much source as external means.[49] Thus a humanistic philosophy of prudential living remains one viable option for Renaissance thinkers.

Yet again, may not the choice of nicodemism stem more from a spirituality that remains indifferent to external forms? In that case the difference between Mass and Lord's Supper would become nothing worth moving for. Movement, the notorious Aristotelian κατα δύναμιν so bothersome to philosophers of action (Marx) and selfhood (Kierkegaard), is essentially an inward category; outward mobility is not causally connected with it. Thus to stay and believe differently than ecclesiastical authority dictates is a matter not of conscience but of indifference. Modern research on Nicodemism, associated especially with the names of Ginzburg, Cantimori and Rotondo, reflects its complexity, and underlines the need to examine further the role of "nicodemite" as both hesychast and adiaphorist. This will involve also reflection on Stoic elements in the Fathers, especially the indifferentism attendant on their low view of emotion, and the part this tradition played in Renaissance and Reformation.

Thus a rough schema of the phenomenon might include the following three categories:

Reject the structures, with the supporting dogma, and seek an alternative. Therefore leave, to find inward peace through outward reformation.

Reject structures and dogma, but consider both indifferent to true religion of the heart. Therefore remain, finding inward peace regardless of outward conformity.

---

[49] R. Belladonna, "Aristotle, Machiavelli, and Religious Dissimulation: Bartolomeo Carli Piccolomini's *Trattati Nove Della Prudenza*" in McLelland, ed. *Peter Martyr and Italian Reform* (Waterloo: WLU 1980), 33 ff. She shows that Carli's *Trattate nove della prudenza* (in MS) reflects the Valdesian sort of mystical consciousness, while his *Regola* (1542) is an imitation of the *Alfabeto* of Valdés.

Reject structure and dogma but through fear of persecution and lack of absolute inwardness, remain in outward conformity and inward distress.

Thus, Ochino and Vermigli belong to the first category, Valdés and Contarini to the second, and the Pseudonicodemites to the third. So the decisive criterion is not courage, but indifferentism. The later Adiaphora controversy, like the Iconoclast controversy in the East, sought to separate the substantial from the accidental or the essential from the occasional. But indifferentism raises ontological questions about the very significance of bodily forms in relation to divine and human spirit.

Conclusion

In Peter Martyr's relationship to the Valdésians of his youth and the Anti-trinitarians of his maturity, we see the influence of "Italian Evangelism." Questions remain however, about the nature of its spirituality, what sort of mystical experience and theology this involves, and the sort of "deception" it may entail. Time and again it falls back on Spain—Erasmianism in Spain, mysticism in Spain, Valdés in Spain, and many others from that soil were fruitful for things of the spirit. Let the last word be this summary of Philip McNair:

> Whilst Spanish Popes desecrated the Chair of St Peter, it was a Spanish Cardinal who began the work of reformation in Europe at a time when Luther's name was still unknown. It was in Spain that the sensitive plant of mysticism was nurtured which was to blossom in the salons of Naples. It is to Spain that the roots of the Socinian hemlock may be traced. It was from Spain that Italy received her three major prophets, for it was Spain which exported that penetrating triumvirate of good and evil: Michael Servetus, Ignatius Loyola, and Juan de Valdés.[50]

---

[50] PMI, 16.

THE *PRECES SACRAE* OF PETER MARTYR VERMIGLI

Emidio Campi

Introduction

Among the works of Peter Martyr Vermigli one of the most fascinating is without doubt the collection of prayers published posthumously in 1564 by his faithful disciple from Zürich, Josias Simler (1530–1576) with the title *Preces sacrae.*[1] Proof of the vitality of this prose paraphrase of the book of psalms is the fact that there were a further ten editions before 1620, four in Latin,[2] two in English,[3] two in French,[4] one in German[5] and one in Czech.[6] The *Preces* are a historical document of a certain importance for the history of Protestantism in the protomodern age. As will be seen later, their composition goes back to the time of the war of Charles V against the Lutheran princes united in the League of Schmalkald. They were then translated into French during the bloody wars of religion between

---

[1] Preces sacrae ex Palmis Davidis desumptae per D. Petrum Martyrem Vermilium Florentinum, sacrarum literarum in scholar Tigurina professorem, Tiguri, Excudebat Christophorus Froschouerus, anno D.D.LXIIII (da ora in poi Preces, seguito dal numero della pagina).

[2] Due ristampe del 1566 e 1578, presso Froschauer, nonché una ristampa in: Petri Martyris Vermilii, Locorum communium theologicorum, ex ipsius diversis opusculis collectorum, Tomus Tertius, in quo reliqua omnia eius opuscula, tam edita quam antea non edita continetur. Cum indice copiosissimo, Basileae, ad Perneam Lecythum. M.D.XXCII. Ad esse si aggiunge l'edizione riveduta del 1604: Preces sacrae ex Psalmis Davidis primum per Petrum Martyrem collectae. Nunc vero ex autographis correctae, e sylvas. Homiliarum selectiss. Et nunquam ante editarum Rodolphi Gualtheri p.m. De vera precum ratione et usu Locupletae, Tiguri, apud Iohannem Wolphium. M.D.CIV.

[3] *Christian Prayers and Holy Meditations as Well for Private as Public Exercise* (London, Middleton, 1568, reprint, Cambridge 1842) (this is a partial edition which includes the first five prayers only); *Most Godly prayers compiled out of David's Psalms* (London, William Seres, 1569).

[4] *Sainctes Prieres recueillies des Pseaumes de David* (Geneve, Jean Durant 1577); *Saintes priers recueillies des Pseaumes* (La Rochelle, Pierre Haultin 1581).

[5] Heilige und trostliche Gebatt uß den Psalmen Davids gezogen durch den Gottsaligen und hochgelehrten Doct. Petrum Martyrem der heiligen Geschrifft Professorn zü Zürych in der Froschow. M.D.LXXXIX.

[6] *Modlitby Swaté z žalmůw Dawida Proroka Božjho od Oswjceného Muže . . .* (Prag, 1620).

Catholics and Huguenots in France. The Czech translation came
out in the same year as the battle of the White Mountain, which
had such devastating effects both on Bohemia as a nation and on
the *Unitas Fratrum*, that is, the reformed church to which Comenius
belonged. But the *Preces* are also a precious instrument to obtain
some insight into the spiritual world of Peter Martyr Vermigli, revealing besides the more well-known face of the exegete and theologian
the less familiar one of the believer.

Dating

It is thanks to Josias Simler that the text of the *Preces sacrae* was not
entirely forgotten, and his decision to publish them is proof of the
exceptional esteem in which the Zürich theologian held Vermigli. In
the preface he describes the reasons for his decision:

> Last year, while I was examining the writings of our teacher, the pious
> and learned Peter Martyr, and was gathering together in his library
> some papers with notes in his handwriting, I came across some that
> were out of place and ruined. In them were sacred prayers written in
> his own hand. After examining them carefully, I considered them wor-
> thy of publishing, even though I knew they had not been written for
> this purpose. I was led to do this for several reasons. The first is that
> Martyr recited these prayers in public, at the end of the lessons at the
> academy of Strasbourg, when the council of Trent had started and in
> Germany a serious civil war of religion had broken out, (*Nam primum
> quia illo tempore, quo et concilium Tridenti inchoatum fuit et religionis causa grave
> et intestinum belllum in Germania exortum est, Martyr has preces finitis lection-
> ibus in schola Argentinensi publice habuit*). It is right to publish them now
> that the council of Trent has finished, now that there is a great need
> to call on God with ardent prayers that there may not arise a simi-
> lar conflagration. Secondly, the prayers in this booklet are clear and
> wander very little from the words of psalms something I judge to be
> of great importance in prayers. In fact these prayers in part expound
> in a concise and clear way the theme of many psalms, and in part
> explain many obscure and difficult passages through a lucid para-
> phrase . . .[7]

Although at first sight the pure simplicity of these statements would
suggest an easy dating of the *Preces*, the question is instead more

---

[7] Preces, 2v.

complex. Even though the date of their printing is certain,[8] that of their composition is a lot less clear. Do they go back to Vermigli's first stay in Strasbourg (Oct. 1542–Oct. 1547),[9] according to Simler's notation, repeated by Charles Schmidt[10] and recently confirmed by John Patrick Donnelly?[11] Or were they written during his second stay in Strasbourg (Oct. 1553–July 1556), as Marvin W. Anderson has argued?[12] Klaus Sturm's indecision[13] does not help resolve the doubt. Curiosity about the dating has also grown because scholars have so far limited their observations to the presence in these prayers of a widespread sense of crisis, a complex of psychological circumstances that can be linked to some well-known coeval events, instead of closely examining the contents.

Certainly the task is not easy, because the order in which the prayers were put together by Simler is not chronological but follows the numbering of the psalms. Moreover, precisely because of the characteristics of the literary genre to which they belong, the *Preces* do not lend themselves to an easy identification of concrete facts; on the contrary, they contain many allusions and examples of polysemies, which though on the one hand conserve all the flavour of the period, on the other they represent a serious obstacle to the interpretation. And yet, behind the figurative language, one can clearly understand the existence of an entanglement of ecclesiastical and political problems, and something of this comes out between the lines.

The starting point for our analysis is Simler's explicit reference to the initial phase of the Council of Trent. But it has to be said straight away that the statement has no precise correspondence in the text.

---

[8] Simler's preface is dated: "*12 Calendas Iuli anno salutis 1564*".

[9] On Vermigli's activity during his first stay at Strasbourg, cf. Klaus Sturm, *Die Theologie Peter Martyr Vermiglis während seines ersten Aufenthalts in Strassburg, 1542–1547* (Neukirchen-Vluyn, 1971) e, da ultimo, PPRED, 42–49.

[10] Charles Schmidt, *Peter Martyr Vermigli: Leben und ausgewählte Schriften* (Elberfeld, 1858), 71–73.

[11] John Patrick Donnelly (ed.), *Peter Martyr Vermigli, Sacred Prayers Drawn from the Psalms of David*, Sixteenth Century Essays & Studies, vol. 34 (Kirksville, Missouri 1996), XVI–XVII (The Peter Martyr Library 3).

[12] PMRE, 285, 300.

[13] Sturm (see note 9), 35, 275.

The most significant allusion is the paraphrase of psalm 58b,[14] the
only prayer in which can be found the word *concilium*. There is a
sudden and violent outburst against those who, with the support of
the council, plot deception and snares against the true church. At
first glance, this brief text could be connected to the first phase of
the historical assizes (1545–1547), thus supporting Simler's testimony.
In reality, there is nothing exceptional or characteristic allows us to
attribute it with certainty to that precise period. It is instead a vague
stereotype formula that does not give an exact account of the problems and the contrasting positions. It is also frequent in Protestant
writings during all the various phases of the council work, inviting
us to exercise some cautious reserve. There is on the other hand
another text which seems a little more interesting, even though there
are no explicit references to the Trent meetings—the highly allusive
prayer that was inspired by psalm 4.[15] Here the author of the prayer
confesses his distress that the "powerful in this world" have come
together to make vain the gospel, but at the same time he inter-
cedes that they might recognise the "nature of the true church,"
thus reinforcing the initial assertion and conferring to the whole
prayer an open resolution. It is clear that the reasoning gains weight
if placed in correlation with the initial phase of the council. We
could even ask ourselves if the paraphrase is not to be considered
as an answer to the bull *Laetare Jerusalem* of 19 November 1544 which
established the objectives of the Trent assizes. Unfortunately these
are only fleeting impressions, plausible but not certain hypotheses.
Notwithstanding Simler, it has to be said that the *Preces* are practically silent on the subject of the council, and there is very little ver-
bal and thematic consonance with the assembly of Trent.

But there is much more to be gleaned from this collection of

---

[14] Preces, 64v. (Psal. 58b): "*Antichristus et omia eius membra, Deus Opt. Max. iam nihil
aliud voluunt animo contra Ecclesiam tuam, quam iniquitates et iniustissiam cogitate, cumque
speciem sibi faciant et haberi velint Concilium pietatis atque religionis, re tamen ipsa nil moli-
untur nisi mendacia . . .*".

[15] Ibid., 7r–v (Psal. 4): "*Hoc in praesentia coram te deploramus, potentiores huius mundi
summis uniti conatibus, ut gloriam Euangelii et religionis tuae in dedecus, imo in nihilum redi-
gant, ob inania studia et spes fallaces, quas sibi proposuerunt. Utinam, Deus, illis paterfaceres
ac demonstrares formam verae Ecclesiae, quam tibi delegisti quamque audis, cum fideliter suis
precibus et clamoribus te invocat. Forte sentirent, magis commoverentur sibique caverent, ne in illam
peccarent . . .*".

apparently uniform prayers if our attention moves from Trent to Strasbourg. Here and there in the *Preces* there are numerous allusions that could refer to the sharp tension between the preachers in Strasbourg and the city authorities on the question of church discipline. It is strange that until now no one has paid attention to this reality as the traces are more frequent than those regarding the council. To understand this well it is not sufficient to read the text, which is obviously reticent about revealing the internal contrasts that tear the city of Strasbourg; it is necessary to refer to other historical sources. Especially from the studies by Bellardi, Brady, Hammann and Greschat[16] on this subject, we know that as from 1544 Bucer and his closest collaborators defend the right to create communities of professing believers within the multi-faceted church to correct its most evident defects in doctrine and ethical behaviour: they will become the "Christliche Gemeinschaften." And we know how the city council, helped by the division among the pastors and jealous of its controlling power over the church, opposed Bucer's project and prevented with every means possible its realisation.

The *Preces*, even with their purely allusive phraseology, enable us to catch glimpses of that exhausting battle between a group of preachers (the author of these prayers takes their side) and the city council. In this way the paraphrase of psalm 2, instead of being an abstract reflection on power in general, expresses through the use of key words, a pungent criticism of the city authorities: *Hoc tempore sentimus, Deus Opt. Max, non solum antichristum, sed omnem vim et potentiam mundi adversum te conspirasse et Christum tuum: ut qui putent evangelium et ecclesiae instaurationem esse vincula intollerabilia et iugum durissimum, idcirco annituntur omnibus rationibus, ut fidelium societates disrumpant et omnem abijciant disciplinam.*[17] On the other hand there is an insistent appeal to the peace of God to protect the church from the evil of discord.[18]

---

[16] Werner Bellardi, *Die Geschichte der 'Christlichen Gemeinschaft' in Strasbourg (1546–1550): Der Versuch einer zweiten Reformation* (Leipzig, 1934), 10–22; Thomas A. Brady, Jr., *Ruling Class, Regime and Reformation at Strasbourg (1520–1550)* (Leiden, 1978), 250; Gottfried Hammann, *Entre la secte et la cite. Le project d'Eglise du Reformateur Martin Bucer (1491–1551)* (Geneva, 1984), 79–80, 363–367, 431–433; Martin Greschat, *Martin Bucer. Ein Reformator und seine Zeit (1491–1551)* (Munich, 1990), 218–226, 272, n. 13.

[17] Preces, 4v (Psal. 2).

[18] Ibid., 162r (Psal. 133): "*[Ecclesia] vehementer frangitur atque debilitatur, si, qui in ea instar fratrum debuissent cohabitare, dissidiis exulcerent aut contentionibus a seipsis divellantur.*

Elsewhere, like a kind of motto, there is the wish that the Strasbourg church live a "second reformation" (Bellardi), and this theme is found several times in the coeval texts of Bucer.[19] The tendency emerges with all the necesssary clarity in the paraphrase of psalm 103,17–18. It reveals a personality endowed not only with remarkable exegetical acumen, but with an exquisite ability to suggest a contemporary application, in which a whole theology is manifested: *Foedus tuum inter nos et te renovari experiamur, et eo restituto, summu studio contendamus vitae sanctitate mandata et legem tuam exprimere.*[20] This request is echoed by an intercession that is incompatible with the centralizing mentality of the Strasbourg magistrates, but which is in perfect harmony with Bucer's ecclesiastical program of reform for doctrine and life: *Excitet* (sc. Jesus) *sibi spontaneos atque ultroneos cooperatores ad tam praeclarum, eximium atque utilissimum opus, qui zelo dignitatis et existimationis eius accensi veritatem doctrinae confirment, mores instaurent et integritatem vitae in populo fideli restituant.*[21] It is sufficient to translate into German the expression *ultroneos cooperatores* to recognise in it the so-called "Kirchenpfleger," that is, those lay members of the church called to collaborate with the pastors in leadership.

The *Preces*, therefore, re-echo the troubles in the Strasbourg church around the mid-forties. They are part of a wider picture of crisis amongst a leadership torn between two contrasting aspirations: the creation of a church composed of professing believers as well as the preservation of the medieval idea of the *corpus christianum*. Through the *Preces* we get the idea that as the situation worsens Vermigli is not inactive. At least in the public prayers, those themes that were so precious to Bucer reappear on his lips with clear approval; and although he himself is enthusiastic about Bucer's cause, he works to settle the discord. As well as confirming the reasons for Bucer's extraordinary esteem of the Florentine theologian, this also provides a certain reference point for establishing the date of the composition of the *Preces*.

Optamus itaque, tuo Beneficio ea nobis detur pax, ut instar membrorum in eodem corpore tuo, quod est Ecclesia, coalescamus"; cf. ance 89r (Psal. 82 b); 147v (122); 162v (Psal. 132b); 163v (Psal. 133c); 178r (Psal. 147).

[19] Cfr. DS 17, 235, 28: "eine ware Christliche reformation": 228, 27–28 ". . . zü Christlicher reformation nottwendiglich."

[20] Preces, 112v (Psal. 103b).

[21] Ibid., 124r–v (Psal. 110b).

But without doubt it is just as certain that there is a thematic link between this work of Vermigli and the war of Schmalkald (1546–1547). Simler's indication seems so convincing that successive writings have taken it up without carrying out any textual verification, limiting themselves more to considerations of a psychological type. In fact, many prayers regularly reflect the Italian's intense participation in the state of mind of his Strasbourg colleagues regarding the military expedition of Charles V. Allusions, for the most part; but allusions that create atmosphere, point to exceptionally grave circumstances, and stimulate interesting comparisons. For example, it is not at all illogical to feel the influence of those war events, which affect the destinies themselves of Strasbourg and the church, in this prayer: . . . *O Deus, te obsecramus per viscera infinitae misericordiae tuae, ut respicere digneris gravia discrimina, in quae deducta est anima nostra; da veniam, precamur, nostris peccatis ac nostrum cor facile ac proclive reddas ad faciendum mandata tua et a laqueis nos eripias, quos inimici sancti nominis tui tetenderunt nobis; et quos in sempiternam haereditatem tuam tibi vendicasti, ne opprimi et calamitose perire sinas. . . .*[22] But is that all that can be gleaned in the *Preces*? If it is unfortunately not possible to trace in them with absolute clarity the various phases of the conflict, we can, however, legitimately suspect the existence of some important moments through some residuous traces. It seems therefore likely that we can consider the paraphrase of psalm 118 as an extreme echo of the change of front by the ambitious Maurice of Saxony, whose crossing over to the Catholic camp from the Lutheran one in June 1546 was decisive for the defeat of the Schmalkaldians.[23] Nor do we believe we delude ourselves if we say that the composition on psalm 122,[24] with

---

[22] Ibid., 140r (Psal. 119). Cfr. Ibid., 148r (Psal. 123): "*Nulla populo tuo manent, omnipotens Deus, amplius auxilia nisi de coelo: nam adeo inualuerunt Antichristi vires et infesta eius consilia, ut parum absit, quin vera pietas et tuus legitimus cultus extinguatur et funditus deleatur . . . Miserere nostril, o Deus, hoc tempore, Miserere nostril, ut quem non lateat, quantis opprobiriis et contumeliis passim afficiatur Ecclesia tua. Non progrediatur longius fastus et contemptus impiorum . . .*"; ibid., 151r (Psal. 124c): "*Violentia et impetus eorum, a quibus oppugnamur, est ceu incitatissimae aquae dum repente campos inundant, illorum crudelitas feritatem belluarum adaequat . . . Quare prout debemus, quod e tantis periculis gregem tuum et simplicem et imbecillem hactenus liberaveris, gratias agimus . . .*".

[23] Ibid., 133r (Psal. 118b): "*Tam gravibus calamitatum procellis, omnipotens Deus, assidue pulsamur, ut solum misericordiae tuae acceptum referendum sit, quod sub eis non prosternamur . . . Quare cum videamus fallacy spe lactari, qui conficunt hominibus, hanc iudicamus esse piorum hominum summam sapientiam, ut nulli mortalium posthac fidant, sed in te uno spem suam collocent.*"

[24] Ibid., 147r (Psal. 122): "*. . . nam prout est (sc. Antichristus) perditus et profligates, nihil*

the explicite reference to the fall of Jerusalem, seems to be inspired
by the circumstance of the submission of Strasbourg to Charles V
in March 1547. And finally there is no way we can mistake the
prayer on psalm 80,[25] perhaps the best in the whole collection, for
a general passage of edification. A sense of deep distress characterises
the composition, and the anaphora *quousque* increases the gravity in
a more intense and widespread way than in the other prayers. One
image dominates the oration: the *delicata et electa vinea Domini* set on
fire and mutilated by the tyranny of the Antichrist. And the strong
invocation *Exurgas ipse et venias nos servandos* irresistably directs our
thoughts to the final decisive phase of the war of Schmalkald if not
more precisely to the battle of Mühlberg, 24 April 1547, when the
Protestant allies were overwhelmed by the imperial troops.

In this way we have ascertained only the existence of a certain number of prayers whose composition goes back probably to
1544–1547, that is, to the time of Vermigli's first stay in Strasbourg,
confirming on the basis of some internal clues the contemporary testimony of Simler. We have not yet determined if it is valid for the
whole collection. We will try to give an answer to this question
through an analysis of the formal characteristics of the *Preces*.

Formal characteristics

The *Preces* are composed of 296 prose paraphrases of 149 psalms[26]
to which Simler has added as an appendix a eucharistic prayer attributed to Vermigli,[27] but which has nothing in common with the rest
of the collection, or better, which seems to be an isolated fragment
whose origin is unknown even to the compiler. The prayer relative
to psalm 87 is missing, and if it was written, as it probably was, it

---

molitur alius, nisi ut sancta Hierusalem, quae utcumque et reaedificari et instaurari coepta est,
denuo collabatur, imo funditus cadat, quo puro cultui et sanctae invocationi amplius non pateat
locus. Te optime pater, qui probe vides, quantum iste impius misceat et turbet, rogamus ardenti
animo atque vehementi affectione, ut, quae ad Hierusalem, id est Ecclesiae tuae sanctae pacem
faciunt, procurare veis . . .". See also the four paraphrases of psalm 78, which are thoroughly homogeneous, where the reference is about the Egyptian captivity.

[25] Ibid., 87r (Psal. 80).

[26] I cannot see how Donnelly, *Sacred Prayers* (see note 11), p. XVII, establishes
the number of 297. To me, the internal division which he proposed is not clear.

[27] Precatio D. Petri Martyris contra artolatreian & omnem superstitionem, s.p.

has gotten lost. Only 39 psalms have a single prayer, more often there are various prayers on the same psalm. Seventy-eight psalms have two, while 27 possess three; for psalms 68 and 78 we have four prayers, on psalm 18 there remain five, on psalm 105 six. Psalm 119 constitutes a special case, in that it is subdivided into nineteen parts, each of which is constructed as a separate prayer and over each one there are two letters of the Hebrew alphabet.

In the Latin edition from 1564 the normal length of each single prayer is one page, regardless of the number of verses in the psalm. For example, the paraphrase of psalm 15 roughly corresponds in size to that of psalm 34, whose text is four times longer. We do not notice any particular imbalance in the exposition of the various types of psalms: the two prayers relative to the famous penitential psalm 51 have the same dimensions as those of the kingly psalm 2. The reader immediately gets the impression that every prayer was carefully studied to attract and hold the attention of the audience. The tone is always elevated and at times reaches heights of lyrical emotion;[28] the phraseology is sober although it is not without metaphors,[29] for the most part borrowed from Biblical language; the lexicon is elegant but at the same time simple and clear. There are no evident contrasts in style or content between one composition and another. This confers to the collection a formal order that not only corresponds well to the author's disciplined work method, already pointed out with admiration by his contemporaries, but also to the didactical and pastoral use of the *Preces*, aimed at training the students in that *sapiens atque eloquens pietas*[30] tenaciously pursued by the academy of Strasbourg from its foundation in 1538.

Where there are various prayers on the same psalm, each time the explanation is taken up again from the beginning and the paraphrase is always at a literal level. There are absolutely no shades of meaning based on anagogy and allegory, although a christological

---

[28] Cfr. Preces, 111v (Psal. 102b): "*Prospicias, oramus, e sublime habitaculo tuo, et intuere calamitates nostras, gemitumque audias eorum, qui vinciuntur, caeduntur et excrunciantur mirabilibus modis propter nomen tuum, salvesque oves tuas ex tantis periculis, quae non solum morti, verum execrationi extremae devotae sun tab Antichristo, ut quandoque filii tui coram te valeant quiete et tranquille agree . . .*"

[29] Ibid., 37r–38r (Psal. 36); 100r (Psal. 93); 151r (Psal. 124c).

[30] Anton Schindling, *Humanistische Hochschule und freie Reichstadt. Gymnasium und Akademie in Strassburg 1538–1621* (Wiesbaden, 1977), 163.

reading of the Old Testament logically leads the author in some cases to refer to a type of the Christ.[31] Nor can we note any attempt to develop a mystical reflection that ends up completely emptying all material circumstances and interests of life; on the contrary, there is a strong sense of history, a perception of the concrete nature of situations and their development.[32] There are no references at all to patristic sources or classical writers, even though they were very familiar to Vermigli and thus frequent in other works of his. As Simler had already rightly noted, the composition of the paraphrase has two main objectives which are not totally distinct from each other but which never coincide: to help the understanding of the text not only from the point of view of language but also of content, and to provide a contemporary application through a continual reference to examples drawn from daily experience. The exegete knows how to establish links in the text, similarities between two situations, drawn together by a simple *nunc*,[33] by the participle adjective *praesens*,[34] by the expression *hoc tempore*[35] or by the correlative *quemadmodum . . . ita*.[36] The attempt to give a contemporary value to the text is not limited to those cases introduced by these traditional grammatical means; often the link with the present is instituted in an indirect way, with reference to the stability of the divine promises, to the covenant.[37]

As well as similarities in style, it is worth mentioning the significant uniformity in structure of the various parts of the work. The first thing to be said is that the prayers are always addressed to God, in most cases using the term *omnipotens Deus*, sometimes with the expression *Deus Opt. Max.*, very occasionally with the title *coelestis Pater*;[38] while they close every time with the phrase *per Iesum Christum dominum nostrum. Amen.* Continuing our observation, in almost all the paraphrases, apart from the length and content, we can distinguish three

---

[31] Preces, 23r–24v (Psal. 22, 22b, 22c); 123v–125r (Psal. 110, 110b, 110c).

[32] Ibid., 4v (Psal. 2); 82r–v (Psal. 77c).

[33] Ibid., 28r (Psal. 26); 47r (Psal. 44b); 48r (Psal. 45); 67v (Psal. 40); 116r (Psal. 105c).

[34] Ibid., 31r (Psal. 30), or the locution *in praesentia*: 42v (Psal. 40); 16v (Psal. 44); 107v (Psal. 99b).

[35] Ibid., 33v (Psal. 32); 121v (Psal. 109), or the locution *his diebus*: 123v (Psal. 110).

[36] Ibid., 82r (Psal. 77b); 117r–v (Psal. 105f); 130r (Psal. 114).

[37] Ibid., 95r–v (Psal. 89, 89b); 115r (105); 125v (Psal. 111).

[38] Ibid., 29r–30v (Psal. 27, 28b, 29); 122r (Psal. 109b).

parts: worship, confession of sin and intercession. Without propos-
ing a direct dependence, it seems to us that such a structure re-
echoes the classical "Roman collect," that is, the brief oration recited
by the priest in the first part of the mass to summarise the vows of
the faithful. Almost always the prayers begin with an evocation of
God that can be summed up in the proclamation of his incomparable greatness and goodness, of his active presence in the world.
There follows the recognition of one's own moral unworthiness and
the confession of the unfaithfulness of the church. They end with
the request for forgiveness, in which the nightmare of deserved judgment disappears and the soul begins to hope again and longs for
action. The cases in which this order is reversed or the parts are
not clearly distinct are few.[39] An example can help to make this
structure clearer. The two prayers relative to psalm 103[40] begin with
an exhortation to bless God and not forget his benefits, both spiritual and material. The praise is linked to a consideration of the
human reality towards which God's work is addressed. And here the
author of the prayer describes man in all his transiency and fragility,
in his insurmountable imperfection. As there is no illusion about
man, he can only intercede that God will manifest himself to the
faithful through his free covenant, appointing them as people called
to have a relationship with himself. Living in the light of this alliance
involves on the one hand a knowledge of one's own dependence on
God, and on the other the observance of his commandments.

These considerations are of fundamental importance, because they
provide us with a criterion of formal evaluation for determining the
period of composition of the *Preces*. If in fact it has been possible to
establish many and such common peculiarities of language and style
among the single prayers—of which only some, it is important to
remember, can be dated between the years 1544 and 1547—this
constitutes the first element in support of extending this dating to
the whole collection, that is, to the first stay in Strasbourg. There
is another step to be taken to be quite sure: an examination of the
theological contents.

---

[39] Cf., for example, ibid. 15v–16r (Psal. 13); 17r–v (Psal. 16).
[40] Ibid., 111r–112v (Psal. 103, 103b).

Theological aspects

The wealth of theological themes developed in the *Preces* is abundant and this is obviously not the time and place to discuss it. If it can be useful for anyone in the future, we are going to mention three aspects: the conception of God, hamartiology, and ecclesiology.

We have already referred to the insistence with which the expression *omnipotens Deus* is repeated in the paraphrases of the psalms. This could lead us to think that the conception of God expressed by Vermigli is simply a surviving residue of his Padua studies: an Aristotelism filtered by Thomas Aquinas. But this heredity, which continuously appears in the *Preces* as in other contemporary works of the Florentine theologian,[41] is tempered by an integral Biblicism that introduces a fertile criterion, provided it is not confused with the idea of a demiurge. God is *omnipotens* not because the idea of omnipotence in itself is particularly worthy of the Divinity. In its inevitable inadequacy, the Aristotelean-scholastic anthropomorphism wants to express rather the Biblical concept of the creator God who from the beginning has manifested his will to save,[42] the God who leads his creatures with supreme power, supreme wisdom and supreme love towards their good. Such a thought is expressed in a whole range of variations that go from one extreme to the other: from the trusting glorification of the sovereign power of God,[43] to the recognition of the painful and disconcerting aspects of life that seem to contradict his will.[44] If the omnipotence of God does not appear evident, as it should, believers know that this is evidence of man's sinfulness, and not of the existence of obscure evil forces that interfere with the action of God. Above the troublesome present reality, they perceive the providential government of He who governs history and the world: *Quamvis impij videantur, omnipotens Deus, interdum tantopere concitari ... non est tamen, quod fideles multum perterrefiant, quando quidem ipse*

---

[41] Cfr. Sturm (see note 9), 91–95.

[42] Preces, 114r (Psal. 104b): "*Non latet fideles tuos, omnipotens Deus, quod omnia condideris ab initio ad electorum salutem . . .*"; 10r–11r (Psal. 8, 8b); 178v–179v (Psal. 148)

[43] Ibid., 21r (Psal. 19): "*Admirabilis potentia, sapientia ac bonitas, quibus natura tua, omnipotens Deus, cumulatissime praedita est, nobis ubique se offert in rebus abs te conditis. Coelum sane cum omnibus ornamentis suis, temporum vicissitudines, stellarum et potentissimi solis iubar voces merae sunt et doctrina omnibus populis communis, a qua maiestatis tuae praeconia amplissime celebratur*"; cfr. ance 34v–35v (Psal. 33, 33b).

[44] Ibid., 73v–74r (Psal. 69).

mundanarum rerum imperium suscipisti et gubernaculis universi orbis pro tua sapientia moderaris.[45] In the most desperate of circumstances, exhausted by anguish, they wait for the help that comes only from God, who is, from the beginning and forever, omnipotent: *Summa anxietate, omnipotens Deus, in his nostris difficillimis casibus auxilium expectamus, ad te unum sustollentes oculos nostros, cuius potentia, ut novimus, creata coelum et terram, sic etiam credimus posse e praesentibus periculis eripi.*[46] The attribute *omnipotens*, in the sense that we have outlined, therefore, aims at affirming the sovereignty of God over the world, while at the same time serves to give a direction to the piety and worship of believers toward their Lord. In this respect, the single prayers in the collection represent a harmonious composition, and can be considered a chorus of voices that call on God waiting for his deliverance.

As we have already seen above, ample space is given to confession of sin in every single paraphrase of the psalms. Let us now look at the content of these texts to establish if there are any links between them through the same theological categories. We take for granted that the prayers contain no doctrinal formulations about the origin, extension or consequences of sin, but only allusions or reminders of the subject. However, if they are read carefully, they reveal an amazing affinity with Zwingli's conception of sin,[47] which Vermigli had already known about since the time he stayed in Naples. Like Zwingli, he too shares the traditional Augustinian-Thomistic distinction between original sin and present sins.[48] But above all, like the Zürich reformer, instead of indulging in a fatalistic conception of sin inherited from Adam, he assumes it into the historical sphere of responsibility of every single person. Thus, in the first place, the Latin term *peccatum*, mostly used in the plural, describes those acts voluntarily commited by man in opposition to God's law, or rather, his attitude of fundamental revolt and disobedience.[49] Secondly, sin is seen as

---

[45] Ibid., 107r (Psal. 99b).

[46] Ibid., 145r (Psal. 121).

[47] Cf. Gottfried W. Locher, *Huldrych Zwingli in neuer Sicht* (Zürich, 1969), 239–244; W. Peter Stephens, *The Theology of Huldrych Zwingli* (Oxford, 1986), 146–153.

[48] Ibid., 46r (Psal. 43b): "*Nam licet in nobis ipsis, dum hanc miserrimam vitam colimus, nil sit roboris aut firmitatis, cui valeamus inniti, cum vitio nativo ac infinitis ad illud peccatis adiectis infoeliciter premamur*".

[49] Preces, 105v (Psal. 98b): "*... in te peccavimus, tam impudenter leges tuas transgressi sumus, ac tibi saepius admodum rebelles fuimus ...*". See also, 14r (Psal. 11); 22r (Psal. 19b); 54v (Psal. 50); 109r (Psal. 101).

covetousness in all its shades of meaning, from ambition to obtain
wealth to carnal desires, which prevent man from carrying out the
divine will.[50] Finally, in an even deeper sense, the term is used to
indicate that lack of faith in God which ends up basing the certainty
of forgiveness on man and obscuring the comforting promise of grace
through the gospel.[51] On the contrary, faith is aware that it cannot
escape God's condemnation, calls on his infinite mercy to obtain the
forgiveness of sins,[52] believes and proclaims that real redemption is
possible only by God: *apud te solum tam credamus, quam praedicemus veram
esse redentionem.*[53] It is almost superfluous to point out that the texts
mentioned pose in an exemplary way the problem of the relationship between confession and forgiveness of sins in the *Preces*. In this
case we also have to conclude that there is a substantial theological
unity in the thoughts expressed.

The homogeneity of the collection from the point of view of ecclesiology is even more evident.[54] The *Preces* leave no margin for an
interpretation of the church as a visible hierarchical-juridical organ-
ism. Neither do we find the term "body of Christ," which is instead
present in other works,[55] to indicate the church in its invisible aspect,
in its profound spiritual reality. Only once is it described with the
New Testament image "bride of Christ";[56] in a few cases it is associated with the adjective "elect."[57] In almost all the prayers the noun
is accompanied by the possessive pronoun *tua*. This is never intended

---

[50] Ibid., 53v (Psal. 49b); 111v (Psal. 103); 116v (Psal. 105d).

[51] Ibid., 28r (Psal. 26): "... *quod tibi parum confidimus, vanis hominibus et carnis aux-
iliis nos commisimus neque recessimus a coetu noxiorum atque impuris actionibus et minibus et
moribus contaminates Euangelium tuum sanctum foedavimus* . . ."; 29r (Psal. 27): "*Verum
quod infirmiter credimus ac saepe nutat nostra in te fiducia, hinc fit, ut simus adeo trepidi atque
meticulosi.*"

[52] Ibid., 159v–160r (Psal. 130b): "... *quis, obsecro, poterit ad tuum tribunal consistere?
Quare cum apud te summa sit, imo infinita clementia . . . ita precamur, ut ea nostrae iniquitates
redimantur. Hac unica spe in singulos dies atque in singulas horas nutrimur, confidimusque te
veri Israelis, hoc est Ecclesiae tuae nunquam obliturum. Da igitur, ut remissionem peccatorum tanquam solidum syncerumque fructrum huius fiducie as te consequamur. Per Iesum Christum dominum
nostrum, Amen.*"

[53] Ibid., 159v (Psal. 130).

[54] Cf. the sharp considerations by Luigi Santini, *Appunti sull'ecclesiologia di P.M.
Vermigli e la edificazione della Chiesa*, in: Bollettino della Società di Studi Valdesi, Nr.
104, 1958), 69–75.

[55] Cf. Sturm (see note 9), 118.

[56] *Preces*, 48r (Psal. 45).

[57] Ibid., 7v (Psal. 4); cf. also 46v (Psal. 44); 78r–v (Psal. 75b).

in the sense of an idealisation of the empirical reality of the church, ever disputable and imperfect, neither as a proclamation of any privileged position. The aim is to underline the free act of God who creates the church and vivifies it through the work of the Holy Spirit purifying it from its sins.[58] The possibility that the church, or at least part of it, could fall short, could cease to be the church of God, is not altogether excluded. The *Preces* are full of references to the *Antichristus et omnia eius membra* who oppress the people of God. Like many Protestants of his time, Vermigli believes that the Antichrist has by now taken up his dwelling in the Roman ecclesiastical institution. But this disturbing conclusion does not assume the apocalyptical tones of Luther, nor is it expressed with that excessive factiousness that can be found in the writings of Vergerio. Indeed an irenic affirmation appears here and there: *Appareat e coelesti Zion auxilium, ut, cum nos a captivitate peccati, diaboli et mortis vindicaris, et refiatur et exultet universa Ecclesia.*[59] Moreover the author of the prayers does not even seem indulgent towards the churches that arose from the reformation movement. There are abundant reminders in the *Preces* of their imperfection: *peccavimus enim graviter tuisque summis beneficijs supra modum fuimus ingrati, vocatione, Evangelio, Sacramentis abusi sumus, contemnendo facultatem nobis oblatam, tibi libere iuxta verbum tuum inserviendi.*[60] And on the contrary, they are full of exhortations to these churches to remain under the judgment of the gospel, to let themselves be continuously reformed by the word of God. Which is the real church according to Vermigli? The answer—by necessity brief, given the literary genre of the *Preces*—is that it can be recognised through the signs of the Word and the sacraments;[61] besides these the Florentine theologian often remembers discipline, intended as integrity of life and practice of brotherly love.[62]

Space does not allow us to extend the analysis to other important theological themes, such as predestination[63] or the concept of

---

[58] Ibid., 46v (Psal. 44): "*Summa bonitate, omnipotens Deus, ecclesiam tibi ex multis gentibus collegisti, manu tua plantatam non humanis viribus: tuo favore et Spiritu a peccatis est repurgata; evasit hactenus diaboli crudeles insultus, abs te adiuta et fortiter defensa.*"

[59] Ibid., 16v (Psal. 14).

[60] Ibid., 13r–v (Psal. 10).

[61] Ibid., 84v (Psal. 79); 146v (Psal. 122); 167v (Psal. 136).

[62] Ibid., 124v (110b); 162v–163v (Psal. 133b, 133c). See also note 18.

[63] Ibid., 97v–98r (Psal. 104b): "*Sin obis gratulamur, omnipotens Deus, tam exuberantem*

covenant.[64] Despite this, in the light of what we have gleaned so far, it is possible to say that amongst the various prayers that make up the *Preces* there exists an affinity that is not only a formal one of language and literary style, but also theological. But having ascertained, at least for some of them, the date of composition, this means that there can remain no doubt about the fact they were all born in the same setting, that is, they were composed in a particular perspective, that of the destiny of the church and the city of Strasbourg between the years 1544 and 1547. In their integrity the *Preces* reveal all the anguish and worry about the situation, but at the same time they are the expression of an unshakable trust in the One who, in the greatest of adversity, remains and will remain victor.

---

fovoris tui copiam, ut nos, quos amore summon prosequeris, ante iacta mundi fundamenta delegeris, priusquam montes fierent aut orbis formaretur, destinari ad tua aeterna bona percipienda . . ."; 97r (Psal. 90); 113v (Psal. 104b); 131v (Psal. 117).

[64] Ibid., 95r–97r (Psal. 89, 89b, 89c); 111v (Psal. 103); 114v–115r (Psal. 105); 125v (Psal. 111); 161r–v (Psal. 132, 132b).

LAW AND ORDER: VERMIGLI AND THE REFORM OF ECCLESIASTICAL LAWS IN ENGLAND

John F. Jackson

Introduction

Peter Martyr Vermigli's importance to England's reformation is no where more evident, than in his contributions to the programme of canon law reform. By 1553, the government had imposed reforms of both liturgy and doctrine in the *Book of Common Prayer* (1549 and 1552) and the *Articles of Religion* (1552). However, the law of England's ecclesiastical courts was still the *Corpus Iuris Canonici* and this body of canon law was the one thing that kept England tied, however reluctantly, to Rome. The desire to reform the canon law in England actually began prior to the break with Rome in 1529, but never materialized.[1] By 1552, however, with liturgy and doctrine now reformed, the government could turn to the important task of revising England's ecclesiastical law. Thomas Cranmer led the way in this project, working with a drafting committee and, more importantly, calling upon the talents of Peter Martyr Vermigli in the editing process. Martyr's expertise as a theologian is without question, yet his work on this project indicates that he had talents beyond theology, and that work on canon law reform suited his abilities quite well.

Among Vermigli's friends and fellow reformers from the Continent was Heinrich Bullinger, prominent among European reformers of

---

[1] See Gerald Bray, *The Anglican Canons: 1529–1947*, Church of England Record Society, vol. 6 (Boydell Press: Woodbridge, Suffolk, 1998). Henry VIII actually edited the 1529 canons which were never adopted. Canons were also formulated in 1535, but again, were never adopted. Bray refers to these latter reforms as the 'Henrician Canons' though both the attempts in 1529 and 1535 can be considered as attempted reforms under Henry's reign. See Gerald Bray, *Tudor Church Reform*, Church of England Record Society, vol. 8 (Boydell Press: Woodbridge, Suffolk, 2000). This latter volume contains Bray's most recent translation of the proposed canon law reforms of 1553, known as *Reformatio Legum Ecclesiasticarum*, along with the 1535 canons. All references to the text of the *Reformatio* herein, unless otherwise stated, are from that volume and are cited as *RLE*.

the mid-sixteenth century and certainly one of the evangelicals better informed about events in England in the early 1550's.[2] We know
something of the process of canon law reform in England because
of the letters that Bullinger received and to which he responded.
Correspondence from Bullinger's friends like John Ab Ulmis, Martin
Micronius, Ralph Skinner and Richard Cox, provided him with news
of political upheavals, such as the fall of Somerset—"how wretched
and miserable is the life of courtiers!"—and the state of religion in
England as well as progress towards reform of the English church.[3]
Bullinger had learned that form and administration of public prayers
and the sacraments had again been altered to conform to the 'rule
of God's word', and of the move afoot to establish godly discipline
in England and finally supplant Rome's rule over the administration
of ecclesiastical laws.[4] He must have remembered the enthusiasm for
the project when Ralph Skinner wrote to him that the church had
'lately called the committee together, and appointed certain persons
to purify our church from the filth of antichrist, and to abolish those
impious laws of the Roman Pontiff, by which the spouse of Christ
has for so long a time been wretchedly and shamefully defiled . . ."[5]

Late in 1551, work was underway in earnest, for a third time, to
draft new canons and create a system of ecclesiastical laws better
suited to its evangelical character. The project was the responsibility of a working party that was part of a committee of 32—probably the *synodum* that Skinner was referring to—commissioned by statue
to reform the canon law in England. The enterprise was under the
direct control of Archbishop Thomas Cranmer who desired that
England more fully participate with the wider group of reformed
churches on the Continent and whose 'Europe-wide vision' was to
unite England with these evangelical churches so that together they

---

[2] I have used the term 'evangelical' in this essay in the same sense as that of
Prof. MacCulloch, to refer to the reformers in general. This avoids the necessity of
explaining the many theological positions taken by those on the Continent and in
England and detracting from the purpose of this work. See Diarmaid N.J. MacCulloch,
Thomas Cranmer: A Life (Yale, 1996), 2.

[3] 10 January 1552, *Epistolae Tigurniae: De Rebus Potissimum Ad Ecclesiae Anlicanae
Reformationem pertinentibus conscriptae, AD 1531–1558*, Parker Society (Cambridge,
1847), 195.

[4] From Windsor, 5 October 1552, *Epistolae Tigurniae*, 143 and *Original Letters Relative
to the English Reformation, 1531–1558*, 2 vols., ed. Hastings Robinson for the Parker
Society (Cambridge, 1846–47), vol. 1, 123.

[5] 5 January 1550, *Epistolae Tigurniae*, 207 and *Original Letters*, 314.

could oppose what was coming out of the council of Trent. The reform of canon law was one more step towards that goal.[6]

There had long been a desire that the English church have its own ecclesiastical laws. Parliament on more than one occasion in the sixteenth century, authorized canon law reform and two previous attempts produced canons, but these collections were never enacted into law. Yet now, in this new reign of Edward VI, neither effort would have fit the mood of the Edwardian church and so following Cranmer's launching of the project in December 1551, work began again in the winter and early spring of 1552.

These delays belie Cranmer's enthusiasm for reform since he had long been an advocate of new canons. He had been around long enough to have seen the rise and fall of previous attempts to draft acceptable ecclesiastical laws. Reform actually started four years before Henry VIII maneuvered the break with Rome and began when Parliament proposed reforms in 1529 aimed at the Church and its clergy. Convocation was aware of the ominous portent of the government's actions and convened at Canterbury in early November 1529. As the first of the 'reformation' parliaments were meeting, Convocation was attempting to head trouble off at the pass and proposed their own reforms of the church and ecclesiastical practice.[7] They were solely the work of the Church, however, and were never authorized or adopted by Parliament, despite Henry VIII's personal involvement in reading them and making suggestions for changes sometime after July 1530.[8] Parliament then passed a statue authorizing canon law reform, *The Act for the Submission of the Clergy* in 1534 and following this, Convocation surrendered its independent authority to promulgate ecclesiastical laws apart from the permission of Crown and Commons.[9] Following this, in 1534, Richard Gwent and a committee of drafters prepared another set of canons that, according to F.D. Logan, were finished by about October 1535.[10] These

---

[6] MacCulloch, *Cranmer*, 101–3.

[7] See Stanford Lehmberg, *The Reformation Parliament 1529–1536* (Cambridge, 1970), 86–99, for more on the reformation parliaments and the reaction of Convocation to their complaints and debates.

[8] The King's edits appear on P.R.O. s.p. 1/57, fols. 112 ff., and 119–123.

[9] 25 H. VIII c. 19.

[10] British Library, Additional MS. 48040, fols. 13–102v., formerly the Yelverton MS 45. See F. Donald Logan, 'Henrician Canons', *Bulletin of the Institute of Historical Research*, 47 (1975), 99–103.

canons met the same fate as those of 1529 and were never adopted. Cranmer was aware of and had access to these in the drafting of the *Reformatio* and some appear to be an influence on certain of its texts.[11] The fact remained that neither of these revisions ever saw the light of day and even the governmental attempts at policy changes in canonical practice had not altered the fact that the law of England's church and its courts was still the canon law of Rome.

Though Cranmer was well aware of this history, despite past failures and the ostensible inattention to this project, John Strype was not exaggerating when he claimed that '[o]ur archbishop, seeing the great evil and inconvenience of canons and papal laws, which were still in force and studied much in the kingdom, had in his mind now a good while to get them suppressed or to reduce them to a narrower compass, and to cull out of them a set of just and wholesome laws, that should serve for the government of the ecclesiastical state.'[12] Nevertheless, despite a long-standing desire, Cranmer was still encumbered with canons that were clearly part of the 'pope's law' and not the canons that he envisioned for a reformed English church.

Here was true irony. Despite past attempts at reform, it was apparent that there was an uncomfortable connection between Rome's authority and the existing English canon law. Regardless of the temporary changes wrought by statue and royal proclamation, the existing system was still tied in sentiment to the Pope and there was no shortage of voices reminding the government of this. In 1543, William Turner argued that the canon law, in both form and practice, stood as a sovereign corpus, antithetical to the King in a nation where the relationship between Church and State was defined in terms of obedience to the monarch, not to Rome.[13] England would need to be rid of the 'pope's law' once and for all to have a fully reformed church. Turner argued that a law code based on a system that exalted papal authority was incompatible with an evangelical church because, "[w]hosoeuer holdeth still the popes doctrine holdeth stil the pope. But ye hold still the popes doctrine whils ye hold stil the popes canon law the popes decretalles & the ordinances . . . the pope made."[14]

---

[11] See Gerald Bray, ed., *Tudor Church Reform*, xxxix–xli.
[12] John Strype, *Memorials of Cranmer* (Oxford, 1848–54), vol. 1, 294.
[13] See Richard Rex, "The Crisis of Obedience: God's Word and Henry's Reformation" *The Historical Journal* 39, 4 (1996): 863–894.
[14] William Turner, *The huntyrs and fynders out for the romishe fox* (Bonn, 1543) STC 24353.

Peter Martyr Vermigli himself was aware of this state of affairs as he wrote to Bullinger from Lambeth on 8 March 1552, where Cranmer had brought him to work on the collection of revised canons to be presented to Parliament. He reported with no uncertainty that the temporary measures adopted by the government had failed to eradicate the influence of Rome's canon law. He noted that the King had decreed the collecting of new canons early on, at least since the gospel had been received and the Pope banished from England. In this new atmosphere, England, he insisted to the receptive Bullinger, should no longer be ruled by these ". . . pontifical decrees, and decretals, Sixtine Clementine, and other popish ordinances of the same kind . . .". Yet he realized that much work needed to be done since ". . . the administration of these laws has for the most part prevailed up to this time in the ecclesiastical court, under the tacit authority of the pope, though many other laws were enacted by which the external polity of the church might be regulated."[15] Martyr hoped for a complete exorcism of this canonical ghost of Rome that haunted England still. His hope, one that he shared with the Archbishop, was to come together with the evangelical churches on the continent and with these new revised canons, do England's part to help "banish the Tridentine canons from the churches of Christ."[16]

Later that month, Peter Martyr again wrote to Bullinger of his enthusiasm, confident that England would soon be out from under the thumb of these 'popish ordinances.'[17] His theological commitment to ecclesiastical discipline as one of the marks of the true church was clear. His work in helping to realize the dream of creating canons that were fitting for this emerging evangelical English church was significant and, seemingly, determined. His own writings demonstrate that he shared a commitment to proper church discipline in general and possessed an in-depth knowledge and understanding of medieval canon law and civil law as well. The text of the revised canons are testimony to Martyr's expertise, not only as a theologian, but as one who was obviously well versed in law as well; something that must have been invaluable to Cranmer in the drafting and editing stages of the canons.

---

[15] 8 March 1552, *Epistolae Tigurniae*, 330–331, *Original Letters*, 503–5.
[16] Ibid.
[17] 8 March 1552, *Original Letters*, 503.

The Spectre of Past Failures

Irrespective of their sincerity and commitment, Cranmer and Martyr had no mean task on their hands in taking up the challenge to reorder England's ecclesiastical laws. The Archbishop and the Regius Professor were aware of the long history of failure and inaction, something that must have given them a sense of foreboding, even as they were confident that things would be different this time. Against this backdrop, Peter Martyr earnestly sought Bullinger's prayers for the drafting and presentation to Parliament of these 'pious and holy laws' that John Foxe later dubbed the *Reformatio Legum Ecclesiasticarum*.[18] His awareness of the seriousness of England's desire and need to reform their canon law, and of the international significance of these canons was not in doubt and he reminded Bullinger of the importance of his labours at Lambeth.[19] Archbishop Cranmer had written to Bullinger himself, as well, telling him of the dream and urging that "[w]e must not therefore suffer ourselves to be wanting to the church of God in a matter of such importance."[20] Both men were well aware that Rome's shadow hung over England's Church because of the failure to that date to complete and adopt a suitable set of canons to govern its church, canons that would free England from the *de facto* authority of Roman canon law.[21]

All did not begin well, however, and if Martyr had any apprehensions, they may have surfaced in the summer of 1552. He wrote to Bullinger again on 14 June from Oxford, but this time he was concerned over a matter that involved the Sacraments, Baptism and the Eucharist.[22] His concern was over the theology of Sacraments and whether they conferred grace, and he was keen to ensure that the correct answer to the question was spelled out in detail in the canons. This episode highlights an unusual aspect of this revision, in that it contains detailed sections on doctrine and not just laws. This also shows that Martyr had active input into the discussions

---

[18] "... non solum enim oportet Deum rogare, ut pie sancteue conscribantur leges ...", *Epistolae Tigurniae*, 201.

[19] MacCulloch, *Cranmer*, 501–3.

[20] 20 March 1552, *Original Letters*, vol. 1, 23.

[21] Cranmer, 503.

[22] George C. Gorham, *Gleanings of a few Scattered Ears From the Period of the Reformation in England ... AD 1533 to 1588* (London, 1857), No. lxxxii, 280–283.

that led to the drafting of canons, and it is likely that he would have been listened to with regard to the issue involving the canon on Sacraments.[23]

Martyr noted that this controversy was significant and caused delays in producing the revision—"But the chief reason why other things which were purposed but not effected was that the subject of the Sacrament stood in the way."[24] His concern was not over the doctrines of transubstantiation or of real presence, since he recognized that those had been laid to rest. However, some wanted to specify that grace was given in the Sacrament. He opposed this and was concerned about how far the canon should go in explaining and specifying that a person receiving a Sacrament would only receive worthily if they already possessed the faith of which the Sacrament acted as a sign. Martyr was opposed to any idea that either Baptism or the Eucharist directly conferred grace apart from '. . . the efficacy of faith'.[25] He wanted this carefully and fully set forth in the canon so to avoid the spreading of superstition.[26] His own commitments to the doctrine of predestination and election led him to his conclusions and he wanted the issue dealt with clearly.

There were apparently two sides to this argument and, while Martyr does not name his detractors, Diarmaid MacCulloch, writing on this incident, speculates that it may have been either Bishops Goodricke or Ridley. The exact extent of Martyr's influence on this issue is unknown. The canon that was written was not in opposition to Martyr's theology, and, while perhaps not as specific as Martyr' might have wished for, the *Reformatio's* canon gives no hint that the Sacraments themselves confer grace. Sacraments are, according to this canon, first and foremost *signum est institutem a Deo*, a sign instituted by God. The various sections of the canon refer confidently to the 'grace of Christ' (*gratia Christi*) and the 'grace of the Holy Spirit' (*gratia Spiritus Sancti*), but steer clear of any suggestion that the Sacraments themselves confer grace.[27] The theology contained in this canon would have been acceptable to Martyr. It must have been,

---

[23] Ibid., 236–41 (*De Sacramentis*).
[24] Ibid., 281.
[25] Ibid.
[26] See *Epistolae Tigurnae*, 80–1, and *Original Letters*, vol. 1, 123–4.
[27] Ibid., pp. 226–9.

since he offered no marginal comments or edits, indicating that he was satisfied with the canon as written. Noting Martyr's concern for this issue, he is likely to have voiced his opposition to a draft that would have hinted at sacramental grace.

MS Harleian 426 and Peter Martyr's Influence

In October of 1552, as the final edits were being made at Lambeth Palace, Cranmer and Martyr were working with a draft that the committee had prepared with which he and Cranmer would work at Lambeth. There is an extant copy of that draft, in the British Library, MS Harleian 426. This is the only extant example of the canons from October 1552, the time in which Cranmer and Martyr were at Lambeth working on them. Martyr was on the committee of 32 assigned the job of revising and was also a member of the drafting subcommittee along with the Archbishop, the Bishop of Ely, Thomas Goodricke, Richard Cox, the civil lawyers Rowland Taylor and William May together with John Lucas and Richard Goodricke—both of whom were common lawyers.[28] Peter Martyr's biographer, Josiah Simler indicated that perhaps Rowland Taylor directly worked on the draft as well, but Martyr's and Cranmer's handwriting are the most prominent of the editors. Martyr was obviously well versed in various aspects of canon law. This draft was, after all, first and foremost a legal document and the Regius Professor seems to have been comfortable with his job as editor. Martyr's direct contribution to the text of the *Reformatio Legum Ecclesiasticarum* is evident. He took an active part in editing several sections, and his handwriting is on the draft in various places. Vermigli's hand is prominent and Gerald Bray in his critical edition of the *Reformatio* has speculated that in several instances, Cranmer may have begun to edit certain canons and later turned them over to Martyr to finish.[29]

---

[28] See Gerald Bray, *Tudor Church Reform*, pp. xli–l; Edward Cardwell, *The Reformation of the Ecclesiastical Laws as Attempted in the Reigns of King Henry VIII, King Edward VI, and Queen Elizabeth* (Oxford, 1850), vi–ix; Leslie Raymond Sachs, 'Thomas Cranmer's *Reformatio Legum Ecclesiasticarum* of 1553 in the Context of English Church Law from the Later Middle Ages to the Canons of 1603' (unpublished doctoral thesis, Catholic University of America, 1982), 234–242.

[29] Bray, ibid., lvii–lviii.

As this incident in June demonstrates, Peter Martyr came to this project quite capable of performing his job as an editor and fully convinced of both the necessity and appropriateness of the church providing ecclesiastical laws, having already argued the case in writing. For example, in his commentary on the book of *Genesis*, Martyr asserts an ecclesiology that gave church discipline a prominent role in the life of the church and referred to discipline as one of the marks of the true church.[30] Martyr believed that it was lawful for the church to "make to itselfe, either Canons, or lawes or decrees, or statutes . . ." to foster such principles.[31] Further, various chapters in the *Loci Communes* give clear indication of his commitment to the use of discipline (especially the use of excommunication) to maintain rule over the 'faithful', and to bring obstinant siners and heretics to repentance.[32] He was concerned in the common places to show that discipline was not just about punishment, but conversion as well.

Martyr compared the arguments of those who believed that Bishops had no right to make any laws for the church with those who exalted canon law above civil law in importance. He discussed both arguments without fully accepting either approach and concluded that it was right for the church to make laws—". . . for the Church is a companie and must be ruled by the word of God, especially because it belongeth to the saluation, thereof and to the worhipping of God, for there is need of certaine outward bonds to the end that fellowship of the people maie be retained.' He used St. Paul's first letter to the Corinthians in which he commanded that women should pray with their head covered as an example of a law that promoted the fellowship of the church and that was fitting for the context of that first century community. He also cited the early church's insistence that all Christians should abstain from eating certain foods.[33] Martyr added the fact that when church councils met to formulate doctrine,

---

[30] ". . . quod si quaeras ubi vera sit. Ubi est Christi spiritus, purum Dei verbum, sincere administrata Sacramenta. Ubicunque, vero hac tres nota inueneris, ibidem disciplina Ecclesiastica & sancti mores proculdubio locum etiam habebunt," in *In Primum Librum Mosis, qui Vulgo literarum in schola Tigurina, nunc denuo in lucem edti.* (Zürich, 1579), f. 34v.

[31] CP, 56.

[32] CP, 56 as an example.

[33] CP, 41; see also I Corinthians 11:5 and Acts 15:29.

they also promulgated canons to accompany the doctrine.[34] However, he was careful to distinguish between the force and effect of the church's laws and civil laws.

Martyr argued that ecclesiastical laws were unlike civil laws since they could not bind an individual's conscience. Ecclesiastical laws, he wrote, were 'not of necessitie' and as such, they were subject to alteration, 'accordnge to the times and seasons'. He cites as examples, the laws surrounding the practice of baptism and the Eucharist. The church could change the time, place and manner of practice for these sacraments to satisfy the present need, for example, '. . . whether we ought to communicate standing or sitting, in the morning or the evening . . .'. These were not matters of importance as doctrine or conscience but were standards of practice that would lead to the 'tranquilitie of the Church.'[35] He contrasted this with what he believed were the exigencies of civil law, which according to St. Paul's in Romans 13, all men were obliged to obey. St. Paul instructed the Roman Christians that this was not an obligation imposed by fear of retribution, but because their conscience demanded it. Ecclesiastical laws did not have this force for Martyr and rather existed to promote good—'For in Ecclesiastical thinges, good order must be regarded, but in civill thinges we must obey, although thought perceive not that good order.'[36]

The difference between ecclesiastical law and the law that binds the conscience appears to surface in one of Martyr's marginal notes made during this editing of the *Reformatio*. It arises in the canon on prescriptions (*De Praescriptiones*), a legal device that allows one to either acquire rights to something or frees one from obligations. The section *Malae findei possessor praescribere non potest* regulates one who holds prescriptions through wrong or an act that results in an evil conscience. The section negates that person's prescription unless they repent and show remorse for possessing something that is the right of another. Martyr comments about the demand that such a person repent and be sorry for obtaining or possessing a prescription in such a way. His comment in the margin is that such a demand on a person is not matter for law—*ista non faciunt ad legem*.[37] What Martyr

---

[34] Ibid., 42.
[35] Ibid.
[36] Ibid., 44.
[37] Bray, *RLE*, 632–633.

meant by this is not specified, but it is consistent with his view that ecclesiastical laws do not bind the conscience. The case of a person repenting for unscrupulous behaviour does involve conscience, it may involve civil laws governing fraud, to be obeyed, and it would certainly be a matter of personal spiritual integrity for the unjust holder of a prescription. Certainly Martyr would agree that the gospel might lead one to repent of such a condition, but that would not make it a matter for ecclesiastical law in his view.

Theologian and Lawyer?

That Martyr would have weighed in on various theological issues such as the nature of Sacraments in relation to grace is not surprising. However, the scholarly focus on him as a theologian has diverted attention away from his expertise in law. Though Martyr was not a lawyer he was obviously well versed in the canon law and Roman law. One may argue that Simler's biography of him was a bit over the top in its assessment of Martyr, but it is difficult not to appreciate the breadth of Martyr's knowledge and understanding by simply looking at the edits in the *Reformatio*. Simler was probably not far off the mark when he noted that because of the Regius Professor's 'singular learning and incredible skill at many things, he was summoned by the archbishop of Canterbury at the king's behest.'[38] Cranmer could have called upon one of the lawyers on the committee to edit the legal sections of the canons, and one might assume that they would have been better suited for the task. Yet Martyr's skills even in law are evident in his edits, and no doubt, Cranmer was familiar with his work in the *Loci Communes*, perhaps with his discussions of marriage and divorce, where Martyr discussed various pertinent canons from both Justinian and the *Corpus Iuris Canonici*.[39]

An example in the *Reformatio* that demonstrates the breadth of his knowledge of law is, again, found in the canon *De Praescriptionibus*. This section of the canon deals with the rules as to when a prescription will cease, can be interrupted or hindered—*Praescriptio vel*

---

[38] LLS, 33.
[39] See generally *Loci Communes*, Part II, cap. X, et. Seq.

interrumpi potest vel cessare vel impediri.[40] Martyr supplies a rather lengthy marginal comment on the issues and handles the legal material by creating a short primer on these subjects.[41] The note is a detailed explanation about when a prescription can be broken or hindered or interrupted. He discusses the role of possession in prescriptions that are incorporeal and when courts are involved in the matter, and he defines the legal occasions when a man is said to possess quietly. Martyr demonstrates in this section the legal sophistication of someone well-versed in law and the note is sophisticated, more in the nature of a reading from one of the Inns of Court.[42]

Two other examples show martyr's grasp of procedural law, *De Sententia et re Iudicatae* and *De Appellationibus*—'Of the Sentence and Judgment Rendered' and 'On Appeals'.[43] *De Sententia* covers various rules that judges must follow in ruling on cases before them. Martyr's comments deal with several issues including the procedure a judge is to follow when conscience leads him to question evidence and place a priority on his conscience, when plaintiff's evidence is to be received against an accused, the proper form for passing sentences, interlocutory sentences, when a judge may alter a sentence and the impugning of a sentence. In *De Appellationibus* Martyr's edits are fewer, but run throughout this rather lengthy procedural canon. He apparently inserted a canon as well, that covers appealing a case that had been heard by several judges.[44] These two canons do not provide exciting reading and martyr's work on them is not that of a master theologian. Additionally, this added canon did not appear in the final version. It is, however, the confident editing of someone comfortable with substantive legal norms and procedural rules and who understood the rules governing the journey of a case through a court.

One of Martyr's proposed additions to the text in the canon *De Iudiciis contra Haeresis* provides a brief glimpse of what may be considered a pastoral concern for those who have strayed into heresy

---

[40] Bray, *RLE*, 636–7.

[41] Ibid., for the text.

[42] Compare this for example, with Spelman's readings on *Quo Warranto*, specifically his section on prescriptions, delivered in Lent 1519 at Gray's Inn. J. H. Baker, ed., *John Spelman's Reading on Quo Warranto: delivered in Gray's Inn (Lent 1519)* Selden Society vol. 113 (Seldon Society: London, 1997), 84–89.

[43] Bray, *RLE*, 698–734.

[44] Ibid., 705, *Quomodo a pluribs iudicibbus appelletur.*

and obstinately refuse to recant.[45] He adds this proposal to section on contumacious heretics, and takes a harsh line on punishment, requiring that those guilty should be punished by exile (*exilium*) or life imprisonment (*perpetuo carcere . . . vel ad aeternas carceris deprimatur tenebras*), indicating, to put it in a modern idiom, that they should never see the light of day. However, Martyr's enthusiasm is tempered in a brief but telling sentence that may be a window on his pastoral concern. He adds that there also could be another means of punishment as would be given at the discretion of a magistrate and then suggests that whatever is done should be that which is most likely to lead to the person's conversion (*ut maxime illius conversioni expedire videbitur*).[46] His desire to exact harsh punishment is meant to lead the heretic to repentance and not simply an act of retribution.

Martyr made numerous other edits that were changes in words or matters of cleaning up the text or reminding the drafters that something in the canon was redundant.[47] However, Martyr's involvement in the *Reformatio* certainly was not limited to his editing of the text. Other canons that bear no marks of his editing are, doubtless, indebted to Martyr's writings on the subject. I have already shown his participation in the debates over theology that would define *De Sacramentis* and his consistent attitude about the nature of ecclesiastical law as it relates to matters of conscience. Of the examples that could be discussed, one of the more significant is in the area of marriage law, specifically in Martyr's understanding of the purposes of marriage and his concern for enforcing the need for parental consent before a couple could marry.

Peter Martyr's Legal Expertise and the Issue of Marriage

In the *Reformatio*, the canon *De Matrimonio* both defines and controls marriage, setting out the rules that were necessary for a couple to follow before they could be considered both legally and validly married.[48] The subsection, *Matrimonium quid sit* defines marriage, giving it both a theological and legal basis.

---

[45] Ibid., 632–3. '*Ista non faciunt ad legum*'.
[46] Ibid., 214–222. See *De contumacibus haereticis*, 218–219.
[47] See, for example, *RLE*, 682 et. seq.
[48] Ibid., 246–251.

> Matrimony is a legal contract, which by the command of God creates and affects a mutual and perpetual union of a man with a woman, in which each of them surrenders power over his or her body to the other, in order to beget children, to avoid prostitution and to govern life by serving one another. Nor is it our will for matrimony to any longer to take place by promises or contracts, however many words they may have or whatever accompaniments there may be, unless it is celebrated according to the form we have appended here.[49]

Like the *Prayer Book*, the *Reformatio* recognizes that there are three purposes to marriage not just two. The third purpose of marriage is 'governing life by serving one another'. Noting that the canon on marriage incorporates the *Prayer Book* by reference, means that this third purpose relates to Cranmer's marriage service which recognized that the third purpose of marriage was that of 'mutuall societie, helpe and coumfort, that the one oughte to haue of thither, both in two persones present . . .'.[50] Now marriage was to be seen as a good in and of itself, and even the act of sex in marriage was part of the mutual union of support.

Martyr's own writings are consistent with the *Reformatio* and might have been a source of significant influence on its text. The *Reformatio* calls marriage a mutual and perpetual union and uses the word '*coniunctionem*'. It emphasizes, in addition to procreation and the avoiding of sexual immorality, that marriage is for the mutual governance of the life of the couple through service to one another (*vel ad vitam mutuis officiis gubernandam*). Peter Martyr's own writings suggest close parallels. Martyr himself posited three purposes for marriage in the *Loci Communes*. He drew upon Justinian and posited that marriage was '. . . a coniuncion of man and woman, an inseparable conversation of life, and a communicating of the lawe of God and man', a definition he felt was adequate on its own, but could be 'made perfect' by the Scriptures.[51] Martyr also provided three purposes for

---

[49] Bray, *RLE*, 246–7, '*Matrimonium est legitimus contractus, mutuam et perpetuam viri cum femina coniunctionem Dei iussu inducens et perficiens, in quo tradit uterque alteri potestatem sui corporis, vel ad prolem suscipiendam, vel ad ortationem evitandam, vel ad vitam mutuis officiis gubernandam. Nec nam nullis promissis aut contractibus matrimonium posthac procedure volumes, quotcunque verbis et quibuscunque concurrentibus, nisi fuerit hac formula quam hic subüciendam esse curavimus.*'

[50] 'The First Prayer Book of Edward VI', in *The First and Second Prayer Books of Edward VI* (The Prayer Book Society: London, 3rd ed., 1999), 252.

[51] CP, 418 "*. . . matrimonium vero, vt habetur in Libro I Institutio Iustinian cum de patria*

marriage—'for the increasing of children, for the taking away of whoredome, and that thereby the life of man might have helpes and commodoties'[52] in order to beget children, to avoid prostitution and to govern life by serving one another.'

Both the *Reformatio* and Martyr follow other reformers in using the word 'coniuncion' to describe marriage. This word implicates sexual union, but implies something more than just the physical act of love. Martyr's approach was in keeping with his scholastic training and was obviously borrowing from Aquinas, who called marriage a *coniunctio maris et feminae*, and himself quoted Justinian. To Aquinas marriage was one of a list of basic human goods that came from the first principle of practical reason. Professor John Finnis has shown that what is interesting about the use of this word in Aquinas, is that the earliest manuscripts use this word rather than *conmixio*. In both cases, the words refer to sexual intercourse, but the latter word is narrowly confined to just the sexual act itself. In the choice of a word *coniunctio*, there is an understanding that sex within marriage is more than just a physical act, it is also 'the whole conjoining of lives in marriage, a consortium and community of two lives that is appropriate to the conception, gestation, and education of children . . . and is in any case a natural form of human friendship.'[53] In his letter of 1551 to Martin Bucer's widown, Vermigli affirmed that marriage involved more than just duty, sexual or otherwise. He referred to it as the closest of human bonds, an intimate relationship between friends where 'everything is shared with candour and sincerity so that whoever is human would wish these friendships to be indissoluble and everlasting.'[54]

That the *Reformatio* used the word *coniunctionem* and includes the third purpose of marriage is not surprising. Both Martyr and the drafters of the *Reformatio* promoted marriage in its fullest terms which included this third purpose of mutual union, in contrast to the Roman canon law's approach to marriage. Generally, Medieval writers on

---

potestate agitur, & in ff. de ritu nuptiarum, definitur esse coniunctio maris & feminae, individual vitae consuentudo, communicatioque iuris diuini atque humani.'

[52] Ibid. '*Proinde addatur, hanc maris & feminae coniunctionem a Deo fuisse institutam, ut liberi propagarendum, Scortatio tolleretur et auxilia commodaque humanae vitae inde haberentur'.*

[53] John Finnis, *Aquinas: Moral, Political and Legal Theory* (Oxford, 1998), 98. See *ST*, I–II, q. 94, a 2c and *RLE*, 246.

[54] Peter Martyr Vermigli to the Widow of Martin Bucer, LLS, 115.

marriage taught that there were only two purposes in the union, procreation and the avoiding of fornication. At times the purpose of companionship and mutual aid is mentioned, but this was not the norm. There is no doubt that marriage in the Middle Ages was often thought of as a second class option to celibacy, in part because of the role of sex. Sex within marriage could become sinful if pursued for the sake of lust, or for its own sake. 'Impersonal lust' was to have no part in the legitimate exercise of conjugal rights within marriage.[55] Popes Gregory the Great and Alexander III, in recognizing that fulfillment of the conjugal debt that husband and wife owed each other was not sin, nonetheless, assumed the existence of 'lustful intercourse'. This was intercourse engaged in merely for pleasure and it was a venial sin.[56] Even in his enthusiasm for marriage, William Harrington, an earlier sixteenth century priest, cautioned that though sex within marriage turned an otherwise sinful act into 'no synne', there were 'certayne cases: in whiche sometyme it may be venyall synne and sometyme deedly synne . . .'.[57] Likewise, Cranmer earlier in his career was not so bold about the subject of married love and was even somewhat embarrassed by the subject of sex. In 1531, he seemed 'prudish', asserting that the marriage bed was first to be used for necessity, not pleasure.[58]

Not everyone prior to the Reformation held this view. Some commentators prior to the Reformation saw sex as an important, though not exclusive, part of the creation of a marriage. Many writers discussed the positive role of sex in marriage long before the Reformation. Even St. Thomas Aquinas saw marital intercourse as a virtuous choice that did not need to be motivated by the desire to procreate. One could engage in sex to fulfill the conjugal debt towards the other spouse, but to Aquinas this was not just a matter of duty. Each could seek from the other, faithfulness which was the 'willingness and commitment to belong to, and be united in mind and body with, one's spouse in the form of *societas* or friendship that we call marriage.'[59] James Brundage has shown that there were several

---

[55] Ralph Houlbrooke, *The English Family, 1450–1700* (Oxford, 1984), 102–3.

[56] Elisabeth M. Makowski, 'The conjugal debt and medieval canon law', in Michael M. Sheehan, ed., *Marriage, Family and Law in Medieval Europe* (Toronto, 1997), 129–143, 130–132.

[57] William Harrington, *Commendacions of Matrimonie* (1528), 201.

[58] MacCulloch, *Cranmer*, 58–9.

[59] Finnis, *Aquinas*, 144–5.

examples of writers who celebrated sex within marriage, such as Hugh of St. Victor.[60] However, not until the Reformation was this trend reversed.[61] The reformers made sexual union an important part of marriage, but not just that, it was also about inner spiritual qualities which, as Heinrich Bullinger believed, were the qualities of the mind, character that was fit and honest and showed a virtuous life.[62] This is one of the reasons why *Matrimonium quid sit* is significant, and Martyr's ideas would not have gone unnoticed in this area. Certainly, he would have been well satisfied with the changes in marriage law that the *Reformatio* proposed.[63] However, the issue of parental consent in marriage also provides another area that points to Martyr's thinking as a source for the *Reformatio's* canons on marriage.

The drafters provided a subsection, *Matrimonium sine consensus parentum non valere*, which established parental consent as a necessary hurdle to clear before a couple could enter into a marriage contract. A couple could not contract a valid marriage without consent of the parents or guardian. Any attempt to do so would be futile since the result would be invalid, null and void from its inception by force of this canon. Children could marry only by the 'authority' of their parent or guardian.[64] What was significant about this was the certainty it provided as opposed to the practice that developed from the canon law.

Roman canon law had also held parental consent up as a significant requirement for marriage. However, since marriage was there viewed as a sacrament, it meant that it was the couple, as the ones entering into the sacrament, and their intentions towards each other, that was paramount in determining whether a legitimate marriage contract had been formed. Thus, a couple who promised marriage to each other using words of present intention to marry (*de praesenti*) could overcome a lack of parental consent. Even from the earliest reforms of the eleventh century, the Church emphasized that couples

---

[60] James Brundage, *Law, Sex and Christian Society in Medieval Europe* (Chicago University Press: Chicago, 1987), 194–197.

[61] Ralph Houlbrooke, *English Family*, 98; James Brundage, *Law, Sex and Christian Society*, 552.

[62] Eric J. Carlson, *Marriage and the English Reformation* (Oxford, 1994), 114–115.

[63] Bray, *RLE*, 246.

[64] Ibid., 248–249.

themselves should be free to contract marriage without outside inter-
ference, including parents. Their consent was not necessary in the
final analysis, to form a valid marriage.[65] This meant that marriage,
for all practical purposes, was released from arbitrary parental control, though the ideal of parental consent remained.[66]

The drafters of the *Reformatio* clearly intended to move the ideal
of obtaining parental consent that the canon law had expressed, into
practice. *Matrimonium sine consensus* is included in the section defining
marriage, and is there to strengthen parental or guardian influence.
Parental consent under the *Reformatio's* regulation was a requirement
that, if ignored, would leave a couple with a marriage that was void.
It would have produced the opposite result from the canon law in
that an attempt to marry without parental consent would be illegal
and the union invalid. If a couple tried to create a marriage contract without parental consent, they were automatically entering into
a contract that was void. A couple wishing to contract a valid marriage had no choice but to first win their parents permission, a
process that the drafters believed was consistent with 'Holy Scripture,
godliness and justice.'[67]

Peter Martyr expressed these ideas about parental consent in his
commentaries, most notably those on I Corinthians 7. In them, he
analyzed several passages that related to parental consent and that
mirrored what the drafters had done in the canons. Martyr built his
case from 'Holy Scripture' and demonstrated why parental consent
was necessary to form a valid marriage. He cited passages from
Genesis, Exodus, Numbers, and II Samuel; he also used examples
such as Samson, Adam and Eve, Abraham and Isaac.[68] He argued
that God established marriage in creation, acting in a parental capacity, and arranged marriage for Adam and Eve. He used Abraham
and Isaac, as well, both as examples of a father arranging a marriage for his son. Likewise, Moses was the mediator of God's law,
which directly commands children to honor their father and mother,
establishing, Martyr argues, a duty of honesty and thankfulness towards
parents. *Matrimonium sine consensus* is consistent with Martyr's demon-

---

[65] James Brundage, *Law, Sex and Christian Society*, 183.
[66] Stephen Ozment, *When Father's Ruled: Family Life in Reformation Europe* (Harvard, 1983), 27.
[67] Bray, *RLE*, 249.
[68] LC, 431–432.

stration that the power of the father lay in piety and the duty of obedience to the father extended to all matters not prohibited by God's law, but especially in the area of marriage.

Martyr no doubt, understood the problems associated with Rome's approach to marriage contracts and the issue of parental consent as well, something the *Reformatio's* canon attempts to alleviate. He criticized Rome's application of canon law since it tried to foster the value of parental consent, yet undermined its own intentions by allowing marriages to be considered valid in the absence of that consent. He considered that Rome had reduced parental consent to a matter of honesty rather than one of necessity and had exalted liberty beyond that which Scripture required, ignoring the commands of God. He attacked the fact that while marriage without parental consent may not have conformed to all the legal requirements, it was nonetheless valid, assuming the right words of present consent were used. Church courts were determined to uphold marriages, despite lack of parental consent, if there was evidence that the couple exchanged the words of present consent and this was simply unacceptable to Martyr.[69]

It was this absence of making parental consent a prerequisite condition of marriage that Martyr found unacceptable. He posited that the drafters of the *Copus Iuris Canonici* should have consulted the older canons promulgated closer to the age of the early church. These canons and decrees, he argued, were not 'deceived' or 'corrupt', and they forbade marriages to take place without parental consent. Martyr says that the ancient canons say that marriages made without parental consent were not marriages at all, but '. . . whoredomes, dishonest companings, adulteries and fornicacions.'[70] As in the *Reformatio*, Martyr's position was that parental consent was not merely desirable, but necessary. It is this certainty that all marriages made without parental permission are not marriages. The *Reformatio* provided such a change in law that would have fulfilled all of Martyr's requirement for the use of parental consent. The force of his arguments is not lost on this section. Certainly he is not the only example of a reformer making such arguments, since Martin Bucer, Heinrich Bullinger and Thomas Becon also argued for a greater and more certain role for

---

[69] Ibid., and see Frank Pederson, *Romeo and Juliet of Stonegate: A Medieval Marriage in Crisis* (Borthwick Institute, 87: 1995), 2–8.

[70] Bray, *RLE*, 432.

parental consent in marriage. However, the similarities in his arguments with the text of the *Reformatio* and his proximity to the drafting and editing process cannot be ignored.

Another suggestion of Martyr having influence beyond his edits
has been made by Gerald Bray in a note to the subsection, *De qui
Vetus Testamentum aut totum reiiciun, aut totum exigent,* part of the canon
on heresies. He suggests that denouncing Anabaptists in the canon
on heresy may have been a result of the influence of Peter Martyr
due to his experience with Anabaptists while on the Continent.[71]
The subsection containing the note refers to those who rejected the
books of the Old Testament in the bible and found them to be
inconsistent with the New Testament. The canon specifically mentions Marcion and Valentinus, both of whom were branded as heretics
in the second-century and whom writers like Irenaeus opposed, accusing Marcion, for example, of 'blaspheming the God whom the Law
and the prophets proclaimed.[72] After setting out the nature of the
heresy which was the belief that the 'Old Testament was held to be
absurd, wicked and discordant with the new', the section simply says
that 'many people can be found in our time' who believe this.'[73]
However, the canon then names Anabaptists as a particular group
who believe this.

Certainly Anabaptists had caused no small amount of trouble for
evangelicals on the Continent, witnessing the Germany city of Münster
which came under the influence of radical Anabaptists around 1535.
Since Anabaptists were one cause that united Catholics and evangelicals, a joint expeditionary force of Lutherans and Catholics
marched against that city and unseated the heretics. Martyr certainly
would have not been opposed to silencing these theological ideas,
and perhaps would have agreed with the naming of Anabaptists in
the canon. But it is doubtful that he was either an influence upon,
or participated in the drafting of, this canon. Other sources are more
likely. Cranmer himself had been 'at the forefront of efforts...' to
counter the influence of Anabaptists in England, and this insert may

---

[71] Bray, *RLE,* see *De Haerisibus,* 188–189.
[72] Irenaeus, 'Against the Heresies', in Cyril C. Richardson, ed., *Early Christian
Fathers,* Library of Christian Classics, vol. 1 (Westminster Press: Philadelphia, 1953),
367.
[73] *RLE,* 189.

reflect his own activism against this group as well as Martyr's.[74] The Continental movement against Anabaptists in 1538 was spearheaded by Martin Bucer, who was in England by the 1550's and had been appointed Regius Professor at Cambridge.[75] Perhaps his influence is evident here. Bishop Ridley, another committee member, had exerted great effort to distance his views on the Eucharist from those of the Anabaptists as well.[76] Another possibility, and more likely than Martyr, is that Jan Laski may have had a part to play in this canon. In any case, there was widespread agreement on this issue and its inclusion would have caused Martyr no problem. However, there are others whose influence may have been more direct in this case.

Conclusion

As much of the history surrounding the *Reformatio*, exactly who gave it its shape remains clouded. Harleian MS 426 shows the presence of several hands, most likely those of Cranmer, Vermigli, Haddon and John Foxe. Thus we have, at least direct evidence of Peter Martyr's contribution, and some, such as Cardwell, suggest that Cranmer and Martyr 'took the whole responsibility upon themselves.'[77] However, whether that is true is impossible to say with certainty, since there is no direct evidence of involvement beyond this draft copy. Peter Martyr is the focus of Bishop Burnet's comments on the canons, as he lists him and confirms that he was in Lambeth in March of 1552 working on the *Reformatio*.[78] However, to lay the whole credit at the feet of the Archbishop and Peter Martyr is certainly an exaggeration. Yet, it may not be much of one, since it is clear that Martyr's direct contact with the manuscript is not the full

---

[74] MacCulloch, *Cranmer*, 145–146.

[75] Ibid., 230–232. MacCulloch has also noted that Bucer and Cranmer worked together on a commentary of St. Matthew's gospel in the late 1540's and that part of Cranmer's concern in the project was how the doctrine of predestination and election impacted Baptism, with particular attention given to the issue of infant baptism since, as MacCulloch notes, Cranmer was concerned to oppose Anabaptist doctrine on this issue. Thus, Bucer and Ridley (see note following) seem to be stronger contenders for influence on this section.

[76] MacCulloch, *Cranmer*, 392.

[77] Edward Cardwell, *The Reformation of the Ecclesiastical Laws as attempted in the reigns of King Henry VIII, King Edward VI and Queen Elizabeth I* (Oxford, 1850), viii.

[78] Gilbert Burnet, *The History of the Reformation of the Church of England*, rev. E. Nares (New York, 1842), 208–9.

story of his participation in reforming the canon law. Much of his
'participation' appears to be in his contribution of lectures and theological ideas while he was in England, which were later collected
and published in the *Loci Communes* and other printed works. It would
be wrong to underestimate the significance of his influence in England
in the early 1550's and his position as Regius Professor only adds
to the weight that his opinions would have received among reformers.

Yet, the study of Peter Martyr and his relationship to canon law
reform in England, also gives new light to his genius as a scholar
and the breadth of his learning. His education, which included a
strong scholastic influence, places him in a prime position to edit
the canons since he brought to the project both a theological mind
and the skills of Scriptural exegesis. But, the extent of Martyr's editing on the *Reformatio*, begs the question for this author, did his education include formal legal training and experience as well? Father
John Patrick Donnelly has done extensive study, not only on Martyr's
education and library holdings, but he has also studied the authors
that Martyr cites in his writings.[79]

Father Donnelly's conclusions indicate that Martyr was trained
in the scholastic method, in theology and the Scriptures, but not in
law. However, Martyr refers to at least five prominent lawyers in
his works including Gratian, Boniface VIII and, most notable,
Hostiensis. He cites to the latter three times, the same number of
times as he cites both St. Anselm and St. Bernard, indicating Martyr's
knowledge and understanding of the importance of this canonist.
Further in his handling of the issue of adultery in the *Loci Communes*
he cites both canon and civil law sources no fewer than 200 times.
Thomas Becon, one of Cranmer's chaplains, cited and discussed
Martyr's opinions as support for his own work on the issue of adultery, calling the Regius Professor, 'that precious pearle and marvelous margarite of the christen common weale . . . a man in all
necessary and lettred artes and sciences of singular knowledge.'[80] It
is hard to imagine that among the 'lettred artes and sciences' Becon
refers to, that there was not a concentrated study of or experience

[79] CAS, 15–25 and 178–180.
[80] Thomas Becon, 'The booke of Matrimony' in *The Workes of Thomas Becon* (John
Daye: London, 1564), rev. 1710, fol. 623.

in legal matters, both ecclesiastical and civil. Martyr does not simply understand the texts; he handles them as would a lawyer.

There are, of course, other explanations that might be given for this. It might be suggested that many reformers—one thinks of Marin Bucer as an example—often quoted from the canon law. It was a well known document. Indeed it was not unusual to be versed in canon law in that the *Corpus Iuris Canonici* was a useful source to locate texts dealing with many subjects, as it systematically collected them. Cranmer himself, no lawyer, dealt with many notable legal matters and made his own collection of canons.[81] It may further be suggested that Martyr's administrative experience gave him a disposition to law and that what we are seeing is that disposition as it developed into the 1550's. But, none of these explanations satisfy the reality of the extent of the expertise with which Martyr makes his edits.

Further, it remains that Cranmer had other lawyers, both civil and common, on the drafting committee that he could have called upon to edit sections like *De Praescriptiones* or *De Appellationibus*. Why not use Rowland Taylor who was both LL.D. from Cambridge and an advocate of Doctor's Commons?[82] Or perhaps William May. May spent time as a fellow at Trinity Hall, Cambridge—the premier college for civil lawyers in the sixteenth century, was active as a vicar-general and had direct experience in many facets of ecclesiastical law, and on high profile cases. Why is obviously impossible to answer, yet it is significant that these were choices that Cranmer did not make. He did, instead, allowed Peter Martyr, a theologian, to edit legal material and his edits appear as one would expect from someone skilled in legal practice. He is not simply one predisposed to enjoy playing with the law. Perhaps what this suggests, is that further study about Martyr's career and education remains to be done. What we do know from the evidence in the *Reformatio* is, that Cranmer could have had no better fellow editor alongside him at Lambeth in 1552, and his trust and turning over the work that he did to Martyr, shows his confidence in him.

---

[81] Lambeth MS 1107.

[82] Admitted advocate on 3 Nov. 1539. See G. D. Squibb, *Doctor's Commons: A History of the College of Advocates and Doctor's of Law* (Clarendon: Oxford, 1977), 149.

The Failure of the Project and a Prophecy Fulfilled

Richard Cox, the Vice-Chancellor at Oxford who presided over the disputations, a drafting committee member and good friend of Martyr's, noted in October of 1552 to Heinrich Bullinger, that there was no appetite in England for the severe institutions of Christian discipline . . .'.[83] Though the draft was nearing completion, it was as if Cox had uttered a prophecy—the end of this affair would soon come and it was not a happy one. The fate of the *Reformatio* meant that neither Cranmer nor Martyr had the chance to see Cox proved wrong. A draft beyond the Harleian MS 426 would have been completed by early 1553 and Cranmer submitted it to the government to enact. Instead, the Duke of Northumberland acting as a member of the House of Lords, 'scornfully sabotaged the proposal' and scolded Cranmer in the process.[84] Dudley was probably getting back at Cranmer because of various Court sermons during Lent preached by Ridley and Haddon and others, which had caused a fury with the Privy Council.[85] The result was that England failed to revise its canons and would fail again in 1571, though others would try in vain to resurrect the *Reformatio*. England was destined, at least for the foreseeable future, to remain under the spectre of Rome's ghost in the form of the *Corpus Iuris Canonici*; and its decretals and labyrinthine procedures that Martyr detested, would continue to haunt her ecclesiastical courts for some time to come.

---

[83] Cox to Bullinger, 5 October 1552, *Original Letters*, vol. 1, 123.
[84] MacCulloch, *Cranmer*, 533.
[85] Ibid., 532–535.

PETER MARTYR VERMIGLI AND POPE BONIFACE VIII: THE DIFFERENCE BETWEEN CIVIL AND ECCLESIASTICAL POWER

Torrance Kirby

In his *Commentary on the Two Books of Samuel*, Peter Martyr Vermigli confidently asserts the thesis that "the charge of Religion belongeth unto Princes."[1] He appeals to the authority of Aristotle for whom political association (*koinonia politike*) is the highest form of community (*teleia koinonia*) on the grounds that it aims at the highest happiness and the highest good; the ultimate goal (*telos*) of the *polis* is "to provide that the people may live well and vertuously." And, Vermigli observes, "no greater vertue there is, than Religion."[2] Through this identification of the Christian commonwealth with Aristotle's community of virtue, Vermigli attributes the care of religion to the sovereign power (*to kurion*) which directs the life of the state towards its appointed end. He appeals moreover to Aristotle's claim that government, that is the exercise of sovereign power, is the principal and architectonic art of all practical activity.[3] There is

---

[1] This is the title given to his *scholium* on *I Samuel* 28:3. *In Duos Libros Samuelis Prophetae . . . Commentarii.* (Zurich: C. Froschauer, 1564), cited as SAM. See CP, Book 4.14.2, 246.

[2] Vermigli gives no precise reference, but very likely is referring to the opening discussion in the *Politics* where it is argued that the *polis* is the perfect form of community (*teleia koinonia*) on the grounds that it aims to realise happiness (*eudaimonia*) in the highest degree through the practice of virtue. "If all communities aim at some good, the state or political community, which is the highest of all, and which embraces all the rest, aims at good in a greater degree than any other, and at the highest good." Aristotle, *Politics*, 1.1 (1252a3–6). See also *Pol.* 3.6 (1278b15–24) where "well-being" (*eu zein*) is defined as the "chief end both of individuals and the state."

[3] Aristotle, *Ethics* I.2 (1094a17–1094b10) According to Aristotle, the art (*techne*) which aims at the highest good "is most truly the architectonic art. And politics appears to be of this nature; for it is this that ordains which of the sciences should be studied in a state, and which each class of citizens should learn and up to what point they should learn them . . . now, since politics uses the rest of the sciences, and since, again, it legislates as to what we are to do and what we are to abstain from, the end of this science must include those of the others, so that this end must

indeed a hierarchy of practical "Arts" among which the art of government stands preeminent:

> Wherefore seeing the office of a Magistrate is the chiefe and principall science, he ought to rule all the partes of a commonweale. In deed he himself exerciseth not those [particular] Arts, but yet ought he to see that none doe corrupt and counterfeit them. If a Phisitian cure not according to the prescript of Galen or Hypocrates, or if an Apothecarie sell naughtie and corrupt drugges, the Magistrate ought to correct them both. And if he may doe this in other artes, I see no cause why he may not doe it in Religion.[4]

Vermigli follows up this Aristotelian analysis of the Magistrate's office with a list of Old Testament kings and Roman emperors who "shewed verie well that religion belonged unto their charge."[5] In a letter to Queen Elizabeth on the occasion of her accession to the throne of England in 1558 Vermigli urges her to take command in the reform of the Church since it is the duty of a godly Prince to defend both tables of the "law divine."[6] He interprets the two tables of the decalogue in Deuteronomy as representing the ordering respectively of religion and matters of civil obligation; both are committed to the power of the godly Magistrate. Furthermore, in a paraphrase of Romans 13 Vermigli maintains that the Magistrate is God's own Vicar or representative and for this reason "everie soule ought to be subject unto the higher power."[7]

In his *Commentary on Romans* chapter 13 Vermigli commences the discussion with a formal and thoroughly Aristotelian definition of the subject matter in hand:[8]

---

be the good for man ... though it is worth while to attain the end merely for one man, it is more noble and more godlike (*kallion kai theioteron*) to attain it for a nation or for commonwealths (*poleis*)."

[4] CP 4.14.2, 247. See also Vermigli's Introduction to *In Primum, Secundum, et Initium Tertii Libri Ethicorum Aristotelii ad Nichomachum* (Zurich: C. Froschauer, 1563), translated by J. C. McLelland, *Philosophical Works of Peter Martyr*, Peter Martyr Library, vol. 4 (Kirksville, MO: Sixteenth Century Essays and Studies, 1996), 12, 13.

[5] CP 4.14.2, 247.

[6] CP, vol. 5, 61. See Marvin Anderson, "Royal Idolatry: Peter Martyr and the Reformed Tradition," *Archiv für Reformationsgeschichte*, Jahrgang 69 (1978): 186, 187.

[7] The magistrate stands "in the stead and place of God." CP 4.14.2, 247.

[8] In *Epistolam S. Pauli Apostoli ad Romanos ... Commentarii* (Basel: P. Perna, 1558), cited as ROM. The translation here is mine; see "The Civil Magistrate: Peter Martyr Vermigli's Commentary on Romans 13," in PMRD, 223. See also the *scholium* "*De Magistratu*" which appears at the conclusion of his commentary on

A magistrate is a person elected by God so that laws and peace may
be protected, evil may be repressed by means of penalties and the
sword, and virtue maybe promoted by every means. In this the efficient
cause[9] is God; the final cause or purpose is the protection of the laws
and peace from the troubles associated with vice and corruption as
well as the increase of virtues.[10] The formal cause is the order constituted in human affairs by divine providence. The material cause is
a man, an individual person, since whoever is chosen to be a magistrate is selected from among men.

Emphasis on the divine provenance of the Magistrate's authority is
the keynote of this political segment of the commentary. According
to Vermigli "those who condemn the magistrate are against God to
their own considerable harm."[11] While there are manifold constitutional forms—and here he cites the Aristotelian six-fold classification
of monarchy, aristocracy, and polity along with their corrupt ana-
logues tyranny, oligarchy and democracy[12]—all are divinely sanc-
tioned, for as the Apostle asserts, "there is no power but of God."
Regardless of the manner of the magistrate's selection, whether "done

---

Judges 19, based on lectures given at Strasbourg 1553–56. *In Librum Judicum . . .
Commentarii doctissimi . . .* (Zurich: C. Froschauer, 1561), cited as IUD; CP 4.13, fol.
226–235; the sixteenth-century translation of Anthony Marten is reprinted in Robert
M. Kingdon, *The Political Thought of Peter Martyr Vermigli : Selected Texts and Commentary*,
Travaux d'Humanisme et Renaissance, no. CLXXVIII (Geneva: Droz, 1980). A
magistrate is "a person chosen by the institution of God to keep the laws as touching outward discipline, in punishing of transgressors with punishment of the bodie,
and to defend and make much of the good."

[9] In this formal definition Vermigli employs Aristotle's teaching concerning the
"four causes." See, e.g., *Physics* 2.1 (192b8–193b22) and *Metaphysics* 5.2 (1013a24–
1013b28).

[10] This twofold goal of the magistrate's power is well articulated by Thomas
Cranmer in the intercessory prayer in the Communion Order of the Second Book
of Common Prayer of King Edward VI (1552) which came into force in England
during Peter Martyr's tenure as Regius Professor of Divinity at Oxford: "We beseche
thee also to saue and defende all Christian Kynges, Princes, and Governoures, and
speciallye thy servant, Edward our Kyng, that under hym we maye bee godlye
and quietly governed: and graunt unto hys whole counsayle, and to all that be
putte in aucthoritie under hym, that they may truely and indifferently minister justice, to the punishement of wickednes and vice, and to the mayntenaunce of God's
true religion and vertue." *The First and Second Prayer Books of King Edward VI* (London:
J. M. Dent, 1913), 382.

[11] PMRD, 224.

[12] Aristotle, *Politics*, 3.7 (1279a22–1279b10). See PMRD, 226; see also Robert M.
Kingdon, *The Political Thought of Peter Martyr Vermigli*, 3: "And although the latter
three kinds are extremely corrupt and defective, yet God is the author even of
them. For there is in them a force and power to govern and to coerce men which
certainly could by no means come to be unless by God."

by consent of the Senate, by the voyces of the people, or by the
will of the souldiers, or else by succession of inheritance" these human
forms of political process are all "mere instruments" whereas in fact
"the proper cause of magistrates is God himself."[13] Like the sun and
the moon, the office of the magistrate is ordained by God's providential design.[14] The magistrate is to be acknowledged as the supreme
vicegerent of God on earth since "the Prince is appointed to be in
God's place, *between* GOD and men."[15] This function of the magistrate as *mediator* of divinely ordained governance constitutes a key
axiom in Vermigli's subsequent account of the complex relation
between civil and ecclesiastical power.

While the magistrate's power is defined as deriving from an infinite
divine sanction, the proper sphere of its exercise is nonetheless very
carefully circumscribed. It is restricted specifically to "lawes touching outward discipline" as distinct from those which more directly
concern "the inwarde motions of the minde."[16] By virtue of this thoroughly Augustinian distinction between spiritual and external spheres
of power, Vermigli links his treatment of the authority of the Magistrate
to his basic soteriological assumptions regarding the right relation
between the orders of nature and grace. While there are other kinds
of offices which also depend upon the direct institution of God, they
need not conflict with the appointed function of the Magistrate to
rule in the *forum externum*.

> It is the office of ministers through the Word of God to pearse even
> to the *inward motions of the minde*: because the Holy Ghost joineth his
> power, both to the right preaching of his word, and also to the sacra-
> ments which are ministered in the Church. The magistrate only exer-
> ciseth *outward discipline* and punishment upon transgressors. The minister
> in the name of God, bindeth the guilty and unpenitent, and in his
> name excludeth them from the kingdome of heaven, as long as they
> shall so remaine. The Magistrate punisheth with outwarde punish-
> ments, and when need requireth, useth the sword. Both of them nour-
> ish the godly, but diversely.[17]

Both civil and ecclesiastical jurisdiction serve the "safetie" or nour-
ishment of the people, but this "safetie" is interpreted as intrinsically

---

[13] Kingdon, *The Political Thought of Peter Martyr Vermigli*, 28.
[14] Ibid., 30.
[15] Ibid., 12.
[16] Ibid., 26.
[17] Ibid., 26 (my italics).

twofold, namely as belonging either to the operation of grace and eternal salvation, or to the order of nature and temporal peace. This distinction between spiritual and external jurisdiction recalls Augustine's delineation of the twofold peace of the earthly and heavenly cities.[18]

Vermigli then proceeds to observe that such an identification of the civil magistrate with the divinely ordained "higher power" of Paul's Epistle is challenged by certain "ecclesiasticall men," as he calls them, proponents of papal authority who maintain their exemption from the jurisdiction of the "publike and ordinarie power" of the civil magistrate.[19] Perhaps he has in mind such apologists of the papal *plenitudo potestatis* as Reginald Pole,[20] a contemporary of Vermigli's in Italy before the latter's flight, who addressed himself as follows to King Henry VIII in a pamphlet critical of his claim to headship of the Church in the *Act of Supremacy* of 1534:

> Your whole reasoning comes to the conclusion that you consider the Church a *corpus politicum* ... Great as the distance is between heaven and earth, so great also is the distance between the civil power and the ecclesiastical, and so great the difference between this body of the Church, which is the body of Christ, and that which is the body politic and merely human.[21]

---

[18] On this see, for example, *De Civitate Dei*, XIX. 12–17.

[19] IUD, Kingdon, *The Political Thought of Peter Martyr Vermigli*, 30: "But the Papistes and they which will be called Ecclesiasticall men, will not give eare hereunto: for they cry, that they are exempted from publike and ordinarie powers, whereas yet the Apostle used no exception, when he said, Let every soule be subject to the higher powers." See also CP 4.2.10 & 11, fol. 33–35: "the Clergie and Ecclesiasticall men contend, that they by the benefite of Princes are exempted from tributes and customes." Vermigli cites *Decretales Gregorii IX*, "Non minus" 3.49.4 in *Corpus juris canonici*, edited by Emil Friedberg (Leipzig: B. Tauchnitz, 1879), vol. 2, col. 654, 655; and Boniface VIII's Bull of 1296 "*Clericis Laicos*" under the title *De Immunitate ecclesiarum* in *Liber Sextus decretalium cum Clementinis*, Friedberg, vol. II, cols. 1287, 1288.

[20] Pole was a cousin of Henry VIII, studied in Padua in the 1520s during Vermigli's time there, was created a cardinal by Paul III in 1536, and conferred at the Conference of Ratisbon in 1541 with Gasparo Contarini in a failed attempt to conciliate the Protestants. He was one of three papal legates at the Council of Trent and was consecrated Archbishop of Canterbury in 1556 under Queen Mary. In "Royal Idolatry," 192, Marvin Anderson notes that Vermigli owned a copy of Vergerio's 1555 Strasbourg edition of Reginald Pole's treatise *De Unitate Ecclesiae*.

[21] *Ad Henricum Octavum Britanniæ regem, pro ecclesiasticæ unitatis defensione, libri quatuor* ... (Excussum Romæ: Apud Antonium Bladum Asulanum, 1538); repr. in Juan T. Rocaberti, *Bibliotheca maxima pontificia* (Rome, 1698), XVIII, 204: "Tota tua ratio concludit te Ecclesiam existimare corpus politicum esse quod si ita est: equidem hac in parte crimine malitiae te libero, sed idem perniciosa ignorantia obcaecatum esse dico. Quantum enim distat caelum a terra, tantum inter civilem potestatem, et ecclesiasticam interest: tantum hoc corpus Ecclesiae, quod est corpus Christi, ab

On the ground of his supposition of the inherent superiority of the spiritual to the temporal sword Pole rejects Henry's claim to supreme ecclesiastical jurisdiction over the Church of England. Pole's ecclesiology expresses a fundamentally disparate interpretation of the sense of Romans 13 when compared with Vermigli's. The reformer, however, chooses not to dispute directly with his contemporaries, but rather to examine the arguments for the Papal supremacy set out in early fourteenth-century canon law.[22] While Vermigli cites a variety of sources from the canon law, he undertakes a particularly extensive analysis of the Bull *Unam Sanctum* promulgated by Pope Boniface VIII at the Roman Council of October 1302 during his dispute with Philip the Fair, King of France.[23] This document sets out a series of dogmatic propositions which culminates in the assertion of Papal supremacy. *Unam Sanctum* is remarkable both for succinctness and theological clarity and thus proves to be most useful to Vermigli in his summary of the scholastic rationale for the subordination of temporal to spiritual power.[24]

---

illo, quod est politicum, et mere humanium differt." Translated by E. Kantorowicz, *The King's Two Bodies: A Study in Medieval Political Theology* (Princeton: Princeton University Press, 1957), 229. See also Reginald Pole, *De Summo Pontifice Christi in terris Vicario, eiusque officio & potestate* (Louvain: Apud Ioannem Foulerum Anglum., 1569); facsimile reprint, (Farnborough: Gregg, 1968).

[22] See IUD, "Of a Magistrate, and of the difference betweene Civill and Ecclesiasticall Power," Kingdon 31 ff., CP 4.13.7–9 and 14 ff.; ROM, "The powers that be are ordained of God," Kingdon, 5, 6; SAM, CP 4.3.10 "Whether two heads may be in the Church, one visible and another invisible." For a discussion of Vermigli's use of the *Corpus iuris canonici* see Robert M. Kingdon, *The Political Thought of Peter Martyr Vermigli*, viii & ix.

[23] The Bull was formally issued on 18 November of the same year. The original is no longer in existence; the oldest text is to be found in the registers of Boniface VIII in the Vatican archives, *Reg. Vatic.*, L, fol. 387. There is no doubt of the genuineness of the Bull. *Unam Sanctam* is incorporated under *Extravagantes Decretales Communes*, I.8.1, "De Maioritate et Obedientia" in the *Corpus juris canonici*, edited by Emil Friedberg (Leipzig: B. Tauchnitz, 1879); reprinted (Graz: Akademische Druk-u. Verlagsanstalt, 1955; 1959), vol. 2, col. 1245–46. An English translation of the Bull is available in Brian Tierney, *The Crisis of Church and State, 1050–1300* (Toronto: Toronto University Press, 1988), 188–189; see also Tierney's discussion of the dispute between Boniface and Philip, 180–185. *Unam Sanctam* is available electronically in the *Internet Medieval Sourcebook*, ed. Paul Halsall, <http://www.fordham.edu/halsall/source/b8-unam.html.>

[24] It is now thought likely that the great canonist and theologian Giles of Rome was the chief architect of the text of the Bull. For a discussion of the authorship of the Bull see David Luscombe, "The '*Lex Divinitatis*' in the Bull '*Unam Sanctam*' of Pope Boniface VIII," in C. N. L. Brooke, et al., eds., *Church and Government in*

At the outset of his discussion of the Bull Vermigli remarks that it is "a worlde" (*pretium*) to read the arguments of those "ecclesiasticall men" who seek exemption from the jurisdiction of the Magistrate. While the translator intended to convey the sense of "marvel" or "wonder," there is something appropriate about his use of the term "worlde." For in the Bull's appeal to the hierarchical logic of the "*Lex Divinitatis*" of the sixth-century Christian neoplatonist Pseudo-Dionysius the Areopagite, Boniface VIII formulates a distilled expression of a "political ontology"—indeed of a complete cosmic vision—which is deeply, though as we shall see, not totally at odds with the Augustinian assumptions underpinning Vermigli's own thought. Through his polemical use of the Bull, Vermigli succeeds in elevating the conflict between the traditional scholastic interpretation of Romans 13 and his own reformed reading of the text to the profound level of a theological tension between the two leading traditions of Christian Platonism, viz. the Pseudo-Dionysian and the Augustinian.[25] At the Augustinian pole, emphasis is placed upon the utter incommensurability between the orders of grace and nature. Vermigli, along with the reformers generally, follows Augustine in looking directly to the incarnate Christ to accomplish an *immediate* union of the soul with God by grace alone in a "forensic" justification. Luther, for example, adopts a consciously Augustinian stance in his criticism of the lack of an explicitly christological mediation between the soul and the divine in the Pseudo-Dionysian spirituality.[26] By

---

the Middle Ages (New York: Cambridge University Press, 1976), 215. Aegidius Romanus or Giles of Rome, Archbishop of Bourges (1243–1316), was the author of *De ecclesiastica potestate* (*On Ecclesiastical Power*), edited and translated by Arthur P. Monahan, Texts and Studies in Religion, vol. 41 (Lewiston/Queenston/Lampeter: The Edwin Mellen Press, 1990); there is another recent translation by R. W. Dyson (Woodbridge, Suffolk: Boydell Press, 1986). Giles, known as *doctor verbosus*, presents here a considerably extended version of the argument of the Bull; he also dedicated the treatise to Boniface.

[25] For a particularly helpful discussion of the historical interplay between the political theologies of Augustine and Pseudo-Dionysius, see Wayne J. Hankey, "'Dionysius dixit, lex divinitatis est ultima per media reducere:' Aquinas, Hierocracy and the 'Augustinisme Politique'," *Medioevo* XVIII (1992), 119–150 and *idem* "Augustinian Immediacy and Dionysian Mediation in John Colet, Edmund Spenser, Richard Hooker and the Cardinal de Bérulle," in Dominique de Courcelles, ed., *Augustinus in der Neuzeit* (Turnhout: Brepols, 1998), 125–132, 159, 160. See also Louis Dupré, *Passage to Modernity: an Essay in the Hermeneutics of Nature and Culture* (New Haven: Yale University Press, 1993) 167–189.

[26] Paul Rorem, *Pseudo-Dionysius: A Commentary on the Texts and an Introduction to their Influence* (Oxford: Oxford University Press, 1993), 126, 220. Luther notes that there

contrast, at the pole of Pseudo-Dionysian spirituality, the orders of
grace and nature constitute a contiguous, ascending hierarchy wherein
the soul's approach to God is accomplished by a graduated process
of *mediation*. Consistent with this latter approach, the hierarchical
mediation of certain communal, liturgical and sacramental functions
is deemed necessary in the "transformational process" of salvation.[27]
The tension between these two great theological traditions of Christian
Platonism lies at the very heart of Vermigli's critique of the fourteenth-century canonists' interpretation of Romans 13 and, by extension, of the hermeneutic embodied in the ecclesiology of the Council
of Trent.

Unam Sanctum, as the Bull's title suggests, is concerned chiefly with
the unity of the Church.[28] To this end Boniface propounds the doctrine of the papal plenitude of power (*plenitudo potestatis*) and consequently upholds first and foremost the subordination of temporal to
spiritual jurisdiction:

> For according to the Blessed Dionysius, it is the law of divinity (*lex
> divinitatis*) that the lowest things are led to the highest by intermedi-
> aries. Then, according to the order of the universe, all things are not
> led back equally and immediately, but the lowest by the intermediary,
> and the inferior by the superior . . . Therefore if the terrestrial power
> err, it will be judged by the spiritual power.[29]

---

is only minimal reference by the Pseudo-Dionysius to the mediatorial role of Christ
in human salvation and an almost total absence of reference to Christ crucified.

[27] See, e.g., Pius IV, *The Tridentine Creed* (1564), translated in Martin D. W. Jones,
The Counter Reformation: Religion and Society in Early Modern Europe (Cambridge: Cambridge
University Press, 1995), 70; text may be found at <http://www.newadvent.org/
fathers/0808.htm>.

[28] The reference is to the Nicene Creed: "et [credo] in *unam sanctam* catholicam
et apostolicam ecclesiam."

[29] *Corpus iuris canonici*, ed. Friedberg, II, col. 1245–46: "One sword ought to be
subordinated to the other, and temporal authority subjected to spiritual power. For,
since the Apostle said: 'There is no power except from God and those that are,
are ordained of God' [Rom 13:1–2], they would not be ordained if one sword were
not subordinated to the other and if the inferior one, as it were, were not led
upwards by the other. For according to the Blessed Dionysius, it is the law of divinity that the lowest things are led to the highest by intermediaries. Then, according
to the order of the universe, all things are not led back equally and immediately,
but the lowest by the intermediary, and the inferior by the superior . . . Therefore
if the terrestrial power err, it will be judged by the spiritual power; but if a minor
spiritual power err, it will be judged by a superior spiritual power; but if the highest power of all err, it can be judged only by God, and not by man . . . This authority is not human but rather divine, granted to Peter by a divine word and reaffirmed
to him and his successors . . . Therefore whoever resists this power thus ordained
by God, resists the ordinance of God [Rom 13: 2], unless he invent like Manicheus

The document epitomizes the scholastic interpretation of the Gelasian ecclesiology of the "two swords" as shaped by Hugh of St. Victor, Bernard of Clairvaux, Albertus Magnus, St. Bonaventure and Thomas Aquinas, all of whom were deeply influenced by the Pseudo-Dionysian spiritual and theological tradition.[30] In Vermigli's summary of this alternative exposition of Romans 13, the ecclesiology of the Bull is reduced to a single, straightforward syllogism:[31] all power is ordained by God; all powers are hierarchically ordered with respect to one another according to the *lex divinitatis*; therefore, given Christ's affirmation in the gospel of the sufficiency of the two swords,[32] the spiritual sword must by necessity regulate the temporal.[33] The syllogism thus hangs on the interpretation of the precise manner of divine ordination, that is *how* exactly the higher powers are "ordained of God." According to Giles of Rome, the putative architect of the *Unam Sanctam*, "if the lower things were brought to the highest in the same way an intermediary is, there would be no right order in the universe."[34] On this account, the temporal authority cannot claim an "immediate" relation to the divine source of power without

---

two beginnings . . ." See Tierney, *Counter Reformation: Religion and Society in Early Modern Europe*, 188, 189. David Luscombe notes the close similarity between the logic employed here and the argument put forward by Giles of Rome in his treatise on ecclesiastical power, "Lex divinitatis in Unam Sanctam," 206, 215–217. See also Giles of Rome, *De ecclesiastica potestate*, I.4, 17–20 and Arthur Monahan's introduction, xxvii.

[30] Luscombe, "Lex divinitatis in Unam Sanctam," 208–217. Hugh of St. Victor, *On the Sacraments of the Christian Faith*, trans. Roy J. Deferrari (Cambridge, Mass.: Medieval Academy of America, 1951), 2.2.4–7, 256–258 and *idem, Commentariorum in Hierarchiam Coelestem S. Dionysii Areopagite, Patrologia Latina*, 175, 1099. Bernard of Clairvaux, *Five Books on Consideration: Advice to a Pope*, transl. J. D. Anderson and Elizabeth T. Kennan (Kalamazoo: Cistercian Publications, 1976). See "Super Dionysium de caelesti hierarchia" in Albertus Magnus, *Opera omnia* (Monasterii Westfalorum: In Aedibus Aschendorff, 1951–), t. 36, pars 1. For Aquinas's formulation of the *lex divinitatis* see *Summa Theologica* IIa, IIae Q. 172, art. 2. See also Monahan's introduction to Giles of Rome, *De Ecclesiastica Potestate*, ix–xxvii.

[31] J. Rivière, *Le problème de l'église et de l'état au temps de Philippe le Bel: Étude de théologie positive*. Spicilegium Sacrum Lovaniense, VIII (Paris: E. Champion, 1926), 396.

[32] Luke 22:38.

[33] In a series of important monographs Walter Ullmann has designated this the "descending theme" in medieval discourse on ecclesiastical power. See *Principles of Government and Politics in the Middle Ages*, 3rd ed. (New York: Methuen, 1974); see also Walter Ullmann, *Law and Politics in the Middle Ages: an Introduction to the Sources of Medieval Political Ideas* (Ithaca, NY: Cornell University press, 1975), 30 ff.

[34] *De Ecclesiastica potestate*, I.4, transl. Monahan, 18.

violating the "order of the universe," for according to the *lex divini-tatis* the due subordination of the lower things to the highest is noth-ing less than a cosmic law. For Vermigli, however, who follows a distinctly Augustinian logic, the first principle of order does not con-sist primarily in a gradual, hierarchical mediation but rather in a simple, binary distinction between two principal species of subjec-tion, namely the political/external and the spiritual/internal. Unlike Boniface's appeal to a subordination of the temporal to the spiritual power according to the *lex divinitatis*, Vermigli's two species of power cannot be ordered hierarchically, as remarked previously, owing to their incommensurability. Thus there are simply "two subjections," one civil and the other spiritual.

According to Boniface, however, such an assertion of the incom-mensurability of the two swords risks the charge of Gnostic dualism. The papal plenitude of power "is not human but rather divine, granted to Peter by a divine word and reaffirmed to him and his successors . . . Therefore whoever resists this power thus ordained by God, resists the ordinance of God [Rom 13:2], unless he invent like Manicheus two beginnings . . ."[35] On the one hand, it might appear, at least superficially, that Vermigli's Augustinian insistence upon the incommensurability of the "two subjections" has led him precisely into the Manichean dualism envisaged by Boniface. On the other hand, however, Vermigli's ascription of ecclesiastical supremacy to the Magistrate appears to conflate the civil and ecclesiastical power and thus to raise the contrary logical difficulty. Both his first prin-ciples and his practical conclusions take issue with the hierarchical logic of the *lex divinitatis* as interpreted in *Unam Sanctum*.

How, then, in the light of these difficulties, does Vermigli inter-pret the alternative Augustinian dialectic of the "two subjections?" He argues that princes are to be called not only "Deacons or Ministers of God, but also Pastors" of the people.[36] As pastors the magistrates have the care of holy things. On the basis of this claim alone it would seem that the inversion of the Bull's logic is complete; the Prince is divinely appointed to the office of Supreme Hierarch, that is the Magistrate whose highest care is for the souls of his subjects:

[35] *Unam Sanctam*, Friedberg, vol. 2, col. 1246.
[36] Kingdon, *The Political Thought of Peter Martyr Vermigli*, 27. See Anderson, "Royal Idolatry," 171.

"For we doe not imagine that a Prince is a Neteheard [cowherd] or Swineheard, to whom is committed a care onlie of the fleshe, bellie, and skinne of his subjectes, yea rather he must provide that they may live vertuouslie and godlie."[37] As we have seen, according to Vermigli's Aristotelian understanding of the commonwealth as the community of virtue (*teleia koinonia*), the promotion of "true religion" is the magistrate's highest care. Where in this argument is the Augustinian distinction between the "two subjections?" In making his case Vermigli both complicates and clarifies the question by arguing for a *mutual* subjection of civil and spiritual jurisdiction:

> The civill power ought to be subject to the word of God which is preached by the Ministers. But in lyke manner the Ecclesiasticall power is subject unto the civill, when the ministers behave themselves ill, either in things humane, or things Ecclesiasticall. For these powers are after a sort interchangeable, and sundrie wayes are occupied about the selfesame things, and mutuallie helpe one another . . . *The Ecclesiasticall power, is subject unto the Magistrate, not by a spirituall subjection but by a politicke.* For as touching the Sacraments and Sermons, it is not subject unto it, because the Magistrate may not alter the word of God, or the Sacramentes which the Minister useth. Neither can he compel the Pastors and teachers of the church to teach otherwise, or in any other sort to administer the Sacraments, than is prescribed by the word of God. Howbeit Ministers in that they be men and Citizens, are without all doubt subject together with their landes, riches, and possessions unto the Magistrate.[38]

Preservation of the right distinction between "spiritual subjection" and "political subjection" demands recognition of the inherently equivocal nature of ecclesiastical power. To the extent that ecclesiastical jurisdiction is involved in the "lawes touching outwarde discipline" it is properly subordinated to the rule of the Civil Magistrate. At the same time, the Magistrate is bound to submit to the jurisdiction of that aspect of ecclesiastical power which is exercised in matters concerning "the inwarde motions of the minde."[39] Thus in

---

[37] Kingdon, *The Political Thought of Peter Martyr Vermigli*, 34.

[38] Ibid., 35, my italics.

[39] Ibid., 26. In the exercise of spiritual jurisdiction, Christ alone is Supreme Hierarch: "For he is our King . . . [who] is now gone up into heaven, yet doeth governe this kingdome of his, indeed not with a visible presence, but by the spirit and word of the holie scriptures." CP 4, 60. See Anderson, "Royal Idolatry," 163.

the internal and invisible realm of the *civitas Dei*, power is immediately derived from the divine source without the mediation of the
magistrate; in the external and visible realm of the *civitas terrena*, on
the other hand, civil and ecclesiastical jurisdiction are united in the
Prince or magistrate. This distinction between two species of ecclesiastical subjection reveals how Vermigli is able both to overthrow
and to retain the logic of hierarchical mediation. Closely following
Augustine he upholds christocentric *immediacy* in the relation between
soul and God in the internal sphere of "spiritual subjection." In the
external sphere of "politike subjection," however, the logic of hierarchical mediation continues to lend stability to the institutions of
the Christian commonwealth. According to Vermigli, bishops, doctors, elders and other ecclesiastical rulers are subject to the architectonic correction of the sovereign power "as when David, Joas,
Hezekiah and Josiah reformed the religion and priestes."[40] Those
"ecclesiasticall men" who deny the supremacy of the magistrate in
ecclesiastical matters:

> still dreame of one civill power that is Ecclesiasticall, and of an other
> that is profane. The one of the which they attribute unto the Pope,
> and the other unto the Magistrate: but all in vaine: for as much as
> pertaineth unto Ecclesiasticall power, the civill Magistrate is sufficient.
> For he, as saith Aristotle, in his Politikes, must provide, that all men
> doe their duetie: both laiers, phisitians, husbandmen, Apothecaries:
> among whom we may also recken minister and preachers . . . For the
> church hath Elders, who must provide in what order all things ought
> to be doone, and that all things be in order the Magistrate ought to
> provide.[41]

Vermigli's overriding concern in his rejection of the traditional exemp-
tions of the clergy is unity and order in the commonwealth which
comprises "all sorts and conditions of men." Hierarchy is to be maintained, therefore, not as a principle governing the relation *between*
the spiritual and temporal realms, but rather as the means for secur-
ing the stability and unity of all matters concerning "outward discipline." Thus Vermigli rejects Reginald Pole's claim that civil and
ecclesiastical power are as far distant from one another as heaven

---

[40] CP 4, 61.
[41] SAM, I. Sam. 8.7, "Whether two heads may be in the Church, one visible
and another invisible." CP 4.3.5, fol. 38; compare 4.13.7.

and earth and, in his *Commentary on Samuel*, observes that the title of headship claimed by King Henry VIII in relation to the Church of England is indeed justified.[42]

What conclusions, then, may we draw from this inquiry? First of all—and most remarkably—the uniting of civil and ecclesiastical juris-diction in the person of the Civil Magistrate becomes for Vermigli the very instrument whereby the binary Augustinian distinction between the "two kindes of subjection" is finally and safely secured. Indeed the clear distinction between the orders of Grace and Nature reflected in Vermigli's own reformed soteriology appears to lead him to this formulation of the constitutional arrangement of civil and ecclesiastical power. In this argument there is, moreover, a remark-able conjunction of Aristotelian and Augustinian political theory. Through Vermigli's Augustinian critique of the Dionysian *lex divini-tatis* as interpreted in the Bull *Unam Sanctum*, ecclesiastical power is rendered simultaneously both more radically spiritual *and* more human and worldly: the power exercised by ministers through the Word in the "inward motions of the minde" is sharply distinguished from that wielded by the Magistrate through the sword in matters of "outward discipline."[43] Conversely, civil power has become sacralised, chiefly owing to its unmediated link with the divine fount of power. And while Boniface VIII's interpretation of the Dionysian *lex divinitatis* has been repudiated, the hierarchical principle itself has nonetheless been reconfirmed in a secular guise. Indeed, owing to Vermigli's adher-ence to the Aristotelian conception of the architectonic function of political power, the logic of hierarchical mediation is reaffirmed by him as essential to the stable ordering of external political commu-nity, both civil and ecclesiastical. It is the hierarchical principle itself which demands the subordination of ecclesiastical persons to the rul-ing authority of the Civil Magistrate in all matters which touch "out-ward discipline." In his interpretation of Romans 13 Vermigli's Augustinian christocentrism is normative in shaping his rejection of

---

[42] "And this perhaps is it, why the king of England would be called head of his own Church next unto Christ. For he thought that that power which the Pope usurped to himselfe was his, and in his owne kingdome pertained to himselfe. The title indeed was unwonted and displeased manie godlie men: howbeit if we con-sider the thing it selfe, he meant nothing else but that which we have now said." CP 4.3.6, fol. 38. See note 21 above.

[43] Kingdon, *The Political Thought of Peter Martyr Vermigli*, 26.

the hierarchical mediation between the orders of nature and grace, between the realms of the "two subjections." At the same time, however, within the order of nature, that is within the external, temporal realm of political existence, the hierarchical rule that the lower is led back to the higher through the intermediate power continues to hold. In the realm of "the inwarde motions of the minde," however, "Christ alone is given to be head of the Church for the Church is a celestial, divine, and spirituall bodie; . . . for regeneration and remission of sinnes doe flowe from the spirite of Christ and not from man. . . . So that everie sense and moving of the church floweth from Christ alone, not from any mortall man."[44] In the realm of "politike subjection," on the other hand, the magistrate assumes the role of Supreme Hierarch, the very *"lex animata"* who gives life and orderly motion to the manifold members of the body politic:

> And kings maie be called the heads of the Commonweale . . . For even as from the head is derived all the sense and motion into the bodie, so the senses by good lawes, and motions, by edictes and commandements are derived from the prince unto the people. And this strength exceedeth not the naturall power. . . For vertue springeth of frequented Actions. So when as princes by lawes and edictes drive their subiects unto actions, they also drive them unto vertues. But the spirit of God and regeneration are not attained by manie actions, but onelie by the blessings of God.[45]

Thus Vermigli's rejection of the hierarchical *lex divinitatis* is best understood as qualified. By this argument, the goals of unity, order and peace pursued by Boniface VIII by means of the assertion of the papal plenitude of power are sought equally by Vermigli in the Christian commonwealth, albeit through the due subordination of all subjects, in all matters civil and ecclesiastical, to the supreme Magistrate. In this way the *lex divinitatis* is reinterpreted within an Augustinian and Aristotelian framework as a key stabilising principle in early-modern, secular political life.

---

[44] CP 4.3.2, fol. 36.
[45] CP 4.3.1, 2 fols. 35, 36.

NOTES ON CONTRIBUTORS

Scott Amos, Ph.D., University of St. Andrews (Scotland), is Assistant Professor of History at Lynchburg College, Lynchburg, Virginia. He is the co-editor with Andrew Pettegree and Henk van Nierop of *The Education of a Christian Society: Humanism and the Reformation in Britain and the Netherlands* (Ashgate, 1999). His research interests are in pre-modern biblical interpretation and especially the thought of the reformer, Martin Bucer.

Emidio Campi, Ph.D., University of Zürich, is Director of the Institut für Schweizerische Reformationsgeschichte, Professor of Reformation History at the University of Zürich, Switzerland and the general editor of the Bullinger project. Among his many publications, he has served as editor of *Heinrich Bullinger und seine Zeit. Eine Vorlesungsreihe* (Zürich, 2004) and as co-editor with Frank A. James III and Peter Opitz of *Peter Martyr Vermigli: Humanism, Republicanism, Reformation* (Geneva, 2002).

John Patrick Donnelly, S.J., received his Ph.D. from the University of Wisconsin/Madison and is Professor of History at Marquette University, Milwaukee, Wisconsin. His research has centered mainly on His the author of *Calvinism and Scholasticism: Vermigli's Doctrine of Man and Grace* (Brill 1976) and *Ignatius Loyola: Founder of the Jesuits* (Library of World Biography, 2003). He is a leading authority on Loyola and Peter Martyr Vermigli and serves as a General Editor of the Peter Martyr Library.

John L. Farthing, Ph.D., Duke University, is Professor of Religion and Classical Languages at Hendrix College, Conway, Arkansas. His publications include *Thomas Aquinas and Gabriel Biel: Interpretations of St. Thomas in German Nominalism on the Eve of the Reformation* (Duke University Press, 1988). He is a leading expert on the theology of Jerome Zanchi.

Donald Fuller, M.Div., Princeton Theological Seminary and M.B.A., University of Chicago, is President of Ad Fontes, LLC, Orlando,

Florida and a free lance scholar with a special research interest in Peter Martyr Vermigli.

Richard C. Gamble, Dr. Theol., University of Basel, is Professor of Systematic Theology at Reformed Theological Seminary/Orlando. He is the editor of the 14 volume Encyclopedia, *Articles on Calvin and Calvinism* (Garland, 1992) and is past president of the Calvin Studies Society.

John F. Jackson, J.D., Capital University and D.Phil., Oxford University, is Curate in the parish of Kidlington, Oxfordshire. Before entering Church of England orders, he was Professor of Law at Capital University. His doctoral dissertation is on He has published both in the field of law and theology.

Frank A. James III, D.Phil. in History, Oxford University and Ph.D. in Theology, Westminster Theological Seminary, is President and Professor of Historical Theology at Reformed Theological Seminary/Orlando. He has published extensively on the Reformation, including *Peter Martyr Vermigli and Predestination* (Oxford University Press, 1998) and co editor with Heiko A. Oberman, *Via Augustini: Augustine in the Later Middle Ages, Renaissance and Reformation* (Brill, 1992). His also a General Editor of the Peter Martyr Library.

Gary Jenkins, Ph.D., Temple University, is Professor of History at Templeton Honors College, Eastern University, St. David's, Pennsylvania. He is the author of *The Life and Times of Bishop John Jewel*, (St. Andrews University Press, forthcoming 2004) and is a leading expert on the English Reformation.

W. J. Torrance Kirby, D.Phil., Oxford University, is Professor of Church History at McGill University, Montreal, Canada. He is a widely recognized scholar on Richard Hooker. He authored *Richard Hooker's Doctrine of the Royal Supremacy* (Brill, 1990) and edited, *Richard Hooker and the English Reformation*, (London and Dordrecht, 2003.)

Norman Klassen, D.Phil., Oxford University, is Associate Professor of English at Trinity Western University, Langley, British Columbia, Canada. His area of expertise is medieval literature and Christian Humanism. His book, *Chaucer on Love, Knowledge and Sight* was published by Brewer in 1995.

Peter A. Lillback, Ph.D., Westminster Theological Seminary, is Senior Pastor of Proclamation Presbyterian Church in Bryn Mawr, Pennsylvania and adjunct Professor of Historical Theology at Westminster Theological Seminary in Philadelphia. His is the author of *The Binding of God: Calvin's Role in the Development of Covenant Theology* (Baker, 2001).

Joseph C. McLelland, Ph.D., New College, Edinburgh, is Professor Emeritus Professor of History and Philosophy of Religion and Christian Ethics at McGill University and The Presbyterian College, Montreal, Canada. He is the author of many works including *The Visible Words of God: An Exposition of the Sacramental Theology of Peter Martyr Vermigli* (Edinburgh, 1957) and (as editor) *Peter Martyr Vermigli and Italian Reform* (Wilfrid Laurier University Press, 1980). He is a General Editor of the Peter Martyr Library.

Douglas H. Shantz, Ph.D., University of Waterloo, Ontario, is Chairman of the Department of Religious Studies and Associate Professor of Christian Thought at the University of Calgary in Calgary, Alberta, Canada. He is the author of *Crautwald and Erasmus: A Study in Humanism and Radical Reform in Sixteenth Century Silesia* (Valentin Koerner, 1992).

Daniel Shute, Ph.D., McGill University, is Director of the Library and adjunct Professor of History at the Presbyterian College at McGill University in Montreal, Canada. He is the editor and translator of Vermigli's *Commentary on the Lamentations of the Prophet of Jeremiah*, vol. 6 in the Peter Martyr Library. His special interest is the Rabbinic sources of Vermigli's exegesis.

John Thompson, Ph.D., Duke University, is Professor of Historical Theology at Fuller Theological Seminary in Pasadena, California. His research has concentrated principally on gender issues and the history of interpretation in the Reformation, especially John Calvin. He is the author of *Writing the Wrongs: Women of the Old Testament among Biblical Commentators from Philo through the Reformation* (Oxford University Press, 2001).

BIBLIOGRAPHY

Primary Sources

Aquinas, Thomas. *Expositio in Onmes S. Pauli Epistolas*, "Ad Romanos" Section 2 and 4, *Opera Omnia*. New York: Musurgia, 1949.
——. *Summa Theologica*. Blackfriars edition. New York: Macraw Hill Book Company, 1963.
Becon, Thomas. *The Workes of Thomas Becon*. John Daye: London, 1564.
Bernard of Clairvaux, *Five Books on Consideration: Advice to a Pope*, (trans.) J. D. Anderson and Elizabeth T. Kennan. Kalamazoo: Cistercian Publications, 1976.
Beveridge, Henry and Bonnet, Jules (eds.) *Selected Works of John Calvin: Tracts and Letters*. Grand Rapids, Mich., 1983.
Brenz, Johannes. *De personali unione duarum naturarum in Christo, . . . Patris*. Tübingen 1561.
Bucer, Martin. *Enarrationes Epistolae D. Pauli ad Romanos*. Basil, 1562.
Calvin, John. *Calvini Opera Selecta*, (eds.) Peter Barth and Wilhelm Niesel, 5 vols. Munich, 1926–36.
——. *Christ the End of the Law, Being the Preface to the Geneva Bible of 1550*. Thoman Weeden (trans.) London: Henry George Collins, 1848.
——. *Commentaries on the Twelve Minor Prophets*, trans. [and ed.] John Owen, V., *Zechariah and Malachi* (Edinburgh: Calvin Translation Society, 1846–1849.
——. *Commentarius in epistolam Pauli ad Romanos*. T. H. L. Parker, D. C. Parker (eds.) Geneva: Droz, 1999.
——. *Commentary on Genesis*. Calvin Translation Society. Grand Rapids: Baker Book House, 1979.
——. *De vitandis superstitionibus . . . excusatio ad Pseudonicodemos . . .* Geneva: J. Girard, 1549.
——. *Dilucida explicatio sanae doctrinae de vera participatione carnis et sanguinis Christi in sacra coena ad discutiendas Hehusii nebulas*. Geneva, 1561.
——. *Ioannis Calvini Opera Quae Supersunt Omnia*, G. Baum, E. Cunitz and E. Reuss (eds.) in *Corpus Reformatorum*, vol. XXXXIII. Brunsvigae: C. A. Schwetschke et Filium, 1876.
——. *Tractatus Theologici Omnes*, Tom. VII. Amstelodami, Apud J. Schipper, 1667.
Cartwright, Thomas. *A replye to an answere made of M. Doctor Whitegifte againste the admonition to the Parliament*. 1573.
Cranmer, Thomas. *Answer to a Craftie and Sophisticall Cavillation* (London, 1553).
——. *Defense of the True and Catholike Doctrine of the Sacrament*. London, 1550.
Crowley, Robert. *A briefe discourse against the outward apparell and Ministring Garmentes of the Popishe Church*. 1566.
"De Maioritate et Obedientia" in the *Corpus Iuris Canonici*, edited by Emil Friedberg. Leipzig: B. Tauchnitz, 1879; reprinted, Graz: Akademische Druk-u. Verlagsanstalt, 1955; 1959.
Early Christian Fathers, Library of Christian Classics. Westminster Press: Philadelphia, 1953.
Epistolae Tigurniae: De Rebus Potissimum Ad Ecclesiae Anlicanae Reformationem Pertinentibus Conscriptae, A.D. 131–1558. The Parker Society. Cambridge: Cambridge University Press, 1847.
Fisher, Edward. *The marrow of modern divinity: touching both the covenant of works, and the*

covenant of grace, with their use and end, both in the time of the Old Testament, and in the time of the New etc. London: Printed by R. Leybourn; 2nd ed. 1646.

Gardiner, Stephen. *Confutatio Cavillationum, quibus sacrosanctum.* Paris, 1551.

Gillespie, George. *A dispute against the English-popish ceremonies, obtruded upon the Church of Scotland.* Leiden: Printed by W. Christiaens, 1637.

———. *A treatise of miscellany questions: wherein many usefull questions and cases of conscience are discussed and resolved.* Edinburgh: Printed by Gedeon Lithgovv, 1649.

Harding, Thomas, *A Reiondre to M. Iewels Replie.* Antwerp: Ioannis Fouleri, 1566.

Hesshusen, Tileman. *De praesentia Corporis Christi in Coena Domini contra Sacramentarious.* Jena, 1560.

Hugh of St. Victor, *On the Sacraments of the Christian Faith.* Roy J. Deferrari (trans.) Cambridge: Medieval Academy of America, 1951.

Jewel, John. *An Apology of the Church of England.* J. E. Booty (trans.) Ithaca: Cornell University Press, 1963.

———. *The Works of John Jewel.* J. Ayre (ed.), 4 vols. The Parker Society. Cambridge: Cambridge University Press, 1845–50.

Ker, Neil. "The Library of John Jewel," *The Bodleian Library Record,* IX no. 5 (1977).

Lambert, François. *Commentarii de propehtia, eruditione atque linguis, deque litera et spiritu.* Strasbourg, 1526.

Luther, Martin. *D. Martin Luthers Werke. Kritische Gesamtausgabe.* J. C. F. Knaake, et al. Weimar: Hermann Bohlaus Nachfolger.

———. *Luther's Works: American Edition.* Jaraslov Pelikan and Helmut T. Lehmann (eds.) Philadelphia: Fortress Press; St. Louis: Concordia.

Melanchthon, Phillip. "De Ecclesia et de Autoritate Verbi Dei Philippo Melanthone Auctore," in H. E. Bindseil, ed., *Corpus Reformatorum,* vol. 23. Halis Saxonum: C. A. Schwetscke et Filium, 1855.

Milton, John. *The tenure of kings and magistrates: proving that it is lawfull . . . to call to account a tyrant . . . and . . . to depose and put him to death etc.* London, 1649; second edition, 1650.

———. *Tetrachordon: expositions upon the foure chief places in Scripture, which treat of mariage, or nullities in mariage: Wherin The doctrine and discipline of divorce, as was lately publish'd, is confirm'd by explanation of Scripture, by testimony of ancient fathers, of civill lawes in the primitive church, of famousest reformed divines, and lastly, by an intended act of the Parlament and Church of England in the last yeare of Edvvard the Sixth.* London, 1645.

Owen, John. *Commentaries on the Epistle of Paul to the Romans,* ed. John Owen. Edinburgh: Calvin Translation Society, 1848.

Parker, Matthew. *Parker's Correspondence.* Cambridge: Cambridge University Press, 1853.

Pole, Reginald. *Ad Henricum Octavum Britanniæ regem, pro ecclesiasticæ unitatis defensione, libri quatuor . . .* Excussum. Romæ: Apud Antonium Bladum Asulanum, 1538; reprint in Juan T. Rocaberti, *Bibliotheca maxima pontificia.* Rome, 1698.

———. *De Summo Pontifice Christi in terris Vicario, eiusque officio & potestate.* Louvain: Apud Ioannem Foulerum Anglum, 1569; facsimile reprint, Farnborough: Gregg, 1968.

Pollet, J. V. (ed.) *Martin Bucer: Etudes sur la correspondance,* 2 vols. Paris: Presses Universitaires, 1958–62.

Reinolds, John. *A Letter of D. Reinolds to his Friend Concerning his Advice for the Studie of Divinitie.* London, Iohn Beale, for Ionas Man. 1613.

Robinson, Hastings (ed.) *Epistolae Tiguinae de rebus potissimum ad Ecclesiae Anglicanae Reformationem Pertientibus conscriptae.* Cambridge: Parker Society, 1848.

Rorem, Paul. *Pseudo-Dionysius: A Commentary on the Texts and an Introduction to their Influence.* Oxford: Oxford University Press, 1993.

Schaff, Phillip. *Creeds of Christendom, With History and Critical Notes.* Grand Rapids: Baker, 1977.

Simler, Josiah. *Oratio de vita et obitu viri optimi, praestantissmi Theologi D. Petri Martyris Vermilii, Sacrarum literarum in schola Tigurina Professsoris*. Zurich, 1563.

Sparke, Thomas. *A Brotherly Perswasion to Unitie and Uniformitie in Iudgement and Practise touching the Received and present Ecclesiastical gouerment, and the authorized rites and ceremonies of the Church of England*. London: Nicolas Okes, 1607.

The First and Second Prayer Books of Edward VI. The Prayer Book Society. London, 3rd ed., 1999.

The Prayer-Book of Queen Elizabeth, 1559. The Ancient and Modern Library of Theological Literature. Griffith, Farran, Okedent, Welsh, London: 1890.

The Second Prayer Book of King Edward VI, 1552. The Ancient and Modern Library of Theological Literature. Griffith, Farran, Okedent, Welsh, London: 1891.

The Zurich Letters. (ed.) Hastings Robinson, 4 vols. in 2. The Parker Society. Cambridge: Cambridge University Press, 1842–5.

Turner, William. *The huntyrs and fynders out fo the romishe fox* (Bonn, 1543).

Vermigli, Peter Martyr. *Brevis Epitome (sive Analysis) disputationis de Eucharistia in Gardinerum*. Zurich, 1561.

——. *Christian Prayers and Holy Meditations as Well for Private as Public Exercise*. London, 1569; reprint, Cambridge 1842.

——. *Commonplaces*. London: John Day, 1583.

——. *Defensio Doctrinae veteris & Aposolicae de Sacrsancto Eucharistiae Sacramento . . . Adersus Stephani Gardineri . . .* Zurich, 1559.

——. *Dialogue on the Two Natures in Christ*, ed. and tr. J. P. Donnelly. Peter Martyr Library, 2. Kirksville, 1995.

——. *Dialogus de utraque in Christo natura*. Zurich, 1561.

——. *Epistolae duae, ad Ecclesias Polonicas, Iesu Christ . . . de negotio Stancario*. Zurich: C. Froschauer, March, 1561.

——. *In Duos Libros Samuelis Prophetae . . . Commentarii*. Zurich: C. Froschauer, 1564.

——. *In Epistolam S. Pauli Apostoli ad Romanos*, 3d ed. Basil, 1568.

——. *In librum Iudicum*. Zurich, 1569.

——. *In Mosis Genesim . . . Commentarii*. Basel: Johann Herwagen, 1554.

——. *In Primum Librum Mosis Qui Vulgo Genesis Dicitur Commentarii . . .* Zurich: C. Froschoverus, 1569.

——. *In Primum, Secundum, et Initium Tertii Libri Ethicorum Aristotelii ad Nichomachum*. Zurich: C. Froschauer, 1563.

——. *In Selectissimam S. Pauli Priorem Ad Corinthios Epistolam. Tiguri, 1551*.

——. *Life, Letters and Sermons: Peter Martyr Vermigli*, ed. and trans. John Patrick Donnelly. Peter Martyr Library, 5. Kirksville: Thomas Jefferson State University Press, 1999.

——. *Loci Communes D. Petri Martyris Vermilii*. Londini: Excudebat Thomas Vautrollerius Typographus, 1583.

——. *Locorum Communium Theologicorum . . .* Basel, 1580.

——. *Melachim id est, Regum Libri Duo posteriores cum Commentarijs* Zurich, 1566.

——. *Most fruitfull & learned Commentaries . . .* London: John Day, 1564.

——. *Philosophical Works of Peter Martyr*, (ed. and tr.) J. C. McLelland. Peter Martyr Library, vol. 4. Kirksville: Sixteenth Century Essays and Studies, 1996.

——. "Praefatio," *In Selectissimam S. Pauli Priorem Ad Corinth. Epistolam D. Petri Martyris, Florentini, ad Sereniss. regem Angliae, &c. Edvardvm VI. Commentarii doctissimi*. Zurich: Froschauer, 1551.

——. *Sainctes Prieres recueillies des Pseaumes de David*. Geneve, jean Durant, 1577.

——. *Saintes priers recueillies des Pseaumes* (La Rochelle, Pierre Haultin, 1581.

——. *Theological Loci: Justification and Predestination*, ed. Frank James III, Peter Martyr Library VIII. Kirksville: Truman State University Press, 2003.

——. *The Oxford Treatise and Disputation on the Eucharist*, (trans. and ed.) Joseph C. McLelland. Peter Martyr Library, VII. Kirksville: Truman State University Press, 2000.

——. *Whether it be Mortalle Sinne to Transgresse Civil Lawes, which be the Commaundementes of Civill Magistrates.* London: Richard Jugge, 1566.

Westphal, *Farrago confusanearum et inter se dissiduntium opinoinum de Coena Domini, ex Sacramentariorium libris congesta* (Magdeburg, 1552.

Whitgift, John. *An Ansvuere.* London: Henrie Bynneman, for Humfrey Toy, 1573.

——. *The Works of John Whitgift,* 3 vols. The Parker Society. Cambridge: Cambridge University Press.

Zanchi, Girolamo. *Operum Theologicorum,* 8 vols. (Geneva, 1605).

Zwingli, Huldrich. *Eine klare Unterrichtung vom Nachtmahl Christi.* Zurich, 1526.

Zwingli, Huldrych. *In Epistolam ad Romanos Annotationes* in *Opera . . . Latinorum Scriptorum.* Zurich: Schulthess, 1838.

Secondary Sources

Abray, Lorna Jane. *The People's Reformation: Magistrates, Clergy and Commons in Strasbourg, 1500–1598.* Ithaca, New York, 1985.

Amos, N. Scott. "'It is Fallow Ground Here': Martin Bucer as Critic of the English Reformation," *Westminster Theological Journal,* 61 (1999): 41–52.

Anderson, Marvin. *Evangelical Foundations: Religion in England, 1378–1683.* American University Studies. New York: Peter Land, 1987.

——. *Peter Martyr Vermigli: A Reformer in Exile (1542–1562): A Chronology of Biblical Writings in England and Europe.* Nieukoop, 1975.

——. "Peter Martyr, Reformed Theologian (1542–1562): His Letters to Heinrich Bullinger and John Calvin', *Sixteenth Century Journal,* 4 (1973): 41–64.

——. "Royal Idolatry: Peter Martyr and the Reformed Tradition," *Archiv für Reformationsgeschichte,* 69 (1978): 157–201.

——. "Vermigli, Peter Martyr," in *The Oxford Encyclopedia of the Reformation.* New York: Oxford University Press, 1996.

Armstrong, Brian. *Calvinism and the Amyraut Heresy: Protestant Scholasticism and Humanism in Seventeenth-Century France.* Madison: University of Wisconsin Press, 1969.

Ateek, Naim, Marc H. Ellis and Ruether, Rosemary (eds.), *Faith and the Intifada: Palestinian Christian Voices.* Maryknoll, N.Y.: Orbis Books, 1992.

Backus, Irena. "Calvin's judgment of Eusebius of Caesarea: an Analysis," *Sixteenth Century Journal,* 22 (1991): 419–437.

——. "Martin Bucer and the Patristic Tradition," in Christian Krieger and Marc Lienhard (eds.), *Martin Bucer and Sixteenth Century Europe.* Leiden: E. J. Brill, 1993.

Backus, Irena and Chimelli, Claire. eds. *La Vraie Piete: Divers traites de Jean Calvin et Confession de foi de Guillame Farel* (Geneva, 1986).

——. "Patristics," in *the Oxford Encyclopedia of the Reformation* New York: Oxford University Press, 1996.

——. "Ulrich Zwingli, Martin Bucer and the Church Fathers," in Irena Backus (ed.), *The Reception of the Church Fathers in the West* Leiden: Brill, 1997.

Bainton, Roland. *Women of the Reformation in Germany and Italy.* Minnesota: Augsburg, 1971.

Baker, J.H. (ed.) *John Spelman's Reading on Quo Warranto: delivered in Gray's Inn (Lent 1519)* Selden Society vol. 113. Seldon Society: London, 1997.

Baker, J. Wayne. *Heinrich Bullinger and the Covenant.* Ohio: Ohio University Press, 1980.

Barth, Karl. *Briefe, 1961–1968.* J. Fangmeier and H. Stoevesandt (eds.) Zürich: Theologischer Verlag, 1975

——. *Church Dogmatics.* G. T. Thomson, T. F. Torrance and G. W. Bromiley (trans.) Grand Rapids: Eerdmans Publishing, 1936.

Bataillon, M. *Introduction au Diálogo de Doctrina Cristiana de Juan de Valdés.* Paris: Vrin, 1974.

——. "Juan de Valdés Nicodemite?" in *Aspects du Libertinisme au XVIe Siecle*. Paris: Vrin, 1974, pp. 93–103.

Becker, Jürgen. *Paul, Apostle to the Gentile*, O. C. Dean, Jr. (trans.) Louisville: Westminster/John Knox Press, 1993.

Bellardi, Werner. *Die Geschichte der Christlichen Gemeinschaft' in Strassburg (1546–1550)*. Leiden, 1978.

Bengel, J. A. *Gnomon Novi Testamenti*, 3rd ed. Tubingen: Ludov. Frid. Fues., 1855.

Bierma, Lyle Dean. "The Covenant Theology of Caspar Olevian." Ph.D. dissertation, Duke University, 1980.

Boland, Vivan, O. P. *Ideas in God according to Saint Thomas Aquinas: Sources and Synthesis*. Studies in the History of Christian Thought, LXIX. Leiden: E. J. Brill, 1996.

Bouwsma, William. *Venice and the Defense of Republican Liberty*. Berkeley and Los Angles: University of California, 1968.

Bozza, Tomasso. *Il Beneficio di Cristo e la Istituzione della religione cristiana di Calvino*. Rome, 1961.

——. *Il Benificio di Cristo*. Nuovi studi sulla Riforma in Italia, vol. 1 Rome, 1976.

——. *Introduzione al`Beneficio di Cristo*. Rome, 1963.

Brady, Thomas A., Jr. *Ruling Class, Regime and Reformation at Strasbourg, 1520–1555*. Studies in Medieval and Reformation Thought, XXII. Leiden, 1978.

Brandy, Hans Christian. *Die späte Christologie des Johannes Brenz*. Tübingen: J. C. B. Mohr, 1991.

Bray, Gerald. "Attitudes towards Jews in Patristic Commentaries on Romans," in A. N. S. Lane (ed.), *Interpreting the Bible: Historical and Theological Studies in Honour of David F. Wright*. Leicester: Apollos, 1997.

——. (ed.) *Romans, Ancient Christian Commentary on Scripture, New Testament*, VII. Downers Grove: InterVarsity Press, 1998.

——. *The Anglican Canons: 1529–1947*, Church of England Record Society, vol. 6. Woodbridge, Suffolk: Boydell Press, 1998.

——. *Tudor Church Reform*, Church of England Record Society, vol. 8. Woodbridge, Suffolk: Boydell Press, 2000.

Bromiley, G. W. (ed.) *Zwingli and Bullinger: Selected translations with introduction and notes*. Philadelphia: Westminster Press, 1953.

Brown, David. *The Restoration of the Jews: The History, Principles, and Bearings of the Question*. Edinburgh: Alexander Straham & Co.; London: Hamilton, Adams, & Co., 1861.

Brundage, James. *Law, Sex and Christian Society in Medieval Europe*. Chicago University Press: Chicago, 1987.

Buhler, Peter. "Der Abendmahlsstreit der Reformatoren und seine aktuellen Implikationen" *Theologische Zeitschrift*, 35 (1979): 228–241.

Burnett, Gilbert. *The History of the Reformation of the Church of England*, 3 vols in 6 (London, 1820).

Bynum, Caroline Walker. *Fragmentation and Redemption: Essays on Gender and the Human Body in Medieval Religion*. New York: Zone Books, 1992.

Campi, Emidio. *Michelangelo e Vittoria Colonna: un dialogo artistico-teologico ispirato da Bernardino Ochino*. Torino: Claudiana Editrice, 1994.

Cantimori, Delio. *Eretici italiani del Cinquecento: Ricerche storiche*. Florence: G. C. Sansoni, 1939.

——. 'La riforma in Italia' in E. Rota (ed.), *Problemi storici e orientamenti storiografici*. Como, 1942.

——. *Prospettive di Storia ereticale italiana del Cinquecento*. Bari: Laferza, 1960.

Caponetto, Salvatore. *Benedetto da Mantova. Marcantonio Flaminio: Il Beneficio di Cristo*. Torino: Claudiana, 1975.

——. *The Protestant Reformation in Sixteenth Century Italy*. Anne and John Tedeschi (trans.) Kirksville: Thomas Jefferson University Press, 1999.

Cardwell, Edward. *The Reformation of the Ecclesiastical Laws as Attempted in the Reigns of King Henry VIII, King Edward VI, and Queen Elizabeth.* Oxford: Oxford University Press, 1850.

Carlson, Eric J. *Marriage and the English Reformation.* Oxford: Blackwell Publishers, 1994.

Clark, Francis. *Eucharistic Sacrifice and the Reformation.* Westminster: Newman Press, 1960.

Collett, Barry. *Italian Benedictine Scholars and the Reformation: The Congregation of Santa Giustina of Padua.* Oxford: Oxford University Press, 1985.

Collinson, Patrick. *Archbishop Grindal, 1519–1583: The Struggle for a Reformed Church.* Berkeley: University of California Press, 1979.

———. "England and International Calvinism: 1558–1640," in Menna Prestwich, ed. *International Calvinism: 1541–1715.* Oxford: Oxford University Press, 1985.

———. *The Elizabethan Puritan Movement.* Patrick Collinson, 1967.

Copeland, Rita *Rhetoric, Hermeneutics, and Translation in the Middle Ages.* Cambridge: Cambridge University Press, 1991.

Corda, Salvatore *Veritas Sacramenti: A Study in Vermigli's Doctrine of the Lord's Supper.* Zurich, 1975.

Cottrell, Jack W. "Covenant and Baptism in the Theology of Huldrych Zwingli." Ph.D. Dissertation, Princeton Theological Seminary, 1971.

Cottret, Bernard. "Une semiotique de la Reforme: Le consensus Tigurinus et La Breve Resolution . . . (1555) de Calvin" *AESC,* 39 (1984): 265–85

Cranfield, C. E. B. *A Critical and Exegetical Commentary on the Epistle to the Romans.* Edinburgh: T. & T. Clark, 1975–1979.

Critchley, Simon. *Ethics – Politics – Subjectivity: Essays on Derrida, Lévinas, and Contemporary French Thought.* London: Verso, 1999.

Curtis, Mark. *Oxford and Cambridge in Transition: 1558–1642. An Essay in Changing Relations between the English Universities and English Society.* Oxford: Oxford University Press, 1959.

Delhaye, Philippe and Stabile, Giorgio. "Virtù," *Enciclopedia Dantesca,* Antonietta Butano, et al. Rome, 1976.

Dent, C. M. *Protestant Reformers in Elizabethan Oxford.* Oxford: Oxford University Press, 1983.

Deppermann, Klaus. *Melchior Hoffman: Social Unrest and Apocalyptic Visions in the Age of Reformation.* Edinburgh: T. & T. Clark, 1987.

De Usoz i Rio, Luis (ed.) *Ziento I diez consideraziones de Juan de Valdés.* Madrid, 1863.

Diestel, Ludwig "Studien zur Foderaltheologie" in *Jahrbuch fur Deutsche Theologie,* 10 (1865): 266.

Di Gangi, Mariano. *Peter Martyr Vermigli, 1499–1562: Renaissance Man, Reformation Master.* Lanham, Maryland, 1993.

Dodds, E. R. *Proclus: The Elements of Theology: A Revised Text with Translation, Introduction, and Commentary.* Oxford: Oxford University Press, 1963.

Dolores Warwick Frese and Katherine O'Brien O'Keeffe (eds.) *The Book and the Body.* Notre Dame: University of Notre Dame Press, 1997.

Donnelly, John Patrick. *A Bibliography of Peter Martyr Vermigli.* Sixteenth Century Essays and Studies, XIII. Kirksville: Sixteenth Century Publishers, 1990.

———. *Calvinism and Scholasticism in Vermigli's Doctrine of Man and Grace.* Leiden: E. J. Brill, 1976.

———. "Calvinist Thomism", *Viator,* 7 (1976): 441–455.

———. "Immortality and Method in Ursinus's Theological Ambiance," in Dirk Visser, (ed.), *Controversy and Conciliation: The Reformation and the Palatinate, 1559–1583.* Allison Park: Pickwick Publications, 1986.

———. "Italian Influences on the Development of Calvinist Scholasticism," *Sixteenth Century Journal,* 7 (1976): 81–101.

———. "Marriage from Renaissance to Reformation: Two Florentine Moralists," *Studies in Medieval Culture* 9 (1977): 161–71.

——— and Kingdon, R. M. *A Bibliography of the Works of Peter Martyr Vermigli*. Kirksville: Sixteenth Century Journal Publishers, 1990.

Dorner, J. A. *History of Protestant Theology*, G. Robson and S. Taylor (trans.) Edinburgh: T. & T. Clark, 1871.

Dupré, Louis. *Passage to Modernity: an Essay in the Hermeneutics of Nature and Culture*. New Haven: Yale University Press, 1993.

Dupré, L. and Saliers, D. E. *Christian Spirituality III: Post-Reformation and Modern* NY: Crossroads.

Eels, Hastings. *Martin Bucer*. New York: Russell & Russell, reprint 1971.

Elton, G. R. (ed.) *The New Cambridge Modern History*, vol. II of *The Reformation, 1520–1559*, 2nd ed. Cambridge: Cambridge University Press, 1990.

Farthing, John L. "*De coniugio spirituali*: Jerome Zanchi on Ephesians 5.22–33," *Sixteenth Century Journal*, 24 (1993): 621–652.

Fenlon, Dermot. *Heresy and Obedience in Tridentine Italy: Cardinal Pole and the Counter Reformation*. Cambridge: Cambridge University Press, 1972.

Finnis, John. *Aquinas: Moral, Political and Legal Theory*. Oxford: Oxford University Press, 1998.

Firpo, Massimo. "The Italian Reformation and Juan de Valdés," *Sixteenth Century Journal*, 27 (1996): 353–364.

———. *Riforma protestante ed eresie nell'Italia del Cinquecento: Un profilo storico*. Rome-Bari: Laterza, 1993.

Fitzmyer, Joseph A. *Romans: A New Translation with Introduction and Commentary*. Anchor Bible, XXXIII. New York: Doubleday, 1933.

Foucault, Michel. *Ethics: Subjectivity and Truth*. Catherine Porter (trans.) New York: The New Press, 1997.

Fraenkel, Peter. *Testimonia Patrum: The Function of the Patristic Argument in the Theology of Philip Melanchthon*. Geneva: Librairie E. Droz, 1961.

Frere, W. H. and C. E. Douglas (eds.), *Puritan Manifestoes: A Study of the Puritan Revolt*. London: S. P. C. K., 1954.

Ganoczy, Alexandre. *La Bibliotheque de l'Academie de Calvin: Le Catalogue de 1572 et ses Enseignements*. Geneve: librairie Droz, 1969.

Gilly, C. "Juan de Valdés: Ubersetzer und Bearbeiter von Luthers Schriften in seinem *Diàlogo de Doctrina*" in *Archiv für Reformationsgeschichte*, 74 (1983): 257–305.

Ginzburg, C. *Il nicodemismo—Simulazione e dissimulazione religiosa nell' Europa dell' 500*. Turin, 1970.

Gleason, Elisabeth G. "On the Nature of Italian Evangelism: Scholarship, 1953–1978," *Sixteenth Century Journal*, 9 (1978): 3–25.

Gollwitzer, Helmut. *Coena Domini: Die altlutherische Abendmahlslehre in ihrer Auseinandersetzung mit dem Calvinismus, dargestellt an der lutherische Frühorthodoxie*. Munich: Kaiser, 1988.

Gordon, Bruce. "Peter Martyr Vermigli in Scotland: A Sixteenth-Century Reformer in a Seventeenth-Century Quarrel" in Emidio Campi, Frank A. James, III and Peter Opitz (eds.) *Peter Martyr Vermigli: Humanism, Republicanism and Reformation*. Geneva: Librairie Droz, 2002.

Gorham, George Cornelius. *Gleanings of a few scattered ears, during the period of the Reformation in England . . .* London: Bell and Daldy, 1857.

Greef, W. de. *The Writings of John Calvin.*, L. Bierma (trans.) Grand Rapids: Baker Book House, 1993.

Gregory, Charles David. *Theodore of Mopsuestia's Commentary on Romans: an Annotated Translation*. Ph.D. thesis, The Southern Baptist Theological Seminary, 1992.

Greschat, Martin. *Martin Bucer. Ein Reformator und seine Zeit (1491–1551)* Munich, 1990.

Haaugaard, William P. "Renaissance Patristic Scholarship and Theology in Sixteenth-Century England," *The Sixteenth Century Journal*, 10 (1979): 53.

Hagen, Kenneth "From Testament to Covenant in the Early Sixteenth Century" in *Sixteenth Century Journal*, 3 (1972): 1–20

Hall, Basil. "Martin Bucer in England" in D. F. Wright (ed.) *Martin Bucer: Reforming Church and Community*. Cambridge: Cambridge University Press, 1994.

Hammann, Gottfried. *Entre la secte et la cite. Le project d'Eglise du Reformateur Martin Bucer (1491–1551)*. Geneva, 1984.

Hammond, Henry. *Paraphrase and Annotations upon All the Books of the New Testament, Briefly Explaining all the Difficult Places Thereof*, IV. Oxford: University Press, 1845.

Hankey, Wayne J. "'Dionysius dixit, lex divinitatis est ultima per media reducere:' Aquinas, Hierocracy and the 'Augustinisme Politique'," *Medioevo*, XVIII (1992): 119–150.

Healey, Robert M. "Waiting for Deborah: John Knox and Four Ruling Queens," *Sixteenth Century Journal*, 25 (1994): 381.

Heidegger, Martin. *Basic Writings*. New York: Harper and Row, 1995.

Henriksen, William. *Israel in Prophecy*. Grand Rapids, Mich.: Baker Book House, 1968.

Heppe, Heinrich *Reformed Dogmatics: Set Out and Illustrated from the Sources*. Grand Rapids: Baker, 1978.

Herkenrath, Erland. "Peter Martyr Vermiglis Vorarbeit zu einer zweiten christologischen Schrift gegen Johannes Brenz 1562," *Blätter für württembergische Kirchengeschichte*, 75 (1975): 23–31.

Herminjard, ed., *Correspondance des Reformateurs dans les pays de langue francaise*. Geneva, 1893.

Hesselink, John. "The Millennium and the Reformed Tradition," *Reformed Review*, 52 (1998–1999): 101.

Hobbs, R. Gerald. "François Lambert sur les langues et la prophétie," in *Pour retrouver François Lambert: Bio-bibliographie et études* Pierre Fraenkel (ed.) Baden-Baden and Bouxwiller: Valentin Koerner, 1987.

——. "Martin Bucer et les Juifs," in C. Krieger and M. Leinhard (eds.), *Martin Bucer and Sixteenth Century Europe: Actes du Colloque de Strasbourg (28–31 août 1991)*. Leiden: Brill, 1993.

Hodge, Charles *Systematic Theology*, 3 vols. Grand Rapids: Eerdmans Publishing Company, 1977.

Hopf, Constantin. *Martin Bucer and the English Reformation*. Oxford: Blackwell, 1948.

James, Frank A. III. "A Late Medieval Parallel in Reformation Thought: *Gemina Praedestinatio* in Gregory of Rimini and Peter Martyr Vermigli," in Heiko A. Oberman and Frank A. James (eds.), *Via Augustini: Augustine in the Later Middle Ages, Renaissance and Reformation*. Leiden: Brill, 1991.

——. "*De Iustificatione*: the Evolution of Peter Martyr Vermigli's Doctrine of Justification." Ph.D. dissertation, Westminster Theological Seminary, Pennsylvania, 2000.

——. "Juan de Valdés Before and After Peter Martyr Vermigli: The Reception of *Gemina Praedestinatio* in Valdés' Later Thought," *Archiv für Reformationsgeschichte*, 83 (1992): 180–208.

——. *Peter Martyr and Predestination: The Augustinian Inheritance of an Italian Reformer*. Oxford Theological Monographs. Oxford: Oxford University Press, 1998.

——. "Peter Martyr Vermigli: at the Crossroads of Late Medieval Scholasticism, Christian Humanism and Resurgent Augustinianism," in Carl R. Trueman and R. S. Clark (eds.), *Protestant Scholasticism: Essays in Reassessment*. Exeter: Paternoster Press, 1999.

Jessey, Henry. "A Philo-Semitic Millenarian on the Reconciliation of Jews and Christians: Henry Jesse and his *The Glory and Salvation of Jehudah and Israel (1650)*," in David S. Katz and Jonathan (eds.), *Sceptics, Millenarians and Jews*, vol. I. Leiden: Brill, 1990.

Jones, Martin D. W. *The Counter Reformation: Religion and Society in Early Modern Europe*. Cambridge: Cambridge University Press, 1995.

Jung, E.-M. "On the Nature of Evangelism in Sixteenth-Century Italy, *Journal of the History of Ideas*, 14 (1953): 511–527.

Kantorowicz, E. *The King's Two Bodies: A Study in Medieval Political Theology*. Princeton: Princeton University Press, 1957.

Katz, David S. *Philo-Semitism and the Readmission of the Jews to England 1603–1655*. Oxford: Clarendon Press, 1982.

Kidd, B. J. *Documents of the Continental Reformation*. Oxford, 1911.

Kingdon, Robert M. "Death for Adultery," in *Adultery and Divorce in Calvin's Geneva*. Cambridge: Harvard University Press, 1995.

———. *The Political Thought of Peter Martyr Vermigli: Selected Texts and Commentary*. Geneva, 1980.

Kittelson, James M. "Johannes Marbach," in *Oxford Encyclopedia of the Reformation*. New York: Oxford University Press, 1996.

———. "Marbach vs. Zanchi: The Resolution of Controversy in Late Reformation Strasbourg," *Sixteenth Century Journal*, 8 (1977): 32.

Knappen, (ed.) *Two Elizabethan Puritan Diaries*. Studies in Church History, vol. II. Chicago: The American Society of Church History, 1933.

Köher, Walther. *Zwingli und Luther: Ihr Streit über das Abendmahl nach seinen politischen und religiösen Bezeiehungen*, 2 vols. Liepzig, 1924.

Kristeller, P. O. *Renaissance Thought and Its Sources*. Columbia University Press, 1979.

Lang, August. *Der Evangelienkommentar Martin Butzers und die Grundzüge seiner Theologie*. Leipzig, 1900.

Laver, Mary S. "Calvin, Jews, and Intra-Christian Polemics." Ph.D. dissertation, Temple University, 1988.

Leeming, Bernard S. J. *Principles of Sacramental Theology*. London: 1956.

Lehmberg, Stanford. *The Reformation Parliament 1529–1536*. Cambridge, 1970.

Le Neve, John. *Facti Ecclesiae Anglicanae, 1541–1857, VI Salisbury Diocese*. London: University of London, Institute of Historical Research, 1986.

Lévinas, Emmanuel. *Otherwise than Being or Beyond Essence*. A. Lingis (trans.) The Hague: Nijhoff, 1981.

Levison, Frederick. *Christian and Jew: the Life of Leon Levison, 1881–1936*. Edinburgh: Pentland Press, 1989.

Lillback, Peter A. *The Binding of God: Calvin's Role in the Development of Covenant Theology*. Grand Rapids: Baker Academic, 2001.

———. "The Continuing Conundrum: Calvin and the Conditionality of the Covenant," *Calvin Theological Journal*, 29 (1994): 42–74.

———. "Ursinus' Development of the Covenant of Creation: A Debt to Melanchthon or Calvin?" in *The Westminster Theological Journal*, XLIII (1981): 247–88.

Lindsey, Hall. *The Road to Holocaust*. New York: Bantam Books, 1989.

Loach, Jennifer. "Reformation Controversies" in James McConica (ed.), *The History of the University of Oxford*, vol. III of *The Collegiate University*, Oxford: Oxford University Press, 1986.

Locher, Gottfried W. *Huldrych Zwingli in neuer Sicht*. Zürich, 1969.

Logan, F. Donald. 'Henrician Canons,' *Bulletin of the Institute of Historical Research*, 47 (1975): 99–103.

Lohr, C. H. "Metaphysics as the Science of God" in C. Schmitt and Q. Skinner (eds.), *The Cambridge History of Renaissance Philosophy*. Cambridge: Cambridge University Press, 1988.

Luscombe, David "The '*Lex Divinitatis*' in the Bull '*Unam Sanctam*' of Pope Boniface

VIII," in C. N. L. Brooke, et al., *Church and Government in the Middle Ages.* New York: Cambridge University Press, 1976.

MacCulloch, Diarmaid. *Thomas Cranmer: A Life.* New Haven and London: Yale University Press, 1996.

——. *Tudor Church Militant: Edward VI and the Protestant Reformation.* London: Allen Lane/The Penguin Press, 1999.

MacIntyre, Alasdair. *After Virtue: A Study in Moral Theory* 2nd ed. London: Duckworth, 1985.

Mann, Nicholas. "The Origins of Humanism," in Jill Kraye (ed.), *The Cambridge Companion to Renaissance Humanism.* Cambridge: Cambridge University Press, 1996.

Marcus, Leah S., Janel Mueller, and Rose, Mary Beth (eds.) *Elizabeth I: Collected Works.* Chicago: University of Chicago Press, 2000.

Martin, Bill. *Humanism and Its Aftermath: The Shared Fate of Deconstruction and Politics.* New Jersey: Humanities Press, 1995.

Martin, John. "Salvation and Society in Sixteenth-Century Venice: Popular Evangelism in a Renaissance City," *Journal of Modern History*, 60 (1988): 205–233.

——. *Venice's Hidden Enemies: Italian Heretics in a Renaissance City.* Berkeley: University of California Press, 1993.

McCoy, Charles S. and Baker, J. Wayne. *Fountainhead of Federalism: Heinrich Bullinger and the Covenantal Tradition.* Louisville: Westminster/John Knox Press, 1991.

McGinn, D. J. *The Admonition Controversy.* New Brunswick: Rutgers, 1949.

McLelland, Joseph C. "Calvinism Perfecting Thomism? Peter Martyr Vermigli's Question," *Scottish Journal of Theology*, 31 (1978): 571–8.

——. "Covenant Theology—a Reevaluation" *Canadian Journal of Theology*, 3 (1957): 184–85.

——. "McLelland on Six Degrees of Reform," *Peter Martyr Newsletter*, 10 (Reformed Theological Seminary, Orlando, October 1999): 4.

——. (ed.) *Peter Martyr Vermigli and Italian Reform.* Waterloo: Wilfrid Laurier Press, 1980.

——. "Peter Martyr Vermigli: Scholastic or Humanist" in McLelland, (ed.), *Peter Martyr Vermigli and Italian Reform.* Waterloo: Wilfrid Lauerier Press, 1980.

——. *The Visible Words of God: An Exposition of the Sacramental Theology of Peter Martyr Vermigli, A.D. 1500–1562.* Edinburgh: Oliver and Boyd, 1957.

McNair, Philip. *Peter Martyr in Italy: An Anatomy of Apostasy.* Oxford, 1967.

——. "Peter Martyr in England" in Joseph C. McLelland, ed., *Peter Martyr Vermigli and Italian Reform.* Waterloo: Wilfrid Laurier University Press, 1980.

Meeks, Wayne A. "On Trusting an Unpredictable God: A Hermeneutical Meditation on Romans 9–11," in John T. Carroll et al., *Faith and History: Essays in Honor of Paul W. Meyer.* Atlanta: Scholars Press, 1990.

Meijering, E. P. *Melanchthon and Patristic Thought.* Leiden: E. J. Brill, 1983.

Menchi, Silvana S. *Erasmo in Italia, 1520–1580.* Turin: Bollati Boringhieri, 1987.

——. "Lo stato degli studi sulla Riforma in Italia," *Wolfenbütteler Renaissance Mitteilungen*, 5 (1981): 35–42, 89–92.

Mergal, A.M. "Evangelical Catholicism as Represented by Juan de Valdes," in *Spiritual and Anabaptist Writers*, Library of Christian Classics XXV. Louisville: John Knox, 1967.

Milton, Anthony. *Catholic and Reformed: The Roman and Protestant Churches in English Protestant Thought, 1600–1640.* Cambridge: Cambridge University Press, 1995.

Moenckeberg, Karl. *Ioachim Westphal und Iohannes Calvin.* Hamburg, 1865.

Moltmann, Jurgen. "Foderaltheologie," in *Lexikon fur Theologie und Kirche* (1960), 190

Monahan, Arthur P. editor and translator, *De ecclesiastica potestate*, Texts and Studies in Religion 41 (Lewiston/Queenston/Lampeter: The Edwin Mellon Press, 1990).

Moo, Douglas J. *Epistle to the Romans.* Grand Rapids: W. B. Eerdmans Publishing Co., 1996.

Moore, Thomas V. *The Prophets of the Restoration.* New York: Robert Carter, 1856; reprinted Carlisle: The Banner of Truth Trust, 1979.

Morgan, *Godly Learning: Puritan Attitudes towards Reason, Learning, and Education, 1560–1640.* Cambridge: Cambridge University Press, 1986.

Morris, Leon. *The Benefit of Christ, Valdés and Don Benedetto.* Portland, Oregon, 1984.

Muller, Richard A. "Calvin and the Calvinists: Assessing Continuities and Discontinuities between the Reformation and Orthodoxy," *Calvin Theological Journal,* 30 (1996): 125–60.

——. *Christ and the Decree: Christology and Predestination in Reformed Theology from Calvin to Perkins.* Grand Rapids: Baker Books, 1988.

——. *Dictionary of Latin and Greek Theological Terms: Drawn Principally from Protestant Scholastic Theology.* Grand Rapids: Baker Book House: 1985.

Murray, Iain H. *The Puritan Hope: A Study in Revival and the Interpretation of Prophecy.* Carlisle: The Banner of Truth Trust, 1971.

Nauert, Charles G. *Humanism and the Culture of Renaissance Europe.* Cambridge: Cambridge University Press, 1995.

Nestingen, James Arne. "Gnesio-Lutherans," *Oxford Encyclopedia of the Reformation.* New York: Oxford University Press, 1996.

Nevin, John W. *The Mystical Presence and Other Writings on the Eucharist.* Philadelphia: United Church Press, 1966.

New Catholic Encyclopedia. Washington, DC: The Catholic University of America, 1967.

Nichols, James (ed.), *Puritan Sermons: Being the Morning Exercises at Cripplegate, St. Giles in the Field and in Southwark by 75 Ministers of the Gospel.* Wheaton, Ill: R. O. Roberts, 1981.

Nieto, José. *Juan de Valdés & the Origins of the Spanish & Italian Reformation.* Geneva: Droz, 1978.

——. (ed.) *Valdés' Two Catechisms: The Dialogue on Christian Doctrine and the Christian Instruction for Children.* Lawrence: Coronado Press, 1981.

Oberman, Heiko. *The Harvest of Medieval Theology.* Grand Rapids: Eerdmans, 1967.

Olin, John C. *The Catholic Reformation: Savonarola to Ignatius Loyola.* NY: Harper & Row, 1969.

Olsen, V. Norskov. *The New Testament Logia on Divorce: A Study in Their Interpretation from Erasmus to Milton.* Tübingen: J. C. B. Mohr, 1971.

Overell, M. A. "Peter Martyr in England 1547–1553: An Alternative View," *Sixteenth Century Journal,* 15 (1984): 87–104.

Ozment, Stephen. *When Father's Ruled: Family Life in Reformation Europe.* Harvard, 1983.

Palacios, M. A. *Saint John of the Cross and Islam.* E. H. Douglas and H. W. Yoder (eds.) NY: Vantage, 1981.

Payton, James R. Jr. "Bucer and the Church Fathers" Unpublished Manuscript, 1991.

——. "*Sola Scriptura* and Church History: The Views of Martin Bucer and Melanchthon on Religious Authority in 1539" Ph.D. dissertation, University of Waterloo, 1982.

Peel Albert and Leland H. Carlson (eds.), *Cartwrightiana.* London: Published for the Sir Halley Stewart Trust [by] Allen and Unwin, 1951.

Peters, F. E. *Greek Philosophical Terms: A Historical Lexicon.* New York: New York University Press, 1967.

Petroff, Elizabeth A. *Body and Soul: Essays on Medieval Women and Mysticism.* New York and Oxford: Oxford University Press, 1994.

Pettegree, Andrew. *Foreign Protestant Communities in Sixteenth Century London.* Oxford: Oxford University Press, 1986.

Plath, Uwe. *Calvin und Basel in den Jahren 1552–1556.* Zürich, 1974.

Primus, J. H. *The Vestments Controversy.* Kampen: J. H. Kok, 1960.

Quistorp, Heinrich. *Calvin's Doctrine of the Last Things.* Richmond: John Knox Press, 1955.

Rabil, Albert Jr. *Declamation on the Nobility and Preeminence of the Female Sex.* Chicago: University of Chicago Press, 1996.

Rankin, W. Duncan "Carnal Union with Christ in the Theology of T. F. Torrance." Ph.D. dissertation, University of Edinburgh, 1997.

Rashdall, Hastings. *The Universities of Europe in the Middle Ages,* vol. 2. 1936; reprint, F. M. Powicke and A. B. Emden (eds.) Oxford: OUP, 1997.

Reid, J. K. S. *Calvin: Theological Treatises.* London, 1954.

Rex, Richard. "The Crisis of Obedience: God's Word and Henry's Reformation," *The Historical Journal,* 39 (1996): 863–894.

Ritschl, Otto "Entwicklung des Bundesgedankens in der reformierten Theologie des 16. und des 17. Jahrhunderts" in *Dogmengeschichte des Protestantismus.* Gottingen: Vandenhoeck & Ruprecht, 1926.

Rivière, J. *Le problème de l'église et de l'état au temps de Philippe le Bel: Étude de théologie positive.* Spicilegium Sacrum Lovaniense, VIII. Paris: E. Champion, 1926.

Robinson, Hastings (ed.), *Original Letters Relative to the English Reformation.* Cambridge: University Press, 1847.

Robinson, Jack H. *John Calvin and the Jews.* New York: Peter Lang, 1992.

Rorty, Richard "Remarks on Deconstruction and Pragmatism," *Deconstruction and Pragmatism.* Chantal Mouffe (ed.) London: Routledge, 1996.

Rott, Jean. "Le Sort des Papiers et de la Bibliothèque de Bucer en Angleterre." *Revue d'Histoire et de Philosophe Religieuses,* 46 (1966): 346–67.

Rowe & Wainwright (eds.) *Philosophy of Religion: Selected Readings.* NY: Harcourt Brace Jovanovich, 1973.

Rubin, Miri. *Corpus Christi: The Eucharist in Late Medieval Culture.* Cambridge: Cambridge University Press, 1991.

Sachs, Leslie Raymond 'Thomas Cranmer's *Reformatio Legum Ecclesiasticarum* of 1553 in the Context of English Church Law from the Later Middle Ages to the Canons of 1603.' Ph.D. thesis, Catholic University of America, 1982.

Schelkle, K. H. *Paulus Lehrer der Väter: Die Altkirchliche Auslegung von Römer 1–11.* Dütmos-Verlag, 1956.

Schindlin, Anton. *Humanistiche Hochschule und freie Reichstadt. Gymnasium und Akademie in Strassburg, 1538–1621.* Wiesbaden, 1977.

Schmidt, Charles. *Peter Martyr Vermigli: leben und ausgewählte Schriften.* Elberfeld, 1858.

Schmitt, Charles B., et al. *The Cambridge History of Renaissance Philosophy.* New York: Cambridge University Press: 1988.

Secor, Philip B. *Richard Hooker, Prophet of Anglicanism.* Tunbridge Wells, Kent: Burns & Oates; Toronto: Anglican Book Centre, 1999.

Seeger, Cornelia. *Nullité de mariage, divorce et séparation de corps a Genève, au temps de Calvin: Fondements doctrinaux, loi et jurisprudence.* Lausanne: Société d'Histoire de la Suisse Romande, 1989.

Shutte, Anne Jacobson. "Periodization of Sixteenth-Century Italian Religious History: The Post-Cantimori Paradigm Shift," *Journal of Modern History,* 61 (1989): 269–284

Southern, A. C. *Elizabethan Recusant Prose, 1559–1590.* London, 1950.

Southern, R. W. *Medieval Humanism and Other Studies.* Oxford: Blackwell Publishers, 1970.

Spinks, Bryan D. *Two Faces of Elizabethan Anglican Theology: Sacraments and Salvation in the Thought of William Perkins and Richard Hooker.* Drew University Studies in Liturgy, No. 9. Lanham, Maryland and London: The Scarecrow Press, 1999.

Squibb, G. D. *Doctor's Commons: A History of the College of Advocates and Doctor's of Law.* Oxford: Clarendon Press, 1977.

Staab, K. "Paulus kommentare aux der griechischen Kirche," *Neutestamentlich Abhuandlungen,* 15. Münster, 1933.

Staedtke, Joachim. *Die Theologie des jungen Bullinger. Studien zur Dogmengeschichte und Systematischen Theologie.* Zwingli, 1962.

Steinmetz, David. *Calvin in Context.* New York: Oxford University, 1995.

Stephens, W. Peter. *The Theology of Huldrych Zwingli* (Oxford, 1986)

Stevenson, William B. "The Problem of Trinitarian Processions in Thomas's Roman Commentary," *The Thomist* 64 (2000).

Strehle, Stephen. *Calvinism, Federalism, and Scholasticism: A Study of the Reformed Doctrine of Covenant.* Bern: Peter Lang, 1988.

Strohl, Henri. "Bucer et Calvin," *Bulletin du Société de l'Histoire du Protestantisme français* 87 (1938): 354

Strype, John. *The History of the Life and Acts of the Most Reverend Father in God, Edmund Grindal. . . .* Oxford: Clarendon Press, 1821; reprint New York: Burt Franklin Reprints, 1974.

Sturm, Klaus. *Die Theologie Peter Martyr Vermiglis waehrend seines ersten Aufenthalts in Strassburg 1542–1547.* Neukirchen, 1971.

Tamburello, D. *John Calvin and the Mysticism of St. Bernard.* Louisville: Westminster/John Knox Press, 1994.

Taylor, Charles. *Philosophical Arguments.* Massachusetts: Harvard University Press, 1995.

Thomas, Keith V. "The Double Standard," *Journal of the History of Ideas*, 20 (1959): 195–216.

Thompson, John Lee. *John Calvin and the Daughters of Sarah: Women in Regular and Exceptional Roles in the Exegesis of Calvin, His Predecessors, and His Contemporaries.* Geneva: Librairie Droz, 1992.

Tierney, Brian. *The Crisis of Church and State, 1050–1300.* Toronto: Toronto University Press, 1988.

Todd, Margo. *Christian Humanism and Puritan Social Order.* Cambridge: Cambridge University Press, 1987.

Trinterud, Leonard. *Elizabethan Puritanism.* New York: Oxford University Press, 1971.
——. "The Origins of Puritanism", *Church History* 20 (1951): 37–57.

Tyacke, Nicholas. *Anti-Calvinists: The Rise of English Arminianism. c. 1590–1640.* Oxford: Oxford University Press, 1987.

Tylenda, Joseph N. "Christ the Mediator: Calvin versus Stancaro," *Calvin Theological Journal*, 8 (1973): 5–16.
——. "Girolamo Zanchi and John Calvin: A Study in Discipleship as Seen Through Their Correspondence," *Calvin Theological Journal*, 10 (1975): 101–41.
——. "The Calvin-Westphal Exchange: The Genesis of Calvin's treatises against Westphal," *Calvin Theological Journal*, 9 (1974): 182–209.
——. "The Controversy over Christ the Mediator: Calvin's Second Reply to Stancaro," *Calvin Theological Journal*, 8 (1973): 131–157.

Ullmann, Walter. *Law and Politics in the Middle Ages: an Introduction to the Sources of Medieval Political Ideas.* Ithaca: Cornell University Press, 1975.
——. *Principles of Government and Politics in the Middle Ages*, 3rd ed. New York: Methuen, 1974.

Urban, Waclaw "Die großen Jahre der stancarianischen 'Häresie' (1559–1563)" *Archiv für Reformationsgeschichte*, 81 (1990): 309–318.

Van Engen, J. *Devotio Moderna: Basic Writings*, trans. and intro. NY: Paulist, 1988.

Van Oort, Johannes. "John Calvin and the Church Fathers," in Irena Backus (ed.), *The Reception of the Church Fathers in the West*, Leiden: Brill, 1997.

Van 't Spijker, Willem. "Bucer als Zeuge Zanchis im Straßburger Prädestinationsstreit," in Heiko A. Oberman, (ed.) *Reformiertes Erbe: Festschrift für Gottfried W. Locher zu seinem 80 Geburtstag.* Zürich: Theologischer und Buchhandlungen, 1992.

Vogt, Herbert. "Martin Bucer und die Kirche von England" Ph.D. dissertation, Münster, 1968.

Wallace, David. *Chaucerian Polity: Absolutist Lineages and Associational Forms in England and Italy*. Stanford: Stanford University Press, 1997.

Welti, Manfred *Breve storia della Riforma italiana*. Casale Monferrato: Marietti, 1985.

Wendel, François. *Calvin: The Origins and Development of His Religious Thought*. London, 1963.

White, Peter. *Predestination, Policy, and Polemic: Conflict and Consensus in the English Church from the Reformation to the Civil War*. Cambridge: Cambridge University Press, 1992.

Williams, Arnold. "Milton and Renaissance Commentaries on Genesis," *Modern Philology* XXXVII: 270.

Williams, George H. *The Radical Reformation*, 3rd ed. Kirksville: Sixteenth Century Journal Publishers, 1992.

Williams, Rowan *The Wound of Knowledge: Christian Spirituality from the New Testament to St John of the Cross*, 2nd ed. London: Darton, Longman, and Todd, 1990.

Wotschke, Theodor. *Geschichte der Reformation in Polen*. Leipzig: Rudolf Haupt, 1911; reprint, New York: Johnson Reprint Corporation, 1971.

Yule, George. *The Puritans in Politics: The Religious Legislation of the Long Parliament, 1640–1647*. Courtenay Library of Reformation Classics. Sutton Courtenay Press, 1981.

INDEX

Abrahamic covenant, 72–75, 77–78, 85, 87, 149
Acontius, Jacobo, 182
Adam and Eve, 144–45
adiaphora, 50, 54–55, 155, 250
Admonition controversy, 53–55, 63
adultery, 150–51, 288
afterlife, 24
Albertus Magnus, 221, 223, 299
Alcaraz, Pedro Ruiz de, 240, 244
Alexander III, Pope, 282
Alumbrados, 240, 242
Ambrose, 53, 61, 117, 136, 144, 153, 194
Ambrosiaster, 142n7
Amerbach, Boniface, vii
Ames, William, 66
amillennialism, 171
Anabaptists, xxiv, 71–73, 94, 112n75, 156, 157, 181–86, 195, 286–87
Anderson, Marvin, 27, 43n57, 59, 64, 117, 253, 295n20
Anglican sacramental theology, 84, 94n89, 96
Anselm, 243
anthropology, 23, 221, 227–28
anti-Judaism, 174
anti-Semitism, 168, 173–74
antichrist, 265
appetites, 207
Arians, Arianism, 185, 188, 192, 194
Ariminum, Council of, 129, 132
Aristotelianism, 197–98, 210, 262
Aristotle, 23, 63–65, 68–69, 124–25, 148, 174, 185, 198–201, 206–8, 212, 220n14, 249
   politics, 291–93
Arius, 185, 188, 194
Arminians, 61
Armstrong, Brian, 6, 64–65
Asper, Hans, xiii, xxv
Augsburg Confession, xviii–xix
Augustine, xiii, 62, 66n85, 117–18, 127–30, 132, 136–37, 144, 194, 243, 297
   on image of God, 140–42

on the Jews, 162–63, 175
on two cities, 295, 300, 303
Averroist Aristotelianism, 124–25

Backus, Irena, 119, 123
Bacon, Nicholas, 58
Baille, Robert, 61
Bainton, Roland, 147n25
baptism, 79, 82–83, 89–91, 149
baptismal regeneration, 94n89
Barrett, William, 60
Barth, Karl, 175, 243
Basil, xvii
Bataillon, Marcel, 240
Beale, William, 62
Becker, Jürgen, 167
Becon, Thomas, 285, 288
Bellardi, Werner, 255–56
Bellarmine, 62
Bembo, Pietro, xv
Bengel, J. A., 167n30
Bernard of Clairvaux, 7, 62, 243, 299
Beza, Theodore, xiv, xxi, 5n11, 6, 18, 62, 65, 69, 105, 242
Bible
   and worship, 216
   authority, 229n46
   Vermigli on, 127–29
Bibliander, Theodore, xx–xxi
biblical humanism, 211
Biel, Gabriel, 243
Bierma, Lyle, 76
bilateral conditional covenant, 76
body, 201–2, 210
Boland, Vivan, 218n9, 219n12
Bonaventure, 299
Boniface VIII, Pope, 296–304
Book of Common Prayer, 37, 44, 57, 94n89, 236
Bouwsma, William, 239
Brady, Thomas A., 255
Branthwaite, William, 60
Bray, Gerald, 172, 267n1, 274, 286
Brenz, Johannes, 14, 67, 110, 178–80, 186, 188, 195, 222
Brown, David, 172
Brundage, James, 282

Studies in the History of Christian Traditions

(formerly Studies in the History of Christian Thought)

EDITED BY ROBERT J. BAST

46. GARSTEIN, O. *Rome and the Counter-Reformation in Scandinavia*. 1553-1622. 1992
47. GARSTEIN, O. *Rome and the Counter-Reformation in Scandinavia*. 1622-1656. 1992
48. PERRONE COMPAGNI, V. (ed.). *Cornelius Agrippa, De occulta philosophia Libri tres*. 1992
49. MARTIN, D. D. *Fifteenth-Century Carthusian Reform*. The World of Nicholas Kempf. 1992
50. HOENEN, M. J. F. M. *Marsilius of Inghen*. Divine Knowledge in Late Medieval Thought. 1993
51. O'MALLEY, J. W., IZBICKI, T. M. and CHRISTIANSON, G. (eds.). *Humanity and Divinity in Renaissance and Reformation*. Essays in Honor of Charles Trinkaus. 1993
52. REEVE, A. (ed.) and SCREECH, M. A. (introd.). *Erasmus' Annotations on the New Testament*. Galatians to the Apocalypse. 1993
53. STUMP, Ph. H. *The Reforms of the Council of Constance (1414-1418)*. 1994
54. GIAKALIS, A. *Images of the Divine*. The Theology of Icons at the Seventh Ecumenical Council. With a Foreword by Henry Chadwick. 1994
55. NELLEN, H. J. M. and RABBIE, E. (eds.). *Hugo Grotius – Theologian*. Essays in Honour of G. H. M. Posthumus Meyjes. 1994
56. TRIGG, J. D. *Baptism in the Theology of Martin Luther*. 1994
57. JANSE, W. *Albert Hardenberg als Theologe*. Profil eines Bucer-Schülers. 1994
59. SCHOOR, R.J.M. van de. *The Irenical Theology of Théophile Brachet de La Milletière (1588-1665)*. 1995
60. STREHLE, S. *The Catholic Roots of the Protestant Gospel*. Encounter between the Middle Ages and the Reformation. 1995
61. BROWN, M.L. *Donne and the Politics of Conscience in Early Modern England*. 1995
62. SCREECH, M.A. (ed.). *Richard Mocket, Warden of All Souls College, Oxford, Doctrina et Politia Ecclesiae Anglicanae*. An Anglican Summa. Facsimile with Variants of the Text of 1617. Edited with an Introduction. 1995
63. SNOEK, G.J.C. *Medieval Piety from Relics to the Eucharist*. A Process of Mutual Interaction. 1995
64. PIXTON, P.B. *The German Episcopacy and the Implementation of the Decrees of the Fourth Lateran Council, 1216-1245*. Watchmen on the Tower. 1995
65. DOLNIKOWSKI, E.W. *Thomas Bradwardine: A View of Time and a Vision of Eternity in Fourteenth-Century Thought*. 1995
66. RABBIE, E. (ed.). *Hugo Grotius, Ordinum Hollandiae ac Westfrisiae Pietas (1613)*. Critical Edition with Translation and Commentary. 1995
67. HIRSH, J.C. *The Boundaries of Faith*. The Development and Transmission of Medieval Spirituality. 1996
68. BURNETT, S.G. *From Christian Hebraism to Jewish Studies*. Johannes Buxtorf (1564-1629) and Hebrew Learning in the Seventeenth Century. 1996
69. BOLAND O.P., V. *Ideas in God according to Saint Thomas Aquinas*. Sources and Synthesis. 1996
70. LANGE, M.E. *Telling Tears in the English Renaissance*. 1996
71. CHRISTIANSON, G. and IZBICKI, T.M. (eds.). *Nicholas of Cusa on Christ and the Church*. Essays in Memory of Chandler McCuskey Brooks for the American Cusanus Society. 1996
72. MALI, A. *Mystic in the New World*. Marie de l'Incarnation (1599-1672). 1996
73. VISSER, D. *Apocalypse as Utopian Expectation (800-1500)*. The Apocalypse Commentary of Berengaudus of Ferrières and the Relationship between Exegesis, Liturgy and Iconography. 1996
74. O'ROURKE BOYLE, M. *Divine Domesticity*. Augustine of Thagaste to Teresa of Avila. 1997
75. PFIZENMAIER, T.C. *The Trinitarian Theology of Dr. Samuel Clarke (1675-1729)*. Context, Sources, and Controversy. 1997
76. BERKVENS-STEVELINCK, C., ISRAEL, J. and POSTHUMUS MEYJES, G.H.M. (eds.). *The Emergence of Tolerance in the Dutch Republic*. 1997
77. HAYKIN, M.A.G. (ed.). *The Life and Thought of John Gill (1697-1771)*. A Tercentennial Appreciation. 1997
78. KAISER, C.B. *Creational Theology and the History of Physical Science*. The Creationist Tradition from Basil to Bohr. 1997
79. LEES, J.T. *Anselm of Havelberg*. Deeds into Words in the Twelfth Century. 1997
80. WINTER, J.M. van. *Sources Concerning the Hospitallers of St John in the Netherlands, 14th-18th Centuries*. 1998
81. TIERNEY, B. *Foundations of the Conciliar Theory*. The Contribution of the Medieval Canonists from Gratian to the Great Schism. Enlarged New Edition. 1998

82. MIERNOWSKI, J. *Le Dieu Néant.* Théologies négatives à l'aube des temps modernes. 1998
83. HALVERSON, J.L. *Peter Aureol on Predestination.* A Challenge to Late Medieval Thought. 1998.
84. HOULISTON, V. (ed.). *Robert Persons, S.J.: The Christian Directory (1582).* The First Booke of the Christian Exercise, appertayning to Resolution. 1998
85. GRELL, O.P. (ed.). *Paracelsus.* The Man and His Reputation, His Ideas and Their Transformation. 1998
86. MAZZOLA, E. *The Pathology of the English Renaissance.* Sacred Remains and Holy Ghosts. 1998.
87. 88. MARSILIUS VON INGHEN. *Quaestiones super quattuor libros sententiarum.* Super Primum. Bearbeitet von M. Santos Noya. 2 Bände. I. Quaestiones 1-7. II. Quaestiones 8-21. 2000
89. FAUPEL-DREVS, K. *Vom rechten Gebrauch der Bilder im liturgischen Raum.* Mittelalterliche Funktionsbestimmungen bildender Kunst im *Rationale divinorum officiorum* des Durandus von Mende (1230/1-1296). 1999
90. KREY, P.D.W. and SMITH, L. (eds.). *Nicholas of Lyra.* the Senses of Scripture. 2000
92. OAKLEY, F. *Politics and Eternity.* Studies in the History of Medieval and Early-Modern Political Thought. 1999
93. PRYDS, D. *The Politics of Preaching.* Robert of Naples (1309-1343) and his Sermons. 2000
94. POSTHUMUS MEYJES, G.H.M. *Jean Gerson – Apostle of Unity.* His Church Politics and Ecclesiology. Translated by J.C. Grayson. 1999
95. BERG, J. VAN DEN. *Religious Currents and Cross-Currents.* Essays on Early Modern Protestantism and the Protestant Enlightenment. Edited by J. de Bruijn, P. Holtrop, and E. van der Wall. 1999
96. IZBICKI, T.M. and BELLITTO, C.M. (eds.). *Reform and Renewal in the Middle Ages and the Renaissance.* Studies in Honor of Louis Pascoe, S. J. 2000
97. KELLY, D. *The Conspiracy of Allusion.* Description, Rewriting, and Authorship from Macrobius to Medieval Romance. 1999
98. MARRONE, S.P. *The Light of Thy Countenance.* Science and Knowledge of God in the Thirteenth Century. 2 volumes. 1. A Doctrine of Divine Illumination. 2. God at the Core of Cognition. 2001
99. HOWSON, B.H. *Erroneous and Schismatical Opinions.* The Question of Orthodoxy regarding the Theology of Hanserd Knollys (c. 1599-169)). 2001
100. ASSELT, W.J. VAN. *The Federal Theology of Johannes Cocceius (1603-1669).* 2001
101. CELENZA, C.S. *Piety and Pythagoras in Renaissance Florence the* Symbolum Nesianum. 2001
102. DAM, H.-J. VAN (ed.), *Hugo Grotius, De imperio summarum potestatum circa sacra.* Critical Edition with Introduction, English translation and Commentary. 2 volumes. 2001
103. BAGGE, S. *Kings, Politics, and the Right Order of the World in German Historiography c. 950-1150.* 2002
104. STEIGER, J.A. *Fünf Zentralthemen der Theologie Luthers und seiner Erben.* Communicatio – Imago – Figura – Maria – Exempla. Mit Edition zweier christologischer Frühschriften Johann Gerhards. 2002
105. IZBICKI, T.M. and BELLITTO, C.M. (eds.). *Nicholas of Cusa and his Age: Intellect and Spirituality.* Essays Dedicated to the Memory of F. Edward Cranz, Thomas P. McTighe and Charles Trinkaus. 2002
106. HASCHER-BURGER, U. *Gesungene Innigkeit.* Studien zu einer Musikhandschrift der Devotio moderna (Utrecht, Universiteitsbibliotheek, MS 16 H 94, olim B 113). Mit einer Edition der Gesänge. 2002
107. BOLLIGER, D. *Infiniti Contemplatio.* Grundzüge der Scotus- und Scotismusrezeption im Werk Huldrych Zwinglis. 2003
108. CLARK, F. *The 'Gregorian' Dialogues and the Origins of Benedictine Monasticism.* 2002
109. ELM, E. *Die Macht der Weisheit.* Das Bild des Bischofs in der *Vita Augustini* des Possidius und andere spätantiken und frühmittelalterlichen Bischofsviten. 2003
110. BAST, R.J. (ed.). *The Reformation of Faith in the Context of Late Medieval Theology and Piety.* Essays by Berndt Hamm. 2004.
111. HEERING, J.P. *Hugo Grotius as Apologist for the Christian Religion.* A Study of his Work *De Veritate Religionis Christianae* (1640). Translated by J.C. Grayson. 2004.
112. LIM, P.C.-H. *In Pursuit of Purity, Unity, and Liberty.* Richard Baxter's Puritan Ecclesiology in its Seventeenth-Century Context. 2004.
113. CONNORS, R. and GOW, A.C. (eds.). *Anglo-American Millennialism, from Milton to the Millerites.* 2004.
114. ZINGUER, I. and YARDENI, M. (eds.). *Les Deux Réformes Chrétiennes.* Propagation et Diffusion. 2004.
115. JAMES, F.A. III (ed.). *Peter Martyr Vermigli and the European Reformations:* Semper Reformanda. 2004.
116. STROLL, M. *Calixtus II (1119-1124).* A Pope Born to Rule. 2004.

117. ROEST, B. *Franciscan Literature of Religious Instruction before the Council of Trent.* 2004.
118. WANNENMACHER, J.E. *Hermeneutik der Heilsgeschichte. De septem sigillis* und die sieben Siegel im Werk Joachims von Fiore. 2004.
119. THOMPSON, N. *Eucharistic Sacrifice and Patristic Tradition in the Theology of Martin Bucer, 1534-1546.* 2004.
120. VAN DER KOOI, C. *As in a Mirror. John Calvin and Karl Barth on Knowing God.* A Diptych. 2004.

Prospectus available on request

BRILL — P.O.B. 9000 — 2300 PA LEIDEN — THE NETHERLANDS